AF519673

PROBLEMS OF TRIBAL EDUCATION IN INDIA
Issues and Prospects

PROBLEMS OF TRIBAL EDUCATION IN INDIA

Issues and Prospects

MIDATALA RANI

Department of Studies in Political Science
University of Mysore
Mysore-6

KANISHKA PUBLISHERS, DISTRIBUTORS
NEW DELHI-110 002

KANISHKA PUBLISHERS, DISTRIBUTORS
4697/5-21 A, Ansari Road, Daryaganj
New Delhi-110 002
Phones : 2327 0497, 2328 8285
Fax : 011-2328 8285
E-mail: kanishka_publishing@yahoo.co.in

First Published 2009

ISBN 978-81-8457-120-2

PRINTED IN INDIA

Published by Madan Sachdeva for Kanishka Publishers, Distributors, 4697/5-21A, Ansari Road, Daryaganj, New Delhi-110 002, Typeset by Sunshine Graphics, Delhi, and Printed at Rajdhani Printers, Delhi.

Dedicated

To
Prof. G. Ravindra
&
Pushpa G. Ravindra

ACKNOWLEDGEMENTS

I whole heartedly thank Professor T.G. Talwar, Vice Chancellor, University of Mysore, Mysore for the constant encouragement and administrative support. I would like to express my gratitude to Professor G. Ravindra, Joint Director, NCERT, New Delhi, and Dr. Pushpa Ravindra, for their love and affection. I am thankful to Dr. K. Sashidhar Rao, retired Principal, IASE, Hyderabad, Prof. V. Ramakrishna and Dr. V. Lalitha for their guidance and academic support. I cannot forget many of the tribal teachers, officials, parents, administrators who helped me in various ways. Without their help this work might not have been completed. I thank the library staff of University of Mysore, Mysore, Tribal Cultural Research and Training Institute (TCR&TI), Hyderabad; Directorate of Tribal Welfare, Bangalore; Anthropological Survey of India, Mysore; Andhra Pradesh State Archives, Taranaka, Hyderabad, for providing me the relevant documents, reports and research material.

I sincerely thank Professor M. Umapathy, retired Professor, Department of Studies in Political Science, University of Mysore; Professor P.S. Jayaramu, Department of Political Science, Bangalore University; Professor B.M. Bayeen, Department of Political Science, Gulbarga University; Professor R. Balasubramanian, retired Professor, Department of Political Science, University of Madras, for their encouragement.

I am equally thankful to Professor G.T. Bandage, Principal, Regional Institute of Education, Mysore and Sri B.C. Basti, for their academic guidance. I also thank Dr. Malli Gandhi, Regional Institute of Education (NCERT), Mysore for his encouragement and support. I thank Sri Madan Sachdeva, Director, Kanishka Publishers for accepting to publish the present work. Finally I cannot forget the help rendered by Dr. D.C. Nanjunda Venugopal and Sri. B.K. Venkatesh, for their timely help. The unending encouragement and comfort I have received from my aged mother Smt. M. Ranganayaki needs a special mention and thanks.

MIDATALA RANI

PREFACE

India achieved about 70 per cent of literacy according to 2001 census. Though the progress could have been better, considering several constraints, it is not a mean achievement. However, the rate of literacy among marginalised sections, in particular adivasis, is much lower when compared to scheduled classes and other backward communities (buhujans). This apart, the type of education provided to them, the curriculum and reading materials is quite conventional, not much different from the other general sections of society. It may sound offensive but it is atrocious, to say the least. It is an accepted norm by all educationists that the curriculum, pedagogical methods and related reading materials should be learner-friendly and learner-specific. The fact that even after nearly six decades of independence, such steps are not initiated, should make us more responsive to this urgent need. The adivasi children are fed with the same curriculum, language, reading materials and tools of teaching similar to that of children in the main stream. This is not only un-scientific but at variance with accepted pedagogic methodology. Separate reading materials should have been developed incorporating socio-economic and cultural ethos/genius of adivasis. This is not to isolate them from the main stream society but to sensitise them about their rich and age old cultural heritage. Intensely debated for several years, the mainstream theory is not favoured today. Integrating them, not isolating them into the broad based and extended civil society is an accepted norm. However, anthropologists world over are of the considered view that while providing all benefits that modern civilization today offers, care should be taken to preserve their core culture. Education provided should not uproot them from their cultural backdrop and, on the other, all steps should be taken to preserve it. Their cultural wealth including their day-to-day life styles, recreational and performing art forms, medicinal plants, herbs and roots, justice-delivery system, martial qualities along with their peace loving and hospitable nature should be protected and preserved. In this volume, an attempt is made to analyse various dimensions of tribal education in India. The author has pooled up the insights gained from various studies on tribal education scenario in India for the last three decades. The collection of essays in this book explores problems, prospects and the educational process of scheduled tribes in India. The present work throws light on the specific problems related to tribal education such as the lessons that can be learnt through the findings, curriculum needs, problems of education among the ex-criminal/de-notified tribes, problems of education of primitive tribal groups, human rights perspective of tribal education, curriculum transaction, problems for the tribal dialects, literacy of scheduled tribe children, multilingual education in tribal schools, functioning of Ashram Schools, school absenteeism among tribal children and the Government Policy towards the development of tribal education in India. This book will be extremely useful for the policy makers, administrators, social scientists, educationists, teacher educators and those who are interested in the area of tribal education.

AUTHOR

Contents

1

Studies on Tribal Education Done in India: A Collection of Findings

Introduction

Education has an acculturating role. It refines sensitivities, activities and perceptions that contribute to national cohesion, scientific temper and independence of mind and spirit, thus furthering the goals of socialism, secularism and democracy enshrined in our Constitution. Education is an essential factor for national development. Today, it is regarded as a national activity. It is regarded as a powerful instrument of social, economic, political and cultural changes. The role of education is to impart knowledge, develop skills and inculcate right type of attitudes, values and interests. The Kothari Commission suggested that education should relate to the life, needs and aspirations of the people. It has to increase productivity, achieve social and national integration, step up the process of modernization and develop social, moral and spiritual values among the future citizens. It is observed that the destiny of India is now shaped in the classrooms. Martin Luther, the German social reformer has rightly said that the progress and prosperity of a nation depends not on the abundant of its revenues or on the strength of its fortifications, but in many education, enlightenment and character.

Education is a fundamental right of all citizens. The fifth Constitutional Amendment Act has made primary education as a fundamental right to the children of 6 to 14 years of age. The Government of India and the State Governments are taking steps to fulfill this right. It is a fact that education is an essential programme for economic growth and development of the society and it is an investment and a human capital. It enhances individual's well being. Literacy is proved to be a key variable for the development of the society and success of democracy. Illiterate people tend to have low self-esteem and low social status. Because of their illiteracy they cannot reap the fruits of democracy. Education is of value not only for the person who acquires it, but also for others. Widespread of education helps to resolve social problems like poverty, ignorance, illiteracy, diseases, population growth and environmental degradation. To march towards bright future the only hope rests with educational persons. Mahatma Gandhi was of the opinion that education is the basic tool for the development of consciousness and reconstruction of the society.

Modern educationists believe that every individual is endowed with certain innate abilities or potentialities and these are to be brought out to achieve a harmonious development. The purpose of education is to promote the development of a well integrated person capable of exercising such responsibilities in the society as his powers allow. Education has to make the individual physically strong, intellectually alert, emotionally stable, culturally sound and socially efficient. According to National Policy on Education (NPE, 1986), Education has to produce self assured, more productive, more capable and more thinking type of citizens. It is not the imitative mind that is to be developed, but it is creative mind that is to be developed. In the present day society wherein we find heavy developments of science and technology, it is not the technical know-how that is to be developed, but life know-how is to be developed. Education is the business teaching as to how to live but not as to how to make a living. Value based education is the need of the hour. 'The progress of a nation is decided and determined not in the legislatures where passions and prejudices wrap of judgement and vitiate the laws that may be framed, not in courts where punishments were often harden than reform offenders, not in factories where man become mechanized, but in schools where the minds of the future citizens are monitored and where the habits and attitudes are shaped'. It was stated that 'School plays a major role in monitoring the ideas, habits and attitudes of the children in order to produce well-balanced personalities'. The present day school has to perform number of functions. It has to teach the 7'Rs – Reading, Writing, Arithmetic, Recreation, Rights, Responsibilities and Relationships. It has to transmit the cultural heritage of the previous generation to the present generation, conserve the culture and advance culture. The school has to recognise the individual differences, provide opportunities for the full development of the children, kindling the minds of the students and develop a passion for social justice.

There are three important components in the educative process. These are the teacher, the pupil and the subject matter or content of education. The teacher is the main dynamic force in the system of education. He is the Director of the teaching-learning process. He has to plan for teaching, organise it, execute it and evaluate its success in terms of learning outcomes of children. The second important component is the pupil. To educate the pupil is the ultimate objective of the instructional process. In this context, the child's abilities, capacities, capabilities, and his psychological aspects are to be taken into account. Today, there is a shift from epistemic approach to reconstructionist approach, from teacher-control and subject centered approach to that of child-centered approach. The present emphasis is on the adoption child-centered, activity-centered and competency based teaching-learning process. Student is the centre of the education system. John Dewey felt that: 'the child is the starting point, the center and the end. His growth and his development is the ideal of education'. Dr. A.P.J. Abdul Kalam, the former-President of India, has stated: 'What is more important is that teachers should not transmit their frustration to their students, but should constantly try to upgrade their skills and encourage the children to think big'. The child should be the focal point in the system of education. The third important component is the subject matter or the content of education, known as curriculum. The curriculum or the content or the subject matter of education is to be handed over to the child by means of a method. Method is a process of establishing a contact between the subject matter or content of education and the child. The teacher needs the mastery of the subject matter which he is going to teach and also possess a sound knowledge of the pedagogical concerns. Curriculum is the path of the realisation of objectives of education. It includes both the subjects for intellectual development and also for the other types of development. It comprises of classroom activities as well as extra-classroom activities. It includes curricular activities as well as co-curricular activities and extra-curricular activities. Curriculum is the totality of experience. It is the sum total of all the educational experiences provided to the child by the school through instruction either within the four walls or outside. It includes scholastic as well as co-scholastic activities. Curriculum is a tool in the hands of an artist (teacher) to mould his material (student) in accordance with his ideals (objectives) in his studio (school)—said Cunningham. In the words of Jawaharlal Nehru 'Education has mainly two aspects, the cultural aspect which makes a person grow and the productive aspect which makes a person do things. Both are essential'. Thus it is incumbent on the part of education to train every individual as a well integrated person and a useful citizen.

It is an inescapable fact that in countries around the globe during the past decades, notable efforts were made to universalise primary education. But millions of children continue to remain deprived of the benefits of education. This is due to variety of causes. Millions of children have no access to primary schooling. Millions of children fail to complete basic education. Millions satisfy the attendance requirements but do not acquire essential knowledge and skills. Thus these millions comprise of poor, rural and remote populations, nomads, indigenous people and girls. The educational development of the disadvantaged population groups acquired great seriousness in India. The children who drop out before the completion of primary education lapse into illiterates.

The disadvantaged population groups are the victims of multiple handicaps due to various reasons such as: 1. they do not have access to basic educational infrastructure like schools, teachers and books, 2. the content of education imparted through the curriculum is not fulfilling their specific learning needs, 3. the nature of curriculum transaction of schools is not conducive to their learning styles and 4. the model of schooling and education presented to the disadvantaged is alien to the cultural needs of these groups. The school itself is against the interests of the disadvantaged population. The educationally disadvantaged groups fail to see any point and purpose in education. They remain outside the school, drop out of it or fail to achieve the desirable learning levels. Scheduled Tribes form a large group of population in Indian society. Due to several historical, economic and social reasons tribal groups remained socially and economically backward. According to 1991 census the total population of Scheduled Tribes in India is 67.7 millions. Out of 613 tribal groups, 62.7 million tribal population are living in rural areas. 5 million population are living in urban areas. The total tribal population is more than 8 per cent. The national literacy rate of scheduled tribe population according to 1991 census is 29.06 per cent. The female literacy rate is 18.19 per cent and the male literacy rate is 40.65 per cent. This indicates the low literacy rate among the tribal population compared with the national literacy rate of 52.19 per cent. Education of tribals is an important task before the Government of India.

Scheduled Tribes in Andhra Pradesh

There are 33 Tribal groups in Andhra Pradesh with a total population of 41,99,481 (6.3%). Of the total tribal population 39 per cent of the population belong to Sugali Community spread dominantly in Warangal, Nalgonda, Khammam, Mahabub Nagar and Nizamabad districts. Next to this nearly 11 per cent population comprise of Koyas inhabited in Khammam, Warangal, West Godavari, East Godavari and Adilabad districts. Around 9 per cent population each comprise of Yanadi and Yerukala communities dominant in Nellore, Chittoor, Prakasam, Guntur, Anantapur, Krishna and Nellore districts. Bagata, Bhils, Gond, Hill Reddi, Kammara, Kondadora, Khond, Kotia, Kulia, Mali, Mukadora, Porja, Reddidora and Valmiki are mostly inhabited in Visakhapatnam district. Gadaba, Jatapu are dominant in Vizianagaram district. Savara community is dominant in Srikakulam district. Kondakapu and Kondareddi are more in number in East Godavari district. Adilabad district is inhabited by Andh, Gond, Naikpod, Kolam, Mannedora, Pardhan and Thoti, tribal communities. Chenchu, Katunayakan and Yerukalas are dominant in Guntur district. Koya and Nayakpod are more in number in Khammam district. Chittoor district has Rona/Rena tribal community. Yanadis are inhabited in Nellore district. The tribal groups in A.P. can be classified into seven cultural zones which are as follows:

Table–1
Cultural Zones of the Scheduled Tribes in Andhra Pradesh

Sl. No.	*Cultural Zone*	*Districts Comprising the Cultural Zone of ST Population*	*Predominant Tribal Groups Inhabited in the Districts*
1.	Vamsadhara–Vigavati basin	Srikakulam and Vizanagaram	Savara, Khond, Gadaba
2.	Machkhand–Gouthami basin	Visakhapatnam	Bagata, Gouda, Kotia, Mannedora, Mukadora, Kondadora
3.	Godavari basin	East Godavari, West Godavari, Karimnagar	Koya, Konda Reddy and Naikpod
4.	Penaganga–Pranahita basin	Adilabad	Gond, Pardhan, Thoti, Kolam and Andh
5.	Nallamalai basin	Mahabubnagar, Kurnool and Prakasam	Chenchu
6.	Rayalaseema	Anantapur, Chittoor and Telangana	Sugali/Banjara
7.	Guntur–Nellore seema	Guntur and Nellore	Yerukala and Yanadi

Jatapu, Kondadora, Mukadora, Mannedora, Sugali, Yerukala, Koya, Gond, Pardhan, Yanadi are some of the major tribal groups and Savara, Gadaba, Thoti, Chenchu, Kolam, Konda Reddy, Poraja and Khond are some of the primitive tribal groups existing in Andhra Pradesh. Cultivation, settled cultivation, shifting cultivation, Podu cultivation, agriculture, agricultural labour, collection of National Timber Forest Products (NTFP) are some of the major occupations of tribal groups. Besides this, the tribal population are involved in the occupations like hunting, honey collection, cattle rearing, manufacture of agriculture implements, basket making, rope-making, selling bangles, beads, making garlands, construction work, digging of earth, forest labour work, petty business, scavenging and labour work. The Savara tribal population are most preponderant tribal group population and their families are nuclear type. The Khonds speak *'Kui'* language. Gadabas believe in transmigration. Bagatas are called as warrior community. The Koyas speak *'Kui'* dialect and Telugu Language. Sammakka and Saralamma are worshipped by them. Naikpods are experts in flatting trees. Pardhans are the custodians of Gond Tradition. Thotis are famous for selling medicinal herbs. Hunting and Honey collection are the main occupations of the Chenchus. The Yerukalas are the Sooth sayers. The tribal population speaks different tribal languages. The tribal dialects spoken by the respective tribal groups in Andhra Pradesh are: Kubi, Kuli, Kuri, Koi, Kolami, Gondi, Sugali, Adibasi Oriya, Savara, Gudaba and Koravanj.

Table–2
Tribal Dialects in Andhra Pradesh

Tribe	*Tribal Dialect*
Kondadora	Kubi dialect
Kondakapu	Kuli dialect
Khonds	Kuvi dialect
Koya	Koi dialect
Kolami	Kolami dialect
Gond	Gondi
Sugali	Lambadi dialect
Adivasi Oriya	Adibasi Oriya dialect
Savara	Sabara dialect
Gadaba	Gadaba dialect
Yerukula	Koravanji

There are certain special characteristic features in the tribal culture among the scheduled tribes of Andhra Pradesh. The special features of the tribal culture are: geographic isolation/isolated societies, simple way of life, treat nature with respect, subject to customary laws/without law and order department, they control themselves, own code of conduct, truthfulness and honesty, closed system, subsistence economy, festivals throughout the year, early marriages (13-15 years for boys, 10-14 years for girls), own dialect, polygamy, divorce, limited exposure to outside world, beliefs and superstitions, limited needs and aspirations, economic characteristics including food gathering/hunting/fishing/shifting cultivation/terrace cultivation, low skills/very little specialization/low productivity/no work training, lacks abstract thinking, child is looked as potential earner but not a learner, women looked as economic assets and learning through imitation but not through instruction. Thus tribal communities lead a simple life, subject to customary laws. They have limited exposure to the outside world. They give more importance to immediate gains. They talk different dialects based on their own traditions and customs. They give importance to the celebration of festivals, which generally fall throughout the year. Whenever there is a festive occasion in the village all the villagers both elders, youngsters and children participate in it.

Education of Scheduled Tribes in Andhra Pradesh

The literacy rate among tribal population in Andhra Pradesh as per 1991 census is 16.96 (25.25 males and 8.68 females). The literacy rate among the Primitive Tribal Groups (PTGs) is very poor and needs urgent attention. There are 72,009 habitations in the state of which 15,690 are with less than 200 population. Still there are 7189 (11.43%) habitations where the children have to attend the primary school having a distance of more than 1 km.

Table–3
Habitations without Primary Schools

Population Slab	*Villages not Having Primary Schools in Tribal Villages (Andhra Pradesh)*
200-250	1,520
100-200	1,747
100 and below	1,537
Total	4,804

There are as many as 35,333 habitations not having upper primary schools or upper primary sections and 42,356 habitations without high schools in the state. Most of these habitations are tribal habitations. Thus access is a serious problem in tribal areas. Nearly 12 per cent of the children in the age group of 5-10 and 24 per cent of children in the age group of 11-15 need to be enrolled. Hence achieving cent per cent enrolment in tribal areas demand suitable strategies. The following details provide the information relating to the dropout rates of tribal children.

Table–4
Enrolment and Dropouts of ST Children

Total ST children (5-10 age group)	8,43,572
Total ST children who are in school	7,42,779
Total ST children out of school	1,00,793
Total ST children % of enrolment	88.05%
Total ST children (11-15 age group)	4,36,470
Total ST children who are in school	3,33,247
Total ST children out of school	1,03,223
Total ST children % of enrolment	76.35%
Total dropout of ST children of classes 1 to 5	65.77%
Total dropout of ST boys from classes 1 to 5	63.22%
Total dropout of ST girls from classes 1 to 5	69.02%
Total dropout of ST children of classes 1 to 7	80.82%
Total dropout of ST boys of classes 1 to 7	78.17%
Total dropout of ST girls of classes 1 to 7	84.42%

There is high dropout rate among tribal children at Class 5 stage and more so in case of Class 7 stage. The dropout rates at higher classes result in high wastage of human resources, and financial allocations. This situation demands implementation of certain area specific strategies and basic changes in the system of education. At Class 5 level there is more dropout in Adilabad, Mahabubnagar, Medak and Nizamabad districts. So also at Class 7 level there is more dropout rate in Adilabad, Nellore, Mahabubnagar, Vizianagaram, Medak, Prakasam, Warangal, Nizamabad and Nalgonda districts. The Midterm Assessment Survey (MAS) of the 14 DPEP Phase II districts reveals the fact that the minimum per cent score of Class 1 Language is 60.31 per cent, the minimum per cent score of Class 1 Mathematics is 65.87 per cent, the minimum per cent score of Class 4 Language is 47.06 per cent and the minimum per cent score of Class 4 Mathematics is 31.58 per cent.

In Class 1 Language achievement, the performance of ST students excelled others in the districts of Guntur, Prakasam and Ranga Reddy. It is observed that the performance of ST students is more than other students in Khammam, Mahabubnagar, Medak, Prakasam, and Srikakulam districts in Class 1 Mathematics. In Cuddapah, Mahabubnagar, Nalgonda, Prakasam and Ranga Reddy districts ST students exceeded others in their achievement in Class 4 language. The achievement levels of ST students are found to be more than others in Anantapur, Cuddapah, Mahabubnagar and Prakasam districts in Class 4 Mathematics. However there is an urgent need to raise the achievement levels of the students belonging to ST groups.

Problems of Tribal Children

The problems faced by the tribal children in education can be clarified under five areas (viz.) Economic factors, Social factors, Cultural factors, School factors and Administrative factors. Poverty of parents, lack of parental demand, child labour, lack of Early Childcare Education (ECE) facilities are some of the economic factors, which stand in the way of education of the tribal children. Illiteracy of the parents, early marriages, community loyalties and lack of awareness are some of the problems which retard the educational development of the tribal children. Tribal festivals, tribal traditions, value system and problem of language are some of the cultural factors which stand as a hurdle with tribal children's education. There are a large number of school factors and administrative factors, which hamper the educational development of the tribal children. To quote some of them are lack of access, incomplete schools, teacher absenteeism, poor quality of teaching, unserviceable curriculum, unsuitable working hours, etc. and lack of coordination among different managements, delays in supplies and incentives, weak inspectorate, lack of enrolment campaigns, lack of community control, lack of incentives for better performance are some of the school and administrative factors which are standing in the way of the education of tribal children. The following diagrammatic representation provides the specific problems of ST children in their education.

Figure 1: Factors Affecting the Education of Tribal Children

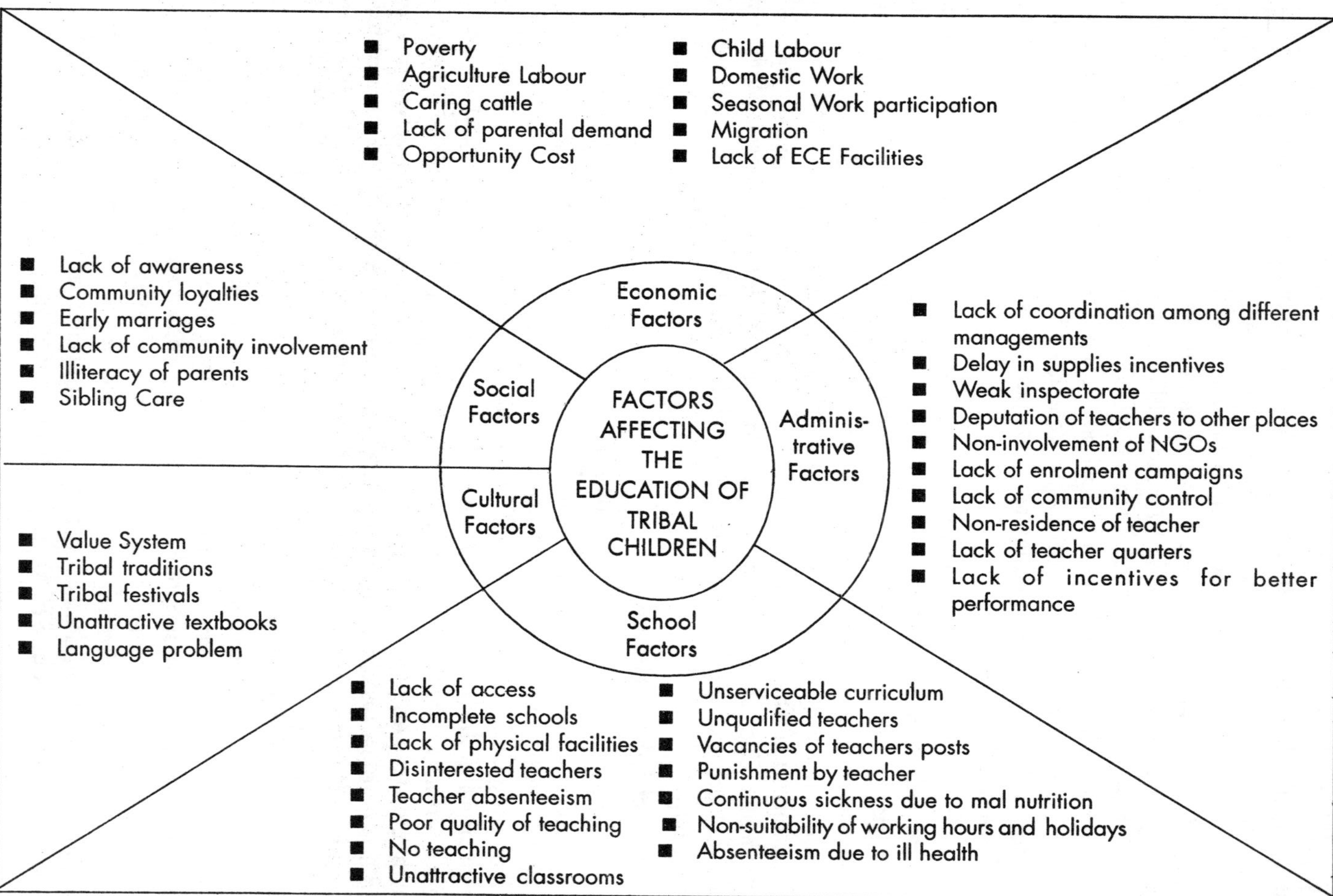

Table–5
District-Wise Problems of Tribal Education

District	*Specific Problems in Tribal Education*
Srikakulam	migration more unenrolled girls engaging children in labour contract work for money
Vizianagaram	more dropouts low parental awareness
Visakhapatnam	lack of access to tribal schools non-residence of teachers working in tribal schools fear of punishment by teachers
East Godavari	out of school children without any work peer group effect
West Godavari	sibling care
Khammam	early marriages
Warangal	parental illiteracy more unenrolled boys
Adilabad	involvement of children in household work
Mahabubnagar	more unenrolled boys and girls sibling care fear of punishment by teachers and illiteracy of parents.

The tribal education scenario can be explained under 12 areas, i.e. administrative structure, access, quality, participation, education and economic development, performance of institutions, finance and cost of education, attitudes, awareness and aspirations, teachers, administration, innovative approaches and approaches and policies.

Studies on Tribal Education

Factors Influencing Parents and Children in Achieving Universal Elementary Education (UEE) in Andhra Pradesh

The study reveals many issues related to the factors influencing Parents and Children in Achieving UEE. The study deals with 1,02,396 teachers covering 22 districts and 75 mandals. The respondents include 3,07,188 parents and 102,396 pupils. Some of the findings pertaining to tribal areas are as follows: economic barriers are not the real barriers for enrolment and retention. Parents illiteracy, peer group effort and unattractive schools are the main causes for drop outs. Most of the out of school children opined that school should be a place of activities with songs, games and good teaching environment. Teachers should avoid punishment in the classrooms and they have to provide attractive atmosphere in the school. Tribal parents are also sending their children to school for education and to have better future. Tribal parents expressed their decrease to earn income as a result of sending their children to school. Tribal parents also expressed their views for the improvement of physical facilities and good teaching in their schools. Tribal parents are not happy to send their children to work. Tribal parents viewed that tribal schools are

Figure 2: Tribal Education Scenario in Andhra Pradesh

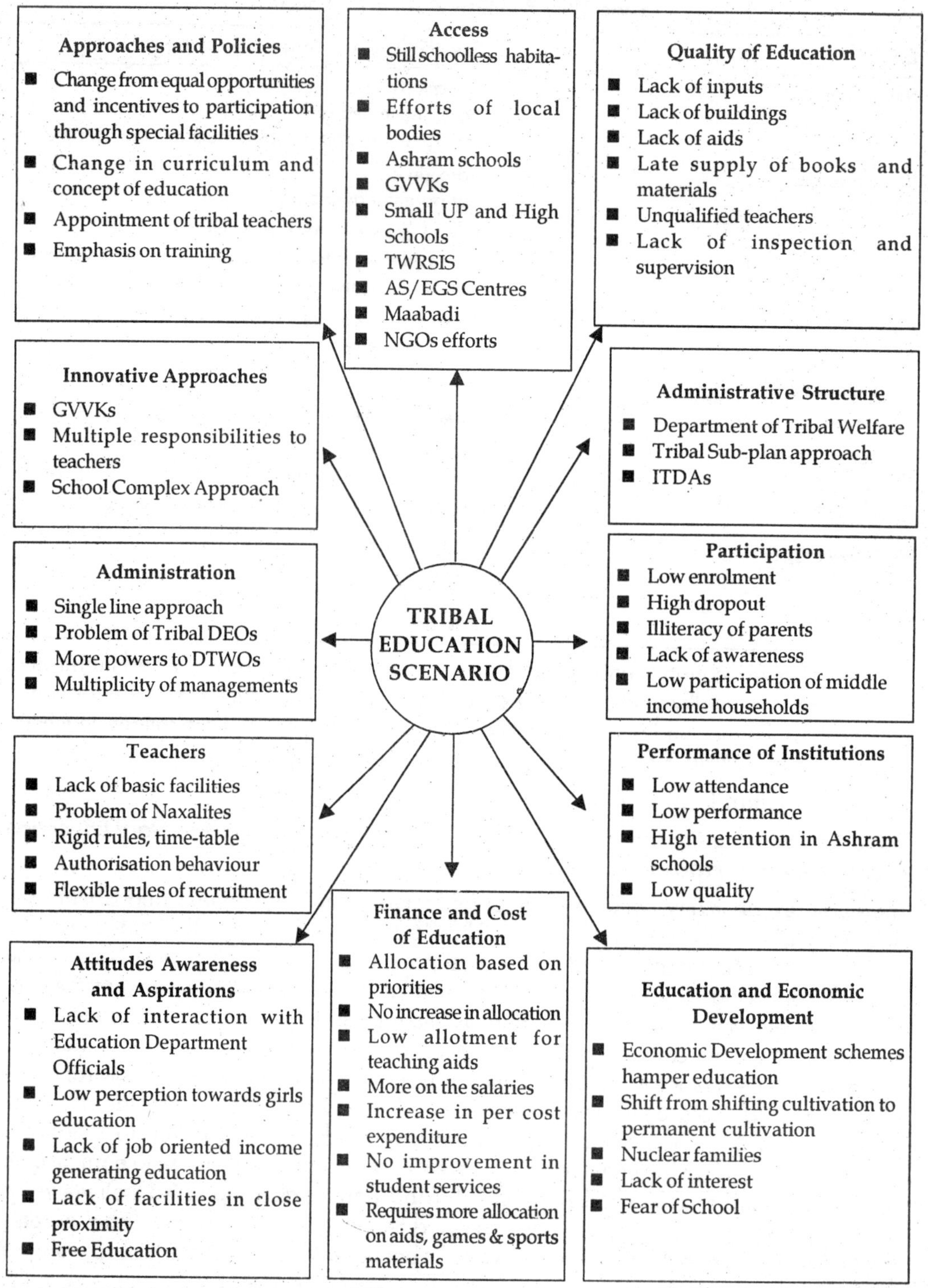

TRIBAL EDUCATION SCENARIO

Approaches and Policies
- Change from equal opportunities and incentives to participation through special facilities
- Change in curriculum and concept of education
- Appointment of tribal teachers
- Emphasis on training

Access
- Still schoolless habitations
- Efforts of local bodies
- Ashram schools
- GVVKs
- Small UP and High Schools
- TWRSIS
- AS/EGS Centres
- Maabadi
- NGOs efforts

Quality of Education
- Lack of inputs
- Lack of buildings
- Lack of aids
- Late supply of books and materials
- Unqualified teachers
- Lack of inspection and supervision

Innovative Approaches
- GVVKs
- Multiple responsibilities to teachers
- School Complex Approach

Administrative Structure
- Department of Tribal Welfare
- Tribal Sub-plan approach
- ITDAs

Administration
- Single line approach
- Problem of Tribal DEOs
- More powers to DTWOs
- Multiplicity of managements

Participation
- Low enrolment
- High dropout
- Illiteracy of parents
- Lack of awareness
- Low participation of middle income households

Teachers
- Lack of basic facilities
- Problem of Naxalites
- Rigid rules, time-table
- Authorisation behaviour
- Flexible rules of recruitment

Performance of Institutions
- Low attendance
- Low performance
- High retention in Ashram schools
- Low quality

Attitudes Awareness and Aspirations
- Lack of interaction with Education Department Officials
- Low perception towards girls education
- Lack of job oriented income generating education
- Lack of facilities in close proximity
- Free Education

Finance and Cost of Education
- Allocation based on priorities
- No increase in allocation
- Low allotment for teaching aids
- More on the salaries
- Increase in per cost expenditure
- No improvement in student services
- Requires more allocation on aids, games & sports materials

Education and Economic Development
- Economic Development schemes hamper education
- Shift from shifting cultivation to permanent cultivation
- Nuclear families
- Lack of interest
- Fear of School

not attractive. Tribal parents are ready to send their children to school if the children desire so. Nearly 40 per cent of the poor and illiterate tribal parents are sending their children to school. However, illiteracy of parents, unattractive school environment and peer group affect are the causes for high drop outs in the agency areas.

Initiatives taken by Integrated Tribal Development Agency (ITDA), Paderu, Visakhapatnam on Tribal Education

The study reveals many issues relating to the tribal education in the agency areas of Andhra Pradesh. The study focuses on the problems faced by the tribal children and schools. They are rampant teacher absenteeism, lack of infrastructural facilities and bilingual problems. To overcome these problems some of the programmes initiated by ITDA Paderu were – conduct of comprehensive education surveys to identify the gaps (teacher/child / habitation/school infrastructure, etc.), opening of Maabadi schools, joyful learning programmes like improving quality of teaching-learning process by introducing the kit developed by Rishi Valley Education Centre, school beautification, supply of additional teaching-learning material; school complex system with Head Masters, Mandal Resource Persons (MRPs) and strong teachers, Project Resource Centre/Project Monitoring Cell, training programmes for tribal teachers, Village Education Committees/Mandal Education Committees (VECs/MECs), mid-day meal programme, conduct of pre-evaluation tests, categorisation of schools into A/B/C categories and comprehensive monitoring system for the Ashram schools and categorising the performance of the Ashram schools into A/ B/C categories.

Development of Culture Specific Co-curricular Activities for Tribal Children in Residential Schools of Andhra Pradesh

All tribal children in Andhra Pradesh more or less face certain common difficulties. The nature and intensity of the educational problems faced by these tribal children varies from one group to another group of tribal population. Certain difficulties they face are peculiar to them. The geographical remoteness and isolation of the tribal habitations is usually accompanied by cultural distinctness of the earliest inhabitants. The tribal population exhibit certain common characteristics. They often live in their cultural meleau. Each Tribal Community has its own distinctive value system, mode of life and social organisation. The tribal groups depend on primitive agricultural practices, grazing, forest and go for hunting and gathering for food and move from one place to other place with their life pattern. It is a great problem to bring these children into schools and keep them in schools for longer time. All tribal groups face impediments like poverty, illiteracy, low health and nutrition. Their habitations are isolated from the main stream of social life. The tribal children need priority treatment as far as their educational interests are concerned. Therefore, the focus of the study was to enable the tribal children to derive maximum benefit from their culture specific co-curricular activities, from the education provided to them so that they live a rich and full life. The study deals with culture specific co-curricular educational activities in residential schools. The study was concerned with revitalization of co-curricular educational activities, development of the triabl specific cultural activities, materials/packages, orientation and training of teachers to improve the methods of teaching by the teachers working in tribal habitations, preservation of tribal culture in the schools, and to involve the tribal community and children in educational process. The study focuses mainly on the tribal schools situated in the interial forest areas. The study addresses to the socio-economic and educational needs and problems of the scheduled tribes. The study is an attempt to redress and ameliorate them, albeit, there have been governmental and non-governmental organizations participating in the upliftment of neglected socio-economically backward communities. Despite the above attempts there remains a great deal of deficiencies and gaps in successfully and usefully bringing the ST students to the main national educational stream. The traditional textbook transaction in the classrooms and laboratories of the school system will not build the capacity of the learner for learning, doing to work together and to be humane holistically. Therefore, the curricular exercises need to be supported, supplemented and contemplated with the contextualised curricular teaching learning episodes. These out of the classroom activities having bearing on the textual concepts should integrate with the formal instruction in the classroom. Co-curricular educational activities would acclimate and acclimatise the first generation, neo-literate learners with self-confidence and self-esteem to express their latent talent potentials and fall in line with the so called forward community learners. Hence, it is contemplated here to develop meaningful, functional and implementable co-curricular educational activities for the benefit of the scheduled caste and scheduled tribe students of the primary classes in the residential schools of Andhra Pradesh. The study examines the kind and variety of culture specific co-curricular educational activities that have been provided in the Residential Schools, Ashram Schools, Tribal Welfare Department and ITDA schools in Andhra Pradesh with a view to protect the tribal culture and to find out their impact on tribal children in the schools in tribal sub-plan mandals.

The important objectives of the Study are to survey the Residential Schools of Andhra Pradesh in order to find out the existing prototype co-curricular educational activities for the Tribal Children; to study the available existing facilities and type of co-curricular activities conducted/organised in the tribal institutions for the total development of the Tribal Children; to develop a package for the improvement of physical, motor, literary, aesthetic, craft, personal, emotional and cultural development of the Tribal Children and to tryout the package for assessing the effectiveness by orientating the teachers from the Selected Residential Tribal Schools in Andhra Pradesh.

The Ashram Schools in Andhra Pradesh have classes from 1st standard. They are co-educational. Ashram Schools are residential in nature and had been viewed to provide congenial atmosphere for teaching learning process and total personality development of the tribal child. But none of the Ashram schools have adequate teachers for academic, non-academic subjects such as craft and physical education. Out of 15 secondary schools in a selected Mandal only seven schools are having one craft and one Physical Education Teacher (PET). Remaining schools neither have drawing/craft nor PET teachers. The Ashram schools are suffering without adequate number of trained teachers. At the same time many of the schools are having low enrolment. The dropout rate is more in higher classes and the maximum dropout rate was found in lower stages in the Residential Schools. The age of the 'child in Class IV would usually be 9-10 years which is crucial to continue the child in school or to withdraw from the school in order to help in their parental occupation. Till the child reaches the age of 9 or 10, they have very marginal role to play in economic contribution of the family and to look after the younger siblings. Therefore, the parents often decide to send their children to Ashram Schools.

The syllabi, textbooks and examination system in Ashram schools are the same as in non-Ashram schools. In all primary and upper primary schools, the school hours and timetable are of routine type. No periods are provided either for work experience, socially useful productive work, vocational training and other cocurricular educational activities. Some of the important questions raised in the study was whether the education in Ashram schools is adequate for educational and total personality development of the child? Does the syllabus and curriculum of the Ashram schools help the tribal children in their life situation and cultural background? The study is an attempt to look into these problems and to suggest the proper ways and means to improve educational conditions in the Residential schools.

The study emphasised that children drop out because of four main reasons. They are grazing the cattle, agricultural labour, cooking at home and looking after the younger children at home. The cultural traits of the tribal groups are also hindering the progress of their children because the parents of these tribal groups take their wards for various festivals and fairs. Due to their long stay at home and away from the school atmosphere the tribal children loose their interest in Education. The problems of access, attainment and participation can be solved if the educational process is made more interesting, more pleasurable and joyful to the pupils. Though some of the experiments conducted by the ITDAs like Back to School Experiment Programme conducted at Chittoor District, Rishi Valley Experiment, Ekalavya Experiment, Educational Development among tribes in the tribal sub-plan area schools in AP, Action Plan in a low literacy tribal pocket, APPEP project etc., these experiments revealed the fact that to attract children and stick them to school, the educative process should be made more interesting and activity oriented. The classroom should not be a slaughter house of minds but it should be a pleasurable activity. Attracting children to schools through culture specific cocurricular activities is one such important activity. Local Culture should be involved in their education to achieve the goals of education and contribute to their might.

Inspite of several efforts made by the Government of India for their educational development, the scheduled tribes lag behind their non-tribal counterparts with respect to coverage by schools, enrolment and out-put figures. Absenteeism, dropouts in large numbers and stagnation characterise tribal education. Majority of the measures taken for educational improvement of the scheduled tribes are based on the assumption that education is valued uniformly and people are not taking advantage of education because of economic constraints. Variables affecting motivation and performance received less attention. Under the expectation that incentives will work automatically, various structural constraints, psychological and cultural problems have been overlooked.

Education is not meant only for acquisition of knowledge. It has social and psychological dimensions. It is the process of development of innate powers of the individual. Education influences the social consciousness of the individual. Mahatma Gandhi said, "True Education is that which draws out and stimulates the spiritual, intellectual and physical facilities of the individual. The emphasis here is on the personality encompassing mind, body and spirit and not just training in the subjects. Good education is one, which creates a sense of self-respect and dignity and inculcates moral, spiritual and social values."

One of the reasons for reluctance on the part of the tribal parents to send their wards to schools is that, those who get educated get themselves alienated from their culture. Education, which does not help the children to appreciate the do's and don'ts of the culture, makes them misfit in the society. Those who got education prefer to avoid manual labour, and are not suitable for the traditional tribal economic pursuits. At the same time, jobs are not easy to come as they are not sufficiently qualified. They set a bad example to those who want to send their children to school. If the school becomes a part of the community and educated children a part of the tribal society, then education will have better acceptance. This can be ensured through better interaction between school and the community, parents and teachers. The aim should be to minimise the alienation of the student so that it will lead to better acceptance. The culture specific co-curricular educational activities facilitates a healthy integration of the child with the society.

In the present system physically, psychologically, linguistically and culturally a tribal child is in a disadvantaged position. Culture is closely linked to language. The gap existing between the language, culture and the curriculum in the school leads to dropouts. The tribal child likes living closer to nature and feels suffocated in the school. The cumulative effect of the rigid school atmosphere, the strange topics in the curriculum, and the formal teaching methods together make education unattractive to the students. Education is considered as a punishment, and the school a prison. Children look forward to running away from the school at the earliest opportunity to play and enjoy themselves.

Early childhood experience is the crucial part of the personality formation of the adult. School can play a very effective role in this context. Self-concept plays a major part in determining ones own success in school and interactions with the world. It results in self-respect or self-esteem. The individual can develop a sense of ability to learn, and a confidence that he can deal with situations, a sense of belonging with the society and environment. Through culture specific co-curricular educational activities, formation of self-concept can be influenced. Tribal manners are part of a desirable personality. Culture specific co-curricular activities not only make education attractive, but also minimise the distance between individual and his culture. It helps in the inculcation of self-respect and eliminates the inferiority complex of the tribal student. One of the offshoots of co-curricular activities is the development of leadership qualities among the students. A person having a balanced personality will be able to present his ideas clearly and confidently. He is receptive to the ideas of others and listens to them attentively. He finally evaluates all ideas carefully and cooperates with others in arriving at democratic decision. Organization of debates and discussions ensures this component. The teacher can propose various topics on local problems, village priorities, community affairs, etc. for discussions and debates. Through various activities, gradual participation of the youngsters in community life can be attempted. The bane of the modern education is that it provides a false sense of prestige among educated. They despise manual work. In tribal areas uneducated are considered as better for work because of this. A sense of dignity of labour need to be inculcated by making them do various kinds of jobs. Playing various games will help in the development of body, spirit of collective action, and leadership qualities. To make the curriculum attractive to children, the habitat, flora, fauna and ecosystem of the region need to be covered under instruction. Part of the teaching need to be informal. Flexible approach is necessary. There should be less curtailment of natural freedom. Then the child does not see the need to escape from the school at the earliest opportunity, as education becomes an enjoyable activity.

The children study history of the distant lands in the classrooms. They can be taught about their own past. If they are made to study about themselves, it will instill among students a sense of pride and self-respect. For example, the Gonds of Andhra Pradesh had a checkered past. Gondwana, a principality was ruled by Gond Kings in the medieval period. The Yadavas of Devagiri, Bahamanis, Imad Shahis of Berar, Nizamshahis and Moghuls ruled the Gond areas. Ruined forts of Gond Chiefs at Utnoor and Sirpur are a reminder that Gond kingdom once flourished had collapsed due to Moghul and Maratha invasions. Influence of Gond, Maratha and Hindu traditions can be seen in the personal names and village names of the region. The Gond rule started in Adilabad in the middle of the 14th century after the fall of Warangal kingdom. Between 1359 and 1600 the Gonds ruled the territory independently. Small revenue divisions known as Mokhasas came into existence under the rulers of Chanda who appointed local prominent Gonds as Mokhasis to look after them. Around 1600 they became tributaries to Moghul rulers of Delhi. They came under the Maratha rule around 1750. The students need to be taken to local historical places and made to understand their significance.

The students can be made familiar with the story of their origin and different internal divisions. This enables a sense of belonging to develop among students. The origin story of Gonds reveals several mythological links. Haimendorf states that Gonds had divine ancestors who were nurtured by goddess Parvati. Encouraging story telling from Gond mythology can enhance language skills. Riddles and proverbs are entertaining and at the same time they reflect the social situation, values coming from generations of experience. The Persapen (supreme deity), and the Akipen (village deity) are very important in the Gond society. The Gond society is divided into four Sagas (Phratry). They are *Nalven, Siwen, Sarven, Yerven* or *Yedwen*. Tribal folklore is rich source of values.

Visits to civic centers both traditional and modern will enhance the understanding of the students, enabling them better participation in adult life. While visiting Panchayats and Rai centers, jatras, pilgrim centers, historical places, towns, etc., the attempt should be to inculcate civic sense in students. The interdependence between individual and society, the functioning of social institutions, like family, neighbourhood, community and village can be explained on the spot. While visiting panchayats, contrast can be brought with courts, police and their functioning. Learning about the village administration and the role of functionaries like Devari, Patel, Havaldar and Panch can be one of the activities. This can sensitise the students to the local system and problems. Mono acting on the role of various village functionaries, dramatisation of historical leaders, organization of mock Panchayat for settlement of disputes can be undertaken. The Panchayat meeting is called for, when any of the villagers commits an act endangering the community, or when individuals seek intervention for solving a dispute. The entire procedure reveals the concern for the well being of the community and the need to maintain social order. The democratic values can be inculcated by making the students visit Panchayats, Rai centers, etc. Recording village history and settlement history will help in expanding the horizons of the students and inculcating a spirit of investigation and development of an aptitude towards systematic presentation. These activities are entertaining and at the same time bring out the talents of the children.

Leisure is very important. Leisure need to be differentiated from idleness, which is just spending or killing time. Whereas leisure refreshes, recreates and provides rest to the body and the mind, time spent on leisure is not wasted. It is essential to increase efficiency and to improve the quality of work done. Leisure for an individual is like lubrication of human machine. It provides diversion. Leisure cannot be for longer than necessary. Children can be encouraged to pursue different leisure time hobbies. Leisure time activities can be drawing and painting of scenes from forest, agricultural activities, village gatherings, jatras, etc. Hobbies like collection and preservation of leaves, flowers and feathers can be encouraged. Toy making can be a very interesting activity for the students. Participating in the village festivals and jatras at pilgrim centers and understanding their significance and organization will help in better appreciation of their culture. Visits to panchayats to understand the dispute settlement process will familiarise students with cultural values and traditions. Learning of local names of seasons, months, measures of distance, volume, etc. will help in better integration of children into local system. Attending marriages and other ceremonies will facilitate the learning of customs and traditions. The democratic values can be inculcated by making the students visit panchayats, rai centers, etc. Projects on festivals, folk dances, leaders, historical places will help in better appreciation of customs, beliefs, values of the people. Projects can be assigned on Gond dances, songs, etc. i.e. why and when they are performed, how they are performed and so on. The Gonds have a rich tradition of arts and crafts which include tattooing, Rangoli, pottery and basket making. Through culture specific cocurricular educational activities, the children can develop a scientific attitude to traditional activities. It makes education an interesting and enjoyable activity by breaking the monotony.

Excursions provide an opportunity for enjoyable outing, to be in the midst of nature and to learn new things, excursions cannot be just site-seeing trips. The students need to be provided adequate information beforehand to make him mentally prepared and receptive. There should be on the spot briefings, discussions and question and answer sessions. The student should be made to reflect on what they have seen and come forward with presentations. A tour dairy or notes taken during excursion will facilitate this. Mathematical concepts can be best taught through method of discovery, from daily life problems, such as finding out cost of inputs, expenditure on family needs etc. Children are instinctively attracted towards natural objects in the surroundings. They can be asked to observe and represent their observations through diagrams and pictures. Introduction to Botany and Zoology can be done in nature by taking the students to nearby forests and fields. Lessons about different animal species can be taken up starting from Gond totems. They can collect leaves, etc. for preparing a herbarium. Collection of feathers can be coupled with identification of birds. Children can be made to identify different trees and their importance. Imitation of sounds especially of animals and birds and identifying them will be liked by students. They can be asked to draw natural objects like animals, plants, humans, etc.

The students are to be taken to nearby administrative centers where agencies working for social welfare are located. Various functionaries of welfare agencies can be requested to address the students. The objectives of various developmental programmes in the fields of agriculture, animal husbandry, health, women and child welfare can be familiarized. How exploitation takes place in economic transactions, marketing of produce need to be a compulsory item. In this regard, the advantages of cooperative, credit institutions, in overcoming exploitation need to be emphasized. Constitutional safeguards, fundamental rights, democratic processes, political parties, government functioning can be explained at appropriate places and occasions.

A communication gap exists between teachers and pupils. Sometimes, the role perception of the teachers and their background prevent from understanding the point of view of tribal children. A gap exists between the students and the teachers who are preoccupied with teaching the curriculum which deals mostly with external world. It is well known that the teachers perceive themselves as agents of modernisation and development and show eagerness to wean the children away from tribal practices, which they consider as undesirable habits. Culture specific cocurricular educational activities are extremely relevant here as they affect the attitude of the school teachers, especially where non-tribal teachers are involved. The non-tribal teachers do not understand the language of the tribals, or appreciate their culture. Through culture specific co-curricular activities, the teacher also gets to know and appreciate the cultural values of the students and works through them in imparting education. The tribal communities perceive themselves as backward, as this stereotype is put into their mind by the non-tribals and is internalised by them. Students have such faith and belief in the teachers that whatever they are taught is taken to heart. When they get to know about their own heritage and culture from the school teachers, it will have tremendous impact on their psyche.

Attempt should be made to convince the teachers and clear their apprehensions in this regard. The teachers may not take culture specific co-curricular educational activities with all seriousness. Having seen many programmes, they may take it lightly as a temporary phenomenon. Teachers also may resent this as additional work. Some also may misunderstand this as, coming in the way of full development of the tribals on par with non-tribals. The teachers need to be properly oriented in this regard.

Literary Activities in Classes 1 and 2 such as names and relationships of the members of family, story narration, identifying the friends and telling their names, introducing the names of Komaram Bhim, Ramji, etc., introducing the names and description of festivals and jataras, telling the double words like Jaldi-Jaldi, Sala-Sala, observing the work carried out by the members of the family, living with friends, relations with the teachers, observing the village environment, knowing the relationships and mutual help among the members of the family, naming the numbers, e.g. Undi, Rendu, Mundu, naming the measures used to measure the food grains, counting the number of numbers in the family, crying the sounds of animals, identifying and naming the animals seen in the environment, knowing about the various materials and implements found in the house and knowing about the different varieties of honey will not only attract the students but also helps them to understand their culture. This may be implemented in the tribal schools.

Similarly for Classes 3, 4 and 5 knowing about the members of the family, recitation of stanzas, writing the stories and telling about them, recitation and telling about the meaning of poems and riddles, identifying a situation that happened in a Jatara, e.g. Keslapur, school festivals, essay writing, on themes like use of forests, local issues, respecting the elders, e.g. father-in-law, mother-in-law, mutual help, e.g. helping each other in the classroom, school, speaking on the death anniversity of Komaram Bhim, Darbar, discussion on leaders, knowing about the historical leaders, viz. Komarum Bhim, Ramji, knowing and speaking about the political leaders, observing the marriage functions and their types, knowing about the tribal traditions, observing the historical monuments and places, knowing about the tribal kings, e.g., Chendrapur, Dubgad, Aheri, knowing about Gond Rajahs of Utnoor, knowing about the tribal festivals, e.g. Pora, Akadi, Deepavali, Manda Avus, knowing about the use of trees, protection of forests, e.g. tree plantation, clean and green, e.g. environmental cleanliness, collection of the names of tribal festivals and telling how they are performed, e.g. Duradi (Holi), Dhibadi (Deepavali), Mandavus (Ugadi), Pora (Polala Pandaga), Nalung (Nalgu), knowing about the measures used for measuring food grains, e.g. Sorai (Sola), Chetti (Avasola), Pirchitte (Pidikedu), knowing about the measures used to measure lengths, e.g. Kuta, Bette, Jana, counting the tamarind seeds and balls, identifying different leaves, observing how the animals are tended, observing the animals found in the village, knowing about various trees and their uses, illustrating various flowers, birds and insects, knowing about the uses of forests and knowing about the sun light.

In higher Classes 6 and 7 the teachers can plan such activities like lecturing on tribal traditions, culture, festivals, mutual help, jataras, agriculture, animal husbandry, family, Komarum Bhim, Ramji, role play, how your village should be? Your school, medical facilities, transport facilities, your needs, etc., discussions on tribal traditions, forests, seeds, etc., model Panchayat, e.g. knowing about the functioning of panchayat in tribal areas, problems and quarrels, e.g. observing how the problems and quarrels are solved by the Panchayat, discrimination among men and women on wage policy, knowing about women's rights, knowing about the status of women in tribal societies, knowing about the preparation of different bronze articles, knowing about the advantages of forests, e.g. collection of forest produce, knowing about decoration articles, e.g. decoration articles of Gussadi dance, discussion on forest produce relating to fruits, e.g. mangoes, eppapuvvu, etc., knowing about the growth of plants and agricultural produce, growing plants in a plot, knowing about various diseases, e.g. cholera, edki fever, toival swelling, etc., organising debates on various social issues, e.g. superstitions, tribal culture, habits and traditions, mutual help, festivals, agriculture, animal husbandry, property rights, family planning, role play, e.g. Komaram Bhim, Ramji, etc., how is your village? Discussion on school, hospital, etc. Qualities of a good citizen, discussion, yes/no discussion, essay writing, strong telling, extension lecture, riddles, poems, Gondiramayanam, varieties of forests, e.g. Chuddur Kheda, trees in a forest, e.g. Tumri Marra, Nelli Marra, seasons and their importance, observation of the environment, knowing about the culture of tribal women, animal sacrifice, discussion on the materials available in plain area houses and tribal area houses, the grains grown in tribal areas, e.g. rice, wheat, etc., manures, e.g. DPT, urea, etc., agricultural implements, protection of grains in tribal areas, animal husbandry, medicines, food habits, etc. can being children closer to their culture.

Cultural activities in primary classes (Classes 1 and 2) such as fancy dress, e.g. acting as father, turban tieing, identification of different musical instruments, identification of different sounds, imitating the animals, imitating different members of family, identifying different colours, identifying different mud models of animals, identifying the names of different festivals, identifying different materials, e.g. chervi, dhadiya, kasundi, playing different games, e.g. Tipla danda, Gilli danda, mingling with other children and playing, knowing the interests and disinterests of tribal children, identifying the four sides, the shape of sun and moon, imitating the animals, their cries and walk, sounds of birds, drawing different figures and colouring them, drawing sky, animals, trees, hills, sun, moon, stars, etc. and colouring them.

In order to promote cultural activities in higher classes conducting ēxcursions, visit to forests, visit to Jatarlu, e.g. Roy centers, games, village service, knowing about time and seasons, mandal development activities, e.g. participation in different types of games, songs, stories activities, singing, stories, mono actions, education contests, drawing, village administration through role play, festivals, worship, village administration, dances, riddles, good and bad omens, traditions, literary interests, introduction to cooking utensils, agricultural implements, musical instruments, dress and clothing, means of transport, rocks and soils, worshipping the Gods and Goddesses, ceremonies after death, marriage ceremonies, introduction to food grains, introduction to week days and months, names of colours, rocks and soils, gods and worshippers, deaths, marriages, fishing, seeds-grains, weeks-months, four sides (Dikkulu), utensils, agricultural implements, musical instruments, garments, means of transport, dances, riddles, good and bad omens and traditions can be introduced to the students.

Similarly in higher Classes 3, 4 and 5: mono action, e.g. Komaram Bhim, drawing figures and colouring them, e.g. forest, animals, flowers, hills, rivers, sky, etc., drawing the figures of animals, e.g. Duval, Eni, clay modeling, e.g. cow, monkey, preparation of horse with wood, preparation of cart, e.g. with Boppaye Bendu, acting as members of family, e.g. Bayyel, Baval, Dadal, doctor and Palil, dancing, e.g. Gussadi, Demsa, Dhandari, Dhudiya, knowing about animals, e.g. Duval, Chitu, Koyelal, preparation of models, collection of materials, e.g. coins, match boxes, Collection of feathers of birds, e.g. Malyati, identifying the time based on the placement of sun, identifying the time based on the position of leaves, identifying the months, identifying the weeks and naming them, observation of the work of wood carpenter and smithy will help the students to understand their culture better.

In Classes 6 and 7 activities such as preparation of different types of models, e.g. with wood, clay, etc., preparation of charts, drawing, wood carving of different figures, preparation of different types of materials, different types of worship, e.g. worshipping Jango, Lingo, etc., observation of birth and death ceremonies, e.g. Parti, Sabha and Karam, knowing about village Goddesses, e.g. Avval Pen, Aki Pen, Rajulk, knowing about the extraction of Eppa oil, knowing the food habits of tribals, death anniversaries, types of ceremonies, e.g. misval, sarus, usage of medicines, drawing of figures, drawing charts, drawing pictures, preparation of models with wood, treating Kappi bird as bad omen, treating Tabbe bird as good omen, cleanliness, ill health, hygiene, communicable diseases and village survey activities will make students appreciate their culture better.

In order to promote handwork and craft activities the following activities may be kept in mind. Stitching, Comb (Kangva), Sukkad (Garita), Dhavi (Teddu), Girki (Babi Gilaka), Dappu, Dholu, Tudum, Dholki, Vette, Pepre, Kalikome, Kikri, Dhakki, Sare (Araka), Kanur (Bandi), Sulludi (Pillanagrovi), Butte (Buttalu), Tatte (Tadakalu), Gade (Gummi), Dabidi Auche (Gampa), Gunti (Villu), Gunti Kulam (Banalu), Seendichapa (Etachrpa), Purki (Burrakaya), Mydaki (Gorintaku), Koherae (Gummadikaya), Kayaguraz, Khnkudi Kaya, Mahaka (Maredukaya), Preparation of models, e.g. hills, rivers, etc., Muske (Chikkalu), Jute thread preparation, Flower garlands, Flower bunches and Decorative articles.

Thus, the main objective of the study was how to keep the tribal children in the schools during the whole academic year and avoid the students absenteeism from residential schools. In order to promote this the following culture spesic activities has been identified by the tribal teachers working in the residential schools.

Physical and motor development activities like Uduthata (Kabadi Aata), Villuaata (Archery Aata), Tillidanda, Yelli-Verukad Aata, Railgadi Aata, Makkan Seti Aata (Tukkudu Silla Aata), Ghoda Aata (Gurram Aata), Mosor Kiskwal Aata (Mukku Gillu Aata), Mudda Mahuswal (Vungaram Aata), Chikko Aata, Mahwal Aata (Dagadu Mutalu Aata), Dubba Karswal Aata (Mattikuppalata Aata), Kor Gandal Aata (Kodi-Godda Aata), Puli Judam Aata, Pammdeyival Aata (Kappa Ginta Aata), Kove Dayival Aata (Koti Komurchi Aata), Bouri Kavawal Aata (Bongaram Aata), Lidda Karswal Aata (Chakali Bana Aata), Sui-Nul Aata (Sudi-daram Aata), Velingkappa Aata (Vennela Kuppalu Aata), Kurchi Kurswal Aata (Kurchi Aata) and Dandi Karswal Aata (Damidi Aata), etc.

Craft activities and handicrafts like stitching, preparation of karyva (comb), sukkud (spoon), gaatikiyval (Teddu), girkd (Gilaka), music instruments—Dappa, Dolu, Tudum, Dolki, Pette, Peprae, Kalikom, with Bendu-Ser (Araka), Kasur (Bandi), Salladi (Pillanagrovi), Butte (Buttalu), Tati (Tadekelu), Tokili (Gullalu), Seti (Chatalu), Dala (Gampalu), Gumti (Villu), Guntikolu (Banalu), Jadapa (Visanikurralu), Purkahaya, Kohirae (Gummadikaya), Namminalu, jute products and lower decoration, etc.

In order to promote cultural activities in tribal schools the following activities are identified. They are as follows: encouraging tribal Gondi songs, do fancy dress, imitation of animals, performing dances (tribal), doing mono actions, going to jataras, conducting lectures on cultures, celebrating festivals, marriage functions, ceremonies, doing role plays, watching animals, Birds, plants and trees, Flora and Fauna and food habits, etc. Excursion activities such as visit to local tourism centres, forts, caves, palaces, play activities, village service and measures – weights, time, etc. were identified and suggested by the teachers to implement them in the tribal schools.

Education Action Plan in Low Literacy Tribal Pockets in Andhra Pradesh

This is an important work to know about the problems of tribal education in India in general and Andhra Pradesh in particular. The main objective of the study is to prepare an action plan encompassing all suggestions, such as requirement of infrastructural facilities, organisational set up and the basic requirements aiming at improving the tribal education quantitatively and qualitatively. For the study a multi method research design was formulated. It is consisting of observation method (both participatory and non-participatory) case study method, focus group discussions and survey method has been used. A three-stage stratified random sampling was adopted for interviewing tribal households in selected villages. Seethampeta mandal of Srikakulam district was selected as a sample for the study. A total number of ten villages in Seethampeta mandal with the larger concentration of Primitive Tribal Groups (PTGs – Khonds and Savaras) were selected for the study. Some of the findings of the study are with regard to the attitude of tribals on education interestingly three-fourths of respondents have indicated positive attitude to educate their children. The sex discrimination continues to exist in the sense that education of the male children takes priority over girl children as they think that a girl child is considered as dependent either on father before marriage or on husband after marriage. The level of education aspired by the respondents for their children is upto 10th class (matriculation) for boys and for girls upto primary level. Majority of the respondents preferred government jobs for their sons and they are educating their children because of government incentives. The main constraints for the tribal education in this mandal are no proper infrastructural facilities in the schools followed by frequent transfers of teachers, educational functionaries, lack of accommodation and mobility of the concerned officials, etc. Majority of the teachers are males (88.7%). However the schools run by Mandal Praja Parishad (MPP) have relatively more female teachers (15.9%) than those run by ITDA (7.8%). The percentage of trained teachers are more in MPP schools than ITDA schools. High participation of tribal students at primary level, low participation at upper primary and high school levels is observed. This means that there are many drop outs in between. The main reasons for the drop out of tribal children are: the tribal parents consider their children as an economic asset. Therefore, sending the children to schools deprives the tribal parents from their earnings from collection of Minor Forest Products (MFPs), roots, fruits, fodder, cattle tending and working in farms; the places of their stay, i.e. huts and small houses do not provide conducive atmosphere to the children to study at home; admission of children in schools are average; an early marriages in case of girls and also the girl child's involvement in bringing at their younger ones; different medium of instruction (other than the tribal dialect) in the schools; inadequate infrastructural facilities within the school and school timings do not match with the working hours of the children. To check dropouts the following measures need to be taken up: starting of pre-school programmes; introducing mid-day meal programme; the course contents should consist of more of songs, plays various games, music, dance and drama, etc. The school activities should be in tune with respective tribal culture and based on local tribal dialect; suitably changing the school timings and vacation period in consultation with tribal parents; keeping the external and internal school environment more picturesque, decorative, and attractive (with proper equipment and infrastructure) for tribal children; actively motivating and involving tribal community in educational programme right from the selection of site for school building and its construction through their contributions in the shape of material, labour, etc.; starting remedial education centers for inclusive coaching to the tribal students so as to make them completely successful in their formal school examinations.

Administration and Management of Primary Schools in Tribal Areas

In the tribal areas the practice of recruiting Vidya volunteers to meet any deficit is not very encouraging. There are two Mandal Resource Persons (MRPs) in each mandal irrespective of the geographic conditions spread over the mandals and the number of schools. This reduces the frequency of visits of the Mandal Resource Persons to schools particularly where the number of schools in his jurisdiction is more than 20 schools. In the tribal areas there is dual reporting structure at the mandal level. The information from schools is sent to ITDAs and on some issues the information will be sent to the Additional Project Coordinator (APC), DPEP/SSA through Mandal Education Officers (MEOs). Similarly the role of the Mandal Education Officer has been marginalised in the ITDA areas. Inter departmental linkages particularly at the district level is low, that is between Education Department, Social Welfare Department and District Rural Development Authorities (DRDA). In the tribal areas inspection of the schools by the Mandal Education Officer (MEO) is non-existing. The teachers are of the opinion that inspection by ITDA authorities was also very limited. Dissemination of training inputs is not taken seriously by the teachers due to the wide difference in educational qualifications between the MRPs and the school teachers. There is considerable delay in information flow from the Integrated Tribal Development Authorities (ITDA)/District Tribal Welfare Officers (DTWOs) to District Education Officers (DEOs), resulting in delay in decision making such as release of textbooks, teaching aids, etc. Participation of the School Education Committees (SECs) in promoting primary education in tribal areas was found very low, the prime reason being high illiteracy and low awareness among the members.

An Investigation into the Problems Associated with the Literacy of Scheduled Tribe Children in Tribal Schools of Vizianagaram District, Andhra Pradesh (1999)

The rationale of the study is that the Scheduled Tribes constitute a major group in Andhra Pradesh for whom access to primary education is the main problem. They live in remote areas of the State and need special focus to solve their problems. The literacy rate of the scheduled tribe children in Andhra Pradesh is very low compared with scheduled caste groups and other backward classes. According to 1991 census, the literacy rate of the Scheduled Tribes of Vizianagaram district is 15.68 per cent (22.53% male and 8.79% female). The female literacy is very poor and needs urgent action. Jatapu, Kondadora, Mukadora, and Mannedora are the major tribal groups in the district and Savara and Gadaba communities are the Primitive Tribal Groups. There are many school-less habitations which are small but scattered in tribal areas. The enrolment percentage of children at primary stage is 71 per cent and dropout rate is 68 per cent which is also high. To fulfill the dream of 100 per cent literacy among Scheduled Tribe children at primary level there is a need to identify their educational problems and find out suitable measures to improve the literacy level of these primitive groups. The high dropout rate among these tribal children are due to various reasons. The children are sent for cattle grazing, agricultural labour, sibling care and lack of interest in education. Besides this, most of the areas are covered with thick forest. Because of the economic and social backwardness the pupils participation in the educational programme is far from satisfactory. The tribal children are faced with the problems of access, attainment, language deficiency and participation. The district has no schools in some habitations and the enrolment percentage is below 60 per cent in some of the trial mandals (Pachipenta—45%). Education of children of primitive tribal communities is a very important concern of our government. Although schools were provided in the tribal areas, attendance was made compulsory for the children of school going age, the expenses on education were met by the governments, children were fed, yet desirable results have not been achieved to improve their standard of living. The solution to the problem depends on how best educational facilities can be provided to them. The educational problems concerning these primitive tribes should be cackled by the apex educational organisations as a part of their extension programmes. It is with this background that it has been decided to study the educational pattern available to these children of Vizianagaram district of Andhra Pradesh with a view to improving the literacy rate in the eight tribal sub-plan mandals of Vizianagaram district of Andhra Pradesh. The study was an attempt to examine the prevailing educational facilities among the schools of eight tribal sub-plan mandals in terms of retention, enrolment, dropouts and physical facilities. However, the major objective of the study was to assess the learning achievement levels of the Savara Tribal students at the end of Classes 1 and 2 in Telugu and Environmental Science and to make an attempt to increase their achievement levels of Classes 1 and 2. The other objectives of the study was to survey the tribal sub-plan Mandals of Vizianagaram district to find out the status of education among the Savara Tribal Students, Teachers and parents, to study the present status of enrolment, retention and dropouts of Classes 1 and 2 Savara Tribal children in the selected schools of Vizianagaram district, to assess the performance level of Savara Tribal children of Class 1 in Telugu and EVS, to assess the performance level of Savara Tribal children of Class 2 in Telugu and EVS, to analyse the school related factors that cause the hindrance in learning achievement level among Savara Tribal children of Classes 1 and 2, to analyse teacher related factors that may contribute to the differences in the learning achievement levels of Savara Tribal children in Classes 1 and 2, to develop the modular material for improving the reading, listening, writing and speaking skills among the Savara Tribal children of Classes 1 and 2 in Telugu and EVS, and to tryout the package for assessing its effectiveness by orientation of teachers from the selected Tribal Schools.

There are 34 Mandals and 4 Municipalities in the district covering sub-plan area of 8 Mandals. The male population of the district is 11,24,152 and female population is 11,16,422. Most of the people are living in rural areas and are dependent on agriculture for their livelihood. Vizianagaram district has been comparatively backward in the field of education. The literacy rate in the tribal sub-plan mandals is very low in girls literacy rate and in the enrolment of school children. In one of the 8 tribal sub-plan Mandals, the enrolment ratio is 60 per cent (Pachipenta 45%) in Gumma Lakshmipuram one of the selected tribal Mandals the teacher student ratio is 1:29. Most of the schools are without buildings, and with just one classroom. The district is facing a number of constraints in the way to achieve the Universal Primary Education (UPE). One of the reason among several problems is the high dropout rate in the tribal schools. It is higher especially in Classes 1 and 2. More dropout children are from the Savara Tribal children due to child labour activities. These tribal children are doing coolie work and agricultural labour. Most of these tribal habitations have a population of less than 200. Some of these habitations have a formal school within a radius of 1 km, but the children are unable to attend the schools regularly due to social and physical barriers. Another main reason for more dropout rate is that the children are assisting their parents in the farm lands in the villages. The tribal parents are creating them as earning members to co-support the family and hence they are not interested to send their wards to the schools. There are a number of girl children who are under sibling care. Some of them are not at all enrolled and others have discontinued in Classes 2 or 3. In order to provide primary educational facilities to the Scheduled Tribe children, whose literacy is poor, 3777 single teacher primary schools were opened in the tribal areas. In these schools, educating scheduled tribe candidates with 10th class qualification were appointed as teachers. In addition to these Grama Vidya Vikas Kendra Schools, 830 Maabadi schools are functioning in the state under the control of Village Tribal Development Agencies (VTDA's). Apart from the above there are 554 schools under the control of Integrated Tribal Development Authority (ITDA) such as Ashram high schools (10) Ashram Up schools (10) Ashram primary schools (19) GVVKs (384) and Mabadi schools (131). Inspite of these efforts, there are 214 school less habitations. In this district there are 16 school complex centres to provide academic guidance to the teachers. The teachers were provided with condensed teacher training for 6 months in different DIETS of the state. The functioning of all these schools is not upto the mark and deficient in the academic front and also regularity in running the schools. The major findings of the study are as follows with regard to schools: The GVVK and Mabadi schools were started in the less populated tribal habitations. The enrolment rate in the Classes I to V is very low. The main reasons found in the survey for high dropout rate is child labour, sibling care, domestic work, lack of proper encouragement from parents, etc. Most of the schools do not have toilets, drinking water facilities, school buildings, etc. 33 per cent of schools were run in the villager's houses. The supply of incentives in the form of books, writing materials, midday-meal rice were not supplied regularly by the authorities. Even supplied, They are not reaching the students. 42 per cent of schools do not have black boards, charts, kits, display materials in the schools. Most of the Savara Tribal Children schools are located at top hill tribal areas. The teachers working in GVVK schools are local tribals with SSC qualification. Some of them are SSC failed candidates. They were untrained teachers. In every Mandal a number of teachers posts are lying vacant. For ex: In Pachipenta Mandal 15 posts of teachers are lying vacant. The tribal teachers are assigned with additional responsibilities like pulse polio programme work, clerical jobs, going to helath camps, etc. Teachers absenteeism is more in the schools. With regard to teachers, female teachers are much less compared to the male teachers. The percentage of female teachers is the lowest in Jiyyammavalasa Mandal. The percentage of ST female teachers are very much low (92 female teachers out of 444 ST teachers). 75 per cent of teachers wanted more inservice training programmes. The salaries of staff, the salaries of new teachers are being paid through demand drafts (DDs). The teachers are experiencing a lot of problems in encashment of DDs and receiving their salaries in time. The delay ranges from 5 to 15 days. The commitment of teachers towards their profession is not uniform. Most of the teachers working in top hill tribal areas were 'nonresidential.' They come from neighbouring villages with a distance of 20-30 kms. In the top hill areas proper road facilities, electric facilities, hospitals, shops were not available. No proper housing facilities exist to stay in the hill areas for teachers. Teaching materials, teaching aids were not there in the 50 per cent of schools. Most of the teachers feel difficult to teach in Savara language. They are non-tribal teachers. The text books are printed in Telugu language. With regard to students, the Savara Tribal Children are not conversant with Telugu language. Most of the children are engaged in seasonal work. Enrolment of girl child is very poor due to sibling care, house watch, etc. Most of the school-going children of 6-14 years of age are working children. Child labour exists in Kurupam, GL puram and pachipenta mandals heavily. Parents engage their children for collecting food grains, cattle rearing, etc. The educational gap during summer and other seasonal holidays had a serious effect on the tribal students. They forget what ever they have learnt in the schools due to the gap. School children are suffering from serious diseases like Cholara, fever and TB. Seasonal festivals had a serious impact on the children. With regard to performance, the girl's achievement level in Class 1 is more than the boys. The girl's performance is highest in EVS than Telugu. The boy's achievement level is highest in EVS than Telugu in Class 1. The girl's achievement level is highest in EVS than Telugu in Class 1. The girl's achievement is high in Class 2. The Girl's performed well in EVS than Telugu. The boys achieved highest in EVS than Telugu in Class 2. The boy's performance is lowest in Class 2. Both girl's and boy's have low achievement levels in Language in Classes 1 and 2.

The implication of the study is that the Savara Tribals are living in the top hill tribal areas are far from the civilization. As long as the disease of illiteracy is with these tribals, development among them cannot be possible. Therefore, it is the, responsibility of both the State and Central Governments to encourage the tribal education and their language and bring them into the mainstream of society. The recent survey shows that there is a need to develop the Savara Tribals. We find, there are many schools with less habitations which are small but scattered in 8 tribal sub-plan Mandal villages. The enrolment, and dropout percentages of the Savara Tribal children are high. There is problem of access and high dropout rate. The schools lack infrastructural facilities. Most of the teachers are untrained and the children are unable to attend the schools regularly due to social and physical barriers. There is a very low profile of Savara Tribal student's achievement. In view of the above problems the following suggestions can be made to improve the educational development of the Savara tribal children in Andhra Pradesh.

1. Alternative schooling facilities should be provided to solve the problem of access. (The Savara Tribal community are engaged in shifting cultivation, Gadaba community is engaged in stone cutting). To provide education to the children of these communities, more multigrade teacher schools are urgently needed. Further, these schools should be provided with well trained teachers.
2. Preparation of bilingual books, charts, dictionaries, glossaries in Savara and Telugu language for classroom use by the teachers to attract children is needed.
3. The teachers should adopt activity—based teaching–learning process.
4. Joyful learning programme should be organised.
5. Supply of incentives in the form of books, writing materials and clothes should be provided by the Government to these tribal children on time.
6. Study tours must be conducted to the VEC members to motivate local tribal community participants.
7. House to house enrolment drives should be conducted.
8. More ECE centres should be opened to increase girl's enrolment and retention.
9. Teacher empowerment programme for attitudinal change should be organised.
10. Teachers knowing tribal language must be appointed in the tribal schools.

11. The lessons taught at the tribal schools must reflect the tribal culture in the text books. While preparing the text books tribal teachers must be involved.
12. DPEP/SSA and ITDA schools are being established by the Government in the remote villages of the tribal areas. However, these schools must be provided with infrastructural facilities along with residential quarters for the teachers to stay with the tribals and improve education among the tribal children.
13. The teachers should set aside the differences of opinion of the education committees and should work for the development of the tribal villages. The officers must visit these schools periodically and study the development of the schools and offer suitable suggestions for improving the literacy rate of the tribal children.
14. Instead of giving 3 kg's Midday meal rice by the Government it is better to start RD Bank accounts with Rs. 50 per child per month. The maturity amount should be given to students who studied upto SSC.
15. Textbooks should be given to teachers atleast one year before, so that the teacher can have an idea of the textbooks.
16. The teachers and the tribal children must be provided with proper health care and medical facilities. More number of primary health care centres should be opened in the top hill areas.
17. Instead of starting the schools in less populated Tribal villages, it is better if the Government start one Ashram school in one place where all the tribal children of 7 to 10 tribal villages can be accommodated and impart education to the tribal children.
18. Every school should have pucca building. Without buildings, furniture and facilities the Government should not start schools in tribal areas.
19. Operation Black Board programmes must be continued in the Tribal areas.
20. More girl child welfare centres may be opened by the government. There are 9, 353 unenrolled girls in the tribal areas. For the welfare of the girl child in Tribal areas girl child welfare activities must be strictly implemented.
21. The Government should curb the child labour in these tribal areas. Parents using their children as child labourers should be strictly punished.

The number of illiterate parents of Class I and II children is more in all sub-plan Mandals of Vizianagaram district. In these selected villages, not even a single mother has received collegiate education. The students are receiving least support from their parents towards their education. Better socio-economic condition of Parents provide better education among the tribal children. The home background especially the parents literacy plays an important role on their children. In retention also Parent's literacy has an impact on the tribal children. There are 1,39,282 girl children of the age group of 6-11 in the district. Out of which 1, 29,929 have been enrolled. The unenrolled girl children are 9,353 in the tribal sub-plan areas. A high percentage of dropouts (70.15%) are due to the parents not wanting their children to study. Especially parents want their girl children engaged in household work and younger sibling care and the boys as child labourers. There is a need for changing the attitude of the parents towards education. In order to achieve universal retention as well as Universal achievement, it is important to improve the literacy level among the parents. In order to improve the literacy rate among these children, the first focus should be on women's education. In this endeavour the local voluntary organisations, NGO's should involve themselves. Teachers working in these tribal areas do not know the tribal language. The medium of instruction is Telugu. Hence their achievement in language is less. Perhaps there is a need to prepare bilingual textbooks, charts, kits glossaries and instruction should be both in Telugu and Savara languages. The lessons taught at the tribal schools and the curriculum must reflect the tribal culture in the textbooks. While preparing the textbooks the tribal teachers must be involved. The language used in the textbooks must be in accordance with the tribal surroundings.

The study has laid bare facts and figures with regard to tribal education in Andhra Pradesh in general and India in particular. The findings of the study will help in discerning the implications. If Mandal-wise perspective plans to improve the conditions of these tribes in top hill areas are drawn carefully and then executed without fail definitely the dropout rate can be reduced to the maximum extent and their achievement level can be improved.

The objectives of the study include to find out the status of education among the tribal students, tribal teachers and tribal parents in the tribal sub-plan mandals of Vizianagaram district, to study the present status of enrolment, retention and drop out of Classes 1 to 5 of the Savara tribal children, to assess the performance levels of Savara children of Classes 1 to 5 in Telugu, Mathematics and EVS, to analyse the school related factors that hinder learning achievement among children of Classes 1 to 5, to analyse teacher related factors that contribute to differences in learning achievement and to develop modular material for improving learning, speaking, reading and writing skills among tribal Savara children of Classes 1 to 5. Eight (8) sub-plan mandals of Vizianagaram district (Gumma Lakshmipuram, Makkuva, Kurupam, Pachipenta, Jiyyammavalsa, Salur, Kumarada and Parvathipuram). One hundred and twenty (120) students each of Classes 1 to 5, and 50 tribal teachers working in three different schools such as Tribal Welfare resdientail schools, ITDA schools and Ashram schools were taken up as the sample for the study. Student achievement tests and teacher schedule with 83 items were used as the tools for the collection of data. The following are the major findings of the study. The reasons for children's drop out are as follows: language problem; lack of equipment in schools such as furniture; blackboard, etc.; modules, charts and kit materials are not used by the teachers; lack of schools in all habitations because of scatteredness of the tribal population; lack of motivation on the part of tribal parents to educate their children; lack of interest on the part of the teachers to work in tribal habitations; lack of door-to-door survey to enroll children; teacher absenteeism; poor teaching; participation of tribal children in seasonal work; migration; female child labour; participation of tribal girl children in domestic work and sibling care; grazing cattle; incomplete schools; unattractive classrooms; professional deficiency of teachers; less qualified teachers; lack of training in child-centered activity oriented instruction to teachers, etc.; the enrolment rate in Classes I and II is low; the main reasons for high drop out rate are child labour, sibling care, domestic work and lack of proper encouragement from parents, etc.; most of the schools are run in villagers houses; the supply of incentives in the form of books, writing materials, mid-day meal rice were not supplied regularly by authorities. Even supplied they are not reaching the students; 42 per cent of the schools do not have blackboards, charts, kits, display materials in the schools; teachers working in GVVKs are local tribals with SSC qualification, some are failed and untrained; in every mandal many teachers posts are vacant; tribal teachers are assigned with additional responsibilities like pulse polio, clerical jobs; census reports and going to camps; teacher absenteeism is more in these schools; female teachers are much less compared to male teachers; percentage of ST female teachers is very much low; inservice training programmes were not conducted for the teachers; the teachers are experiencing lot of troubles in encashment of salary through DDs in time; the commitment of teachers towards profession is not uniform; most of the teachers working in top hill tribal areas were non-residential. They come from neighbouring villages with a distance of 20-30 kms; no proper housing facilities exist to teachers who stay and work in the schools located in the hill areas; 50 per cent of the schools do not have teaching materials and teaching aids; non-tribal teachers working in tribal schools are feeling difficulty to teach in Savara and other tribal languages; the Savara tribal teachers are not conversent Telugu language; most of the tribal children are engaged in seasonal work; involvement of girl child in education is very poor due to sibling care, house watch, crop watch, etc.; most of the school going children of 6-14 years of age are working children; parents engage their children for collecting food grains, cattle rearing, etc.; the educational gap prevail during summer and other seasonal holidays which had a serious effect on the tribal students. They forget whatever they have learnt in the schools due to the gap; seasonal festivals had a serious impact on the children; with regard to the academic achievement, the girls achievement in Classes 1 to 5 is more than that of boys. The girls performance is highest in EVS Mathematics and Telugu. However, both boys and girls have low achievement levels in Classes 1 to 5 in all tribal schools in the agency areas.

A Study on the Functioning of Girijana Vidya Vikasa Kendras (GVVKs) With Special Reference to Integrated Tribal Development Agency (ITDA), Parvatipuram, Vizianagaram District, Andhra Pradesh

This is another important study on tribal education. The main objectives of the study were to know the functioning of the GVVKs in relation to teacher component in the tribal pockets of Vizianagaram district, to find the academic deficiencies of the GVVK teachers, and to suggest suitable measures for the effective functioning of these schools. The study covers a sample consisted of 39 teachers belonging to Kondadora, Mannedora, Jatapu, Savara and Godaba tribal sub-communities spread in seven mandals, i.e., Salur, Parvatipuram, Makkuva, Gummalakshmipuram, Kommarada and Pachipenta Mandals in Vizianagaram district of Andhra Pradesh. The tool used to conduct the study was a questionnaire administered with 458 items. Besides, the questionnaire, personal interviews with some of the teachers were also held. Information was also collected with group interaction. The following are the findings of the study: Of the 39 teachers involved in the study 24 teachers are not residing in the school village whose percentage works out to 62 per cent. In many cases teachers belonging to one community are working in places of different communities, for example, Kondadora in Jatupu habitation, Godaba in Mukadora habitation, Savara in Gadabahabitation, etc. The causes for non-residence of the teachers are lack of houses to reside, non-availability of medical facilities, school is not nearer to the place of residence, spouse working in a different place and village is inhabited by other community members. Teachers working in Grama Vidya Vikas Kendra (GVVK) schools are facing the problem in dealing with the Mathematics subject because of their academic deficiency. In teaching-learning process no aids are prepared and used. GVVK teachers are not provided with any academic guidance or support. Schools lack infrastructural facilities like building, furniture, aids, etc. Teachers are adopting only traditional method of teaching but not activity method. Language problem is also expressed by the subject teachers. They are deficient in Telugu language and also the local dialects. Teachers are not aware of the school readiness programme and joyful learning programmes.

A Study on the Causes for Low Enrolment and High Drop Out in Ashram Schools in Andhra Pradesh

The major objective of the study is to find out the causes for low enrolment and high drop out in Ashram schools of Adilabad district which is under the control of ITDA Utnoor. A questionnaire with 94 items was used as the tool for the collection of data. The following are the reasons found to be the causes for low enrolment and high drop outs in Ashram schools. Children are not habituated to education, ill health, lack of interest on education in case of children, financial backwardness of parents, taking away the children by parents always, disinterestedness on the past of the children to leave their homes, lack of interest on the part of the teacher towards the education of children, language problem, more number of festivals, lack of school programmes to arouse interest towards education, sibling care at home, disinterestedness among teachers towards tribal children and lack of parent-teacher contacts, etc.

A Study on the Causes of Low Percentage of SSC Results in Ashram Schools of Adilabad District

The study reveals very important lesson to be learnt in the field of tribal education. The major objectives of the study is to find out the causes for low percentage of SSC results in Ashram Schools in Adilabad district. A questionnaire with 53 items was used as a tool for the collection of data. Information from 16 Ashram school head teachers, teachers and pupils were collected. The following are fond to be the causes for low percentage of results – non-coverage of syllabus on time and failure to revision the syllabus completed, neglect of IX class, late communication of special coaching facilities, no proper connection of pre-public examination scripts and not informing the students of their defects, dependence of pupils on copying and prevention of copying in public examinations, neglect of the programmes which help in the better preparation of students for the public examination, no working out of question banks, no working out of the last three year public examination question papers, no adoption of students by the teachers, no working out the exercises given at the end of the lessons in the textbooks, by hearting of the material given in the boxes in the textbook, abstaining from school without informing the concerned teachers, not attending the school on time after availing leave for celebrating festivals at home, showing greater interest in co-scholastic activities as against scholastic activities, non-taking of interest by the teachers in English, Mathematics and Science subjects for preparing the students to the public examination through special coaching.

A Study on Adilabad Agency Experiment in Activity Method

The study reveals some of the important issues in tribal education such as access, attainment and participation of tribal students in schools. It is reported that the educational scenario of Integrated Tribal Development Agency (ITDA), Utnoor, Adilabad district was faced with the problem of access, attainment and participation, i.e. lack of schools in some habitations, low standards of teaching learning process and poor people participation in educational activities. To solve the problems of access, attainment and participation an experiment was conducted with the following objectives in the ITDA, Utnoor of Adilabad District in Andhra Pradesh: to provide access for primary education by opening schools with surplus teachers and community participation, to provide quality education by reaching/attaining the minimum levels of learning through the adoption of activity method, to ensure community participation through the constitution of tribal committees, and to study the results of the above three programmes on the quality of education. To realise these objectives the programmes implemented in Adilabad agency district are as follows: with regard to access rationalisation of teachers posts, opening of community schools/Maabadi schools in schooless habitations and encouraging voluntary organizations to open schools are being suggested. With regard to enrolment opening of village census registration, door-to-door survey, incentives to school committees which achieved cent per cent enrolment and retention, constructing two roomed sheds, one for school and the other for the teacher to reside and teacher-doctor programmes are suggested. Similarly, with regard to retention activity based instruction, mid-day meals programmes, constitution of tribal committees, supply of minimum educational material as a package of incentive, residence of teacher in the school village and Contacts with parents about the progress of the children, etc. are suggested. With regard to quality improving the competence of teachers, training in minimum levels of learning, training in activity approach, preparation and supply of instructional modules, supply of instructional kits, preparation and supply of instructional charts, filling up of vacant posts by locals, strengthening of supervision through education counselors, payment of teachers salaries through banks, awal committees to watch the regularity of the school, monthly review of academic work at cluster level, teaching through bilingual charts, daily schedule of academic work in the form of a calendar, frequent orientation in activity method, adoption of Andhra Pradesh Primary Educaiton Project (APPEP) pedagogy and incentives to those who do good work are suggested.

The results of the experiment were studied through questionnaire-cum-observation mode and the findings reveal that the teachers are using activity method in Classes 1 and 5 to realise the minimum levels of learning. The conclusions of the study reveals the fact that the teachers are in touch with I and II Classes syllabus only and trying to realise the Minimum Levels of Learning (MLL) through activity method. Materials supplied like modules, charts, kit materials are used. Awal committees are functioning. Display of charts and materials in the classroom are attracting the pupil. It had also increased the rate of transfer of pupils from Classes I and II and Classes II and III. 96 schools were opened in schooless area habitations with surplus teachers. 37 Maabadi schools were opened. A total number of 449 two round sheds were constructed and the teacher-doctor programme was also availed by the villagers.

School Assessment Study Among the Scheduled Tribal Groups in Andhra Pradesh

The main objectives of the study were; to study the accessibility of education to the children of tribal groups, the changes in the management and monitoring of the school and education system to encourage tribal participation, to develop the communication strategy, to improve the decentralisation process to be more sensitive to the needs of tribal groups and to help

DPEP/SSA to prepare sensitization packages, etc. The sample of the study consisted of 64 villages in 32 mandals in 8 districts. Four mandals in each district were selected. 320 parents of school going age children and 320 parents of non-school going age children were involved in the study. The sample districts include Adilabad, Khammam, Vizianagaram, Visakhapatnam, Warangal, Guntur, Nellore and Mahabubnagar districts. Data was collected from secondary and primary sources. The secondary source consisted of the records and the primary sources consisted of the interviews. Two separate interview schedules were used for the collection of data, one for schooling and another for non-school going age children's parents. Five focused group discussions were also held. The following are important observations of the study. The occupation of the 35 tribal groups including 12 Primitive Tribal Groups (PTGs) were as follows: cultivation (41.2%), agriculture labour (41.6%), household industry (2.6%) and other occupations (9.6%). Repetition of students in higher classes discourages the parents from sending their children to school. Parents like to send their children if the schools function regularly and children show academic progress. Children of six or seven years of age need emotional and psychological support from their parents. The reasons for non-enrolment and drop out of the children are: poor economic conditions, non-interest of the tribal child, non-interest of the parents, lack of schools in the village, because of girl child, ill health of the child, no tradition of sending the child to the school, physically handicapped, to look after younger siblings at home, teacher teasing, unemployment after education, to work in the fields, parents death, single son, nomadism, retaining in the same class and under aged. Children experience school as a punishment for them as they are not allowed to move freely. Some of the other reasons are: teacher absenteeism, isolation and inaccessibility, forest policy of not laying roads and permanent constructions, seasonal variations, naxalite movement, occupations, poor school environment and non-suitable curriculum, etc. Education of the parents also influences on the education of their children. Illiterate parents are not aware of the importance of education. There is positive correlation between wet cultivation and literacy. Dandora is the best means of communication followed by radio and TV announcements and advertisements. Father have major role in decision making regarding their children's education. Reasons for non-residence of students in hostels are: poor accommodation, no sleeping material facilities, no teaching during non-school timings, early serving of food, absence of personnel during nights and the fear of the presence of ghosts and spirits. Tribal communities lack awareness about the educational facilities like Non-Formal Educadtion (NFE), back-to-school, open school and other continuing education programmes being provided by the Government for their development. The causes for teachers irregular attendance are: non-residence, teachers belong to other ethnic groups, adjustment problem, politically influenced, having an understanding with the higher officials, having relation with local leaders, no teaching ability and not attending the school daily after leaving the school. The tribal District Institute of Education and Training (DIETs) lack proper infrastructure and not discharging necessary training inputs to the tribal teachers. Implementing agencies are not able to provide the incentives regularly and in time. 30.30 per cent of the parents in school going category keep their children in hostels and about one third of them are not staying in hostels at night. There is poor maintenance of school records and lack of periodical inspection in tribal schools. 68.96 per cent of the non-tribal teachers and all the tribal teachers feel that training in pedagogy is essential for effective classroom teaching. The suggestions for the improvement of the situation include the following: strengthening and extending Maabadi and GVVK schools based on mandal school mapping, limiting Ashram schools to mandal headquarters/road junctions considering various ecological barriers, strengthening the Ashram schools complexes to provide better supervision, by increasing supervision visits by higher officials for better monitoring and implementation, vacation should be based on local needs and seasonal variations like festivals, collection of MRF and other economic activities where tribal children participate, bringing awareness about the incentives through pamphlets and folk media, providing additional incentives in the form of rice (10 kg per head) per month to the students who belong to PTGs as these groups have low literacy rates, the cooks working in Ashram schools should be given short term training in improved methods of cooking, authorising and prescribing periodical visits to schools and hostels compulsory by the different sectoral officers at district and ITDA levels, preparing separate training modules for DIETs which impart training for teachers working in tribal areas, appointing anthropologists with faculty of DIETs or arranging guest lecturers by anthropologists in teaching learning programmes, also the performance of the teachers should be evaluated in terms of residing in the same village where he/she is working, increasing enrolment, regular attendance and promoting/admitting number of children in Ashram schools and performance appraisal by SEC and a committee of parents selected at random and utilising shandies/places of community festivals and other large gatherings for the propagation of education through different folk media and posters.

A Study on the Educational Development Among Scheduled Tribes in the Tribal Sub-Plan Areas of Andhra Pradesh

The major objectives of the study were: to study the quantitative and qualitative aspects of educational facilities available at primary, middle and secondary stages. The indicators for the quality would be teacher-pupil ratio, teachers' qualifications and infrastructural facilities available for the school. Another important objective was to study the educational status (enrolment, dropouts, non-enrolled) of 6-14 years of age children *vis-à-vis* socio-economic and educational background of their families in tribal sub-plan area mandals. The study also examines the social and educational background of teachers and their attitude towards tribal children and society and their willingness to work in tribal areas. However, the main focus of the study was to study the parental views, perceptions and aspirations regarding education and their awareness and attitude towards education, other developmental programmes and governmental agencies, to study the financial policy of tribal sub-plan and budget allocation to tribal development and education at macro and micro levels and also to examine the unit cost of education item by item at institutional level in different categories of schools in the tribal sub-plan areas, to understand the educational administrative system and interdepartmental coordination in tribal sub-plan areas and to examine the grassroot innovations for educational development in tribal sub-plan areas.

The study was conducted in two separate districts of Andhra Pradesh, i.e. East Godavari and Warangal districts. Twenty (20) villages from both the districts were randomly selected based on multistratified purposive sample. A total number of 521 children in the age group of 6-14 years, 260 teachers working in sub-plan areas and 400 teachers working in Gramina Vidya Vikas Kendras (GVVKs) were involved in the study. Field survey was conducted with structured interview schedules, questionnaires, informal discussions with tribals, administrators, elected leaders and others and observation method had been adopted as tools for the collection of data for the study. The major findings of the study were as follows: with regard to approaches and policies, from mere providing of equal opportunity and incentives the policy had changed to ensure participation through provision of special facilities and improving quality of education in terms of various inputs. In early eighties the major policy concern was how to bring the tribes into the fold of education. For this, attention was drawn to the content and curriculum and suitable teachers for tribal areas. The administrative mechanism for tribal development has undergone many changes. At the state level, the Tribal Welfare Department was bifurcated from the Department of Social Welfare. With the sub-plan approach a separate administrative mechanism called Integrated Tribal Development Agency (ITDA) was established covering a few tribal concentrated blocks in a district. Access for education was a problem. As a result of shift from viability to providing schools in close proximity, the number of primary schools in the sub-plan area had grown phenomenally due to the Integrated Tribal Development Agency (ITDA) initiative. The mandal level administrative units introduced in 1985-86 had also led to the improvement of access to education. The change in the role of tribal welfare department from 'supplementary' to 'pivotal' has helped to increase access to education in close proximity. At the upper primary stage, the emphasis was on providing Ashram schools or hostels rather than opening more schools due to lack of demand. At the secondary school stage large number of schools are run by the local bodies. Tribal Welfare Department was also providing hostels for tribal students. Apart from expanding school facilities, attention was paid to provide better opportunity to talented children by establishing residential schools in each ITDA area. With regard to quality, special efforts of Tribal Welfare Department were confined only to providing schools and did not reflect in providing the inputs for effective learning. It pays inadequate attention with regard to teaching aids, and other infrastructure facilities. Ashram schools are mostly run in uncongenial houses without minimum facilities for residential purpose. Except a few Ashram schools others do not have any teaching aids. Even blackboard and a chalk is a scarce resource. Although Ashram schools have teaching aids and radio facility, they are hardly or ever used. Teachers also do not have proper furniture like chairs and tables. The textbooks, writing materials are supplied to students very late and sometimes at the fag end of the year. The quality of slates and other writing materials is so poor that students cannot use them even for a few days. The uniforms are either large or small to fit to the students. The teachers working in ITDA schools who are tribal youth do not have training. The low proportion of teacher-pupil ratio in tribal schools is due to less number of students. It varies across the schools under different managements. Majority of the schools have single teachers, inspection and supervision of primary schools is not regular. Thus, the quality aspect of education in tribal areas is still in the same condition as it was in 1950s or 1960s. With regard to the extent of participation, more than 70 per cent of boys in both the sample districts were enrolled and attending the school. Among the girls the extent of participation is less compared to the boys. Among the total enrolled children more than 60 per cent was studying in Grades I and II. There is no significant variation in enrolment basing on the geographical location of villages (roadside and interior). The education of the head of the household and education of other adult members has a positive influence on the enrolment of children. The participation of children has a direct bearing with the income and size of land holdings of the household. The lowest and highest income and land holding groups had better participation compared to middle level groups. With regard to education and economic development of the households, the labour distribution in the family cannot afford to spare a child to go to school as the economic schemes provided by the governments are attractive and have to show results to the concerned authorities. This vigorous economic development schemes hinders educational participation until the households reach a threshold level. Lack of interest and fear of school among children was often mentioned as a reason for non-enrolment of the children in tribal schools. In this connection area specific and group specific programmes need to be adopted for education. With regard to performance of institutions although the enrolment is high, the regularity in attending the school is very poor due to frequent and prolonged absenteeism. Ashram schools are better in this regard when compared to other schools. Although there is non-detention policy the students are retained for lack of adequate attendance and performance. The retention is high in local body schools and in lower classes. The extent of drop outs varies among different types of schools in tribal sub-plan areas. The reasons mentioned for poor performance was both economic and educational. As regards finances and cost of education, providing the resources and allocating resources for development according to local priorities has been the major change in the policy. The budget for tribal development has increased with the adoption of tribal sub-plan. The increase in allocation has been largely spent on expansion of facilities and no attention is paid to improve the system or student services. Unless conscious efforts are made to increase the share of allocation to teaching aids, games and sports materials and student services, the equity concept will remain only at access and low participation will remain as a problem. With regard to attitude, awareness and aspirations are concerned, it is very rare that the tribals have any interaction with the education department. Their interaction is mostly confined to agriculture and allied sectoral persons. Except the teachers they did not see any other person belonging to education department. They consider education as a means for their children to get government jobs and occupational mobility. However their perception about girls' education is different from boys. They aspire to have jobs and better life for their children. Considering the aspirations of tribals, the formal education has to be job oriented and income generating. Among various incentives the tribals feel school is close proximity, free education, hostels, Ashram schools and free books are important and without which they cannot educate or go to school. But the pre-metric scholarships and clothes given to primary school children are considered not that important to decide to educate or not to educate their children. With regard to teachers, the performance or willingness of teachers to work in tribal areas is mainly due to extra allowances and staying near to their native places. Lack of basic facilities and naxalite problem are some of the reasons mentioned by those who do not like to work in tribal areas. The younger age teachers are more willing to work compared to older age teachers. The tribal teachers also feel lack of basic facilities in the village as a reason to desire to work in other places. With regard to interaction with the local community, tribal teachers feel free and identify with the community, the non-tribal teachers have limited contact with the community. The policy of appointing tribal youth as teachers seems to be useful to develop interactions between school and community. For tribal teachers poverty is not the only problem but also the school. Teaching and the teachers are not attractive for children to come to school. According to tribal teachers the authoritarian behaviour of the teachers, the rigid rules and fixed school timings discourages the children to come to school. The teachers suggested that educational problems need to be tackled from economic, cultural and social angles. There should be suitable policy for selecting teachers to tribal areas by identifying their reasons to work in their areas. As regards administration, after the establishment of ITDA and introduction of single line administration, the educational administration has become more intricate. Although there is single line administration, the local body functions according to its norms. The Project Officer (PO) and District Tribal Welfare Officer (DTWO) looks after the schools run by ITDA and Ashram schools. The DTWO has financial and administrative powers. He is also responsible for recruitment, placement, and transfer of teachers. He also conducts inspections and supervision. In this midst of different agencies the DEO who is exclusively posted for tribal areas does not get the real importance to carry on with his job. The personality clashes and ego problems come in the way of coordination of the education officer with others. The District Education Officer ITDA is under the final control of PO and his parent department. There is an urgent need to bring all the schools in ITDA under one umbrella and to stream line the academic administration by unifying the multiple agencies. In fact, in tribal areas, compared to non-tribal areas the number of agencies involved are more and the schools are also of different types. The multiplicity of managements results with variation in implementation of policies and plans formulated by the Government. The multiple agencies respond differently to educational needs of tribals. As a result, there is a conflict and friction between education department and agencies particularly with local bodies and the social and tribal welfare departments.

A Study on the Problems of Tribal Children with Reference to Enrolment, Retention and Quality in the Five First Phase District Primary Education Programme (DPEP) Districts of Andhra Pradesh

The important findings of the study are: Universal access could not be provided in tribal habitations with less than 100 population. Overall enrolment of STs in the state is 70 per cent and for girls it is 57 per cent. Children below 5 years and averaged children are also admitted in Class I. Absenteeism of pupils is more pronounced immediately after vacation, during tribal festivals, weekly markets, marriage seasons, peak seasons of agricultural operations and food produce collection. Attendance is being manipulated by the teachers upto 75 per cent mainly to ensure promotion to next class as well as to correlate with the attendance marked for mid-day meal programme. Attendance marked on the day of visit and students actually present substantially vary. In some places the attendance for mid-day meals is 100 per cent while the actual present is around 60 per cent. Parents and other elders feel that absenteeism of teacher is mostly hampering the spirit of education in tribal areas. The school atmosphere also often does not attract children. 59 per cent of the students in interior villages appear totally unclean with shabby hair, without even hair oil, without garments, torn clothes and with scabies and running nose. The instruction of ECE centers are combining their students with 1st and 2nd Class students who are causing disturbance in the class. 81 per cent of the younger generation have realised the value of education. Awareness is more in roadside villages which have frequent interaction with ITDA/educated general population/radio/TV/newspapers, etc. Out of 32 schools studied, 7 schools do not have VEC or SEC, while the remaining are nominated bodies. Interviews with VECs/SECs revealed that 16 per cent are not aware of the existence of the VEC/SEC, 52 per cent are aware but not about the role and responsibilities. 66 per cent of the teachers complained that village community is not cooperative, while 78 per cent of the villagers complained that teachers do not interact with the villagers. Meetings of VECs/SECs were not held in 64 per cent of the villages. In community schools also, the participation of community till the school is started is active but their role after that is not known to them. Only 25 per cent teachers are staying in the same village, 38 per cent commute from places located below 5 km, while 37 per cent reside as a distance of 5 to 15 km. Teachers working in roadside schools stay in the same habitation while most of the teachers working in interior villages stay outside the village. The content of the textbooks do not reflect the tribal culture. Only 9 per cent of the teachers know the dialect of the students with whom they are working. Only 2 per cent of the teachers have lesson plans. On an average 75 per cent of the teachers do not use blackboards. 100 per cent teachers do not use teaching aids. They simply read lessons from textbooks. Using play methods, giving illustrations, observing students while teaching and ensuring their participation, reviewing previous lessons, giving assignments in classrooms and homework, etc. are absent in more than 90 per cent of the schools. Regular supervision is a rare phenomenon for tribal schools. Parents who found their children not learning anything in school started withdrawing the students. Language barriers, untrained teachers, and teacher absenteeism has contributed to poor performance of students. Under aged children admitted for maintaining TP ratio or for MMP are detained till they attain the prescribed age. Drop out rate among ST students is very high at primary level, i.e. 74.05 per cent. There is consistent increase in drop out rate from Class II onwards. The causes being: low intake capacity of Ashram schools, home sickness, reluctance of parents to admit their children in far off places, preference for child labour, unable to cope up with Class III syllabus in Ashram schools and lack of importance to girls education, etc. On an average 60 per cent of the students of Classes I and II are less than 35 per cent marks in Language and Mathematics. Teachers residence outside the school location is a big barrier for the functioning of the school.

Monitoring of Learning Achievement in Tribal Schools of Andhra Pradesh

The DIET faculty members and the School Complex Resource Persons conduct several in service programmes to improve the teaching-learning process in schools. By monitoring the teaching and learning in schools, they can ascertain the extent of effective implementation of instructional practices to enable pupils for their all-round development. In order to capture the monitoring practices and to bring about improvement, the study was conducted. The basic issues addressed pertaining to monitoring of learning achievement in tribal schools of Andhra Pradesh are: what is monitoring? what is academic? what is academic monitoring? what do we expect of education? what are the main objectives of tribal school education? who is responsible for academic monitoring of tribal schools? and how to collect information in academic monitoring of tribal children?

The specific objectives of the study was: to develop an awareness among the DIET/TTI faculty, School Complex Education Resource Persons (SCERPs) and Teachers about the need for monitoring of learning in schools, to develop ability among DIET/TTI faculty/ SCERPs and teachers to device schedules and proforma for monitoring of learning in schools, to develop capacity among DIET/ITI faculty, SCERPs and teachers to train mandal resource persons on monitoring of learning in schools and to enable the DIET/TTI faculty, SCERPs and Teachers for effective monitoring of the learning achievement in tribal schools with effective monitoring proforma, etc.

Some of the areas that influence students' learning are: physical, infrastructural facilities, curricular and co-curricular activities, extra curricular activities, incentives, community participation activities, co-operative learning, cultural activities, school complex programmes, human resource development activities, enrolment, retention and absenteeism, institutional planning, administrative activities and recording instruments.

Monitoring of Physical Infrastructural Facilities: School Campus (adequacy, safety, coordination, efficiency, beauty, economy, adaptability, etc.); school site (surroundings, level, direction, shape, facilities, scope for further expansion); Area and Playground for: Primary Classes–6 sq.ft per child 1 acre playground, Upper Primary Classes–7 sq.ft per child 2 acres playground and Higher Secondary–8 sq.ft per child 5 acres playground; Classrooms (30'×20'×15') Min 1000 sq.ft in MPL Areas. The school will be very ideal with one floor, drinking water facility, toilet facility with running water with good shape (I,L,T,U,E,H), Good Lighting Ventilation, Classroom equipment (desks, chairs, tables, blackboard, map stand, learning corner), library, laboratory rooms for workshops, museum, teaching aids, kits, play materials, etc. are the requirements. The concerned officers who monitor the tribal schools should ensure the availability of these facilities.

Monitoring of Curricular and Co-Curricular Activities–Teaching and Testing: in Academic Subjects: Language(s), Mathematics, Environmental Studies I & II. In Activity Subjects: Health Education, Physical Education, SUPW, Moral Education and Creative activities; in Planning: Annual Planning, Unit Planning, Lesson Planning: content analysis/ specific objectives/teaching-learning activity/teaching-learning materials and evaluation, in Teaching-Learning process: Child centred, Activity oriented and competency based teaching-learning process, in Transaction: Providing learning activities, promoting learning by doing, developing individual, group and whole class activity, recognizing individual differences, utilising local resources and creating interesting classroom. In Co-Curricular Activities: debates, discussions, library work, laboratory work, composition writing, essay writing, project-work, etc. In Testing: unit tests, assignments, terminals, quiz, remedial programmes, diagnostic testing, question paper analysis, script analysis. With regard to the Extra Curricular Activities the following activities were suggested: celebration of birth days of national leaders, celebration of birth days of scientists, organisation of various days, school day/teacher's day/children's day/parents day/alumni day/chaduvula pandaga/world literacy day/UNO day, celebration of national festivals, clean and green programmes, social service activities, community dinning, scouting/NSS/girl guiding, green corpse, adult literary programme and child to child programmes, etc. With regard to Incentive Schemes the activities suggested were: free education, supply of free textbooks, mid-day meals scheme, free distribution of dress, writing materials, note books pocket money to the children of weaker sections, distribution of cycles, book banks, question banks, etc. were suggested. With regard to Community Participation Activities, the School

Education Committees take certain specific roles such as taking measures for the enrollment of unenrolled school children, taking suitable measures to reduce the dropout, ensure effective functioning of the school, quality improvement, providing teaching-learning materials, securing playground, incentive schemes and their utilisation, building construction programmes, appointment of Vidaya Volunteers based on need, utilisation of AV materials supplied to school, organization of play activities, plantation work in school campus, school education fund and they have to provide all possible assistance for the development of the school. Cooperative Learning Programmes such as learning in groups, project work, process skills development, development of personality traits and group assignments may be provided and organised regularly in tribal schools. Cultural activities helps in the tribal children to draw out the innate potentialities in them. Therefore, organisation of activities like music, songs, folk dance, variety shows, drawing and painting, school decoration, organizing exhibitions, sculpture, fancy dress, flower festivals, preparation of charts, models, dramatics, etc. may be organised in the tribal schools. School Complex Programme is another important area to be monitored. The schools complex activities help the children and teachers to remove isolation and ensure effective functioning through mutual help and support. Two tire system develops co-operative efforts, best utilization of human resources, economy in use of material resources, removes the iron certain between the higher level and lower level institutions, helps in providing academic guidance to the constituent schools, provides equipmental assistance, conducting supervision, conducting evaluation, providing extension work and in-service education, discriminating educational information, devising institutional planning, common testing programme, maintaining academic standards and making follow up studies.

Human Resource Development Activities such as in service teacher training at institutional level, on the job assistance programme, organization of exhibitions, teaching learning material exhibitions, exhibition of pupils projects, extension lectures, science fairs, inter school competitions, quiz programmes, brains trust, brain storming sessions, deputation to various programmes, encouraging action research, school magazine, reading competitions, debates/essay writing and story telling competitions needs to be monitored.

Enrolment, retention and absenteeism among the tribal students needs to be checked thoroughly. Enrolment of children in schools at different times other than the beginning of the academic year also stands in the way of their academic achievement. Children who are coming from the non-formal streams are given admission into the main stream at different times as and when they make themselves eligible. The school should have the capacity to hold the interest of the children to continue in the school. For this, particularly the physical structure of the school should be attractive and the teaching learning process should sustain the interest of the child to continue. Child friendly environment should prevail in the school. Any neglect in this aspect results in irregular attendance and frequent absenteeism of the children. The affects of the absenteeism on the academic achievement of the student needs no mention. So monitoring of enrolment, retention and absenteeism of students is also a programme which needs special attention in the present situation especially in tribal schools.

Institutional Planning

The concept of institutional plan is not at all new. However most of the Institutions do not maintain plans. As such Headmasters are requested to recall the objectives. *(i)* to provide understanding of the physical features of the institution, its human and material resource and other resources available around the school for educational utilization. *(ii)* to provide minimum academic programme for the year in respect of all classes. *(iii)* to seek social support for resource mobilization for the Physical improvement of the Institution and Institutional information, Plan of Curricular Activities, Co-curricular Activities, Monitoring and Supervision and Resource Mobilization.

Institutional Information: history from inception, present name and location with details of recognition, strength particulars: class-wise, caste-wise and sex-wise showing physically handicapped children clearly, human resources of teaching and non-teaching staff, details of accommodation and playground facilities and sanitary facilities, present plan in creation of new facilities, details of furniture and equipment (audio-visual, laboratory, library, N.C.C. Scouting and games, etc.), details of educational institutions within a radius of 4 kms, community resources available, plan for additional resources to be made available during the current year.

Plan of Curricular Activities: academic plans of subject teachers, annual plan and unit plan, planning and administration of assignments, unit tests and terminal examinations, plan for written work assigned for pupils, e.g. composition, science records, map-drawing, home work, etc., identification of academically backward children: class-wise, subject-wise, and plans for remedial teaching or supervised study.

Planning of Co-curricular Activities: subject club activities, elocutions, debates, quiz, organisation of exhibitions and seminars, utilisation of community services, utilisation of school library and laboratory, celebration of national festivals, participation in the cultural activities, participation in games and sports, organizations of exercises, activities of students associations, participation in competitions conducted at various levels.

Monitoring and Supervisions: conduct of monthly staff Conference and appraisal of performance by each staff member, review of activities planned under curricular and co-curricular areas periodically, support of academically backward children and convening parent teacher association meetings, review of results at the end of terminal examinations or public examination.

Resource Mobilization: organize SEC meetings, collection of voluntary contributions by way of money and material through SEC, shramadan for improving infrastructure.

Steps Involved in Preparing the Plan: Normative Planning: establishment of objectives mission and goals. Strategic Planning: identification of problems and needs, assessment of resources, determination of priorities, formulation of plan and finalization of plan. Operational Planning: work plan for implementation, monitoring and evaluation and revision of plan.

Aspects of Planning: curricular and academic programmes, co-curricular activities, administrative aspects, inservice programmes and Academic growth of teachers, student welfare services and physical facilities.

Administration Activities: suitability of school timings, collection of fees, maintenance of registers and records, testing programme, student welfare services, teacher welfare services, conduct of parent teacher association meetings, issue of progress sheets, extension services, staff meetings and students self government.

Recording Instruments

There are two recording instruments maintained in the school, viz., the progress record card and the cumulative record card. In the progress record card the attendance put in by the student each month, his academic achievement in terms of marks scored in the unit test, assignments and the terminal examinations is mentioned. This is only instrument which is circulated to parent to know the academic progress of his ward. Cumulative record card is a confidential record maintained by the school which consists of the personality development factors of the students.

Who is responsible for Academic Monitoring of Schools? For the academic monitoring teacher in the school situation, prefect in the dormitory, parent at the house, warden in the hostel and supervisor/administrator/manager in the system. How to collect information in Academic Monitoring? through the observation of class room teaching-learning process-student participation in the process, interview/putting questions, written work-class work/home work, attendance registers, performance in unit tests/terminal tests, assignments, progress cards, cumulative record card, pupil diaries, library work, laboratory work, through peers, group work, pupil products, through teachers, participation in debates/discussions/quiz/celebrations, participation in co-curricular activities, review meetings and analysis of answer scripts of unit tests and terminal tests. Identify strengths and weaknesses: outstanding performance, deficiencies, Academic subjects, Activity subjects, Personality traits.

Assistance for effective Academic progress: suggest few more and higher type assignments to gifted, multi level assignments based on individual difference, arrange for special coaching, arrange for remedial teaching, meetings with school officials/parents/wardens, discussions with school education committees, implementation of prefect system, examination of progress cards/watching, organization of activities like debates/discussions/quiz, working out the questions given in unit tests and terminals, regular library and laboratory work, adoption of APPEP principles, correction of scripts before students, regular habit of studying, arranging extension lecturers, timely supply of text books, writing materials, clothing, timely release of scholarship, nutritious food, health checkup, frequent visits and organization of co-curricular activities more in number.

Academic Monitoring for School Improvement School Wise Proforma

Instructions: Each DIET Lecturer is requested to go through all the aspects given in the proforma in the school which is assigned to him and categorize the school item-wise for all the item's at the time of first visit and monitor the school by way of providing the 'guidance and work with the school staff for the improvement i.e., to bring 'D', 'C' and 'B' items into 'A' category. For each visit the DIET Lecturer should discuss the areas for improvement and give written instructions to the School Head Masters (HMs) so that he/she can review the progress during the next visit on the items focused in earlier visit. (The category 'A' refers to Good, 'B' refers to Satisfactory, 'C' refers to Below Satisfactory and 'D' refers to Nil).

Monitoring Performance for Tribal Schools

Sl. No.	*Item*	*The Category in which the School Falls*			
		A	*B*	*C*	*D*
1.	Maintenance of database viz., names of out of school children, dropouts, irregular students against gender and community from 5-15 years age group children and names of children in the age group of 0-5 in the catchment area				
2.	Out of school children				
3.	Dropouts				
4.	Regular pupil attendance				
5.	Pupil performance in reading				
6.	Pupil performance in writing (observe pupil notebooks)				
7.	Pupil performance in arithmetic				
8.	Development of TLM				
9.	Display of teacher and pupil work				
10.	School premises – clean and green				
11.	School committee involvement				
12.	Improvement of infrastructure through community participation				
13.	Regular conduct of exams/tests and correction of scripts and assignments and issue of progress cards				
14.	Conduct of games and sports				
15.	Conduct of other non-scholastic activities such as SUPW, moral education, art education, creative activities, etc.				
16.	Utilisation of OBB material such as maths kit, science kit, mini tool kit and other TLM				
17.	Utilisation of library books and supplied under OBB and regular issue to children and 'Chaduvu' magazine				
18.	Use of audio visual equipment supplied, i.e. TV, VCCP, RCCP and cassettes				
19.	Teachers rolled in the enrollment of out of school children i.e. never enrolled and dropped out				
20.	Conduct of parent teacher meets – Teachers regular meeting the parents and appraisals				
21.	Teacher preparation – Lesson plans, TLM, etc.				
22.	Use of school and teacher grants				

Please note: The basis for the categorization of 'A', 'B', 'C' and 'D' for particular quantitative items are as follows:

1. Out of School Children: If the percentage of out of school children is below 10 per cent refers to 'A' category, thus 10-15 per cent for 'B', 15-20 per cent to 'C' and above 20 per cent is 'D' (Calculation = Total No. of Out of Schools children in the age group of 5-15/Total No. of School Children in the age group of 5-15 × 100).
2. Dropouts: Number of children who are unrolled during 1999-2000 in the school dropped out during 2000-01—Less than 10 per cent refers to 'A', 10-15 per cent is 'B', 15-20 per cent is 'C', 20 per cent and above is 'D'.
3. Pupil Attendance: 90 per cent and above is 'A', 80-90 per cent is 'B', 70-80 per cent is 'C', below 70 per cent is 'D'.

Monitoring proforma have been suggested to monitor the learning achievement of students in tribal schools of Andhra Pradesh is as follows: statistical information relating to the pupils and teachers present at the time of visit/inspection, observation of physical facilities, monitoring of curricular and co-curricular activities, monitoring of the learning competencies/leavels of students, level of students in learning of the academic activities, utilisation of science laboratory, utilisation of teaching learning materials, laboratory details, monitoring of co-curricular activities, monitoring of non-scholastic activities, monitoring of incentive schemes, monitoring of school-community relations, monitoring of the activities relating to enrolment, retention, attendance, transfer and cooperative learning activities, monitoring of school administrative activities, monitoring of cultural activities, monitoring of the institutional plan, school complex activities, human resource development activities, monitoring of recording instruments, observations of the supervisor on various activities in a nutshell and other activities such as: review register of teachers, vocational education activities, cultural activities, games activities, student review information, teacher review information, parent-teacher activities, special activities, school administration, cooperation of other institutions in school administration, students physical status, visits by officials, visits by non-officials and others, suggestions of visitors/supervisors, observations of the supervisors on the centers, monthly progress sheet of students including: details of teachers and their teaching subjects, details of lessons taught in the month, competencies acquired by students at the end of the month, content of tests/evaluation, students progress sheet from Classes I to V and report of MEO/SCRP on the visit of the school.

Modern educationists believe that every individual is endowed with certain innate abilities or potentialities and these are to be brought out to achieve a harmonious development. The purpose of education is to promote the development of abilities to enable exercising of such responsibilities, in the society as his powers allow. Education has to make the individual physically strong, intellectually sound, emotionally stable, culturally fit and socially efficient. According to National Policy on Education 1986, Education has to produce a self-assured, more productive, more capable and more thinking type of citizens. It is not the imitator that is to be developed, but it is exploratory that is to be developed. Education has to promote productivity, achieve social and national integration, step up the process of modernization, and inculcate social, moral and spiritual values. This is what is expected of education.

In order to achieve these objectives suitable curriculum has been formulated and introduced at different levels of the education system. At the primary stage children are exposed to three academic subjects and five activity subjects. The academic subjects comprise of Language, Mathematics and Environmental Studies (I-Social Studies and II-Science). The activity subjects consist of Health Education, Physical Education, Socially Useful Production Work, Creative Activities and Moral Education. From III level, English is introduced and from Class VI Hindi is also introduced as Second Language. Secondary education begins to expose students to appreciate roles of science, the humanities and social sciences.

Language is a means of communication. Teaching of language should aim at developing the four skills of listening, speaking, reading and writing. Mathematics should be visualized as the vehicle to train a child to think, reason, analyze and to articulate logically. Science education need to develop in the child well defined abilities and values such as the spirit of inquiry, creativity, objectivity, the courage to question and an aesthetic sensibility. It should enable the learner to acquire problem solving and decision-making skills. In our culturally plural society, education should foster universal and eternal values, oriented towards the unity and integration of our people. The value education should help eliminate obscurantism, religious fanaticism, violence, superstition and fatalism.

The teacher who is the main dynamic force in the system of education needs to transact this curriculum by adopting appropriate strategy. Today there is a shift from Epistemic approach to Reconstructionist approach, from teacher centered and subject centered approach to that of child-centered approach. The present emphasis is on the adoption of child centered, activity oriented and competency based teaching-learning process. Student is the center of the education system. "The child is the starting point, the center and the end. His growth and his development is the ideal of education" felt John Dewey. His Excellency the President of India, Dr. A.P.J. Abdul Kalam, has stated "What is more important is that teachers should not transmit their frustration to their students, but should constantly try to upgrade their skills and encourage the children to think big." The child should be the focal point in the system of education. Here comes the role of academic monitoring.

Monitoring is defined as a periodic review and surveillance by Management at every level of the implementation of an activity in order to ensure that the inputs, deliveries, work schedules, targeted outputs and other required actions are proceeding according to plan. It is a process of recording, collecting, processing, and disseminating information to assist project management decision-making. This is carried out to see: Whether various tasks are carried out according to schedule? Whether projects results are likely to lead to the realization of project objectives? Whether project objectives/targets/execution need modification?

Thus monitoring is a managerial function that begins with the start of a project and ends with the completion of the project, but it is a continuous process during the implementation of project. It is an essential tool for successful implementation of project. During the process of monitoring the shortfalls, deviations, and problems and causes for the same are identified so as to take appropriate remedial and corrective action.

Today in school system academics include both theoretical as well as non-theoretical aspects. It includes subjects not only for intellectual development but also other types of development. It includes curricular, co-curricular and extra-curricular activities. It is the sum total of all the educational experiences provided to the child by the school through instruction either within the four walls or outside the four walls.

Academic Monitoring is a periodic review of curricular, co-curricular and extra-curricular activities carried on in the school as scheduled/planned. It is a continuous process of knowing to what extent the objectives are realized, whether the objectives/targets/execution need any or change. It involves measuring, recording, collecting, processing and communicating information to assist the management relating to the teaching-learning process. To bring about certain desirable changes in the behaviour of the child either at the thought level, perception level or psychomotor level is the ultimate objectives of the teaching process. To what extent these are achieved should be known and necessary steps should be taken either to change the strategy or the objectives to be realized. Whether there is any problem with regard to the teaching or problems with regard to learning are to be known and suitable measures are to be taken.

Monitoring involves three important issues (viz) knowing, Identifying, and Assisting. Knowing involves-knowing whether the student is progressing in learning the academic as well as non-academic activities organized in the school, whether the expected learning outcomes are achieved or not, whether the desired behavioural changes have taken place in the child as a result of instruction? Identifying involves-identifying the strengths and weaknesses of the student, the deficiencies, the interests and attitudes etc., Assisting involves-suggesting steps to make good the deficiencies, implementing the programmes to make good the weaknesses, taking up remedial instructional programmes, taking up individual care and attention, arranging for special coaching etc.

Since monitoring is a managerial function, all those who are involved in the project implementation should do monitoring. It is important to appreciate that monitoring is not an individuals' functions but it is a collective function. However to be more specific the responsibility needs to be taken by the following personnel. Teacher in the school situation, Prefect in the dormitory, Parent at home, Warden in the hostel and Supervisor/Administrator/Manager of the System.

Through the following Programmes information for providing academic monitoring of students may be collected. Through the observation of classroom teaching-learning process- student participation in the process, interviews/putting questions, observing and checking the written work, class work and home work, attendance registers, performance in Unit Tests and Terminal Tests, assignments, pupils products, progress cards, cumulative record cards, pupils diaries, library work, laboratory work, project work, through peers, group work, through teachers, through parents, participation in debates, discussion, quiz, programmes, celebrations, participation in co-curricular activities, review meetings and analysis of answer scripts of unit tests and terminal tests etc.

After collecting the data for Academic Monitoring, the next step is identification of strengths, and weaknesses. Some students may be academically sound in some subjects and some others may not. In which areas they are sound and in which areas they are weak is to be identified. Identify outstanding performance and identify deficiencies-in academic subjects, in activity subjects and personality traits.

After identifying the strengths and weaknesses the next step is to provide assistance. The following are the ways through which assistance can be provided: suggest more and higher type assignments to gifted or outstanding students to progress further, give multilevel assignments based on individual differences, arrange for special coaching in time, arrange for remedial teaching, meeting the school officials/parents/wardens, discussions with school education committees, examination of progress cards, organization of activities like debates, discussions, quiz programmes, working out the questions given in unit tests and terminals, regular laboratory and library work, adoption of primary education project pedagogy, correction of scripts before students, regular habit of studying, frequent testing, arranging extension lectures, timely supply of text books, writing materials, clothing, timely release of scholarships, supply of nutritious food, health checkups, frequent visits, organization of co-curricular activities more in number, updation of syllabus, conduct of pre-final examination and correction of answer scripts before the students, working out the question papers of the last three years public examination and questions from question banks, adoption of students by staff, working out the exercises given at the end of the lessons in the textbooks, by-hearting the materials given in the boxes in the textbook, drawing science figures, extra drill, map pointing in social sciences, organization of supervised study programme, organization of brains trust, training in letter writing and comprehension exercises and emphasizing on co-operative learning. The following are the hints for Administrators: Maintain a register with names of students, their personal details and school details. Record their academic progress during personal visits. Interviews, discussions with teachers, progress cards, classroom visits, putting questions etc. Suggest measures for making good the deficiencies noticed based on the visits, putting questions etc. Follow up. Visit at lest once a month the school and hostel and observe the academic progress of the students. Have direct interaction with students. Go through the school inspection reports. Hold review meetings. Maintain contacts with parents. Attend the review meetings organized by Education Department on academic issues. Attend the Headmasters conference organized in the District either at the District Level or Regional Level. Planning and Preparation: discussions with State Administrative and Education Authorities, identification of Tribal Schools/SCERPs/Tribal Teachers/TTI/ DIET faculty, data collection from Tribal Schools/Visit to Teacher Training Centres and discussions with State functionaries for necessary action.

Design and Development of the Training Package: discussion with State Education Experts, DIET faculty, SCERPs and Tribal Teachers on workable activities, identification of Monitoring Areas, draft preparation of Monitoring Package and refinement and finalisation of the Training Package.

Training Programme for TTI/DIET faculty, SCERPs and Headmasters and Tribal Teachers: discussions with State Education Authorities, SCERPs/Tribal Teachers on the implementation and validity, interaction with Tribal Teachers/SCERPs on various areas identified and developed in this Training Package, group Activities, guidance and Suggestions and handing over the Training Package for Field Testing.

Monitoring the Effectiveness of the Training Programme: data collection from Tribal Teachers/SCERPs and DIET faculty abut the effectiveness of the training package, implications of the Training Package and Training Programme and follow up action.

Presently academic monitoring for school improvement and teacher appraisal are being done at primary stage of education. District Institute of Education and Training are entrusted with the Academic monitoring for school improvement and the Mandal Resource Persons with attendance monitoring. However we need to have exhaustive academic monitoring.

The progress of a nation is decided and determined not in the legislatures where passions and prejudices warp judgement and vitiate the laws that may be framed, not in courts where punishments more often harden than reform offenders, not in factories where men become but in schools where the minds of the future citizens are moulded and where the habits and attitudes are shaped.

School plays a major role in moulding the ideas, habits and attitudes of the children and in order to produce well-balanced personalities, the present day school has to perform number of functions. It has to teach the 7 R's - Reading, Writing, Arithmetic, Recreation, Rights, Responsibilities and Relationship. It has to conserve the culture of the society train the children for democracy and develop scientific attitude. The school has to recognize individual differences, provide opportunities for the full development of children, kindling the minds of the students a passion for social justice. To perform these functions to the maximum extent possible the teacher plays an important role in the school system. Physical infrastructural facilities, curricular and co-curricular activities, extra-curricular activities, Incentives, community activities, co-operative learning, cultural activities, school complex programmes, human resource development activities, enrolment, retention and absenteeism, Institutional planning, and administrative activities are the material aspects, activities and programmes exercise a varied influence on the learning achievement of pupils in their tribal or non-tribal localities. A detailed account of these programmes is given below.

The material equipment of a school exercises a marked influence on the academic achievement of the students. No school can function in air. It can function only when adequate material, equipment is provided to it. The school building, classrooms, furniture, science laboratory, library and playground help in the academic achievement of the students. School Environment, Laboratory and Library in particular help in better learning and reinforcement.

At the primary stage the students are exposed to three academic subjects—Language, Mathematics and Environmental studies and five activity, subjects—Health Education, Physical Education, socially useful productive work, creative activities and moral education. At the upper primary and higher school stage students are exposed to three languages—Telugu, Hindi and English, Mathematics, Science and Social Studies and the activity subjects of Health Education, Physical Education, Socially useful productive work, creative activities and Moral Education as in the case Primary stage of education. Languages are taught in order to develop the skills of listening, speaking, reading and writing.

The learning process includes providing teacher generated learning activities, promoting leaning by doing, developing individual, group and whole class activities recognizing individual differences, utilizing local resources and creating an interesting classroom by displaying the teacher's work and student's work. For effective teaching the teacher needs to plan his work by formulating the year plans, unit plans and lesson plans.

The objectives and specifications need to be planned before hand. The competencies are to be identified and they are to be developed among the students. Along with the curricular programmes, co-curricular activities need to be organized for better learning like organizing debates, discussions, library work, laboratory work, composition writing, essay writing, project work etc. These activities result in better academic achievement of the students. The testing programme is also to be organized hand in hand to teaching programme. How for the instructional objectives are realized can be known only through the testing programme. Unit tests, terminal tests and Assignments provide the required feedback to the teacher and the students.

These activities are some thing extra which reinforce learning. Celebration of birth days of National Leaders, organization of school day, teacher's day, children's day, Parent's day, Alumni day, celebration of National festivals organizing community programme and social service activities, etc. reinforce the academic learning of pupils.

Incentive Programmes like distribution of textbooks, dress, mid-day meals, scholarships, bus passes, bicycles to girl children provide an equal opportunity for the students of weaker sections to become on par with other students. Rewards help in developing competitive spirit among the students to learn better.

These activities include Mass Prayer, morning assembly, embroidery, social service in the neighbourhood, first aid, red cross, community dining, labour squads, services on special occasions like fairs, processions etc., village survey, NSS etc. These activities provide a lot of scope for the students to learn moral and ethical values for the harmonious development of the personality of the students.

Learning takes place through interaction either passive or active. Passive interaction takes place by reading books, watching TV, hearing radio etc. Active interaction takes place through individual's interaction. The student learns more with groups rather than as an individual. Co-operative learning is encouraged, which helps the students to discuss among themselves and find solution to problems. Co-operative learning helps in self-expression and in stimulating new ideas. It also develops process skills among the students and also certain personality traits like co-operation, competition, accommodation, assimilation etc.

Organisation of cultural activities in schools helps in drawing out the innate potentialities of the students. Activities such as music, songs, folk dance, drawing and painting, organizing exhibitions, preparation of charts-models, etc., help in the academic development of students. These activities provide opportunities for better understanding of the cultural traditions.

School Complex Programme removes isolation among schools functioning at different levels, say, primary, upper primary and high schools and ensure better co-operation among the teachers of these institutions. In this the primary schools in the vicinity are attached to the nearest upper primary school and the upper primary school complexes are attached to the nearest high school. The facilities of the central schools can be utilized by the constituent schools in the complex. The physical as well as human resources of the central school can be extended for the harmonious development of the students in the vicinity. The teachers and students of the constituent schools can get better guidance and extension services from the nuclear schools.

Teacher's empowerment and student empowerment activities fall under this category. Teacher centres and school complex centers are utilized for this purpose. In-service training programmes for the teachers and extension lecturers for the students are organized which result in improving the teacher efficiency and student achievement. The sources like the library, laboratory, competency based teaching-learning equipment need to be utilized both by the teachers and students.

Enrolment of children in school at different times other than the beginning of the academic year also stands in the way of their academic achievement. Children who are coming from the non-formal streams are given admission into the main stream at different times as and when they make themselves eligible. The school should have the capacity to hold the interest of the children to continue in the school. For this particularly the physical structure of the school should be attractive and the teaching learning process should sustain the interest of the child to continue. Child friendly environment should prevail in the school. Any neglect in this aspect results in irregular attendance and frequent absenteeism. So monitoring of enrolment, retention and absenteeism of students is also a programme which needs special attention in the present situation especially in tribal schools.

Based on the full needs and resources available each institution should prepare its own plan called "The Institutional Plan." Institutional Plan helps us in understanding of the physical features of the institution, its human and natural resources and other resources available around the school for educational utilization. It provides for minimum academic programme for the year in respect of all classes. It also help, to seek social support for resources mobilization for the physical improvement of the institution. The planning and extension of the Institutional Plan also influences the achievement of the students. The headmaster is required to prepare the plan under five areas: Institutional information, Plan of curricular activities, co-curricular activities, Monitoring and supervision and lastly Resource Mobilization Plan of curricular activities including Academic plans of subject teachers, Annual Plan and Unit plans, Planning and Administration of Assignments, Unit tests and terminal examinations, plan for written work assigned for pupils (eg) composition, science records, map drawing, home work etc. It also includes identification of academically backward children class-wise and subject-wise and plans for remedial teaching or supervised study. Planning of co-curricular activities include subject club activities, elocutions, debates, Quiz, organization of exhibitions, seminars, mobilization of community services, organization of excursions, participation in competitions conducted at various classes etc. Monitoring and supervision includes conduct of monthly staff conferences, review of activities planned under curricular and co-curricular areas periodically, review of results at the end of terminal examinations or public examinations etc.

Planning and implementation of administrative activities also influence the academic achievement of the students. This area includes those aspects like suitability of school timings, collection of fees, maintenance of registers and records, testing programmes, student welfare activities, teacher welfare activities, Issue of progress cards, student self-government etc.

There are two recording instruments maintained in the school—the progress record card and the cumulative record card. In the progress record the attendance put in by the student each month, his academic achievement in terms of marks scored in the unit test, assignments and the terminal examinations is mentioned. This is the only instrument which is circulated to the parent to know the academic progress of his ward. Cumulative record card is a confidential record maintained by the school which consists of the personality development factors of the students.

Effective monitoring of these programmes result in better academic achievement of the students. It helps in checking what is happening and know to what extent the academic programmes are implemented. It helps in accountability and development of the institution. Monitoring is not to threaten the teacher but to periodic support to the teacher to work better and for student to achieve better. Hence the need to develop different monitoring performance to collect information relating to what is happening in the schools, analyse information, evaluate the effectiveness, plan as a result and to act.

It is a process of measuring, recording, collecting, processing and communicating information to assist project management decision-making. Monitoring is carried on in terms of whether various tasks are carried out according to schedule, whether project results are likely to lead to the realization of project objectives and whether project objectives/targets execution needs adjustment. It begins with start of a project and ends with the completion of the project. To day in school system it includes theoretical as well as non-theoretical aspects. Academic includes subjects for intellectual development as well as other types of development and it includes curricular, co-curricular and extra-curricular activities.

What is Academic Monitoring? It is continuous/periodic review of curricular, co-curricular, and extracurricular activities carried on in the school as scheduled/planned, Whether the objectives are realized, Whether the objectives/targets/execution needs/ adjustments achieved, Involves measuring, recording collecting, processing and communicating information to assist management relating to teaching-learning process. What are the main objectives of School Education? The main objectives of the school education is to develop literacy and numeracy skills and social awareness, to create scientific attitude, to promote co-operation, tolerance and self control and other values, to promote vocational efficiency and productivity, to develop the qualities of political social, industrial and cultural leadership and to prepare the children for higher education. Academic subjects: Language(s), Mathematics, Environmental Studies –I (Social Studies), Environmental Studies–II (Science). Activity Subjects: Socially Useful Productive Work (SUPW), Health and Physical Education, Creative Activities, Moral Education.

What competencies are to be developed? The competencies that needs to be developed in the academic subjects such as: Language: Hearing, Speaking, Reading, Writing, Vocabulary, Recitation. Mathematics: Understanding the Mathematical concepts, problem solving ability, logical thinking, utilization in real life, creative thinking, diagrammatic representation. Environmental Studies–I (Social Studies): Understanding concepts, comparison contrast causes, relationships, classification, map drawing, map reading, project work. Environmental Studies–II (Science): concepts, understanding–utilization, observation, comparison, contrast, classification, telling causes, drawing figures, Labelling and project work. Socially Useful Productive Work (SUPW): Health, Food, clothing, shelter,

Cultural Activities, Social Service Activities; Health and Physical Education: Body development activities, Physical exercises, Recreational activities and Games and sports; Creative Activities: Drawing and painting; - Decoration and Music; - Drama; Dancing; Moral Education: Discipline: Honesty; Co-operation; Sympathy; patience, Responsibility; Knowledge, understanding, application and skill.

Whether the student is progressing in learning the academic as well as non-academic activities organized in the school. Whether the expected learning outcomes are realized or not. Whether the desired behavioural changes-took place in the child as a result of instruction. Identifying: Strengths and weaknesses, Deficiencies, Interests and attitudes; Assisting: Suggest steps be taken to make good the deficiencies. Implement the programmes to make good the weakness Report higher authorities to take decisions.

Enrolment of children in school at different times other than the beginning of the academic year also stands in the way of their academic achievement. Children who are coming from the non-formal streams are given admission into the main stream at different times as and when they make themselves eligible. The school should have the capacity to hold the interest of the children to continue in the school. For this particularly the physical structure of the school should be attractive and the teaching learning process should sustain the interest of the child to continue. Child friendly environment should prevail in the school. Any neglect in this aspect results in irregular attendance and frequent absenteeism. The affects of the absenteeism on the academic achievement of the student needs no mention. So monitoring of enrolment, retention and absenteeism of students is also a programme which needs special attention in the present situation especially in tribal schools.

From the very beginning, the basic objective of planned development in backward areas has been to accelerate modernization. Development meant imparting better methods in agriculture, animal husbandry, health and other sectors. Development agencies relied on extension methods for popularizing innovations and extracting compliance of the people. The situation was characterized by 'we give you this-you take it'. People remained largely as recipients and beneficiaries. Various studies highlighted the failure of development programmes as there was little participation or involvement of people. In the recent decades, Participatory Approach is emerging as the major strategy in the planning and implementation of rural and tribal development programmes. To achieve sustainable development, empowerment of people through participatory planning and management is being prescribed. Stress is being laid on people's capabilities, knowledge, skills and elimination of external vested interests. Under the influence of international funding agencies, participation is being built in to various schemes. Significant change is taking place in the status of tribals from that of recipients of development to that of partners. Participatory approach aims to involve people in all stages of development i.e. Planning, execution and monitoring. This approach differs from the earlier ones that conceived people's role as recipients of developmental benefits and innovations. As part of this, the participation of tribal people in the running and management of the educational institutions is envisaged. In view of the existing socio-economic conditions in the tribal areas, it is essential to monitor the working of teachers for effective functioning of schools. The parents, who were earlier approaching the school for solving their children's problems, are now being entrusted with the responsibility of solving the school problems.

In the beginning, schools in tribal areas were established mainly by missionaries and Government Agencies. Later voluntary agencies and outsiders started schools. It is significant to note that it is outsiders who have started schools to educate the children of tribals. Ordinary tribals generally avoid Government Officials and outsiders out of fear and apprehension. Though, they enroll their children into schools due to various reasons, they maintain very little contact with the schoolteachers. Because of their daily economic pursuits, there little time for tribal parents to approach the school. They hesitate to meet, discuss, and communicate with teachers due to inferiority complex, and lack of knowledge. They do not expect that they will get a proper hearing from the teachers. But, contact and communication between the parents and schoolteachers is most important, for the better functioning of the school system. This assumes maximum significance when first generation learners who need guidance and encouragement, are involved.

The conditions are not encouraging in schools in tribal areas. Teacher strength infrastructure, training, motivation of teachers and parents are all in short supply. These problems are going to persist. These need not come in the way of attempts for improving the existing situation. The teachers need to realize the participation and involvement of villagers in school affairs. School-home contact is a must in successful schooling. As stakeholders in the school, the villagers are entitled to take interest in the village affairs. Various avenues like DWACRA, self-help groups, Grama Sabhas may be harnessed for educating the parents. Counseling of parents can be undertaken through these bodies.

To overcome the above constraint, there is need for community education in order to better the relations between the school and community. Parent-teacher associations have an important role in this regard. The teachers need to make use of the opportunity, when they meet the community as part of census and survey operations etc. At this stage it self, contacts can be built with the community with proper approach towards tribal parents. Apart from knowing the parents in the villages, it also helps to know their conditions and to build rapport. Generally, in tribal villages, teachers are well-sought persons as they are the knowledgeable and literate persons locally available. This position need to taken advantage of. The teachers need to strive for better participation and involvement of parents after establishing rapport and contact with parents, which can be continued in various ways. An awareness and understanding of the teacher about the problems of parents is very helpful in understanding the limitations of the students.

To attract the villagers to participate in school affairs, the school premises can be used as a continuing education center. With the help of paramedical staff, some of the basic medicines can be kept at the school. Discussions and meetings can be organized in the school on topics that concern the villagers. Agriculture, marketing, health and hygiene are some of the topics. Competitions and games can be organized for parents. These will help in bridging the school-parent distance. By offering the services of the students for village level occasions like festivals, celebrations etc., a sense of involvement can be shown. Through culture specific co-curricular activities, Teaching through local culture and environment, parents can be assured that the children are not going to become better citizens with education. From tribal parents point of view children should not shun manual work, because they are getting educated. They should not get the feeling that children are getting alienated from their own culture. The presence of educated unemployed acts as a deterrent for parents who want to educate their children. Attempts are a must to make him or her aware of the importance of education for every individual. Education is not just for employment. It enhances the self-respect of the individual and makes one self-confident to deal with various situations. These days, the emphasis is on leadership training empowerment of people and capacity building. Education, which facilitates expression and communication ability, is an inseparable ingredient here.

Various mechanisms like parent-teacher associations, village educational committees are functioning to foster better relations between parents and teachers. These bodies provide an opportunity for the parents to air their concerns and extend their suggestions for betterment of teaching and school conditions. At the same time, the teachers can guide the parents and advice them with regards to their wards performance and progress. The educational committees are to act as liaison between school and village. They have the twin responsibilities. Firstly monitoring the school functioning and rendering the necessary assistance for the smooth running of the school. Secondly their job is to ensure enrolment and regular attendance of students and to educate parents in this regard. These education committees and parents associations need some orientation with regard to their responsibilities. They should not see themselves as on some fault finding mission or adopt a rigid ever complaining attitude.

The village education committees can take initiative to annually honor teachers along with students on the basis of their performance. This will facilitate positive relations and attitudes. They need to appreciate the constraints and limitations of the teachers and provide constructive criticism. Generally, they concentrate more on timings, absence of teacher during school hours etc. But, it is equally important to have some understanding of teaching and evaluation methods, uniform coverage of lessons etc.

Many times external monitoring teams concentrate more on food, conditions existing etc., and focus less on the processes of teaching. Time constraint plays a role here. In this context, the local committees become more relevant. At present monitoring is being done by the resource persons at different levels. They have a large area under their jurisdiction. In monitoring the focus has been on expenditure, accounts and physical facilities. Performance is reviewed on the basis of results at the end of the academic year. How to monitor academic processes, except through exams and inspection is the dilemma.

It is highly useful if the monitoring resource persons, inspecting authorities properly appraise these education committees and parents associations about their findings of monitoring and inspection. In view of the inadequacy of external supervision in tribal areas, of the local committees and associations need to take up this job, subject to proper orientation. Teachers should realize that, they need to work together with these committees and parents associations.

The education committees are to be oriented about the basic processes of teaching and running the school. The educational committee members should get some idea about the importance of reading, writing, speaking skills in case of languages; understanding of concepts in the case of non language subjects. They may be oriented to pursue the suggestions and comments given by the resource persons periodically visiting/inspecting the school. Generally the notings made by the resource persons in the visit and inspection books are not cared for by the teachers. The educational committees come into picture here. In view of the problems of transport and communications, it is difficult for resource persons to visit all the schools at desired intervals. This increases the responsibility of the village educational committee. The educational committees can effectively check the absentee and proxy teachers.

Development of Glossary of the Terms used in Telugu, Mathematics and Environmental Science Textbooks at Primary Stage in Andhra Pradesh

Language has been defined as a system of arbitrary vocal symbols by which members of a social group cooperate and interact. By means of language, learning process of culture is effectuated and a given way of life achieves both continuity and change. Without language, the accumulation and transmission of cultural knowledge that differentiates man from other animals could not have been possible. Thus, there is close link between culture and language.

The purpose of the formal education is to provide opportunities to the tribals and to bring psychological integration with the rest of the population. As a result, tribal languages and tribal cultures are ignored in teaching tribal children. In the context of schooling, language skills become a crucial variable for understanding concepts and academic participation. Linguistic competence is more important for tribal children as they find it difficult to follow academic instruction, and communicate with teachers. They are already handicapped due to lack of enough support on the home front. This results in lack of interest ultimately leading to drop outs and failures.

Experts have suggested the need to use home language in the elementary stages of schooling to enable tribal children to gain confidence. They also emphasized on importance of teachers relating the home language of the children to the school language i.e. teachers should use home language of children for explaining difficult concepts. As most tribal languages do not have a script, using regional language script can solve the problem. Many linguists suggest making unwritten language into a written one using local dialect. But this is stupendous task financially. Examples are available from former Soviet Union where State financed construction of tribal languages was undertaken. However, the constraints involved in replicating such exercise in India are: 1. The cost factor, 2. Lack of language experts in tribal languages, 3. Regional and local variations in languages and dialects.

The realization of the importance of instruction in mother tongue is reflected in Article 350A of the Constitution lays down that adequate facility for instruction in mother tongue at the primary stage of education shall be endeavoured to be provided. More than five decades later, the Draft National Policy on Tribals (2004) stated that the following are to be ensured to achieve the objective of reaching the benefit of education to tribals: Tribals are included in the national programme of *Sarva Shiksha Abhiyan* run by the Ministry of Human Resource Development. Schools and hostels are opened in areas where no such facilities exist. At least one model residential school is located in each, tribal concentration area. Education is linked with provision of supplementary nutrition. Special incentives like financial assistance, pocket allowance, free distribution of textbooks and school uniforms are provided. Teaching is imparted in tribals' mother tongue at least up to the primary level. Educated tribal youth are given employment as teachers, wherever possible. Pedagogy is made relevant so that tribals do not find it as alien. Curriculum and co-curriculum include aspects of meta skill up gradation of tribal children. Curricula for meta skill up gradation are to include aspects of tribal games and sports, archery, identification of plants of medicinal value, crafts art and culture, folk dance and folk songs, folk paintings, etc. Emphasis is laid on vocational/professional education. Polytechnics are set up for studies in subjects like forestry, horticulture, dairying, veterinary sciences, and polytechnics. Thus, we can see that Constitution of India and government policies on tribals gave importance for teaching in mother tongue to tribal children in elementary stages.

There are thirty-three scheduled tribes in Andhra Pradesh, apart from nomadic tribes and de-notified communities. In the north coastal districts of Andhra we can see four speech areas as far as tribal languages are concerned, viz., Savara, Kui, Kubi, and Gadaba. The Savara language belongs to Mundari group of languages. Gidugu Rammurthy Panthulu and Gidugu Sitapati studied the language. Through their efforts, a Savara-English Dictionary was prepared and an attempt was made to evolve a script so that the language could be used as a medium of instruction. Kui is spoken by Khonds (Samanthas) and Kubi is spoken by Konda Doras. Gadaba sub-groups speak different Gadaba dialects.

The Koyas speak a language called as Koi, which is very much influenced by Telugu. Gondi language, is similar to Koi, is the language of Raj Gonds. Largest numbers of studies were made on the Gondi language. Kolami is a Dravidian language spoken by Kolams. Several authors have studied Kolami. Banjara is the only tribe in Andhra Pradesh speaking an Indo-Aryan language. Yerukala (Kurru) language is not concentrated in any belt. This dispersal makes it difficult to carve out a speech area.

Majority of the tribal communities in the state speak Telugu. Bagata, Chenchu, Goudu, Konda Kammara, Konda Kapu, Konda Reddi, Koya Dora, Manne Dora, Mukha Dora, Nayak (Nayakapodu), Reddi Dora, Valmiki and Yanadi use Telugu. The Yanadis speak in the language Telugu, but, those who live in the border areas of Tamil Nadu also speak a mixture of both Telugu and Tamil. Communities living in Andhra-Orissa border such as Kotiya, Mulia, Porja, Rona and Savara speak both Telugu and Oriya. Similarly, the communities like Pardhan, Gond and Andh speak Telugu and Marathi (Pardhans speak Gondi also).

There are also tribes, who use Telugu along with their tribal language. They are Gadaba (Gadaba), Gond (Gondi), Koya (Koya), Lambada (Lamani or Lambani), Porja (Parji), Yerukala (Yerukula), Jatapu, Samantha and Khonda (Kuvi). According to Krishna Reddy and Ramachandra Reddy (1987) the linguistic speculation as well as celebration of Holi festival by the Banjaras support the explanation which points out that the Banjaras are of North Indian origin. Their dialect shows connections with North Indian languages like Hindi, Rajasthani and Punjabi.However, the Banjara dialect in South India is mixed with the surrounding Dravidian languages. In all the tribal languages, script has not developed. The tribal dialects are slowly disappearing because of culture contact and the children being educated in schools where medium of instruction is Telugu. Apart from the above, there are also a large number of nomadic and denotified tribes. Languages and dialects of communities like G. Mathura, Parthi, Ara, Dommara, Peddinti Golla, or Budabudakkala have not received much attention.

Table–6
The Tribal Communities of Andhra Pradesh Mainly Belong to Three Linguistic Families

	Family	*Examples*
1.	Dravidian language family	Gondi, Koya, Kolami, Erukula
2.	Mundari language family	Savara and Gadaba
3.	Indo-Aryan language family	Banjara

The following authors carried out studies on tribal languages. Sitapati (1943) on Savara, Emeneau (1955) on Kolami, Krishna Murthi (1969) on Kubi (Kanda Dora), Trivedi (1978) on Chenchu, Pratap (1980) on Naikapods.

Tribal children in Andhra Pradesh are taught in the schools in Telugu, the regional language. Being first generation learners, tribal children lag behind in vocabulary, spelling and reading speed and comprehension. School language is different from home language most of the time. Tribal children who come from homes where the mother tongue used is different from the medium of instruction in the school face problem of understanding and adjustment. Family dialect and peer group dialect affect children's style as they imitate these styles. They learn language by listening from the language environment in the home and community. Thus, by the time they come to the school, they have a set language skills having distinctive usage of syntax, structure, forms and usage. The words and sentences spoken by teacher in the classroom and present in the textbooks create confusion in the minds of the children. They sound strange, difficult to pronounce, remember and understand. When children come to school, they bring with them communication habits different from those expected in the school. The non-tribal teachers not having understanding of tribal languages lack in first hand communication with young children and do not appreciate the difficulties of tribal children. This leads to a communication gap. Misunderstanding, miscommunication between students and teachers leads to negative evaluation of each other.

When the teachers and students do not share the same communication background, they differ in communication strategies and contextual meanings of utterances. To understand classroom lessons, both literary meaning and contextual cues are required, but the latter are culturally determined for tribal children. It is well known that teachers resort to categorization of the children into low and high achieving groups. The teacher does not expect the low group do better, spends less time teaching them, though they actually need more attention. Apart from their socio-cultural disabilities, students from low group are affected by inadequate attention paid by the teacher in teaching. Relationships develop between the teacher and those who have a greater chance to do well in studies. As a result, students lagging behind because of various reasons feel frustrated and tend to withdraw from schools. Language and communication discontinuities between home and school are crucial variable in the adjustment problems faced by children. Language thus becomes a major factor leading to dropouts. Realization of this factor made many psychologists and educationalists to emphasize on teaching in mother tongue to young tribal children.

In Andhra Pradesh, Haimendorf is one of the pioneers to attempt education of tribals in their mother tongue (Haimendorf, 1944). In Adilabad district, Haimendorf found that much of the land alienation was because; the illiterate tribals are cheated in their credit transactions. Wherever present, schools were unattractive to tribals, as the Urdu and Marathi speaking teachers were unable to communicate effectively with tribal children. He started a school in 1943 for Gond youth who knew Urdu or Marathi, for training them as teachers. The teachers were trained to impart teaching in Gondi language using Devanagari script. The trainees were provided stipend during training period and after the completion of training, they were asked to open primary schools in the tribal villages. Readers and Premiers in Gondi, were prepared with the help of trainees. Lessons were mainly based on mythology, folklore and way of life of Gonds. On the pattern of the first training school started at Marlavai, training schools were later started at places like Sudimalla and Kamaram in Khammam district. Teaching in tribal languages has started in tribal areas of North East India in fifties. Central Institute of Indian Languages, Mysore, NCERT, New Delhi, and Tribal Cultural Research Institutes, Integrated Tribal Development Agencies in different states are said to have made some contributions towards preparation of reading material in tribal languages and dialects. The role played by missionaries in different parts of the country also needs to be mentioned here. However, the reading material prepared by various agencies made no significant impact due to the policy of uniform syllabi for tribal students and non-tribal students.

Education through local tribal dialects at least up to second standard is said to be desirable. Notwithstanding the constitutional provision, teaching in tribal languages did not receive much attention. There are no clear instructions on policy guidelines. There are several issues involved in achieving this laudable objective.

The linguistic diversity of tribal population does not allow one pattern of medium of instruction in tribal education. Presence of multi-lingual speech areas poses a problem in imparting education in mother tongue in tribal areas. Most of the tribal languages do not have a script. Instructional material is not available. Speakers of many languages are not a viable number. Non-availability of teachers knowing tribal languages is another constraint.

Parents themselves are apprehensive if their children are taught in mother tongue, they will face problem in switching over to other languages at higher levels. Shift from tribal dialect to regional language from III class onwards will create problems for tribal student whose vocabulary of regional language is not up to the mark. This shift from mother tongue to regional language is considered as over burdening of students. Some suggest the need to have supplementary premiers in state language for those studying elementary classes in tribal languages so that a smooth transition is ensured from tribal language to state language.

Everywhere the trend is to go for English medium schools as it is considered prestigious and adds to prospects. Except for Convents, Public Schools, and a few selected private schools, the medium of instruction is regional language. How a separate system of primary education carried through their mother tongue prepares the tribal children for higher studies in regional languages and English is an issue for debate. Many point out to the fact that Christian missionaries were able to achieve better literacy and education in the tribal areas of northeast, though the medium of instruction is English.

One view is that, the teachers, dealing with tribal children studying in a language other than home language, need to be trained specially and to be provided with incentives for following a bilingual approach in teaching. They need to be provided with glossaries in tribal languages for technical terms. Here one of the problems that need to be overcome is lack of equivalent terms and concepts in tribal languages.

Prominent educationists and various reports on education have recommended that the mother tongue of the child be made his medium of education, Gandhiji stated: "I am convinced that children who receive education in a tongue other than their own commit suicide." Wardha Committee (1937) recommended the use of mother tongue as the medium of instruction. Language Commission (1956) specifically mentioned the need to make Hindi the official language. Tagore viewed that "There is no joy, no expansion, no blossoming of our families without mother tongue."

Need of social integration also supports the claim of the mother tongue. The Emotional Integration and the National Integration Committee have also supported that the regional language of the child should be made his medium of instruction. It is essential to make mother tongue as instruction-medium because: It facilitates learning and teaching. It is a more psychological and natural medium. It is helpful in the intellectual, mental and emotional growth of the child. It enables the children to understand and appreciate their cultural traditions. It will facilitate the process of emotional and national tradition. It will reduce the burden of cramming and verbalism in teaching and learning. It will give pleasure to the children. It enables the school to attract the children and sustain them in school. It has been rightly asserted by Dr. VKRV Rao that: "India would be as any other advanced country in the world in the next fifty years if medium of instruction in schools and universities is switched over to the mother tongue from now."

Our Constitution is based on four important ideals—that is Justice, Liberty, Equality and Fraternity. Justice: Social, economic and political; Liberty of thought, expression, belief, faith and worship; Equality of status and opportunity and to promote among them all; Fraternity: Assuring the dignity of the individual and unity of the Nation. As per 42 Amendment Act, our country is a sovereign, socialist, secular, democratic republic. The following are some of the provisions relating to protection of language. Art 29(1): The Constitution states that the citizens residing in any part of the country but having their own language, script or culture will have the right to maintain them. Art 30(1): All minorities based on religion or language will have the right to set up and administer institutions in their own interest. Art 350: States that every individual has the right to give representation to an officer in the State or Central language. Art 350(A): Advises that education be imparted in the mother tongue, stating that it will be the endeavour of every state, and of every local official within the state, to provide suitable facilities for providing education to the children of linguistic minorities in their mother tongue at the primary stage.

The Constitution has recognized 18 languages in the Schedule of the Constitution—Assamese, Bengali, Gujarathi, Hindi, Kannada, Kashmiri, Konkani, Malayalam, Marathi, Manipuri, Oriya, Punjabi, Sanskrit, Sindhi, Tamil, Telugu and Urdu. Sindhi was added by 21st Amendment Act 1967. Konkani, Manipuri and Nepali languages were added by 71st Amendment Act 1992. There are almost 1652 dialects spoken in India without script. In case of tribal communities there are only dialects without script.

Teaching Learning Process is continuous and involves multi interactions. It is the process of transfer of ideas and concepts to others. The means of transfer of ideas mainly is the language, the language of learner and the language of speaker i.e. teacher. As we are aware that the main principles of learning are: Known to unknown; Simple to complex; and Concrete to abstract and many others. The main questions to be addressed here are: Which is known to the child? Which is simple to the child? Which is concrete to the child?

The children are very comfortable with the language used in the house, with the language of the parents and the words used in the known language. That means the basis for all the principles of learning is the language. The language familiar to the learner enhances the learning. But unfortunately the tribal children are deprived of the use of their mother tongue in the classrooms. The languages used in the houses of the tribal children are entirely different from the language used in the classroom. Whatever principles or strategies, the teacher may adopt, the learning is elusive to the child unless the teacher uses child-friendly language. Hence to build the gap between the home language and the classroom language, use of a glossary in a tribal and Telugu language is more appropriate. Some Experiments done in Teaching School Language through Tribal Dialect were: Adilabad Agency experiment - Development of bilingual charts in Gondi and Telugu language (ITDA, Utnoor). Development of Bridge language inventories in Savara language by ITDA Seetampeta and Parvatipuram and in Banjara by ITDA Eturunagaram, Warangal District, Andhra Pradesh. Development of Bilingual textbooks in Gondi, Savara, Kolami and Lambada in Class I by APDPEP, Hyderabad. Development of textbooks in eight tribal dialects for Class I (100% tribal dialect), Class II (80% + 20%) school language, Class III (60% + 40% SL), Class IV (80% + 20% SL) and Class V 100 per cent school language (Kolami, Gondi, Savara, Koya, Khond, Kuvi, Adivasi Oriya, Banjara). Collections relating to tribal stories, riddles in different tribal dialects in Andhra Pradesh by APDPEP.

In the process of learning, the child has to interact with the teacher, the peer group and the environment. How can a tribal child interact with the teacher, if the language of the teacher is different from the language of the child? The teacher has to understand the child and the child has to understand the teacher. In this process language is the main barrier in the tribal areas. This barrier can be minimized by using glossary. Another important aspect is: How can child interact with the environment if it is totally unfamiliar to him? The environment can be made familiar with the use of available language with the help of a Tribal Language—Telugu Glossary.

Today, the talents of the tribal child should be recognized. This can be drawn out by providing suitable situations. This can be possible through the creation of the Tribal Child Friendly Environment inside and outside the classroom. But the present situation is unknown and complex to the child. This can be transferred into known and simple through a tribal Telugu Glossary. The glossary is useful to the child as a vehicle to transform the Abstract to concrete, Complex to simple and unknown to known situations, etc.

The glossary is useful to acquire skills to' draw the child's inborn qualities and develop talents. The glossary is useful to the teacher as a vehicle to understand the culture, social values, habits of the child and his environment which in turn helps in understanding the child and his parents. The glossary simplifies the complexity of teaching learning process and gives highest satisfaction to the teacher. The effective usage of glossary directs to improve the capacities and capabilities of the teacher, which lays fair path for the raise of the status of the teacher.

The main hurdle in the education of the tribal child is acceptance of education by the tribal community. This is because of the diversity in the language i.e. the Tribal Language and Telugu. The glossary makes a full-stop for the diversity and converges both the languages and helps in accepting the education by the community. The glossary brings the teacher and community nearer which in turn strengthens the community participation in education. The glossary helps to bring educational awareness among the tribal community. The following diagram helps us in understanding of how a Glossary will be of great help to the teachers working in the tribal and non-tribal locality schools, the community aspirations and to develop the child's interests.

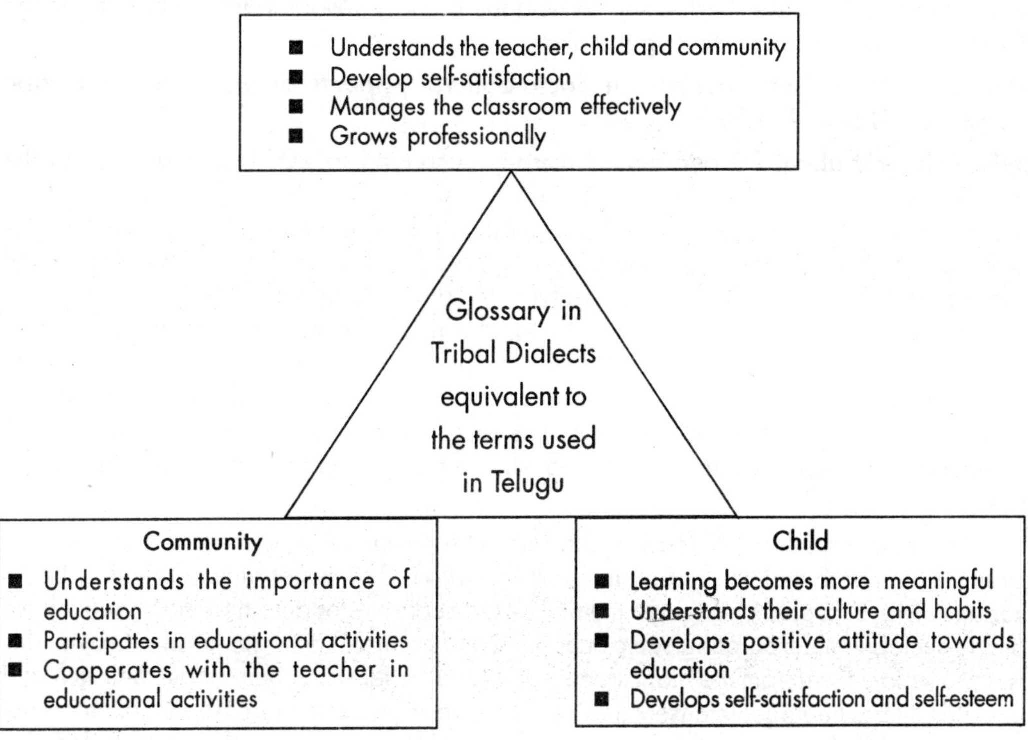

The scheduled tribes constitute a major group in Andhra Pradesh for whom access to primary education is the main problem. They live in remote areas of the state and need special focus to solve their problems. Jatapu, Kondadora, Mukadora and Mannedora are the major tribal groups and Savara and Gadaba communities are the primitive tribal groups. The Savara tribal schools in the agency area is surrounded by thick forests. In most of the schools, Telugu language learning is very poor. The Savara tribal children are not very much conversant in Telugu. The teachers are following Telugu textbooks in primary schools. The Savara tribal children use their own dialect. The teachers know Telugu and they communicate to tribal children in Telugu language. Teachers are facing difficulty in communicating with the tribal students as they use the tribal dialect in responding to the teaching. The teachers are unable to understand the responses given by the tribal students. It has been identified by the Government of Andhra Pradesh that there is a gap between the students and the teachers in understanding the materials supplied by the government. The home language used by the Savara Tribal students is entirely different with that of the Telugu language used in the classroom transaction by teachers. Due to the language gap between the Savara tribal students and teachers, there is a problem of understanding the instruction. There is a mismatch between the teachers and the tribal students. In order to bridge this gap in educating Savara Tribal children, there is a need to prepare a glossary which would help both the tribal student and the teachers. The programme has been identified as a state need. The main objectives of the present study are as follows: To collect the vocabulary used by Savara tribals (proverbs, riddles, names of herbs and other elements of folklore). To find out the equivalent Savara tribal dialect words to the Telugu words used in the Telugu Textbooks. To help the primary school teachers working in the Tribal areas to understand the tribal dialect.

Development of Audio Scripts on Socio-Cultural Aspects of the Scheduled Tribe Groups of Andhra Pradesh

India achieved about 70 per cent of literacy according to 2001 census. Though the progress could have been better, considering several constraints, it is not a mean achievement. However, the rate of literacy among marginalized sections, in particular adivasis, is much lower even compared to scheduled classes and other backward communities (bahujans). This apart, the type of education provided to them, curriculum and reading materials, is quite conventional, not much different from the other general sections of society. It may sound offensive, but it is atrocious, to say the least. It is an accepted norm by all educationists that the curriculum and related reading materials should be learner-friendly and learner-specific. The fact that even after nearly six decades of independence, such steps are not initiated, should make us more responsive to this crying need.

The Adivasi children are fed with the same curriculum, reading materials and tools of teaching similar to that of children in the main stream. This is not only unscientific but at variance with accepted pedagogic methodology. Separate reading materials should have been developed incorporating socio-economic and cultural ethos/genius of adivasis. This is not to isolate them from the mainstream society but to sensitize them about their rich and age old cultural heritage. Intensely debated for several years, the mainstream theory is not favoured today. Integrating them, not isolating, into the broad based and extended civil society is an accepted norm. However, anthropologists world over are of the considered view that while providing all benefits that modern civilization today offers, care should be taken to preserve their core culture. Education provided should not uproot them from their cultural backdrop and, on the other, all steps should be taken to preserve it. Their cultural wealth including their day-to-day life styles, medicinal plants, herbs and roots, recreational and performing art forms, justice-delivery systems, martial qualities along with their peace loving and hospitable nature should be protected and preserved.

The present information is based on three workshops (of five day duration) held at Mysore (RIE) and Hyderabad (SIET). About 30 participants representing different tribes and regions in Andhra Pradesh were invited to attend. Deliberations were held on the present curriculum and texts followed in the adivasi schools upto the primary level. The exercise revealed that both the curriculum and related tools of teaching are the same as those followed in schools in the plains. Also the content is heavily loaded in favour of children of these areas. This is understandable for the focus of curriculum and textbooks hitherto has been based on the life styles of dominant sections of society. Hegemonic culture would always endeavour to dominate the subordinate cultures. This happens in a subtle and imperceptible manner. This needs to be corrected. The ideal situation would be to develop separate curriculum and also reading materials accordingly. It is heartening to note that the Andhra Pradesh Government has initiated steps in this direction. It is a never-too-late situation. We wish that the process would cover grades upto upper primary level and Telugu could be taught as second language.

The present report, as one would perceive, is in the direction of developing ancillary materials in the form of audio cassettes and CDs encompassing the local tribe specific socio-cultural aspects of their life styles. That it should be done cautiously is understood. The positive aspects of their society and culture should get reflected in these audio recordings so as to provide the children with a basic understanding of their cultural ethos and thus cope with the curriculum and textbooks. It is observed, sadly though, that the present day youth among adivasis are being gradually alienated from their cultural roots. They are fast taking to cultural practices and social observances of the non-tribal groups and, if the process continues unabated, the day is not far off when the uniqueness of their culture gets totally eclipsed.

We would like to make a few observations in conclusion. First, the topics for different projects we have undertaken so far are closely related to tribal education in Andhra Pradesh. We feel that they are relevant to the present day needs of Education of adivasi children. Thanks to the NCERT (New Delhi) that these projects are made possible by liberal funding. The NCERT is primarily concerned with monitoring school education under the Central Government jurisdiction, its reports and reading materials are being adopted/adapted by several State Governments. The reports of these workshops which we prepared need be implemented in tribal schools. The State Government Officials in departments of tribal welfare, education and also academic experts in tribal studies are actively associated with these workshops. After implementation, feedback exercise could be undertaken based on which necessary changes could be made. Secondly, the teachers working in tribal areas are the carriers of tribal culture to future generations. Our experience shows they are well informed and adequately equipped to carry forward their cultural traditions to the future generations. Also they occupy a pivotal position in whom the adivasis could repose their trust. As they occupy such a crucial position in the teaching-learning process, it is through them the dissemination of their culture should take place.

Education is chiefly concerned with the development of man, the modification of his behaviour and equipping him in the art of living successfully and efficiently. The ultimate purpose of education is man making. It attempts to develop man in terms of his multidimensional personality. It develops his innate powers from infancy to maturity in such a way that not only he can adjust himself to his environment, but also can control and improve it. Education consists in leading out the innate knowledge, virtues and powers of the child making the potential actual. Thus education is leading out what is within man through knowledge and experience.

Formal education is provided to the child through school. School plays a major role in moulding the ideas, habits and attitudes of children with a view to producing well balanced personalities. A school is not a mere brick and mortar structure showing a miscellany of pupils and of teachers; a school is not a market place where knowledge is doled out to unwilling consumers of varying capacities; a school is not a railway platform where a heterogeneous crowd gathers with diverse objects; a school is not a vigorous reformatory where juvenile suspects are kept under vigilant watch; a school is a spiritual organization with distinctive personality of its own; a school is a vibrant community centre radiating life and energy all round, a school is a wonderful edifice, resting on the foundation of goodwill–goodwill of the public, goodwill of the parents, goodwill of the pupils. John Dewey thinks "The school is primarily a social institution, education being a social process. The school is simply that form of community life in which all these agencies are concentrated that will be most effective in bringing the child to share in the inherent resources of the race to use powers for social ends."

Teach the 3Rs was the conception of a traditional school. The slogan of a present school is Teach the 7Rs i.e. Reading, Writing, Arithmetic, Recreative, Rights, Responsibilities and Relationships. The present school must prepare the students for a democratic society by providing them democratic experiences. It is an important institution that conserves the morals, customs and whys of life and passes it on to the students. Education is the transmission of technical skills and cultural traditions from one generation to the other and the school must discharge this function effectively. Further mere conservation of culture is not enough. It should aim at developing new ways of thought, new ways of action and new ways of feelings. Thus it was to conserve the socio-cultural aspects of the society, transmit them to the new generation and try to develop new socio-cultural aspects and add to the present knowledge so as to enable the individuals lead a happy, prosperous and outstanding life in the society. The schools exist to accelerate the impact of the essential aspects of culture which prevails in the society.

To be born in a human society means to be human, not animal. To be human means to be cultured, to be civilized. The child is to be socialized. Socialization is a process by which the individual is adapted to his social environment and becomes a co-operating efficient member of it. According to Taylor, "Culture is that complex whole which includes knowledge, beliefs, art, morals, law, customs and any other capabilities acquired by man as a member of society." In this sense, culture is much more than the material wealth of a society. It refers to the capabilities acquired by man while they grow as members of society i.e. social and cultural modes. It includes the ways in which men live, their customs, values, social and political attitudes, etc. H. Rugg has stated that culture is what the people in a given society, do, think, feel, believe, desire, fear. Brown considered culture as the total behaviour pattern of the group. Ellwood regards "Culture as something which includes: (1) the whole of man's material civilization, tools, weapons, systems of industry and (2) all the non-material or spiritual civilization such as language, literature, art religion, morality, law and government." Thus culture includes the socio-cultural aspects of the society.

There are 33 tribal groups in Andhra Pradesh. Each community has its own mode of life, its own culture and social behaviour. Each community has its own socio-cultural pattern. This is to be provided and communicated to the future citizens. Education is the only means through which this is to be done. The Indian Education Commission 1964-66 stated thus: "The most important and urgent reform needed in education is to transform it, so as to endeavour to relate it to life, needs and aspirations of the people and thereby make a powerful instrument in social, economic and cultural transformation, necessary for realization of national goals." One of the main steps should be the promotion and understanding of the socio-cultural heritage of the society to the future generation.

The three focal points of the educative process are : *(i)* the instructional goals (the aims of education), *(ii)* the content material (the curriculum) and *(iii)* the instructional procedures (the method). Teaching is the act of instruction and learning is the result of it. The verb teaching connotes two accusatives viz. subject and the individual. Teaching is a process through which certain amount of knowledge is imparted. Certain skills are developed and attitudes, values and interests are inculcated. In the process of teaching for effective learning, the teachers need to adopt certain materials, may be the audio or visual or audio-visual aids. These provide right type of experience to the child. In this connection, Edgar Dale has suggested various aids to provide experiences to the child in the form of a cone.

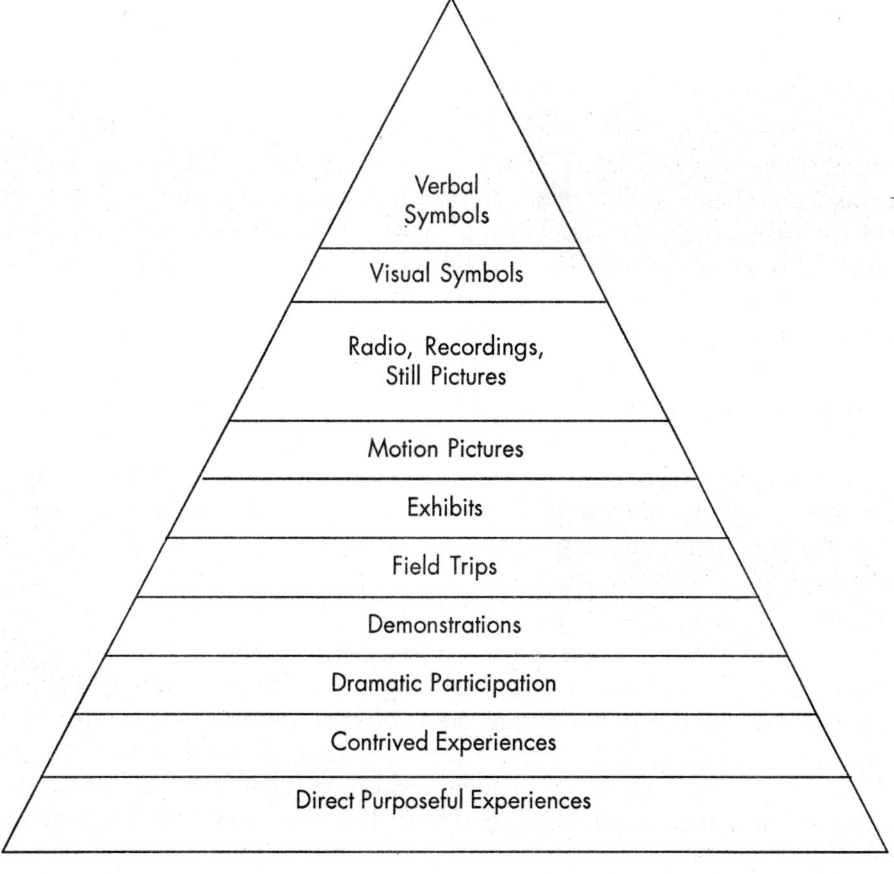

Items 1 and 2 are the activities which help in the acquisition of experiences by doing items 3 to 8 by observing and items 9 and 10 through the presentation of symbols.

Audio CDs provide an important means to provide suitable experiences to the children. To transmit the socio-cultural aspects of the tribal communities and to preserve them and develop them, preparation of audio CD's scripts is taken up.

According to 1991 census, there are 573 Scheduled Tribes in India constituting 8 per cent of the total population. Among States, Orissa has the largest number of Scheduled Tribes (i.e. 62). There are 33 Tribal groups in Andhra Pradesh with a total population of 41,99,481 (i.e. 6.3%). Of the total tribal population, 39 per cent of the population belong to Sugali Community spread dominantly in Warangal, Nalgonda, Khammam, Mahabub Nagar and Nizamabad districts. Next to this nearly 11 per cent population comprise of Koyas inhabited in Khammam, Warangal, West Godavari, East Godavari and Adilabad districts. Around 9 per cent population each comprise of Yanadi and Yerukula communities dominant in Nellore, Chittoor, Prakasam, Guntur, Anantapur, Prakasam, Krishna and Nellore districts respectively. Bagata, Bhils, Gond, Hill Reddi, Kammara, Kondadora, Khond, Kotia, Kulia, Mali, Mukadora, Porja, Reddidora and Valmiki are mostly inhabited in Visakhapatnam district. Gadaba, Jatapu are dominant in Vizianagaram district. Savara community is dominant in Srikakulam district. Kondakapu and Kondareddi are more in number in East Godavari district. Adilabad district is inhabited by Andh, Gond, Naikpod, Kolam, Mannedora, Pardhan and Thoti tribal communities. Chenchu, Kotunayakan and Yerukula are dominant in Guntur district. Koya and Nayak are more in number in Khammam district. Chittoor district has Rona/Rena tribal community member. Yanadi community members are inhabited in Nellore district more in numbers.

Andhra Pradesh has 42 lakhs Scheduled Tribes population (1991 census). Largest tribal population is found in Khammam district (5.59 Lakhs), followed by Visakhapatnam district (4.69 lakhs). The tribal population of Andhra Pradesh increased from 7.67 lakhs to 42 lakhs between 1951 and 1991. The substantial population increase between 1971 and 1981 was because of the recognition of the Lambada, Erukala and Yanadi communities as Scheduled Tribes in the entire state. The Scheduled Tribes Population in the State of Andhra Pradesh increased during the past four decades.

The tribal communities in the state of Andhra Pradesh mostly exhibit proto-austroloid features. Chenchus and Yanadis exhibit some Negrito strain whereas the Khond and Savara have few Mongoloid features. The tribal communities of Andhra Pradesh mainly belong to three linguistic families as follows: Dravidian language family Gondi, Koya, Kolami, Erukula; Mundari language family Savara and Gadaba; Indo-Aryan language family Banjara.

Majority of the communities speak Telugu. Bagata, Chenchu, Gondu, Konda Kammara, Konda Kapu, Konda Reddi, Koya Dora, Manme Dora, Mukha Dora, Nayak (Nayaka podu), Reddi Dora, Valmiki and Yanadi use Telugu. The Yanadis speak in the language Telugu, but, those who live in the border areas of Tamil Nadu speak a mixture of both Telugu and Tamil. Communities living in Andhra, Orissa border such as Kotiya, Mulia, Porja, Rona and Savara speak both Telugu and Oriya. Similarly, the communities like Pardhan, Gond and Andh speak Telugu and Marathi (Pardhans speak Gondi also). There are also tribes, who use Telugu along with their tribal language. They are Gadaba, (Gadaba), Gond (Gondi), Koya, (Koya), Lambada (Lamani or Lambani), Porja (Parji), Yerukula (Kurru/Yerukula), Jatapu, Samantha and Khonda /Kuvi). In all the tribal languages, script has not been developed. The tribal dialects are slowly disappearing because of culture contact and the children being educated in Telugu schools.

Jatapu, Kondadora, Mukadora, Mannedora, Sugali, Yerukula, Koya, Gond, Pardhan, Yanadi are some of the major tribal groups and Savara, Gadaba, Thoti, Chenchu, Kolam, Konda Reddy, Pooja and Khond are some of the primitive tribal groups existing in Andhra Pradesh. The Savara tribal population are most preponderant tribal group population and their families are nuclear type. The Khonds speak 'Kui' language Bagata are called as warrior community. The Koyas speak 'Kui' dialect and Telugu Language. Sammakka and Saralamma are worshipped by them. Naikpod are experts in flatting trees. Pardhans are the custodians of Gond Tradition. Thotis are famous for selling medicinal herbs. Hunting and honey collection are the main occupations of the Chenchus. The Yerukulas are the Sooth sayers.

The State has 21.3 per cent of its total area under forests. However, in areas of tribal concentration, where the tribal sub-plans are being implemented through integrated Tribal Development Agencies, forests constitute 63.43 per cent of the total geographical area. The tribal economies can be characterized as agro-forest based. Depending on their broad traditional economic pursuits, the tribal communities can be categorized under the following types: Food gathering, e.g. Chenchu; Shifting cultivation, e.g. Konda Reddi; Pastoralists, e.g. Gondu, Sigali; Settled cultivators, e.g. Bagatha Valmiki; Artisanal Groups, e.g. Konda Kammara, Erukula.

Different communities pursue a number of subsidiary activities apart from their traditional economic activity. For example, the food gathering Chenchu depended upon hunting and cattle rearing, partially the Sugali (Bajara) and Gond have taken up settled cultivation. Broadly speaking, settled cultivation can be seen in all communities. Communities living in the hilly and forest areas depend upon minor forest produce collection as an important source of supplementary income. Fishing and hunting are seen in all communities for supplementing the food requirements. Basket making, carpentry, black smithy, pig rearing, etc. can be seen in some of the communities. By and large, tribal households have a near subsistence level of economy. Those who undertake settled cultivation are in a better position. Indebtedness is a common feature of economy in most of the communities.

The 33 tribal groups in Andhra Pradesh comprising 6.3 per cent population of the State. Bagata, Bhils, Goud, Hill Reddy, Kondadora, Mukadora, Poorja, Savara, Gadaba, Gond, Pardhan, Kolam, etc. are some of the tribes residing in hilly areas and forests. Shifting cultivation, Podu cultivation, Agriculture, Agriculture labour, collection of non-timber forest produce are some of the major occupations of the tribal groups. Besides these some groups are involved in occupations like hunting, honey collection, cattle rearing, manufacture of agricultural implements, basket making, selling bangles and beads, making garlands, forest labour, etc.

Every community has its own culture. Culture is regarded as social heredity. It includes traditions, morals, laws, customs and other capabilities that are acquired by man as a member of society. It includes both material aspects like housing, clothing, food, festivals, ceremonies, marriages, folk art, etc. as well as non-material aspects like language, family system, relationships, etc. From the sociological point of view, education has to transmit the cultural heritage of the previous generation to the present generation and also it has to conserve it and advance it. Education has to socialize the child and make the child physically strong, intellectually alert, emotionally stable, socially efficient and culturally sound. The special features of the socio-cultural aspects of the ST groups of Andhra Pradesh can be mentioned as follows: 1. Geographic Isolation/Isolated Societies; 2. Simple way of life; 3. Treat Nature with respect; 4. Subject to customary laws/without law and order department, they control themselves; 5. They have their own code of conduct; 6. Truthfulness and honesty are found in them; 7. Closed system; 8. Subsistence economy; 9. Festivals throughout the year; 10. Early marriages (13–15 years boys, 10–14 years girls); 11. Own dialect (Kuli, Kui, Gondi, Lambadi, Kolami, etc.); 12. Polygamy; 13. Divorce; 14. Limited exposure to outside world; 15. Beliefs and superstitions; 16. Limited needs and aspirations; 17. Parents are interested in immediate gains; 18. Economic characteristics include Food gathering/Hunting/Fishing/Shifting cultivation/Terrace cultivation; 19. Low skills/very little specialization/low productivity/no work training; 20. Lacks abstract thinking; 21. Child is looked as potential learner but not a learner; 22. Women looked as economic assets and 23. Learning through imitation but not instruction, etc.

Tribal Communities lead a simple life, subject to customary life. They have limited exposure to outside world. They give more importance to immediate gains. They talk different dialects based on their own traditions and customs. They give importance to the celebration of festivals, which generally fall throughout the year. Whenever there is a festive occasion in the village all the villagers both elders, youngsters and children participate in it, which may disrupt the academic/school schedule of the children.

Imparting education to tribal children is a challenging task in the present scenario, as they have to grow, acclimatizing themselves, in the changing world of new livelihood patterns and lifestyles. The personal growth of tribal children is beset in developing their abilities and faculties to cope up psychologically as well as culturally in the new social milieu. They have to adopt learning through classroom teaching, contrary to the practice of learning their subsistence patterns and value-systems by participating in their culture and gaining knowledge by experience. The medium of education for tribal children in their pristine environments is lived experience, as a member of a social group.

It is, therefore, imperative for the institutions implementing educational programmes to tribal children to give priority in developing suitable mechanisms of reorienting the tribal children to classroom education, and to the realities of the changes into which they are being drawn into. As a matter of fact, the tribal societies and tribal children are already well entrenched in the transition into the realm of tribal- rural-urban, matrix and modern consumerism.

Classroom education for tribal children is crossing a threshold of learning as a practice of interaction with the natural world to a system of textbook learning. This process has already made much headway in the tribal areas. But this kind of education has not evoked the expected enthusiasm among the tribal societies, apparently because it is not emotionally satisfying. Talking to tribal parents, one could sense an obtuse feeling that medium of modern education is a withdrawal of mediation of culture in shaping their life worlds.

As mention has already been made, children in these traditional societies, as a routine, live in harmony with their environments through culturally encoded norms of hands-on learning and gain practical knowledge. Meeting their survival needs is interwoven with tapping the resource zones in their respective ecosystems with a choice and freedom of managing community resources.

Tribal child is a free bird by nature. He enjoys complete freedom unrestricted by his parents or other family members. Tribal children prefer to spend their time moving freely around, swimming in ponds and streams, catching fish, climbing trees, hunting birds, collecting berries, riding on buffaloes, etc. The characteristics of a tribal child are: the tribal child is very bold, friendly in nature and obedient, possesses skills and concentration, likes co-curricular activities, respects the elders, reliable, shows interest towards functions/ festivals, believe superstitions, likes simplicity, treat nature with respect, believe truthfulness and honesty, limited in needs, low aspirants, feel shy with the strangers but free with the known people, like to learn through imitation rather than instruction, do not like to remain confined to four walls of the school and prefers to roam about and play in the open. In tribal communities, very rarely the children are punished. The conflict between the norms of school and socialization at home results in resistance and unwillingness among children to attend the school.

Andhra Pradesh Primary Education Programme (APPEP) which was implemented in the State with the assistance of U.K. Government, has suggested six pedagogical principles, which are being followed in all the primary schools of the State including tribal areas. These principles are providing teacher generated learning activities; promoting learning by doing, discovering and experimenting; developing individual, group and whole class work; providing for individual differences; using the local environment and creating an interesting classroom by displaying children's work and organizing it effectively. The District Primary Education Programmed (DPEP/SSA) went a step further and is emphasizing on Natural Learning experiences drawing out the inborn abilities. While adopting these processes teachers in tribal areas need to keep in view the local cultural aspects to correlate with the teaching items for better learning and sustain interest among the tribal children. The cultural aspects, which can be used in the classroom by the tribal teachers are: Tribal dialect, Tribal play activities, calculation of time, identification of seasons, measures used for calculating distance, weight, volume; agriculture crops grown, pesticides used, cattle rearing methods adopted, body cleanliness and healthy habits, dress and costumes, house keeping, medicines used for ailments, village panchayat/Muthadar systems, solving problems, festivals celebrated, seeds procured, marriage systems, custom of receiving guests, honouring guests, tribal dances, worship, grain bank, agriculture implements, transportation system, interdependence/Give and take, leisure time activities/recreation, protection of crops, shandies, musical instruments, household implements, property rights, food habits, fuel, riddles, songs/folk songs, stories, etc.

These components of tribal culture need to be adopted in the teaching-learning process in the school to create and sustain interest among the tribal pupils. In this regard, the teacher plays an important role. His commitment, the quality of his empathy, the creativity and ability in correlating his teaching with the cultural components of the community go a long way in creating interest and to impart education effectively among the tribal children. Whenever and wherever it is possible, socio-cultural and culture-specific curricular and co-curricular activities need to be organized by the teacher through different modes in the school.

The teachers working in tribal areas must make it a point to invariably refer to the local tribal community, their way of life, habits, economic system, social problems, history of the concerned tribe, changes in their life styles, physical features, difference between tribal and non-tribal groups relating to their physical and mental aspects, their life modes, work practices, their relation with the forests and nature etc. in their teaching-learning process, while dealing with different subjects in the curriculum. This creates interest among tribal children towards education and help in better learning.

Imparting education to tribal children is a challenging task in the present scenario, as they have to grow, acclimatizing themselves, in the changing world of new livelihood patterns and lifestyles. The personal growth of tribal children is beset in developing their abilities and faculties to cope up psychologically as well as culturally in the new social milieu. They have to adopt learning through classroom teaching, contrary to the practice of learning their subsistence patterns and value-systems by participating in their culture and gaining knowledge by experience. The medium of education for tribal children in their pristine environments is lived experience, as a member of a social group.

It is, therefore, imperative for the institutions implementing educational programmes to tribal children to give priority in developing suitable mechanisms of reorienting the tribal children to classroom education and to the realities of the change into which they are being drawn into. As a matter of fact, the tribal societies and tribal children are already well entrenched in the transition into the realm of tribal rural-urban, matrix and modern consumerism.

Classroom education for tribal children is crossing a threshold of learning as a practice of interaction with the natural world to a system of textbook learning. This process has already made much headway in the tribal areas. But this kind of education has not evoked the expected enthusiasm among the tribal societies, apparently because it is not emotionally satisfying. Talking to tribal parents, one could sense an obtuse feeling that medium of modern education is a withdrawal of mediation of culture in shaping their life worlds.

As mention has already been made, children in these traditional societies, as a routine, live in harmony with their environments through culturally encoded norms of hands-on learning and gain practical knowledge. Meeting their survival needs is interwoven with tapping the resource zones in their respective ecosystems with a choice and freedom of managing community resources.

If we look at the ground realities in the context of education of tribal children, it becomes obvious that it is linked to economic equity, which cannot be achieved by mere classroom prescriptions. Attempts at even partially fulfilling the goal of economic equity, bring us back to the enterprise of involving tribal children in making best use of their traditional knowledge in harnessing the resources and biodiversity and sustainable management of environments and livelihoods. The grassroot level of education of tribal children needs a combination of three strands: *(a)* their traditional knowledge of livelihoods; *(b)* imparting skills to make them partners in sustainable management of environments; and *(c)* modern education through primary and secondary schooling, to bring awareness of the world around them and to derive benefit from the new opportunities that are being made available.

The linkage between traditional knowledge of livelihoods and learning can be seen by considering some of the tribal societies in Andhra Pradesh. These communities are hunter-gatherers (Chenchu, Yanadi, Yerukula, Boya); marine fishermen (Voda Balije, Pallekaru, Besta, Jalari); shifting cultivators (Konda Reddi, Kondadora, Konda Kapu, Koya, Khond, Savara, Bhagata, etc.); and pastoralists (Golla, Kuruva, Kuruma). The Gonds (and also Kolams) of Adilabad though have now taken to settled and plains, agriculture, they originally practiced shifting cultivation. In these societies, the process of learning for a child has an orientation to the traditional practices of survival of that group to which it belongs. For instance, children in hunting-gathering societies learn about the food resources in their natural world (e.g. a variety of forest plant foods such as fruits, berries, nuts, flowers, tubers and yams, gums, mushrooms; insects; honey and habits and habitats of big and small game, birds and fishes) and they acquire the skills of hunting and fishing (using nets, a variety of traps, bows and arrows), and gathering, as a customary tradition of making out their living. In the pastoral societies, children learn cattle and sheep/goat herding techniques such as tending of herds, transhumance to pastures and herbal veterinary practices by participating in the pursuit along with the elders. Children in shifting cultivator and peasant societies, likewise, learn about seasonality of crops, sowing and cropping patterns, weeding, control of pests and grain storage from the elders.

Learning in these societies is a behavioural response guided by culture. Culture is institutionalized knowledge, a method of information processing, and also a mechanism in situating individuals within its group and also situating different social groups within a larger social matrix. In these tribal, pastoral and agricultural groups kinship relations and age and sex categories also pattern behaviour. The livelihood norms are cultural traditions with a past-present continuum. Some of the important aspects, which a tribal child learns as a member of a given society, are as follows: Land use pattern, organization of space, territorial divisions and markers. Resource zones, communal sharing and management of resource zones. Social construction of landscapes such as forested, rural and urban, sacral and spatial mobility. Settlement systems, domestic architecture, organization of domestic space and sacral space. Procurement of raw materials and production of artifacts, arts and crafts (material culture). Rituals associated with rights of passage and village rituals. Community participation with reciprocal exchange of foods, goods and services.

Education of children in these tribal societies is a long-term strategy that has been going hand-in-hand with a multitude of tribal development programmes. The guiding principle of state's intervention in development of these communities is poverty alleviation; improving housing, hygiene and sanitation; health care; and education.

A wide spectrum of the tribal groups is becoming increasingly aware of the developmental projects and educational programmes and is expecting proper implementation of these schemes for their benefit. They are adjusting themselves to be partners in a system of hierarchical social order.

Empowerment of women and youth due to the encouragement of progressive bureaucrats has given successful results but such instances are not many. In some districts, women through Sahayaka Sanghams/Self-Help Groups are playing an important role not only in income generation and decision-making but also in literacy programmes.

Elders and youth have come to perceive that literacy and education are important for their future. But they are in a dilemma and ask the question in which way the modern education (primary/secondary) can contribute for the betterment of their livelihoods? To answer such predicaments it might be appropriate to include, in the curriculum, the socio-cultural patterns of the 'tribal cultures' as well as those of the 'others' whose mode of 'education' is being imparted in the tribal schools, for an interactive exchange in the sphere of education. Further educational measures should be addressed in a long-term holistic approach against the background of livelihoods, poverty alleviation and the ongoing processes of social transformation and change in the tribal societies.

There are three important components in the educative process i.e. the teacher, the pupil and the subject matter or content of education. The teacher is the main dynamic force in the system of education. He has to plan for teaching, organize it, execute it and evaluate its success. The second important component is the pupil. To educate the pupils is the ultimate objective of the instructional process. In this regard, the child's capabilities, abilities, interests and his psychological aspects and social environment need to be taken into account. The pupils is to be considered as the starting point, the middle and the end. His growth and his development is ideal of education. The third important factor is the subject matter or content of education, otherwise known as curriculum. Curriculum is the path for the realization of the objectives of education. It includes curricular, co-curricular and extra-curricular activities. It is the sum total of all the educational experiences provided to the child by the school through instruction by the teacher either within the four walls or outside. It includes scholastic as well as co-scholastic activities. Today there is a shift from epistemic model of children's learning to that of constructionist movement which provides a greater scope for children's social experience in acquiring knowledge. The National Curriculum Framework 2005, envisages in the Constructivist perspective. Learning is a process of the construction of knowledge. Learners actively construct their own knowledge by connecting new ideas to existing ideas on the basis of materials/activities presented to them. The teachers' role in children's cognition could be enhanced if they assume a more active role in relation to the process of knowledge construction in which children are engaged. The teacher is a facilitator who encourages learners to reflect, analyse and interpret in the process of knowledge construction.

Teacher education is a continuous process. Teacher's performance is the most crucial input in the field of tribal education. The programmes of teacher education emphasizes the updating of skills, knowledge, methodology of teaching, teaching techniques and enhance the competencies of the teachers. With regard to tribal schools, the teacher should get sufficient academic support in this regard. All the Mandal Resource Coordinators (MRCs), Mandal Resource Persons (MRPs), Integrated Tribal Development Agencies (ITDA) school teachers, School Complex Education Resource Persons (SCERPs), Mandal Education Officers (MEOs) should be provided with the latest teaching equipments for effective implementation of educational programmes in tribal schools. Sufficient training, orientation should be provided to the tribal teachers in the use of education technology in their classrooms. The tribal teachers has to be strengthened to integrate indigenous knowledge in the theory and practice of modern educational thoughts, enhance the proper understandings of modern techniques of evaluation and management of tribal schools, ability to use locally available resources, develop competencies for Teaching Learning Material (TLM), provide resource support to the tribal schools in areas like Education Technology, academic support and guidance to the tribal teachers, etc. The ITDAs PMRCs have to play a vital role for the upliftment of Tribal education. The training programmes of tribal teachers should be shaped in such a way that each tribal teacher is able to fulfill the expectations of the balanced education. Lot of attention has to be paid in this regard.

In Andhra Pradesh, there are Grama Vidya Vikas Kendras (GVVKs), ITDA schools, Ashram schools, Educational complexes, and Tribal Welfare Residential Schools, etc. catering to the educational needs of Scheduled Tribe children. The schools are functioning under the control of the Tribal Welfare Department. Some of the important factors affecting the quality of Tribal Education are lack of better teaching-learning facilities, teaching aids, accountability of teachers, supervisions, unattractive school environment, etc. The efforts of the Tribal Welfare Department was confined only to provide schools. It did not focus its serious attention in providing the better infrastructural facilities and inputs for effective Teaching-Learning facilities in tribal schools. The tribal schools are hampered with good teaching aids and other infrastructural facilities. The schools are lacking minimum educational facilities. Although some Ashram schools have teaching aids, audio-video technology, they are hardly used. Majority of the schools have single teachers, inspection and supervision of the primary schools is not regular. Therefore, there is an urgent need to provide in all tribal schools with all infrastructural facilities like good school building, equipment, aids, educational technology facilities etc. There is an urgent need to improve the inputs in the tribal schools and the prompt supply of incentives on time and keeping the external and internal environment more picturesque, decorative and attractive to the tribal children. The tribal schools should be made attractive and interesting by organizing more tribal culture specific curricular and co-curricular aspects of teaching learning environment in tribal schools.

There are 33 tribal groups in Andhra Pradesh comprising 6.3 per cent population of the state. Bagata, Bhils, Goud, Hill Reddy, Kondadora, Mukadora, Poorja, Savara, Gadaba, Gond, Pardhan, Kolam, etc. are some of the tribes residing in hilly areas and forests. Shifting cultivation, Podu cultivation, Agriculture, Agriculture Labour, Collection of non-timber forest produce are some of the major occupations of the tribal groups. Besides these some groups are involved in occupations like hunting, honey collection, cattle rearing, manufacture of agriculture implements, basket making, selling bangles and beads, making garlands, forest labour, etc.

Andhra Pradesh Primary Education Programme (APPEP), which was implemented in the State with the assistance of U.K. Government, has suggested six Pedagogical principals, which are being followed in all the primary schools of the State including tribal areas.

These Principals are providing teacher generated learning activities; promoting learning by doing, discovering and experimenting; developing individual, group and whole class work; providing for individual differences; using the local environment and creating an interesting classroom by displaying children's work and organizing it effectively. Teachers in tribal areas need to keep in view the local cultural aspects to correlate with the teaching items for better learning and sustain interest among the tribal children.

The cultural aspects, which can be used in the classroom by the tribal teachers, can be listed such as: tribal dialect, tribal play activities, calculation of time, identification of seasons, measures used for calculating distance, weight, volume, agriculture crops grown, pesticides used, cattle rearing methods adopted, body cleanliness and health habits, dress and costumes, house keeping, medicines used for ailments, village panchayat/muthadar systems, solving problems, festivals celebrated, seeds procured, marriage systems, custom of receiving guests, honouring guests, tribal dances, worship, grain bank, agriculture implements, transportation system, interdependence/give and take, leisure time activities/recreation, protection of crops, shandies, musical instruments, household implements, property rights, food habits, fuel, riddles, songs/folk songs and stories.

The components of tribal culture need to be adopted in the teaching-learning process in the school to create and sustain interest among the tribal pupils. In this regard, the teacher plays an important role. His commitment, the quality of his empathy, the creativity and ability in correlating his teaching with the cultural components of the community go a long way in creating interest among the tribal children. Whenever and wherever it is possible, culture specific curricular and co-curricular activities need to be organized by the teacher in the school. In teaching language the teacher has to prepare and use bilingual charts and primers. In dealing with mathematics, the teacher must invariably refer to the ways in which the tribal communities record various measures of length, weight, volume, calculation of time, day, month, year, transactions carried on in shandies, identification of various shapes, etc.

So also in dealing with the science subjects, reference should be made to the various cultural components of tribals like health habits, body cleanliness, house keeping, crops grown, pesticides used, soils, flora, fauna, seeds procured medicines used for ailments, dress, agriculture implements, food habits, feathers used, collection of grains, leaves, musical instruments, housing, household implements, forest produce, seasonal produce, climatic conditions, etc.

In dealing with social studies subject, the teacher should refer to the agricultural crops grown, seasons, geographic conditions, cattle rearing methods, panchayat, solving problems, relationships, interdependence, festivals, marriages, custom of receiving guests, grain bank, transport systems, family systems, property rights, food grains, etc. in his teaching. These helps in creating interest among tribal children and help them in effective learning.

In non-academic subjects of health and physical education, the tribal play activities need to be organized in the school. Archery should form a part and parcel of Physical Education activity. In dealing with moral education reference should be made in teaching to the various modes of worship, ceremonies, customary rights of tribal communities.

Under creative activities tribal dances, mono actions, playing music, singing songs, story composition of tribal cultural components should be given importance. Under socially useful productive work programme place should be given to basket making, preparation of various implements, musical instruments, mat weaving, carpet making, wood work, leather work, gum making, fuel collection, honey collection should be given importance. While dealing with all the above aspects/subjects, teachers working in Tribal schools as far as possible should make use of the various facilities/techniques to inculcate interest in the academic disciplines by using audio-video materials in their classrooms teaching if such facilities are available to them. In case of non-availability of such materials/facilities, arrangements has to be made in consultation with the educational authorities in the States.

Educational programmes should create means for income generation. Promotion of small-scale enterprises, processing or manufacturing units in the tribal areas involving the participation of the concerned social groups, especially youth, would be of great use. Women's Self-Help Groups have demonstrated the potential of such an approach. These societies have a long history of manufacturing items based on forest resources, and barter and exchange of these goods with other groups. Some of these items consist of raw materials for housing; agricultural implements; baskets made of bamboo, reeds, cane and wicker work for household storage, and bins for grain storage; fuel woods; mats; broomsticks; barks for dying and tanning; nuts and seeds for oil processing; gums; honey; lacquer; herbal medicinal products. These items (which fall under the category of Non-Timber Forest Produce) are procured and marketed by the Girijan Co-operatives and middlemen. Children along with elders take part in the collection and supply of these items, which is a contract labour.

These societies have traditional knowledge systems of the use of endemic flora including herbal medicines. Educational inputs coupled with financial support to these groups, by making them stakeholders in the cultivation of such plants and procurement of forest-based raw materials, can be a strategy for development of small scale industries and local entrepreneurial skills. The meaningfulness of modern education and literacy would be appreciated when it is linked with opportunities for income earning.

There are two important aspects of our lives i.e., education and communication. By education, we refer to a process which includes both instructional and non-formal ways of communicating knowledge with the explicit intention of both the teacher and students to promote the latter's future development. It is the need of the society to transfer knowledge about the physical and social environment and the practical skills needed to solve human problems from one generation to another. The transfer or transmission of knowledge from one generation to another is done through many channels of communication with the mass media being typically the modern one. Mass media are essentially defined as all forms of communication which are mediated by an impersonal agency, where direct contact between the sender and receiver of the message does not exist. Radio and television are widely used medium of mass communication. These are the new communication technologies having the most visible and apparent impact. It is also the glamorous medium which has captured the attention of the decision maker and the public alike. Television and radio has been shown clearly as a medium which can be used to teach effectively. Particularly in tribal areas the use of television and radio goes a long way to improve the conditions of the tribal people in the agency areas. The use of Communication Technology like Radio and TV in tribal schools will solve many problems associated with tribal education scenario in Andhra Pradesh. The National Curriculum Framework 2005 emphasised that Educational Technology need to be used at all levels of schools – cluster and block resource centers, district, state and national level institutions in order to provide hands on experience in using Education Technology. Such experiences provided to children, teachers and teacher educations could include something as simple as the audio-recording of an interview with a tribal village elder or to make a video film of the socio-cultural aspect such as festival, a dance or a shandy of a major tribal group–provide children more direct access to multimedia equipment and Information and Communication Technology (ICT) and allowing them to mix and make their own productions and to present their own experiences. It provides children and teachers with new opportunities to explore their own creative imagination.

Each tribal groups has its own specific culture and way of life. Each tribal community has got its own traditions, morals, laws and customs. Presently no effort seems to have been made to transmit the socio-cultural heritage of these groups to their respective new generations. Further organization of socio-culture specific activities in the school creates and sustains interest among tribal children towards schooling. Hence there is a need to identify socio-cultural specific activities for organization in the schools not only to preserve and transmit the cultural heritage but also to create and sustain interest towards education in the school among the tribal children. Preparation of audio scripts on the socio-cultural aspects of the 33 tribal groups of Andhra Pradesh for the development of audio CDs is a step towards this direction.

To conclude the teachers working in the tribal areas must make it a point to invariably refer to the local tribal community, their way of life, habits, economic system, social problems, history of the concerned tribe, changes in their life styles, physical features, difference between tribal and non-tribal groups relating to their physical and mental aspects, their life modes, work practices, their relation with the forests and nature etc. in their teaching-learning process, while dealing with different subjects in the curriculum. This creates interest among tribal children towards education and help in better learning.

There are 33 Scheduled Tribe Communities in Andhra Pradesh (Two more communities have been added by the Government of India recently making the list to 35). The tribal population is 50.25 lakhs constituting 6.56 per cent to the total population of Andhra Pradesh during 2001 census.

Out of 33 communities, 30 communities live in Agency Areas and three live mostly in rural areas outside agency. Tribal population in agency areas is 60 per cent of total population. There are basically nine languages spoken by tribes namely Gondi, Kolami, Koya, Khird, Kiri, Yerukula belonging to Dravidian linguistic family, Savara belonging to Munda linguistic family and Lambadi belonging to Indo-Aryan linguistic family.

Tribals pursue a variety of occupations namely gathering and hunting, shifting cultivation, horticulture, trade and settled agriculture. Each of the occupation has an associated social organization for resource management. Knowledge, belief systems are also associated with each of the activity.

Tribal culture is recognized by rich heritage depicted in song, dance, literature, musical instruments, mythology, etc. Due to modernization, the rich aspects of tribal culture are disappearing at faster rate than earlier. Now the advantage in this disadvantageous situation is that, there is large number of educated tribal youth working as Teachers, Forest Guards, Nurses, Anganwadi workers, etc. at village level. These people can be best resource persons to record the various aspects of culture for future.

The cultural identity is a very important component, which will increase self-confidence among the people of that community. The material and non-material aspects of culture provide best answers to the society in its setting.

Culture changes on its own, but also changes due to culture contact. The contact agents are non-tribals, which include government (directed change). Education, Newspapers, TV, Radio, Leaders, NGOs, etc. provide information to the society. Market provides the goods from outside. Thus changes occur in material and non-material aspects of culture. The culture contact is advantageous and disadvantageous.

Talking of preserving once own culture is not to be taken as a retrograde step. On the other hand, one should take pride in preserving own culture and telling others about it, as it consists of many great aspects.

Knowledge, beliefs, religious ceremonies, dress, decoration, musical instruments, festivals, art, dance, etc. are some of the aspects to be recorded – audio and video. Traditional knowledge of medicinal plants available in the area and their uses is another important aspect of culture to be preserved. These components of tribal life are required to be fully exploited to improve the educational experiences of the tribal children. In order to achieve all the above goals mentioned earlier the tribal schools have to be strengthened. The audio scripts developed in the programme can be of great help to the State Departments which in turn to be distributed for the teachers for the classroom practices in the tribal schools of Andhra Pradesh. The teachers working in the tribal schools should come forward to protect, preserve and use the tribal culture elements in the schools by using the audio-video technology in the tribal schools.

Research Findings

The following are the component wise research findings relating to the problems of tribal education in Andhra Pradesh.

(i) Teachers

1. 62 per cent non-residence in school village, 2. Teacher of one community is working in a tribal habitation of different community, 3. Causes for non-residence of teachers are: *(a)* No house to reside, *(b)* No medical facility, *(c)* Spouse working elsewhere and *(d)* Village inhabited by other community, 4. Unwillingness to work in tribal habitation, 5. Lack of basic facilities, 6. Naxalite problem, 7. Youth are more willing to work than old aged teachers, 8. Lack of suitable policy to select teachers, 9. Teacher absenteeism, 10. Additional responsibilities, 11. Low professional qualification, 12. Vacant posts, 13. No academic guidance, 14. Limited contact with community, 15. Authoritarian behaviour of teacher, 16. Disinterestedness among teachers towards tribal children, 17. Poor teaching, 18. Less qualified teachers, 19. Lack of training in child centred activity oriented, competency

based teaching, 20. Female teachers are much less in number, 21. Problem in encashing salary of DDs, 22. Non-tribal teachers facing the problem of teaching and 23. Tribal teachers are not conversant with Telugu language.

(ii) Quality

1. No emphasis on providing inputs, 2. No teaching aids/blackboards/equipment, 3. Textbooks/writing materials not supplied in time, 4. Frequent transfers, 5. Lack of accountability/mobility, 6. Low number of women teachers, 7. Lack of trained teachers, 8. Home environment not conducive for learning, 9. Non-coverage of syllabus, 10. Neglect of non-detention classes, 11. Late commencement of special coaching, 12. Less qualified teachers, 13. High repetition, 14. Incomplete schools, 15. Gap in education in summer and other seasonal holidays, 16. Migration, 17. Lack of supervision, 18. Lack of regular inspections, 19. Unattractive school environment, 20. Non-revising of previous lesson before introducing new lesson, 21. No homework, 22. Lack of adoption of pupils by teachers, 23. Non-working of exercises given at the end of the lesson, 24. No writing exercises like composition writing, maps drawing, map pointing, drawing diagrams, etc., 25. Seasonal work participation, 26. More interest in co-curricular activities, 27. Irregularity on the part of pupils, 28. Lack of interesting teaching, 29. Language problem, 30. No aids are prepared and used, 31. No on the job support to teachers, 32. No joyful learning, 33. Under aged and over aged children are admitted and 34. Non supply of incentives in time.

(iii) Parental Attitude

1. Lack of awareness of the importance of education, 2. Low level of aspiration, 3. Lack of motivation, 4. Education only to get incentives, 5. Lack of parent, teacher contact, 6. Non-tradition of sending child to school and 7. SECs are not active.

(iv) Curriculum and Textbooks

1. Content of textbooks did not reflect trial culture, 2. Lack of culture specific co-curricular activities, 3. More festivals, 4. No place for tribal folk songs, 5. No activities for preservation of tribal culture, 6. Culture contamination and 7. Interference with tribal traditions.

(v) Access and Participation

1. Small and scattered habitations, 2. Universal access could not be provided in tribal habitations with less than 100 population, 3. Boys enrolment 70 per cent only, 4. Literacy has positive effect on enrolment, 5. Low and high income households better participation, 6. Among the total enrolment 60 per cent were in Classes I and II, 7. Fear of school, 8. Lack of interest in education among children, 9. Regularity is poor among children, 10. Dropout varies in different schools, 11. Retention is high in local body schools, 12. Low interaction of parents with the officials of education department, 13. Teaching and teacher not attractive, 14. Authorisation attitude of teachers, 15. Rigid and fixed rules discourage children, 16. Economic development schemes hamper the education of the children, 17. Lack of teaching aids, 18. Lack of games and sports, etc., 19. Education is not job oriented, 20. Child is an economic asset, 21. Sex discrimination–girl child, 22. High participation at primary school level and low at UPS and HS level leaving dropout between, 23. Over-aged admission, 24. Under-aged admission, 25. Early

marriages, 26. Children not habituated to education, 27. Ill health, 28. School not attractive, 29. Single son, 30. Parents who found their children not learning any thing in school start withdrawing them and 31. Under aged admitted for maintaining TP ratio or for mid-day programme are detained till they attain the prescribed age.

(vi) Administration

1. Lack of academic guidance, 2. Lack of supervision, 3. No aids are prepared and used, 4. School timings do not match the needs, 5. Non-supply for incentives on time, 6. Non-importance to education officers working in agency areas, 7. Multiplicity of managements, 8. Poor reporting system, 9. Weak school complex/MRP system and 10. Lack of interdependence.

(vii) High Dropout and Low Enrolment in Ashram schools

1. Children not habituated to education, 2. Ill health, 3. Lack of interest of children on education, 4. Financial backwardness of parents, 5. Taking away the children by parents always, 6. Children not interested to leave their homes, 7. Lack of interest on the part of the teachers towards the education of tribal children, 8. Language problem, 9. More number of festivals, 10. Lack of school programmes to arouse interest towards education, 11. Sibling care at house, 12. Lack of parent, teacher contact, 13. Day prison school system and 14. Uninteresting curriculum.

(viii) Low Percentage of Results in SSC

1. Non-coverage of syllabus on time and failure to revise the syllabus, 2. Neglect of IX class, 3. Late commencement of special coaching, 4. Non-conduct of pre-final examination, 5. Non-correcting of pre-final examination answer scripts and not informing the students of their difficulties, 6. Dependence of students on copying and prevention of copying in the public examination, 7. Neglect of the programmes which help in the better preparation of students for the public examinations: *(a)* Working out of question banks, *(b)* Working out of the last three year public examination question papers, *(c)* Adoption of students by teachers, *(d)* Working out the exercises given at the end of the lessons in the textbooks, *(e)* By hearting the materials given in the boxes in the textbook, *(f)* Training in map pointing, *(g)* Training in letter writing, *(h)* Doing book works and *(i)* Drawing science diagrams, 8. Absenting from school without informing the concerned teachers, 9. Not attending the school on time after availing leave for celebrating festivals at home and vacation, 10. Showing greater interest in co-scholastic activities as against scholastic activities and 11. Non-interest of the teachers of English, Mathematics and Science subjects in preparing the students to the public examination through special coaching.

Programmes Needed for Improvement of Tribal Education

(i) Policy

1. Shift from providing equal opportunities and incentives to that of ensuring effective participation and quality improvement, 2. Change of the role of Tribal Welfare Department from "Supplementary" to "Pivotal," 3. Encouragement to gifted children, 4. Adopt area specific and group specific programmes, 5. Improve the system of "Student Services", 6. Make education job oriented and income generating, 7. Bring all schools in the tribal area under one single control and administration, 8. Limiting ashram schools to Mandal

headquarters/road junctions considering various ecological barriers and 9. Shift from policy of exclusiveness to that of diversification in admissions.

(ii) Access, Enrolment and Retention

1. Start pre-school education programme, 2. Introduce mid-day meal programme, 3. School to be a place of activities with songs, games and good teaching environment, 4. Teachers to avoid punishments and to provide attractive atmosphere in the school, 5. Strengthen schools, GVVKs, EGS centres, alternative schools based on school mapping, 6. Provide additional incentives in the form of rice to the students belonging to PTGs, 7. Utilise the service of surplus teachers for providing access through rationalization, 8. Organise door-to-door surveys for enrolment, 9. Incentives to SECs which achieve cent per cent enrolment and cent per cent retention, 10. Constitute mothers committees and take their help, 11. Supply of minimum educational material as a package of incentive, 12. Effective monitoring by SECs, 13. Effective monitoring by SCRP and MRPs and 14. Attractive schools.

(iii) Quality

1. Provide in-service training to teachers of tribal areas to make good their academic deficiencies in those subjects as Mathematics, Science and English, 2. Provide constant academic guidance and support to tribal teachers through SCRPs/MRPs/MEO, etc., 3. Provide training in the adoption of activity methods, joyful learning, school readiness programme, etc., 4. Provide non-tribal teachers working in tribal areas with bilingual material to overcome the problem of language, 5. Provide regular inspection and supervision of schools, 6. The policy of appointing tribal youth as teachers needs to be continued, 7. Change in "Day Prison" model of school, 8. Starting special coaching classes well in advance, 9. Strengthen Ashram school complex to provide better supervision, 10. Increasing inspection visits by higher officials for better monitoring and supervision, 11. Vacations should be based on local needs and seasonal variations like festivals, collection of NTFP and other economic activities where tribal children participate, 12. Authorising and prescribing periodical visits to schools and hostels compulsory by different sectoral officers at district and ITDA level as the common goal of all is tribal development, 13. Academic monitoring of schools and students, 14. Use of play methods, giving illustrations, observing students while teaching and ensuring their participation, revising the previous lessons, giving assignment in the classroom and home work, etc., 15. Adoption of the six APPEP pedagogical principles in the teaching-learning process, 16. Adopt NLE approach to draw out the innate abilities of pupils, 17. Organise monthly review meeting on academic work, 18. Training in MLLs and 19. Teaching through bilingual charts and primers.

(iv) Teachers

1. Ensure residence in the school village, 2. Place tribal teachers of a particular community in the tribal schools of that particular community, 3. Adopt joyful learning programmes to remove fear complex among pupils, 4. Provide basic facilities for teachers like quarter, education facilities for their children, etc., 5. Suitable policy of selecting teachers is needed for tribal areas, 6. The performance of the teacher is to be evaluated in terms of *(a)* Residence in the school village where he/she is working, *(b)* Increasing enrolment,

regular attendance and promoting/admitting number of children in Ashram Schools/ Residence schools, *(c)* Performance appraisal by SEC and a committee of parents selected at random, 7. Rationalisation of teachers posts and 8. Commitment and motivation.

(v) Infrastructural Facilities

1. Provide all schools with all infrastructural facilities like building, equipment, aids, etc., 2. Improvement of inputs, 3. Supply of incentives on time and 4. Keeping the external and internal environment more picturesque, decorative and attractive to the tribal children.

(vi) Curriculum and Textbooks

1. Make the school attractive and interesting by organising culture specific co-curricular activities, 2. Textbooks to reflect tribal culture by including lessons, poems, pictures from tribal areas and culture, 3. The course content should consist of more of songs, plays, various games, music, dance and drama, etc., tribal culture based on local tribal dialect and 4. The curriculum should include training in income generating activities to make it useful to the learners with stress on SUPW.

(vii) Community

1. Conduct awareness programmes on the importance of education, 2. Develop awareness on the various schemes of the Government both general as well as educational for tribal development, 3. Change the school timings and vacation period if needed in consultation with tribal parents, 4. Actively motivating and involving tribal community in educational programme right from the selection of site for school building and its construction through their contribution in the shape of material, labour, etc., 5. Bringing awareness about the incentives through pamphlets and folk media, 6. Utilising shan dies/places of community festivals and other large gatherings for the propagation of education through different folk media and posters and 7. Ensure regular functioning of the school and progress of the child by SEC.

Conclusion

How to create and sustain interest among tribal children towards schooling?

Each tribal group has its own specific culture and way of life. Each tribal community has got its own traditions, morals, laws and customs. Presently no effort seems to have been made to transmit the cultural heritage of these groups to their respective new generations. Further organization of culture specific activities in the school creates and sustains interest among tribal children towards schooling. Hence there is need to identify culture specific activities for organization in the schools not only to preserve and transmit the cultural heritage but also to create and sustain interest towards education in the school among the tribal children. Some of the areas relating to tribal culture can be stated as follows.

1. Tribal play activities, 2. Calculation of time, 3. Identification of seasons, 4. Measures used distance, weight and liquid, 5. Agriculture–crops grown, 6. Pesticides used, 7. Cattle rearing methods, 8. Body cleanliness/health habits, 9. Dress, 10. House keeping, 11. Dialect/Language, 12. Medicines used for ailments, 13. Village Panchayat/ Muthadar, 14. Solving problems/quarrels, 15. Festivals celebrated, 16. Seeds procured, 17. Celebration of marriages, 18. Marriage system, 19. Custom of receiving guests,

20. Honouraring guests, 21. Tribal dances, 22. Worship, 23. Riddles, 24. Grain bank, 25. Agriculture implements, 26. Transportation system, 27. Means of communication, 28. Methods followed to arrest epidemics, 29. Interdependence/Give and Take, 30. Participation in politics, 31. Leisure time activities/recreation, 32. Animal sacrifice, 33. Hunting, 34. Protection of crops, 35. Relationships, 36. Shandies, 37. N.T.F.P., 38. Musical instruments, 39. Music, 40. Household implements, 41. Cooking implements, 42. Family system, 43. Reckoning age, 44. Property rights, 45. Food habits, 46. Fuel collection/charcoal, 47. Songs and 48. Stories. These components of culture of the tribal communities need to be organized in the school to create and sustain interest among the tribal pupils towards the educational programmes carried in the school.

Language: 1. Use of bilingual charts and primers, 2. Biographies of tribal leaders, 3. Stories, 4. Riddles, 5. Discussions, 6. Debates, 7. Composing poetry and 8. Writing essays

Mathematics: 1. Measures used length, weight and liquid, 2. Calculation of time, 3. Reckoning age, 4. Day/Month/Year, 5. Transaction in shandies, 6. Barter method/ exchange and 7. Shapes.

Science: 1. Health habits/body cleanliness, 2. House keeping, 3. Crops grown, 4. Animals/birds, etc., 5. Pesticides used, 6. Soils, 7. Flora, fauna, 8. Seeds procured, 9. Medicines used for ailments, 10. Dress, 11. Agricultural implements, 12. Methods used for arresting epidemics, 13. Leisure time activities, 14. Food habits, 15. Collection of leaves, grains, etc., 16. Feathers used, 17. Protection of crops, 18. Musical instruments, 19. Housing, 20 Household implements, 21. Cooking implements, 22. Forest produce, 23. Seasonal produce and 24. Climatic conditions.

Social Studies/Science: 1. Agricultural crops grown, 2. Seasons, 3. Geographic conditions, 4. Cattle rearing methods, 5. Panchayat, 6. Solving problems, 7. Relationships, 8. Interdependence, 9. Festivals, 10. Marriages, 11. Family system, 12. Custom of receiving guests, 13. Honouring guests, 14. Worship, 15. Grain bank, 16. Transport system, 17. Participation in politics, 18. Shandies, 19. NTFP, 20. Family system, 21. Property rights, 22. Fuel collection, 23. Hunting, 24. Livelihood, 25. Food grains, 26. Health and Physical Education, 27. Tribal play activities and 28. Archery.

SUPW: Basket making, preparation of implements, musical instruments, mat weaving, carpet making, wood work, leather work, gum making, fuel collection, honey collection.

Moral Education: 1. Worship, 2. Ceremonies, 3. Customary rights, 4. Creative Activities, 5. Dancing, 6. Painting, 7. Drawing, 8. Mono action, 9. Playing music, 10. Singing songs and 11. Story compositions. Teacher is the main dynamic force in the system of education. The success of tribal education to a large extent depends on him. His commitment, the quality of his empathy, his residence in the habitation go a long way in tribal education development.

Tribal child is a free bird by nature. He enjoys complete freedom unrestricted by his parents or other family members. The present school system is viewed by him as a prison imposing all types of restrictions right from 09.00 A.M till 03.30 P.M. Education should be a pleasurable activity for him. It should not be a slaughterhouse of minds. Specially at lower classes bilingual charts and primers are to be used to attract the children to school and sustain interest in them. Teaching should be based on play methods, and activity oriented using the six APPEP Pedagogical principles.

The school should be a centre for the reflection and protection of the culture of the tribal communities concerned, comprising their traditions, morals, laws, customs, practices etc. Whenever and wherever it is possible, culture specific co-curricular activities need to be organised in the school. Debates, discussions, practices etc., are to be held in the school. Fancy dress, tribal songs, Mono actions, Role-plays, Festivals, Ceremonies etc., need to be held in the school. Under physical education activities tribal games and play activities can be, organised in the school to impress them that school is a part and parcel of their culture.

In order to provide access to the tribal children, presently 'Maabadi', community schools, GVVKs, Alternative schools, Bridge courses on residential and non-residential basis are organised. If there is need, besides the present scheme of small schools and mini schools, flexi schools may also be organised. In places where it is not viable to provide schools, children of these habitations may be given admission in Residential Schools or Ashram Schools directly.

Shandies and other ceremonial functional days and places of community festivals may be utilised to make the tribal communities aware of the importance of education and the facilities provided by the Government for the improvement of education of the tribal children. The developmental schemes initiated by the Government should be made known to them. The curriculum component of the school should include training in income generation activities, which help in developing positive attitude towards the school system. In this connection it is necessary to strengthen the SUPW activities. The recent massive study conducted on the factors influencing parents and children in achieving UEE in AP revealed the fact, that economic causes are not the real barriers for enrolment and retention. Tribal parents are also sending their children to school for education to have better future. Tribal parents expressed, for improvement in physical facilities and good teaching. Tribal parents are also not happy to send their children to work. 11 per cent of the parents of sampled villages expressed that the school is not good. Nearly 40 per cent of the poor illiterate tribal parents are sending their children to school. School dropouts in tribal areas are more at Class II in GVVK or community school or Maabadi. Language barriers, untrained teachers, less qualified teachers, teacher absenteeism had contributed to poor performance of students. Further regular supervision and guidance have become a rare phenomenon for tribal schools. Effective SCRP system and panel inspection system at secondary level needs to be implemented.

One of the research studies reported that parents like to send their children if the schools function regularly and children show academic progress. This is a very pertinent finding. One suggestion is limiting Ashram Schools to the Mandal Head quarters and road functions considering various ecological barriers, which needs **attention** of the Government. Another suggestion is instead of running the Ashram Schools to one particular tribal community, it is suggested to open the schools for admission to other communities also which facilitate interaction with the children of other communities in the society resulting in better education. Timely supply of the incentives, and student welfare services which also help in the educational development of the tribal children.

SECs which are the important management structures at the school level need to be pressed into service to realise the desired results in tribal areas. There is need to continue the existing incentive schemes for some more time. The infrastructural facilities in terms of construction of buildings, supply of equipment, teaching aids needs to be continued. The academic support schemes of school grant, teacher grant, teacher centre grant, is also to be continued.

REFERENCES

1. Abraham, L., 2004, 'Building Cultural Capital to Combat Poverty: Globalisation, Education and the Urban Poor', See, R. Ruzicka, J.H. Ballantine, Roman Jose (Ed.), Education Participation Globalisation, Conference Proceedings, Prague, 2004 Conference.
2. Achar, Draft Report on Tribal Development through Education in Karnataka, 2002, Mysore, Central Institute of Indian Languages (CIIL).
3. Acharya, P., 1981, 'Politics of Primary Education in West Bengal: The Case of Sahaj Path', Economic and Political Weekly, Vol. 16, No. 24.
4. Acharya, P., 1987, 'Education: Politics and Social Structures', In: R. Ghosh and M. Zachariach (Eds.), Education and the Process of Change, New Delhi, Sage Publishers.
5. Acharya, P., 1988, 'Bengali, Bhadralok and Educational Development in Nineteenth Century Bengal', in S. Shukla and R. Kaul (Eds.), Education Development and Underdevelopment, New Delhi: Sage Publishers.
6. Acharya, P., 1988, 'Is Macaulay Still Our Guru ?' Economic and Political Weekly, Vol. 23, Issue 22, May 1988.
7. Acharya, S., 2001, 'Access to Primary Educadtion: Rural Maharashtra and Madhya Pradesh', In A. Vaidyanathan and P.R. Gopinathan Nair (Eds.), Elementary Education in Rural India: A Grassroots View, New Delhi: Sage Publishers.
8. Action Plan for the Education of Tribal Children of Karnataka 1996-2001, Mysore, CIIL.
9. Agarwal, S., 2003, 'CINI ASHA: Building Bridges for Urban Children', in V. Ramachandran (Ed.), Getting Children Back to School: Case Studies in Primary Education, New Delhi, Sage Publication.
10. Aggarwal, J.C. and Aggarwal, S.P., 1982, Role of UNESCO in Education, New Delhi, Vikas Publishing House Pvt. Ltd.
11. Aggarwal, Y., and Sibou, S., 1994, Educating Scheduled Castes: A Study of Inter District and Intracast Differentials. New Delhi: NIEPA.
12. Ahmad, I., 2003, Educational Development of Minorities in India, In J.B.G. Tilak (Ed.), Education, Society and Development: National and International Perspective, New Delhi, NUEPA.
13. Aikara, J., 1997, Learner Achievement in Primary School, Mumbai: Tata Institute of Social Sciences (TISS), Memeograph.
14. Aiyappan, A., Report on the Socio-Economic Conditions of the Aboriginal Tribes of the Province of Madras, New Delhi, Government of India, Management of Publication, 1948.
15. Aiyappan, A., Report on the Socio-Economic Conditions of the Aboriginal Tribes of the Province of Madras, 1948, New Delhi, Government of India.

2

Curriculum Needs of Tribal Children

Introduction

The Education Commission 1964-66 has observed "one of the important social objectives of education is to equalise opportunity, enabling the backward or underprivileged classes and individuals to use education as a lever for the improvement of their condition. Every society that values social justice and is anxious to improve the life of the common man and cultivate all available talent must ensure progressive equality of opportunity to all sections of the population. This is the only guarantee for the building up of an egalitarian and human society by which the exploitation of the weak will be minimised. Tribal communities, which are mostly inhabited in places away from the civilised population, should be provided all possible facilities for education as they form a part and parcel of the society. Even though much effort have been made by the Government at all levels achieving Universal Elementary Education is still a problem specially with the tribal communities. The tribal education is faced with four-fold problem of providing for access, enrolment and retention and providing good quality education. This situation demands the need for developing different types of strategies, innovative practices and measures to achieve UEE among tribal communities. Here Research has to play its role in providing solutions to the problems faced in the field of Tribal Education. The same strategy cannot be adopted in case of all tribal communities because of their cultural diversities and different ways of life. Different types of practices need to be adopted in different tribal communities as suggested by different researchers.

In the field of research there is a shift from positivist scientific approach to that of interpretative ethnographic approach. There is a shift from quantitative methods to that qualitative methods. In order to find solutions to the problems of tribal education the present trend is on the adoption, qualitative models. Presently the project has access to some research findings in the field of tribal education. To quote some of them are to researches done by the TCR & TI, AP, Hyderabad, State Universities, APPEP, DPEP, SCERT etc.

In the present system of education there is a shift from epistemic modal of children's learning to that of constructivist model. That means there is a shift of emphasis from information based and teacher centred education to process centred and learner friendly education. Specially in case of tribal child the system should be learner friendly and tribal culture friendly.

Components in Education Process

There are three important components in the educative process of the tribal children. They are the teachers working in tribal areas, the pupil and the subject matter or content of education. Teacher is the main dynamic force in the system of education. It is he who can put the entire educative process into motion. He is the key man on whom depends the future of the child and mankind. He is the fourth pillar in the tribal habitation, the first being the village ward man, the second the village priest, the third village medicine man and the fourth is the teacher. His/Her is not simply confined to teaching alone. He/She is expected to participate in all the developmental activities of the local tribal community. He/She is the only educated person who has to guide and provide all necessary help to the local tribal community. Generally in tribal areas not only teachers belonging to that community but also non-tribal teachers will be working. The problem with the non-tribal teachers is that they are alien to the local tribal community in which they are posted. They complain of number of problems. With regard to tribal teachers most of them posted do not reside in place of their posting but shift their families to main areas and commute from that place. There by the important problem is non-residence of teachers in the tribal village and teacher absenteeism. Teacher absenteeism is ultimately leading to non-functioning of the school and student dropout and low standards of education. Some other problems include low standards of teachers, lack of physical facilities in schools etc. So teacher component is an improvement area in which there is need for research, as to how to make the teacher work in the tribal school and discharge his role effectively as per his job chart and also provide extension service to the local community.

The second important component of the educative process is the pupils, i.e., the tribal child. He is a free bird in the family. He enjoys complete freedom in this family. He is born intelligent as in the case of other children but he is disadvantaged due to lack of opportunities. "Child is the starting point, he is the centre and the end." His growth and his development is the ideal of education 'felt John Dewey.' In case of tribal child the socialisation process adopted at school. Almost all the philosophers and educationists advocate that the school should reflect the house atmosphere. But for a tribal child the school is entirely a new environment, alien to him, which makes him perplexed. The language in which he is developed as entirely different in school. The freedom enjoyed in the family is restricted in the school. This is a big problem faced by a tribal child. How to overcome this? How to create interest in education among the tribal children? How to retain them in the school? How to make the school attractive to the tribal child? What should be the medium of instruction? All these questions are to be answered. Research should provide answers to these questions. The strategies to be adopted to enroll and retain the tribal children are to be developed. How to make the school tribal child friendly? is to be answered by research.

The third important component of the educative process is the curriculum in tribal schools. Presently at the primary stage children are exposed to three academic subjects (Telugu Language, Mathematics and Environmental Studies) and five activity subjects (Health education, Physical education, Socially useful productive work, Moral education and creative activities). A tribal child who is 5+ is exposed to all these subjects in the school in Class I itself. Are these subjects attracting the child? The curriculum includes both the classroom activities and extra classroom activities. What type of extra classroom activities are to be organised? These questions need answers through Research. Curriculum is handed over to the child by means of method. Method is a bridge between the curriculum and the child. What types of methods are being adopted in the Teaching Learning process also needs a study. Textbook development is another area of research concern. Presently there is a criticism that the textbooks are not child friendly and, culture friendly. How to make them tribal child friendly and tribal culture reflective? How to achieve this is a problem for study. Almost all the South Asian Countries realised the importance of ensuring basic education for XII and the development of vocational and technical skills among children on the present times. Further there is a demand to revamp education according to the developmental needs of tribals. This raises the question that, should the system vocationalised to make more relevant to the tribal children duly including their vocations? This also needs research base.

The other important factor, which influences tribal education, is the parental co-operation. Most of the tribal parents are not aware of the importance of education and the benefits they got out of it. How to make them aware and how to motivate them to send their children to school and retain them till the completion of full school course are the problems to be tackled by research. School Education Committees are formed for each school. How are they functioning? What is their contribution to the educational development of their children also needs to be studied.

Foremost important factor which influence the Tribal Child Education is the Tribal Developmental Programmes. The Government has been implementing many schemes for the welfare of the tribes. The constitutional safeguards, establishment of ITDAs, MADAS, TRICOR etc., and other schemes look into the health, education, economic, social and cultural aspects of the tribal population. How these initiations influence the Tribal community and guide them towards education of their child is the burning problem. Here studies on these issues has to be undertaken and strategies to be developed.

The other intervention is the Non-Governmental Organisations. Education specially the quality education cannot be universalised only through governmental programmes/ schemes. The convergence of the community and other non-governmental organisations is to be ensured. The NGOs are doing much work in the area of education. They are playing a greater role in the tribal area for the social upliftment and cultural preservation and education. This poses a question: "how far these activities contribute towards the education of the tribal community" and "what strategies make the development of the tribal child more effective?"

Another most important area, which needs the concern of all, is the area of quality education. Quality as a matter of fact depends on many factors. Right from the teacher his professional efficiency, his ability to transact with the curriculum using the teaching learning materials, the availability of the TLM, the interests, capacities, capabilities and abilities of the pupil, the school environment, the textbook materials, to the infrastructural facilities exercise a marked influence on the Quality of Education. Education should be a pleasurable activity for the child—specially in tribal areas. Adoption of activity method, Aata-Pata-Mata (games-songs-words) programme, school readiness programme adoption of play-way techniques are some of the programmes adopted to make education interesting to the child. Even the Government of Andhra Pradesh had gone further in publishing textbooks in tribal dialects and adopting the concerned tribal dialect as the medium of instruction to create interest among the tribal children and to stick them to school. Positive results are observed on this innovative practice. Providing effective guidance through School Complex centres is another practice adopted in tribal areas of Andhra Pradesh. Education Guarantee Scheme, publication of Glossaries in various tribal dialects is another programme completed by AP DPEP/SSA. However, what type of measures and strategies are to be adopted to provide quality education to Tribal Students yet needs to be studied. Supervised study, extra drill cooperative methods of teaching are some of the measures to improve quality among children. What other practices are to be adopted to improve quality among the tribal children is an importance area in which some type of research needs to be done.

Curriculum Needs of Tribal Children

Article 46 of the Constitution of India lays down that "The State shall promote with special care the educational and economic interests of the weaker sections of the people, and in particular of the Scheduled Castes and Scheduled Tribes and shall protect them from social injustice and all forms of exploitations." To fulfill this, directive efforts have been and are being made by the Central and State Governments. A large amount of money, resources and time have been spent to achieve this objective, but the results are not up to the expectations. Till recently, this vital problem of the educational development of the tribal people did not attract the attention of the administrators and educationists, but gradually this issue came to lime light and the Government is showing its concern for the educational development of the tribal people.

The educationists believe that every individual is endowed with certain innate potentialities; drawing and achieving a harmonious development is the ultimate objective of education. By education, "I mean all round drawing out of the best in child and man—body, mind and spirit" felt Mahatma Gandhi.

Tribal community leads a simple life, subject to customary laws. They have limited exposure to outside world. They give more importance to immediate gains. They talk different dialects based on their own traditions and customs. They give importance to the celebration of festivals, which generally fall throughout the year. Whenever there is a festive occasion in the village, all of the villagers, both elders and children, participate in it, which may disrupt the academic school schedule of the children.

Some of the main reasons why the educational standard of the tribal students is very low as compared to that of the non-tribal students are the unsuitable textbooks and an unknown medium of instruction.

One of the important causes of educational backwardness of the tribe and their comparatively inferior educational performance has been because they are taught through regional language and not through their mother tongue. If the medium of instruction in the primary schools was the mother tongue of the people, the children could have picked up their lessons easily and produced satisfactory results. The characteristics of a tribal child are: the tribal child is very bold, friendly in nature and obedient, possesses skills and concentration, likes co-curricular activities, respects the elders, reliable, shows Interest towards functions/festivals, belief superstitions, likes simplicity, treat nature with respect, believe truthfulness and honesty, limited needs, low aspirations, lack of abstract thinking, feel shy with the strangers but free with the known people, like to learn through imitation rather than instruction and also tribal children do not like to remain confined to four walls of the school; prefer to roam about and play in the open.

Tribal child is a free bird by nature. He enjoys complete freedom unrestricted by his parents or other family members. Tribal children prefer to spend their time moving freely around, swimming in ponds and streams, catching fish, climbing trees, hunting birds, collecting berries, riding on buffaloes, etc. In tribal communities, very rarely the children are punished. The conflict between the norms of school and socialisation at home results in resistance and unwillingness among children to attend the school.

At the primary stage of education, the curriculum consists of two components i.e., scholastic and non-scholastic. The scholastic comprises languages and non-languages, are examination subjects whereas the non-scholastic comprises SUPW, Health and Physical Education, Creative Activities and Moral Education, which are non-examination subjects. The 30 per cent of the instructional time is allocated for these non-examination subjects.

The textbooks depict mostly the urban and non-tribal culture and ethos while they have no relevance to tribal cultural context. The internal teaching methods adopted in the classroom are strange to the tribal child who has different socialisation pattern in its community where group-learning is prominent, pace of learning is independent. Being most of the first generation learners feel conflict with the rigid and structured school system while their cultural norms are flexible and suitable. This leads to conflict among students resulting with developing culture of silence in learning process.

While adopting the teaching learning process, the teachers in tribal areas need to keep in view the local cultural aspects, to correlate with the teaching items for better learning and sustained interest among the tribal children. Some of the local cultural aspects such as tribal dialects, tribal play-way activities, tribal dances, leisure time activities/ recreational activities, riddles, songs/folk songs, stories, puppetry and field trip activities may be taken up while teaching learning is taking place in tribal school.

The components of tribal culture need to be adopted in the teaching learning process in the school to create and sustain interest among the tribal peoples. The commitment of the teacher, the quality of his empathy, the creativity and the ability in correlating his teaching with the cultural components of the community go a long way in creating interest among the children. Wherever and whenever it is possible, culture-specific curricular and co-curricular activities need to be organised by the teacher in the school. The curriculum have to be organised based on the maxims of teaching, i.e., known to unknown, simple to complex and concrete to abstract, etc. But the curriculum under implementation in tribal areas is same as other areas in the State, which is contradictory to the maxims of teaching. The existing curriculum can be transformed/translated into tribal-specific curriculum with the existing curriculum, the tribal-oriented textbooks need to be developed. As already specified, the curriculum is mainly categorised into three components i.e., languages, non-languages and activity subjects.

Languages

The Language curriculum specifies the mastery in the language competencies through listening, speaking, reading and writing. This can be achieved by providing familiar situations in the early stages of education and gradually introducing unfamiliar situations. The folk songs, the stories, the riddles, the festivals about the local heroes, the language games of their native which are familiar to them certainly creates interest among the tribal child. If all these information is brought from the Tribal Culture and includes the total teaching learning process have to be built on the tribal cultural aspects.

Environmental Studies

The environmental sciences I for Classes I and II curriculum stresses on the following: our body, our family, our home, our school, our neighbours, our earth, sky, etc. can be taught. In the syllabus, the "Our" itself emphasises the inclusion of local specific content but unfortunately, the books are not taken into account the tribal-specificities in the content. Similarly, Environmental Science - II includes, the human body, health and hygiene, the air we breathe, water we drink, food we eat, clothes we wear, shelter we live in, plants and animals around us, agriculture and animal husbandry, etc. can be taught effectively to the tribal children.

To deal with these topics, the resources are plenty in tribal areas. The textbooks deal with the food habits, the clothes, the houses, the animals, and the agriculture alliance to of the tribes in the early stages of education, why should they leave the school? But the existing content is totally unknown to the child. It is quite, but natural, to develop negative attitude towards schooling. There is sufficient provision for non-examination subjects. This is the area where the students can attract towards the school. The good habits, moral values, cultural assimilation, socialisation, development of creativity, physical health, language skills, for that matter, the integrated development of the child can be achieved through these subjects only. The characteristic of a Tribal child also suits to tele activities and the children love the school with all such activities. Nothing will be specified but the creativity of the teacher makes all these activities implementable in the schools. He can initially start the activities from the tribal origin and take them to modernisation.

Tribal Education in Relation to Developmental Needs

Members of Scheduled Tribes who are socially, economically, and educationally disadvantaged have been targeted under post independence legislation to criminate discrimination. According to 1991 Census there are 573 scheduled tribes in India, constituting 8 per cent of population. Among the status Orissa has the largest number of scheduled tribes (62). The following table provides the information relating to the number of scheduled tribe communities in each state in India along with the percentage of population as per 1991 Census.

Often both physically and socially isolated from majority communities scheduled tribes have lower enrolment and achievement rates and higher dropout rates, than the general population. A recent study of 60 schools in two tribal districts in Andhra Pradesh found high absenteeism among tribal children who were enrolled (Sujatha 1995). Absenteeism is higher in Grades II and III. Sujatha points that very young children and those old enough to help with household work are less likely to attend school regularly.

Table–1
Scheduled Tribes in India

State	*Number of Scheduled Tribes*	*Percentage of Population as Per 1991 Census*
Andhra Pradesh	33	6
Assam	14	13
Bihar	30	8
Gujarat	29	15
Haryana	—	0
Karnataka	49	4
Kerala	35	1
Madhya Pradesh	47	9
Orissa	62	22
Punjab	—	0
Rajasthan	12	12
Tamil Nadu	36	1
Uttar Pradesh	5	0
West Bengal	38	6
All India	573	8

— Not available.

Source: Nanda, 1992.

In a massive exercise undertaken as a part of the training programme for teachers conducted in May 2002 under the auspices of Teachers Research Forum DPEP, A.P., Hyderabad, it is reported that Economic causes are not the real barriers for enrolment and retention, poverty is not the real hurdle to education. Parents illiteracy, peer group effect and unattractive schools are the other causes for dropouts. Children opined that school should be a place of activities with songs, games and good teaching environment. Teachers should avoid punishments and they have to provide attractive atmosphere in the school. Tribal parents expressed for improvement in physical facilities and good teaching. In one study it is reported that of the school functions regularly and the teacher attends the school regularly the tribal parents do not have any objectives to send their children to school.

Cultural discontinuity between family and school language of instruction of tribal gap in education Family, community and school factors, all play a part in limiting enrolment, retention and achievement among tribal children. Some tribes still observe traditional "pollution" laws that restrict their interaction with other communities, limiting the acceptability of region schools that would service more than one community. Children from tribal households may come to school less prepared to learn as most of them are first generation students. Further, behaviour required of children at school may be unfamiliar to tribal families. Tribal communities are not aware of the benefits to which they are entitled. The second important factor that students in the why of tribal education is the language of instruction. The language of instruction in the sight most important factor affecting the response of Tribal people to formal education. In a study it is found that on average only 60 per cent of teachers believed that tribal children understood textbook writer in regional language. Government of India policy provides for instruction in the local language although most tribal parents surveyed wanted their children to be educated in the more widely spoken regional language. Also contributing to the tribal gap in achievement are differences in the resources of schools—fewer pukka buildings, less furniture and equipment, fewer instructional aids, fewer teachers educated to grade 10 or above, fewer teachers with recent in-service training etc., Unserviceable curriculum is another problem relating to school quality. The curriculum is not related to the developmental needs of the tribal community.

Modem educationists believe that every individual is endowed with certain innate potentialities, out and achieving a harmonious development in the ultimate objective of education. "By education, I mean all-round drawing out of the best in child and man-body, mind and spirit" felt Mahatma Gandhi. The purpose of education is to promote the development a well integrated person capable of exercising such responsibilities in the society as his powers allow. A harmonious development of the individual is the need of the hour for leading a happy, prosperous and outstanding life in the society.

To bring about a change either at thinking level or feeling level or acting level is the ultimate objective of the teaching learning process. These three refer to the three aspects of man, viz. Head, Heart and Hand, i.e. 3Hs. The present system of education has to emphasise on the, development of 7Rs, i.e. Reading, Writing, Arithmetic, Rights, Responsibilities, Relationships and Recreation.

The National Policy on Education 1986 made it clear that education has to produce self asserted, more productive, more capable and more thinking type of citizens. Education has to develop self-assurance and capacity to think independently on the part of the child. The production capacity of the child is to be-improved. The Vision 2020 document of A.P. Government emphasises on the development of marketable skills among the pupils of secondary and higher education institutions.

There are three important components in the educative process, i.e. the teacher, the pupil and the subject matter or content of education. The teacher is the main dynamic force in the system of education. He has to plan for teaching organise it execute it and evaluate its success. The second important component is the pupil. To educate the pupils is the ultimate objective of the instructional process. In this regard the child's capabilities, abilities, interests and his psychological aspects and social environment need to be taken into account. The pupil is to be considered as the starting point the middle and the end. His growth and his development is ideal of education. The third important factor is the subject matter or content of education, otherwise known as curriculum. Curriculum is the path for the realisation of the objectives of education. It includes curricular, co-curricular and extra-curricular activities. It is the sum total of all the educational experiences provided to the child by the school through instruction either within the four walls or outside. It includes scholastic as well as co-scholastic activities.

Today there is a shift from epistemic model of children's learning to that of constructionist movement which provides a greater scope for children's social experience in acquiring knowledge. As already mentioned for an all-round development of the learners the interface between cognition, emotion and action is necessary. National curriculum framework for School Education 2000, envisages shift of emphasis from information based and teacher centered education to process centered and learner friendly education.

The National Curriculum Framework 2000 advocates the following curriculum at School Education Stage. 2 year Early Child Care and Education (School readiness); in Classes I and II: one Language, Mathematics, Art of healthy and productive living; in Classes III to V: one Language, Mathematics, Art of healthy and productive living and Environmental Studies and in Classes VI to X: Three Languages, Mathematics, Science and Technology, Social Sciences, Work Experience, Art Education, Health and Physical Education, Computer Education. All these curricular programmes provide scope for the inclusion of various items relating to the developmental needs of tribals. Alfred North Whiter Head suggested a rhythm in the system of education. Rhythm between the system of education and the development of the child is to be maintained. Pre-primary, primary, upper primary, Lower Secondary, Higher Secondary, collegiate and Adult Education System is to be in accordance with the stages of development of the individual, viz. infancy, childhood, boyhood, adolescence and Adulthood. Keeping in the stage of development of the child- his needs, capacities, societal needs etc., the system of education is to be developed. Suitable curriculum is to be developed based on the stage of development of the individual.

With regard to tribal communities because of geographic isolation and aloofness from the deviated population and lack of modern facilities they are still backward in all respects still they use primitive methods in their agricultural and economic living activities. The developmental needs of tribal communities fall under the following areas such as: agriculture, horticulture, soil conservation, water conservation, health, education, animal husbandry, forest produce, marketing facilities, protection against exploitation, culture conservation, recreation facilities, employment needs, legal knowledge, medicinal plantation, agricultural implements, housing, clothing, food preservation, collection and prevention of herbs, beads and economic developmental activities. In order to enable them to develop the need of the hour is to have tribal development oriented curriculum in the School Education System. The developmental needs listed need to be integrated in various school subjects, specially social studies, science and socially useful productive work programmes, etc. The Social Science Curriculum may contain the following tribal developmental need programmes. Agriculture: Cultivation, cultivation methods, Tribal Area Cultivation methods such as Herbs cultivation, Podu Cultivation (advantages and disadvantages) and modern methods to be adopted in cultivation. Seri Conservation: Methods of Seri conservation Soil observation in tribal areas. Water Conservation: Methods of Water conservation–drinking water, needs, prevention methods; Forest produce: Methods of collection of forest produce, preservation and marketing. Legal knowledge: Protection against exploitation Governance. Education: Importance of education, need for education, developmental schemes, welfare activities, Reservations, Employment opportunities, etc. Recreation: Recreational activities, productive utilisation of leisure. Culture: Culture issue, protection culture of developed societies, sanskritisation advantages, development by adoption of civilised cultures, etc.

The Science Curriculum may contain the following Tribal Developmental need programmes: Health: Health habits. Food: Food habits cultivation of food crops, vegetation, growth of vegetable gardens, fruit bearing trees, etc. Shelter: Types of shelter, Hiring ingredients of housing. Horticulture: Fruits bearing trees, dry fruit production etc. Medicinal plants: Cultivation of medicinal plants, herbs etc. Animal Husbandry: Cattle rearing practices -Improved systems, mils and Milk Products. Transport: Transport system, improved practices to be adopted in tribal areas for easy transport Road and Rail services, etc. Economic Development Activities: Knowledge of various economic development activities for tribal development should find place in the curriculum.

The following vocational activities should find place in the work experience/SUPW curriculum. Self experienced activities like making design on paper such as ink designs, prints with treads, vegetable prints. Paper work such as making greeting cards, flags of different pieces, geometrical models, floating figures, office envelopes. Card sheet and card board work such as making articles like tumbler, flannel, pencil/pen stand, card board box, letter holder, dustbin, flower basket, file cover. Clay modelling like preparation of toys including dolls, models, collection of intervals such as leaves, shells, flowers, seeds, features. Food and drinks like preparation of drinks such as tea, coffee, neem, . . . squash, sharbat, etc. Preparation of simple food items like Rice, Chapati, Dal, Soup, raising plants in pots and care of clothes like preparation of washing soap, detergent powder, preparation of stationery items like note books, composition books, drawing books, book binding, report to cycle/stove and simple domestic approaches, making chalk with duster, brooms, waste paper basket, dustbin, garment making, spinning, Weaving, cutting, stitching, wood work like wooden tray, book racks, kitchen implements, preparation of neck decorative with beads and production activities like: Basket making, dying, embroidery, flower gardening, kitchen gardening, knitting, leather work, smith/toy making; Making culture specific agricultural tools with wood; Patriots of birds, animals, Preparation of different shapes. Activities such as birds faces, pictures with beads, kite making, toys with mango suds, bamboo work, wood work like making wombs, spoons, Teddu, Gilaka, etc., leather work like – Preparation of Dappu, dolu, Tudum, Dolak, etc., cane work like preparation of Flute, basket, Tadaka, Gampa, etc., decorative items with Beads, preparation of broom sticks, preparation of leaf plates, bee keeping, honey cultivation, preservation of meat, fishing, gum making, cotton collection/preservation, tunki leaf collection/Drying/preservation, candle making, computer knowledge, etc.

Instead of having a separate system of education for tribal communities in relation to their developmental needs it is necessary to include these needs in the existing curriculum itself and introduce certain vocational skill activities to make the tribal students easily adopt to the mainstream plain students. These activities in the school will help them develop and integrate themselves with the mainstream.

Culture and Quality Improvement with Special Reference to Tribal Primary Schools

There are three viewpoints with regard to man. Some consider man as rational in character. He has got the intellect to use. He possesses the ability to think and reason. This philosophy emphasis on the development of cognitive abilities of man. Some People consider man as a spiritual being. He has got the Divine spark or Spirit within himself. Making man conscious of his Self is regarded as the ultimate objective of education. This philosophy emphasizes on the development of affective domain. Some other people consider man as biological in nature. He is regarded as continuous with other animals. This philosophy emphasizes on the development of conative skills. Thus one viewpoint emphasizes on the development of cognitive skills (i.e.,) development of Head, another on the development of affective skills (i.e.,) development of Heart and a third one on the development of conative skills (i.e.,) development of Hand. But now what we want in the present society is a harmonious development of all these three components (i.e.) Head, Heart and Hand.

The National Policy on education 1986 made it clear that education has to produce self assured, more productive, more capable and more thinking type of citizens. Education has to develop self-assurance and capacity to think independently on the part of the individual. The productive capacity of the individual has to be developed.

There are three important components in the educative process. These are the Teacher, the Pupil and the Subject matter. The teacher is the main dynamic force in the system of education. He is the Director of the Teaching - Learning Process. He has to plan for teaching, organize it, execute it and evaluate its success. The second important component is the pupil. To educate the pupil is the ultimate objective or the instructional process. In this context the Child's ability, capacities, capabilities and his psychological aspects are to be taken into account. The pupil is to be regarded as the starting point, the middle and the end. His growth and his development are to be considered as the ideal of education. The third important component is the subject matter or the content of education known as curriculum. The Curriculum or the Content is to be handed over to the child by means of the method. The teacher needs the mastery of the subject matter, which he is going to teach and also possess a sound knowledge of pedagogical concerns. To make teaching more effective and learning more meaningful the teacher must be conversant with the culture of the community, more so in case of tribal areas.

Every community has its own culture. Culture is regarded as Social Heredity. It includes traditions, morals, laws, customs and other capabilities that are acquired by man as a member of society. It includes both material aspects like housing, clothing, food, etc. as well as non material aspects like language, family system, relationships etc. From the sociological point of view education has to transmit the cultural heritage of the previous generation to the present generation and also it has to conserve it and advance it. Education has to socialize the child and make the child physically strong, intellectually alert, emotionally stable, socially efficient and culturally sound.

There are 33 tribal groups in Andhra Pradesh comprising 6.3 per cent population of the state. Bagata Bhils, Goud, Hill Reddy, Kondadora, Mukadora, Poorja, Savara, Gadaba, Gond, Pardhan, Kolam, etc., are some of the tribes residing in hilly areas and forests. Shifting cultivation, Podu cultivation, Agriculture, Agriculture Labour, Collection of non-timber forest produce are some of the major occupations of the tribal groups. Besides these some groups are involved in occupations like hunting, honey collection, cattle rearing, manufacture of agriculture implements, basket making, selling bangles and beads, making garlands, forest labour, etc. The special features of the tribal culture can be mentioned as follows: Geographic isolation/isolated societies, simple way of life, treat nature with respect, subject to customary laws/without law and order department, they control themselves, they have their own code of conduct, truthfulness and honesty are found in them, closed system, subsistence economy, festivals throughout year, early marriages (13-15 years boys, 10-14 years girls), own dialect (Kuli, Kui, Gondi, Lambadi, Kolami, etc.), polygamy, divorce, limited exposure to outside world, beliefs and superstitions, limited needs and aspirations, parent are interested in immediate gains, economic characteristics include food gathering/hunting/fishing/shifting/cultivation/terrace cultivation, low skills/ very little specialisation/low productivity/no work training, lacks abstract thinking, child is looked as potential earner but not a learner, women looked as economic assets, learning through imitation but not instruction, etc.

Tribal Communities lead a simple life, subject to customary laws. They have limited exposure to outside world. They give more importance to immediate gains. They talk different dialects based on their own traditions and customs. They give importance to the celebration of festivals, which generally fall throughout the year. Whenever there is a festive occasions in the village all the villagers both elders, youngsters and children participate in it, which may disrupt the academic school schedule of the children.

The literacy percentage among tribal population falls at 16.96 (25.25% male and 8.65% female). The literacy among the primitive tribal groups is very low and needs concern. The enrolment figures of tribal children indicate the fact that nearly 12 per cent of the children in the age group 5-10 and 24 per cent children in the age group 11-15 need to be enrolled. Further there is high dropout rate among tribal children at V Class stage and more so in case of VII Class stage. The dropout rates at higher classes result in high wastage of human resources and financial allocations. This situation demands culture and context sensitive approaches to educational policy in tribal schools.

At the primary stage of education the curriculum consists of two components (i.e.) academic subjects and activity subjects. Academic Subjects comprise of language (Telugu), Mathematics and Environmental studies (1 Social Studies and 2 Science). At Class III stage English is also introduced. Activity subjects comprise of Socially useful productive work, Health and Physical education, creative activities and moral education.

Tribal child is a free bird by nature. He enjoys complete freedom unrestricted by his parents or other family members. Tribal children prefer to spend their time moving freely around, swimming in ponds and streams, catching fish, climbing trees, hunting birds, collecting berries, riding on buffaloes, etc. In tribal communities very rarely are the children punished. The conflict between the norms of school and socialization at home results in resistance and unwillingness among children to attend the school. Behaviour required of children at school may be unfamiliar to tribal families.

Andhra Pradesh Primary Education Programme (APPEP), which was implemented in the state with the assistance of U.K. Government, has suggested six Pedagogical principals, which are being followed in all the primary schools of the state including tribal areas. These principals are providing teacher generated learning activities; promoting learning by doing, discovering and experimenting; developing individual, group and whole class work; Providing for individual differences; using the local environment and creating an interesting classroom by displaying children's work and organizing it effectively. The

District Primary Education Programme (DPEP) went a further and is emphasizing on Natural Learning experiences drawing out the inborn abilities. While adopting these processes teachers in tribal areas need to keep in view the local cultural aspects to correlate with the teaching items for better learning and sustain interest among the tribal children.

Those cultural aspects, which can be used in the classroom by the tribal teachers, can be listed thus: tribal dialects, tribal play activities, calculation of time, identification of seasons, measures used for calculating distance, weight, volume, agriculture crops grown, pesticides used, cattle rearing methods adopted, body cleanliness and health habits, dress and costumes, house keeping, medicines used for ailments, village Panchayat/muthadar systems, solving problems, festivals celebrated, seeds procured, marriage systems, custom of receiving guests, honoring guests, tribal dances, worship, grain bank, agriculture implements, transportation system, interdependence/give and take, leisure time activities/ recreation, protection of crops, shandies, musical instruments, household implements, property rights, food habits, fuel, riddles, songs/folk songs and stories.

These components of tribal culture need to be adopted in the teaching- learning process in the school to create and sustain interest among the tribal pupils. In this regard the teacher plays an important role. His commitment, the quality of his empathy; the creativity and ability in correlating his teaching with the cultural components of the community go a long way in creating interest among the Tribal children. Whenever and wherever it is possible, culture specific curricular and co-curricular activities need to be organized by the teacher in the school.

In teaching language the teacher has to prepare and use bilingual charts and primers. The writer while working in Gond tribal community, with the help of teachers developed bilingual charts and got them used by teachers, which gave very effective results. In developing the bilingual charts, first figure is given and then its name in their dialect is given and after that the name in state language, Telugu, is given (e.g.) the figure of mother, Awal the name in their dialect (Gondi), Arnma name in state language Telugu is given. Like that figure of leaf, Aki, Aku; figure of pig, paddi, pandi. Like that the bilingual charts were developed using local culture, which helped the children in learning the language easily. The teachers of tribal area developed flash cards, story charts reflecting the tribal culture for use. In Class I language, primers in Lambada, Gond, Kolarn and Savara tribal dialects were developed. The teachers should encourage debates, discussions, composing poetry and writing essays in tribal dialects while dealing with language teaching. Further the students should be exposed to biographies of tribal leaders.

In dealing with Mathematics the teacher must invariably refer to the ways in which the tribal communities recon various measures of length, weight, volume, calculation of time, day, month, year, transactions carried on in shandies, identification of various shapes, etc.

So also in dealing with the science subjects reference should be made to the various cultural components of tribals like health habits, body cleanliness, house keeping, crops grown, pesticides used, soils, flora fauna, seeds procured medicines used for ailments, dress, agriculture implements, food habits, feathers used, collection of grains, leaves, musical instruments, housing, household implements, forest produce, seasonal produce, climatic conditions, etc.

In dealing with social studies subject, the teacher should refer to the agricultural crops grown, seasons, geographic conditions, cattle rearing methods, panchayat, solving problems, relationships, interdependence, festivals, marriages, custom of receiving guests, grain bank, transport systems, family systems, property rights, food grains etc., in his teaching. These helps in creating interest among tribal children and help them in effective learning.

In non-academic subjects of health and physical education the tribal play activities need to be organized in the school. Archery should form a part and parcel of Physical Education activity. In dealing with moral education reference should be made in teaching, to the various modes of worship, ceremonies, customary rights of tribal communities. Under creative activities tribal dances, mono actions, playing music, singing songs, story composition of tribal cultural components should be given importance. Under socially useful productive work programme place should be given to basket making, preparation of various implements, musical instruments, mat weaving, carpet making, wood work, leather work, gum making, fuel collection, honey collection should be given importance.

To conclude the teachers working in the tribal areas must make it a point to invariably refer to the local tribal community, their way of life, habits, economic system, social problems, history of the concerned tribe, changes in their life styles, physical features, difference between tribal and non-tribal groups relating to their physical and mental aspects, their life modes, work practices, their relation with the forests and nature etc., in their teaching–learning process, while dealing with different subjects in the curriculum. This creates interest among tribal children towards education and help in better learning.

Quality Education in Tribal Schools

Efforts Made by DPEP/SSA in Andhra Pradesh

DPEP is the offshoot of APPEP and SSA is the offshoot of DPEP. In addition to the scheme of Operation Blackboard, the major other initiative introduced in A.P. is the Andhra Pradesh Primary Education Project (APPEP). Apart from the construction of improved classrooms to the primary schools and add on facilities, the main thrust of the project has been on Human Resource Development. Teacher training was an important constituent of APPEP. For the first time, all the primary school teachers were given intensive training in child-centered, activity-based teaching–learning process. The following six pedagogical principles followed the basis for the classroom transaction: providing teacher generated learning activities, providing training by doing, discovering and experimenting, developing individual, group and whole class work, providing for individual differences, using local environment and creating and introducing classroom by displaying children's work and organizing it effectively.

As a result of the intensive training on cascade systems under this project, this was a substitutional improvement in the quality of classroom transaction. The teachers started using the activity-based methods in transacting the curriculum. Establishment of Teacher Centres is also a major contribution of the APPEP. During this project period 32 research reports and 18 case study reports were brought out. These were mainly concentrated on the six pedagogical principles. Some of these studies were on the impact of the project on enrolment and retention of students in schools. Evaluation of the project revealed that pupils are learning as much as, or more than before, after APPEP methods are introduced in schools. A similar pattern has emerged in the case of pupils who want to attend schools more than in the part. The percentage of pupils who took different roles in classrooms is also on the increase. Parents appear to be more willing to ensure that their children attend schools regularly. Attendance of pupils has shown a firm upward trend in all the schools where APPEP methodology is followed. A significant impact was also observed on the levels of pupils achievement. Even in tribal areas the teachers were trained in the APPEP pedagogy for ten days and were provided with an allowance to purchase different materials for use in the Teaching–Learning process. In this direction the ITDA, Utnoor during the year 1993-94 made efforts to provide training to all the primary school teachers in Adilabad Agency in APPEP Pedagogy and to adopt child-centered activity oriented interaction. The quality improvement programme in the primary schools of Adilabad Agency area includes the following programmes.

With regard to access: Rationalization of teachers posts. Opening of schools in school-less areas with the excess points identified, opening of community schools/Maabadi schools by encouraging the local community by providing some contribution, and encouraging the voluntary organisations, NGOs, Open Schools, EGS, Rajgond Samithies, Gond Sangarshana Samithies, etc.

With regard to enrolment: Opening of census registers in every school, conducting door-to-door surveys, providing incentives to school committees, which achieved cent per cent enrolment and cent per cent retention, constructing two rooms and sheds, one for school and the other for the teacher to reside by supplying flat and ridge tiles free of cost by ITDA, teacher doctor programme: To train the teachers to giving tablets and capsules to various common ailments of tribals.

With regard to retention: Adoption of activity based instructions, mid-day meal programme, constitution of tribal committees, supply of minimum educational material as a package of incentive, resident of the teacher in the school village and contacts with parents about the progress of their children.

With regard to quality: Improving the competence of teachers. 16-day in-service training in APPEP pedagogy, training in Minimum Levels of Learning, training in Activity approach, preparation and supply of instructional modules, supply instructional kit, preparation and supply of 116 instructional charts, filling up of vacant posts by local tribals, strengthening of supervision through education counselors, payment of salaries to teachers through banks, constitution of rural committees to watch the regularity of teachers, monthly review of academic work at cluster level, teaching through bilingual charts, daily schedule of work in the form of a calendar, frequent orientation in activity method, adoption of APPEP Pedagogy and incentives to those who do good work.

ITDA Paderu took up the following programmes as it has faced with the problem of rampant teacher absenteeism, look of infrastructural facilities and language problem. Conduct of comprehensive education survey to identify gaps (Teacher/Child/habitational school information form), etc., opening of Maabadi Schools, joyful leaning programme, improving quality of teaching–learning process by introducing the kit developed by Rishi Valley Education Centre, school beautification, supply of additional TLM, School Complex

System with Head Master, Mandal Resource Person and strong teacher, Project Resource Centre/Project Monitoring Team, Training Programmes, VECs/MCs, Mid-day Meal Programme, Conduct of Pre-evaluation tests, categorisation of schools into A/B/C and Comprehensive monitoring proformae for Ashram Schools. A/B/C categorization, etc.

As on off shoot of APPEP, DPEP came into being since 1996-97, under two phases Phase I, 5 districts and Phase II, 14 districts. In certain selected mandals and areas the Joint GOI-UNDP project was launched in the remaining four leftover districts. DPEP is a house grown idea to achieve Universal Primary Education by adopting a holistic planning and management approach. Community participation and contextuality are the two important pillars of DPEP. The aim of the programme is to achieve Universal Access, Universal Enrolment, Universal Retention and Universal attainment/achievement. Under this programme for the development of 'tribal education' certain measures have been taken up. Some of these include formation of Tribal Education cells at district level and the District Project Offices and identification of one officer as the Tribal Education Coordinator, one professors post and a lecturers post was created in the state. Project Office to look after tribal education in the state. Some of the programmes initiated by the SPD are as follows: development of bridge language inventories for use by non-tribal teachers working in tribal areas, development of supplementary reading materials like stories, songs, riddles, etc., Savara, Banajra, etc., development of bilingual textbooks for Class I in Savara, Banjara, Gondi and Kolami, development of a module on tribal education, research studies on the problem of Tribals Education by TCR & TI, Hyderabad and Social Assessment Study by S.V.U. Tirupathi, implementation of Education Guarantee Scheme in Tribal Areas, development of Primers in Class I Language in eight tribal dialects, viz., Gondi, Kolami, Savara, Konda, Kuvi, Adivasi Oriya, Koya and Banjara and their use in selected schools in tribal areas of A.P., participation in the four studies conducted by RIE, Mysore on measures to improve literary in tribal areas, organisation of culture specific co-curricular activities, development of monitoring proformae for tribal schools and development of glossary in Savara dialect, development of Glossaries in tribal dialects for use in Language, Mathematics and EVS I & II for Classes I and V in seven dialects (viz.,) Gondi, Kolami, Konda, Kuvi, Adivasi Oriya, Koya and Banjara, impact study on the culture specific textbooks for Class I developed in eight tribal dialects.

In its study conducted on problems of the Tribal Children with reference enrolment, retention and quality in the five Phase I DPEP districts of Andhra Pradesh in the year 1998, the TCR & TI, A.P., Hyderabad reported the following findings. Universal access could not be provided in tribal habitations with less than 100 population, overall enrolment of STs in the state is 70 per cent and for girls it is 57 per cent, children below 5 years and over-aged children are also admitted in Class I, absenteeism of pupils is more pronounced immediately after vacation, during tribal festivals, weekly markets, marriage seasons, peak seasons, of agricultural opinions and food produce collection, attendance is being manipulated by teacher up to 75 per cent mainly to ensure promotion to next class as well as to correlate with the attendance marked for mid-day meals programme, attendance marked on the day of visit and students actually present substantially vary, in some places the attendance for mid-day meals is 100 per cent while the actual present is around 60 per cent, parents and other elders feel that absenteeism of teacher is mostly hampering the spirit of education in tribal areas, the school atmosphere also often does not attract children, 59 per cent of the students in interior villages appear totally unclean with shabby hair, without even hair oil, torn clothes and with scabies and running nose, the instructors of ECE Centres are combining their students with 1st and 2nd class students, who are coming disturbance in the class, 81 per cent of the younger generation have realised the value of education. Awareness is more in roadside villages which have frequent interaction with ITDA/educated general population/Radio/TV/Newspapers, etc., out of 32 school studies 7 schools do not have VEC or SEC while the remaining are nominated bodies, interviews with VECs/SECs revealed that 16 per cent are not aware of the existence of the VEC/ SEC, 52 per cent are aware but not about the role and responsibilities, 66 per cent of the teachers complained that village community is not co-operative, while 78 per cent of the villagers complained that teachers do not interact with villagers, meetings of VECs/SECs were not held in 64 per cent of the villages studied, in Community schools also, the participation of community till the school is started is active but their role after that is not known to them, only 25 per cent of the teachers are staying in the same village, 38 per cent commute from places located below 5 km, while 37 per cent reside at a distance of 5 to 15 kms, teachers working in roadside schools stay in the same habitation while most of the teachers working in interior villages, the content of the textbooks do not reflect the tribal culture, only 9 per cent of the teachers know the dialect of the students with whom they are working, only 2 per cent of the teachers have lesson plans, on an average 75 per cent of the teachers do not use blackboards. 100 per cent do not use teaching aids they simply read lessons from textbooks, using play methods, giving demonstrations, observing students while teaching and ensuring their participation, reviewing previous lessons, giving assignments in classrooms and home work etc., are about in more than 90 per cent of schools, regular supervision is a rare phenomenon for tribal schools, parents who found their children not learning anything in school started withdrawing the students, language barriers, untrained teachers, and teacher absenteeism has contributed to poor performance of students, under-aged children admitted for maintaining TP Ratio are detained till they attain the prescribed age, dropout rate among ST students IS very high at primary level, i.e. 74.05 per cent, there is consistent Increase in dropout rate form Class II onwards, the causes being; low intake capacity of Ashram Schools, home sickness, reluctance of parents to admit their children in far off places, preference for child labour, unable to cope up with Class III syllabus in Ashram schools, lack of importance to girls education, on an average 60 per cent of the students of Class I and II got lets that 35 per cent marks in Language and Mathematics, teachers residence outside the school location IS a big barrier for the functioning of the school.

The following are the findings of the Social Assessment Study conducted by the Sri. Venkateswara University in 2000. The occupation of the 33 tribal groups including 12 PTGs were as follows: 41.2 per cent - cultivation, 41.6 per cent - Agriculture Labour, 2.6 per cent - Household industry and 9.6 per cent - Other Occupations; high representation of students discourages the parents from sending their children to school, parents like to send their children if the school functions regularly and children show academic progress, children of six or seven need emotional and psychological support from their parents, the reasons for non enrolment and dropout of children are as follows: poor economic conditions, non-interest of the child, non-interesting of the parent, lack of school in the village, because of girl child, ill health of the child, no tradition of sending the child to school, physically handicapped, to work after younger siblings, teacher teasing, unemployment after education, to work infield, parents death, single son, nomadic life and remaining the tribal children in the same case, etc.

Most of the tribal children experience school and classrooms as a punishment as they are not allowed to move freely in their localities. However, some of the other reasons are: teacher absenteeism, isolation and unaccountability, forest policy of not laying roads and permanent constructions, seasonal variations, naxalite movement, occupations, poor school environment and non-suitable curriculum, etc.

In urban places the education of parents influences education in their children. But in the condition in tribal areas is illiterate tribal parents are not aware of the importance of education. There is positive correlation between wet cultivation and literacy of the tribals. Therefore Dandora is the best mass of communication followed by radio and TV to spread education among the tribals. In the tribal families father has major role indecision making regarding their children. The major reasons for non-residence of students in Government Hostels are as follows: poor accommodation, non-sleeping material, no teaching during non-school timings, early serving of food, absence of personnel during the nights and presence of ghosts and spirits, etc.

Many of the tribal communities lack awareness about the education facilities like NFE, back-to-school, open school and other continuing education programmes being provided by Government. The teachers do not attend the schools regularly. The main causes for teachers irregular attendance are as follows: non-residence of teachers in tribal localities, teachers working in tribal areas, belong to other ethnic groups, adjustment problem, teachers are politically influenced, teachers are having understanding with officials, having relative with local leaders, no teaching ability and not attending the school daily after having the school. The tribal DIETs lack proper infrastructure and not discharging necessary training inputs to the teachers. Implementing agencies are not able to provide the incentives regularly and in time. 30.30 per cent of the parents in school going category keep their children in hostels and about one third of them are not staying in the hostels at night. Poor maintenance of school records and lack of periodical inspection. 68.96 per cent of the non-tribal teachers and all the tribal teachers feel that training in pedagogy is essential for effective classroom teaching.

The suggestions for the improvement of the situation in tribal schools include the following: Strengthening and extending Mabadi and GVVK schools based mandal school mapping, limiting Ashram Schools to Mandal Headquarters/road side junctions considering various ecological barriers, strengthening the Ashram School Complexes to provide better supervision, increasing surprise visits by higher officials for better monitoring and implementation, vacation should be based on local needs and seasonal variations like festivals, and other economic activities where tribal children participate, bringing awareness about the incentives through pamphlets and folk media, providing additional incentives in the forms of rice (10 kg per head per month) to students who belong to PTGs as these groups have low literacy rate, the cooks working in Ashram Schools should be given short term training to improver the methods of cooking, authorising and prescribing periodical visits to schools and hostels compulsory by the different sectoral officers at district and ITDA schools, preparing separate training modules for DIETs which impart training for teachers working in tribal areas, appointing anthropologists with the faculty of DIETs or arranging just teachers by anthropologists in teaching programme, also the performance of the teachers should be valuated in terms of residing in the same village where he is working, increasing enrolment, regular attendance and promoting/admitting number of children in Ashram Schools and performance appraisal by SEC and a committee of parents selected at random and also utilising strategies/places of community festivals and other large gatherings for the proposition of education through different folk media and posters.

AP DPEP conducted a study on the factors influencing parents and children in achieving DEE in AP and made for following findings: economic barriers are not the real barriers for enrolment and retention, parents illiteracy, peer group effect and unattractive schools are other causes for dropouts, most of the out of school children opined that school should be a place of activities with songs, games and good teaching environment. Teachers should avoid punishments and they have to provide attractive atmosphere in the school. Tribal parents are also sending their children to school for education for better future. Nearly 100 per cent of the tribal parents sample expressed decrease in income as a result of sending their children to school. Tribal parents expressed for improvement in physical facilities and good teaching. Tribal parents are also not happy to send their children to work. 11 per cent tribal parents expressed that the school is not good. Tribal parents are also ready to send their children to school if the child desires so. Nearly 100 per cent of the poor illiterate tribal parents are sending their children to school. Illiterates of the parents, unattractive school environment and peer group affect also stand causes for dropouts in agency areas. School dropouts in 'tribal areas are more in Class II level. Some of problems of tribal education district-wise identified are a follows:

Srikakulam	:	Migration, more unenrolled girls, engaging children in work for money
Vizianagaram	:	More dropouts, low parental awareness
Visakhapatnam	:	Lack of access, non-residence of teachers, fear of punishment
East Godavari	:	Out of School children without work, peer group affect
West Godavari	:	Sibling care
Khammam	:	Early marriages
Warangal	:	Parental illiteracy, more unenrolled boys
Adilabad	:	Involvement of household work
Mahabub Nagar	:	More unenrolled, sibling care, fear of punishment, illiteracy of parents

The Operational Research Group (ORG) which conducted a study on the Administration and Management of primary schools in Tribal areas reported wing findings: In tribal areas the practice of recruiting vidya volunteers to meet any deficits not very encouraging, there are two MRPs in each mandal irrespective of geographic spread of mandals and the number of schools. This reduces the frequency of visits of MRPs to schools particularly where the number of schools in his jurisdiction in more than 20, in the tribal areas there is a dual reporting structure at the Mandal level. The information from schools is sent to ITDAs and on some issues to the APC, DPEP through DEO. Similarly the role of MEO has been marginalised in the ITDA areas, inter-departmental linkages particularly at the district level is low, viz. between Education Department, Social Welfare Department and DRDA, in tribal areas inspection of the schools by the MEO is non-existing. The teachers are of the opinion that inspection by ITDA was also very limited, dissemination of training impacts is not taken seriously by the teachers due to the wide difference in educational qualifications between the MRPs and the teachers, there is a consideration delay in information flow from ITDA/DTW to DEO, resulting in delay in decision making such as release of textbooks, teaching aids, etc., participation of the SEC in promoting primary education in tribal areas was found very low, the prime reason being high illiteracy and low awareness among the numbers.

The study on the functioning of Girijana Vidya Vikas Kendras (GVVKs) with special reference to ITDA, Parvatipuram in 1998 mode the following findings: Of the 39 teachers involved in the study as many as 24 are not residing in the school village whose percentage works out to 62. In many cases teachers belonging to one community are working in places of different community, e.g. Konda Dora in Jatapu habitation. Godaba in Muka Dora habitation, Savara in Gadaba habitation, etc. The causes for non-residence of the teachers are as follows in the cadre of priority: no house reside, no medical facility, school is not is nearer to the place of residence, spouse working in a different place and village is inhabited by other community. GVVK teachers are facing the problem and delaying with the Mathematics subject because of their academic defecting. In teaching–learning process no aids are prepared and used. GVVK teachers are not provided with any academic guidance on support. Schools lack infrastructural facilities like building, furniture, aids, etc. Teachers are adopting only the traditional method of teaching but not activity method. Language problem is also expressed by the teachers. They are deficient in Telugu Language and also in the local dialects. Teachers are not aware of the school readiness programme and joyful learning programme

Sarva Shiksha Abhiyan (SSA) is an offshoot of DPEP. SSA is an effort for UEE by community ownership of school system. The objective of SSA are as follows: All children in school, Education Guarantee Centre, Alternate School, Back to School camp by 2003. All children complete five years of primary schooling by 2007. All children complete eight year Elementary Schooling by 2010. Focus on Elementary Education of satisfactory quality with emphasis on education for life. Bridge all gender and social category gaps at primary stage by 2007 and at Elementary Level by 2010 and Universal retention by 2010.

The guidelines for the implementation of the programme include adoption of local specificity; need based planning, and planning a realistic exercise. The basis features of the programme are institutional reforms, community ownership of school-based interventions, institutional capacity building and community based monitoring with full transparency. It also focuses on education of special groups. The Tribal Education of AP DPEP under the auspicious of SSA took up certain programmes for the development of tribal education in AP which are detailed below.

AP DPEP has developed Glossaries in eight tribal dialects for use by the classroom teachers of tribal areas. The dialects include Gondi, Kolami, Kuvi, Konda, Banjara, Koya, Adivasi Oriya and Savara. The equivalents of Telugu to the concerned tribal dialect of word are developed subject-wise and classwise from Classes I to V. The subjects include Telugu language, Mathematics, Environmental Studies I Social Studies and Environmental Studies II Science. First the Telugu word is given in alphabetical order and then for it the, tribal dialect word is given. The glossaries are distributed to the field.

Tribal Child Learning Guarantee project with the following objectives was launched in tribal schools of AP during the academic year 2004-05. They are: to create child friendly classroom, to familiarize the children with language activities, to make the classroom more lively in terms of having through activities/facilitation, to remove the classroom fear among the children and to make learning guarantee a reality. The project was limited duly to Classes I to II and to two selected mandals in ITDAs of AP. The project emphasis are teaching through activity based, child centered approach and continuous evaluation. Fruitful results are observed on this project. It is also prepared to extent this project took the schools in the Mandal by degrees. It is also proposed to assess the training needs of the teachers working in tribal areas. One of the causes for low achievement of pupils in tribal areas in reported as low performance of teachers working in tribal areas. In this connection it is proposed to assess the academic as well as the pedagogical needs of teachers. For this purpose a schedule was developed of tribal teachers. The project is under the data collection stage.

The Tribal Education cell of SSA has taken up an impact study on the culture specific textbooks for Class I developed in eight tribal dialects, viz., Gondi, Kolami, Kuvi, Konda, Savara, Banjara, Adivasi Oriya and Koya. These primers have been introduced are on experimental basis in 10 selected schools in each dialect ITDA areas of the state. The books were developed keeping in view the following five objectives: to develop interest in education among the tribal students, thereby reducing the percentage in absenteeism of tribal students, to reduce the retention rate of students of staying in the same class for two or more years, though not directly but indirectly to raise the literacy percentage among illiterate tribals, to conserve the culture of the concerned tribal communities and to make acquisition of primary education easy and facilitation by making the home language and school language as one and the same.

The study involved 39 schools, 39 teachers, 394 students and 77 parents. Five tools were developed and used in the study for data collection. The study revealed positive results. The following are some of the findings of the study. The appearance of the books is attractive except in case of Koya and Banjara dialects, the content in the books is reported to the level of the students except in Gondi dialect, the lessons presented are to the experiential level of the students, the figures printed in the books are attractive to the students and are experienced by the students in daily life and they reflect the concerned tribal culture, the letters provided in the books are recognizable of the students except in Savara and Gondi dialects, the poems given in the textbooks are related to the concerned tribal culture except in case of Savara and Kuvi dialects, the words used in the textbooks are known words to the students exception case of Gondi dialect, the examples given in the textbooks are known examples to the students except in case of Gondi dialect, the content in the textbooks motivates the students to learn, the students are participating in the Teaching Learning process actively with exception in Adivasi Oriya, students are able to recite songs relating to their culture with exceptions in some dialects, teaching of these books developed interest towards education among students, teaching of same books resulted in: increase in attendance of students, regularity and punctuality in attending the school, retention of the students in the school till its closure, removal the fear of school from the minds of students in case of students of all dialects. The parents of all dialects responded positively on the concerned books. The parents whole-heartedly welcomed the implementation of the books developed in tribal dialects. The teachers feel the book as handy for those to teach. The teachers feel the need for some type of training to transact with the book. The teachers felt the need for the supply of additional TLM to deal with the book. From evaluation print of view the classroom practitioners expressed that through these primers the four language skills can be developed. There is an increase in enrollment and attendance consequent on the introduction of the books. Full attendance was observed as the day of visit in case of Kuvi dialect schools. The classroom observation revealed that students are able to perform activities themselves except in case of Kuvi and Banjara dialect schools. TLM pertaining to the textbook available in limited way of being used by students except in case of Adivasi Oriya schools. Local resources are utilised in the teaching learning process except in Adivasi Oriya, Koya and Gondi dialect schools. The Focus Group Discussion revealed that the children studying well consequent on the introduction of this new intervention of teaching in their dialect. Parents reported that they form a change in the behaviour of their wards and they are authoring the school content any interruption happily. Parents reported that their children are studying even at house and reciting some poems, riddles and the like at home and reading the words well. Some parents started that the textbook reflected some items relating to their children. Parents feel the need for the improvement of alphabetical charts. Parents also started that they want to read this book and receive education. All the students in all the eight dialects secured more marks in listening competency than in other competencies. This indicates the fact that the textbooks developed in tribal dialects contain suitable content to develop listening skills. Next to listening skill in achievement comes speaking skill, where in more marks are secured than the other two skills, i.e. reading and writing. This to a large extent confirms the fact that the textbook is contributing to the development of speaking skills. The achievement in writing skill is not worthy of mention by way of the eight dialects. This needs special concern. During their interaction with the fill the investigation reported that the figures are not printed in the textbooks in an appropriate manner. In some pages there is no relation between the figures printed and the words mentioned. Students are expressing their happiness and enjoyment over the textbooks printed in their dialect. The students are expressing happiness and enthusiasm and satisfaction on the teacher is teaching in their mother dialect. Same of the mistakes found in the present textbooks should be corrected and republished. As the book contains the pictures and materials known to the children they are learning easily various songs and stories without difficulty. The book is good to the pupils. The alphabetical chart must contain good and attraction pictures to motivate children to learn effectively. The teachers are of the opinion that the book is very good and the pupils are very happy with the book. The two better and three letter words must be in good number in the textbook. Corrections are necessary in the book. The books must contain more forms relating to the concerned tribal culture. The books help in conversing the tribal culture. To implement this book not only in case of Class I students but also in case of adults. Adult literates can be made literate by using this book. From the classroom practicum's point of view the most accepted primer is the Adivasi Oriya primer and the last accepted in Gondi dialect primer and Koya dialect primer. Konda and Kolami primers are well transacted and Koya dialect primer in least transacted.

These are some of the efforts made by DPEP/SSA in achieving quality in Primary Education. The findings of the researches done and the materials developed need to be adopted in the field to achieve the desired results with regard to DEE.

Curriculum at the Primary Stage in the Tribal Schools of Andhra Pradesh

> *"There is strong reason to suppose that no one is designed to speak one or another language. If my children were to have grown up in Japan, they would have spoken Japanese, indistinguishably from natives. The ability to acquire language is basically a fixed, uniform species property."*
>
> **—Noam Chomsky in Powers and Prospects**

India has been the home of many heterogenous ethnic groups of human beings. For thousands of years the tribes lived in solitude having no communication with the outside world. As a result, they had no civilizational impact. This was mainly responsible for their backwardness. The "Primitive Tribes" have their own ways of living, customs, traditions, superstitions, rituals and ceremonies which separate them from other segments of society.

The major constraints of tribal education are scattered population, small size habitation, lack of facilities of transport and communication. The content, curriculum and text books are not relevant to their culture. Medium of instruction, non-availability of teachers knowing tribal languages and economic deprivation are the main reasons for high drop out rate among scheduled tribe children.

Education is a major tool for socio-economic change of all categories of people. Tribal students constitute an important segment of our population. For various socio-economic and historical reasons the tribals continue to live in isolation. The fruits of educational development has not reached them to a desirable extent. An unsuitable curriculum is one of the reasons for this.

The 33 Scheduled Tribes constitute a major group in Andhra Pradesh for whom access to primary education is the main problem. They live in remote areas of the state and need special focus to solve their problems. The literacy rate of the Scheduled Tribe children in Andhra Pradesh is very low compared with Scheduled Caste and other Backward classes. The female literacy is very poor and needs urgent action.

Education of children of primitive tribal communities is a very important concern of our Government. Although schools were Provided in tribal areas and the expenses on education were met by the Government, desirable results have not been achieved to improve their standard of living. The solution to the problem depends on how best education facilities can be provided to them. It is with this background that it has been decided to study the educational pattern available to Scheduled Tribe Children of Andhra Pradesh. The present chapter is an attempt to examine the prevailing school curriculum in the tribal schools. The major objective of this chapter is to assess the learning, achievement levels of the tribal students through the existing curriculum adopted in the tribal schools. This chapter also looks into the problems relating to the school text books, learning materials, curriculum, problems of tribal teachers and the problems of school administration.

Andhra Pradesh is a State with acute problems to be addressed in the field of tribal education. The total Scheduled Tribe population according to 1991 census comprises of 41,99,481 out of which 21,42,817 are males and 20,56,664, are females. The tribal population of Andhra Pradesh constitute 6.31 per cent of the total population. The literacy rate among these tribal groups is 17.16 per cent (males 25.25% and females 8.68%). The dropout rate among the Scheduled Tribe children during 1996-97 was 74.26 per cent out of which 71.16 per cent were boys and 78.71 per cent were girls of Classes I to V.

The high dropout rate among these tribal children are due to various reasons. The children are sent for cattle grazing, agriculture labour, sibling care and lack of interest in education. Besides this, most of the areas are covered with thick forests. Due to the economic and social backwardness the pupils participation in the educational programme is far from satisfactory. The tribal children are faced with the problems of access, attainment, language deficiency and participation.

Most of the tribal people in Andhra Pradesh live in rural areas and predominantly depend on agriculture for their livelihood. The tribal children accompany their parents for agricultural and cooli work. Most of the tribal habitations have a population of less than 200. Some of the habitations have a formal school within a radius of 1 km, but the children are unable to attend the schools regularly due to social, physical and psychological barriers.

One of the main reasons for more dropout rate is that the tribal parents treat their wards as earning members to support the family and hence the tribal parents are not interested to send their children to schools. There are a number of girl children who are under sibling care. Most of the tribal girls were not at all enrolled and the remaining have discontinued in Classes II or III.

In order to provide primary education facilities to Scheduled Tribe children single teacher primary schools were opened. In these schools educated Scheduled Tribe candidates with X Class qualification are being appointed as teachers. In addition to these the Grama Vidya Vikas Kendra Schools (GVVK), Mabadi Schools, Tribal Welfare Schools, and Integrated Tribal Development Authority Schools (ITDA) were actively functioning for the development of the Scheduled Tribe children. However it has been observed that the functioning of these schools, is not up to the mark and deficient in the academic front and also regularity in running the schools.

Most of the tribals are illiterate and do not know the importance of education. In order to encourage regular attendance in the students mid-day meals, free text books and scholarships are distributed to tribal students. Orientation and training programmes were also conducted to the teachers to handle their classes effectively. Still the supervision of these schools in the tribal sub-plan areas is very difficult. Most of the primitive tribal groups such as Gadaba, Kondadora, Mukadora and Savaras use different dialects. But the major language of the people being used is Telugu.

The school is considered as the second home and the teacher is the mother substitute especially in the case of primary school children. But the vital point is how far the students are willing to stay in the class rooms, how many schools are lively, even happy feel and what are the facilities provided to them? Schools have a vital role to play in improving the health of young people and laying the foundation for economic well being of the children.

A school health programme has three components, viz., school based health sciences, health promoting school environment and comprehensive school health education (curriculum). The National Policy Documents on health and education in India have called for improvement in health of children in schools. Despite the enormous potential of schools for health promotion and existence of adequate framework of legislation, the achievements have been disappointing. The reasons for this include low priority to school health promotion by education and health sciences, inappropriate curriculum, teaching methods and poverty. The quality of school health programmes is mainly dependent on the amount of time and effort that the teachers are willing to put into health education and their understanding and skills in running the schools.

The Integrated Tribal Development Authority made an attempt to develop reading materials for the tribal children. To make learning of language more effective the Grama Vidya Vikas Kendra School teachers have prepared bilingual charts with the tribal dialect and the Telugu language. Awareness campaigns and Kala Jatas were conducted by the DPEP etc. However these efforts did not bring desirable achievements in the development in tribal education.

The curriculum for tribal and non-tribal schools are the same and hence do not reflect their customs, habits and environment of the tribal children. The tribal children are unable to follow the language used in the text books. The authors of the text books prepared by the State Council of Educational Research and Training do not take into consideration the tribal cultural traits and their environment. The language used in the text books is entirely different to language of the tribals used at their homes. Therefore there is a communication gap between the teachers and students.

The existence of tribal schools in remote and top hill areas, the geographical hindrances, fear of forest animals, no proper road facilities are some of the reasons for the officers not supervising the tribal schools. As a result, both teachers and students frequently absent themselves from attending the school. The tribal teachers are assigned with additional responsibilities such as wardenship, collection of census reports, clerical jobs etc. The teachers close the schools and attend the jobs assigned by the higher authorities. Under these circumstances the tribal children neglect their schooling and education. Most of the tribal schools are located in the top hill areas. Due to non-availability of housing, electricity and hospitals the teachers do not reside in the tribal areas. The teachers have to walk not less than 20 to 30 kms to reach the top hill tribal schools. Since no school buildings are available the teachers have to conduct the classes in the open areas.

The school curriculum in order to be socially relevant should reflect the ethos and the life styles of the pupils for whom it is meant. In Andhra Pradesh variety of cultures and subcultures exist. Therefore one common curriculum for all groups of pupils may not reflect the cultural values of all. The Scheduled Tribes in Andhra Pradesh have distinct culture of their own. There is a need to have a curriculum which suits their needs and aspirations.

Education for the Scheduled Tribes in Andhra Pradesh cannot be conceived in isolation. They live in distinct socio-cultural environments with their own pattern of culture. The educational objectives for them cannot be different. Within the framework of general objectives of education for the country, the content of education for the tribal children could be devised in such a way that it would suit their needs. The recent advance in Science and Technology has increased the total stock of knowledge. It is necessary to impart Science and Technical knowledge to the tribal students. It is equally essential to ensure that it does not create socio-cultural imbalances in their society II. The content of education for them should not be such as to uproot them from their cultural milieu, Tribal students have to be prepared through education to face the new challenges. The curriculum has to take care of this aspect.

For most of the tribal students primary education is terminal. They do not need a large body of knowledge to meet their socio-economic requirements. Their information bag need not necessarily be over loaded. It is desirable to ensure that the curriculum maintains a harmonious balance between culture based and scientific oriented knowledge.

While developing a curriculum for tribal students two major factors are vey important. Firstly, the tribal culture is essentially different from the surrounding non-tribal culture. Secondly, the tribal areas are geographically a part and parcel of State in which the tribal people live. The interests of the forward group students cannot be vastly different from the tribal children. There should be no difficulty in preparing a modified curriculum for tribal students and within the framework of general objectives and national goals of education.

Education has to act as a tool for socio-economic change. Curriculum will have to be developed in such a way that it becomes relevant to the life styles, needs and aspirations of the tribal students. Decentralisation of curriculum is warranted in view of the socio-economic and cultural differences between the non-tribal and tribal communities.

The tribal child should be able to communicate easily with others through properly articulated speech and writing. For the tribal students the language of communication should be their mother tongue. It is also essential for them to learn the regional language (Telugu) to the extent that they can read and understand.

The tribal child should be able to operate the four fundamental numerical operations and apply them in his life to solve practical problems. The tribal child should be able to appreciate the simple numeral and social phenomena in his environment Emphasis may be laid on the spirit of enquiry, the scientific method, trace the cause and effective relationship, cooperation and betterment of their living conditions. These areas will include the Environmental Studies I and II. Once the basic foundations are laid, it will not be difficult for the tribal child to join the mainstream of general education with the help of bridge courses at the higher stage. The contents in this area must be more functional than the corresponding programme meant for the non-tribal children. The spirit of enquiry, learning by doing and knowledge of his environment are more advantageous for the tribal children. Many social problems that exist in the tribal society need to be emphasized in the curriculum.

The tribal child should be able to lead a healthy life. He should take part in the games and sports effectively. Therefore the content should be based upon the actual present life of the tribal child and not loaded with information necessary for future life. The dictum of 'life best lived to day, is the best preparation for the future' should be followed. A tribal child has natural potentiality for sports and games. This ability should be groomed for raising natural standards.

While writing text books topics like Animals-domestic and wild, family with basic kinship terms, tribal fares and festivals, health and hygiene, folk tales and folk songs, local games and sports, modern transport, different types of cultivation, weekly market, nearest town, leave application, local Gods and temple, village life, diseases and tribal heroes may be considered. The listening and speaking abilities, reading and writing abilities, grammar, and vocabulary has to be developed for the tribal children.

Activities such as sport and simple questions has to be developed to test their knowledge in listening and speaking after a story or event is narrated to a tribal child. Students have to be encouraged to recite their folk songs, poems, to narrate their experiences, describe short stories and folk tales in a natural way and dramatise them. Tribal students have to be encouraged to use polite language. More stress have to be given on both loud and silent reading and they have to be encouraged to comprehend things. Regular hand writing and dictation have to be emphasized. They should be encouraged to write short essays on domestic animals, bullock cart, dibble, hoe, weeder, plough, fairs and festivals etc.

Lessons for the tribal students have to be centered around the known animals and birds, games, different crops, folk tales, people who help us, fairs and festivals, the lives of great people, travelogues, famous places, national understanding, health and hygiene, citizenship, scientific inventions and discoveries, adventures, plantations and forest, etc.

Lessons will have to be developed with a view to inculcating desirable human values in the minds of the people such as the sense of duty, respect for superiors, etiquette, patriotism, kindness, dignity of labour, cooperation etc. Sufficient number of exercises have to be provided in the text books. Exercises pertaining to the four skills-reading, writing, listening and arithematic have to be prepared by the teacher and administer in the classes. Objective types of exercises have to be prepared. The exercise prepared by the teacher should serve the purpose of teaching and evaluation.

With regard to methodology of teaching in the tribal schools the medium of instruction should be the mother tongue at the primary stage. Gradually this can be shifted to the regional language at the higher stages. Integrated Approach have to be adopted. Suitable doing projects connected with the life problems of the tribal child have to be selected and the knowledge contents have to be built around the environmental conditions of the tribal child. This approach will make learning more effective. Iiems that cannot be covered have to be taken up independently by the teacher. The illustrations both verbal and visual have to be selected from the environmental conditions of the tribal localities. Instructional materials and teaching aids have to be improvised by the teacher.

The following suggestions can be made for the development of tribal education and curriculum at the primary stage in the tribal schools of Andhra Pradesh: All schools located in the tribal areas have to be taken up for training in order to develop strategies for the development of tribal education. The teachers both tribal and non-tribal have to be given training on tribal languages and tribal culture. Additional incentives have to be provided for the tribal teachers working in tribal localities. The tribal teachers working in the tribal localities must acquire skills like preparing a local specific curriculum based on the need and aspirations of the locality, able to arrange community participation activities, develop the ability of discovering new strategies for the development of tribal education in tribal localities, projects on different problems of training education, develop the competence in class management, major learning principles of tribal education, understand the role of the school and the tribal home. The teachers must develop an awareness to discover and solve the needs of the tribal groups. The teachers must develop a mind and heart to receive the tribal children. Lastly they should know the modem techniques of evaluation.

Monitoring of Academic Achievement of Students in Tribal Schools of Andhra Pradesh

So far as the tribal education programme is concerned, there is a shift in approaches and policies from the provision of equal opportunities and incentives, to that of effective participation and receiving good quality education on the part of the child. May be a tribal child or a non-tribal child, the present emphasis is on quality improvement in schools. A tribal child should in no way lag behind as regards quality. Here comes the need for effective monitoring of the academic achievement of children in tribal schools.

The present chapter provides a detailed account of the various issues connected with the monitoring of the academic achievement in tribal schools. What is academic monitoring, what is academic monitoring of students, who is responsible for this, what are the steps in monitoring, how to collect information and what type of assistance is to be provided are dealt with in detail. It is reported that the three important steps in monitoring are knowing, identifying and assisting. Some hints are also suggested to the administrators in the process of academic monitoring of students.

Why Education ? Modern educationists believe that every individual is endowed with certain innate abilities or potentialities and these are to be brought out to achieve a harmonious development. The purpose of education is to promote the development of abilities to enable exercising of such responsibilities in the society as his powers allow. Education has to make the individual physically strong, intellectually sound, emotionally stable, culturally fit and socially efficient. According to National Policy on Education 1986, Education has to produce a self-assured, more productive, more capable and more thinking type of citizens. It is not the imitator that is to be developed, but it is exploratory that is to be developed. Education has to promote productivity, achieve social and national integration, step up the process of modernization, and inculcate social, moral and spiritual values. This is what is expected of education.

In order to achieve these objectives suitable curriculum has been formulated and introduced at different levels of the education system. At the primary stage children are exposed to three academic subjects and five activity subjects. The academic subjects comprise of Language, Mathematics and Environmental Studies (I-Social Studies and II-Science). The activity subjects consist of Health Education, Physical Education, Socially Useful Production Work, Creative Activities and Moral Education. From III level, English is introduced and from Class VI Hindi is also introduced as Second Language. Secondary education begins to expose students to appreciate roles of science, the humanities and social sciences.

Each subject in the curriculum has a specific objective. Language is a means of communication. Teaching of language should aim at developing the four skills of listening, speaking, reading and writing. Mathematics should be visualized as the vehicle to train a child to think, reason, analyze and to articulate logically. Science education need to develop in the child well defined abilities and values such as the spirit of inquiry, creativity, objectivity, the courage to question and an aesthetic sensibility. It should enable the learner to acquire problem solving and decision-making skills. In our culturally plural society, education should foster universal and eternal values, oriented towards the unity and integration of our people. The value education should help eliminate obscurantism, religious fanaticism, violence, superstition and fatalism.

The teacher who is the main dynamic force in the system of education needs to transact this curriculum by adopting appropriate strategy. Today there is a shift from Epistemic approach to Reconstructionist approach, from teacher centered and subject centered approach to that of child-centered approach. The present emphasis is on the adoption of child centered, activity oriented and competency based teaching-learning process. Student is the center of the education system. "The child is the starting point, the center and the end. His growth and his development is the ideal of education" felt John Dewey. His Excellency the President of India, Dr. A.P.J. Abdul Kalam, has stated "What is more important is that teachers should not transmit their frustration to their students, but should constantly try to upgrade their skills and encourage the children to think big." The child should be the focal point in the system of education. Here comes the role of academic monitoring.

What is Monitoring ? Monitoring is defined as a periodic review and surveillance by Management at every level of the implementation of an activity in order to ensure that the inputs, deliveries, work schedules, targeted outputs and other required actions are proceeding according to plan. It is a process of recording, collecting, processing, and disseminating information to assist project management decision-making. This is carried out to see: Whether various tasks are carried out according to schedule? Whether projects results are likely to lead to the realization of project objectives? Whether project objectives/ targets/execution need modification?

Thus monitoring is a managerial function that begins with the start of a project and ends with the completion of the project, but it is a continuous process during the implementation of project. It is an essential tool for successful implementation of project. During the process of monitoring the shortfalls, deviations, and problems and causes for the same are identified so as to take appropriate remedial and corrective action.

What is Academic ? Today in school system academics include both theoretical as well as non-theoretical aspects. It includes subjects not only for intellectual development but also other types of development. It includes curricular, co-curricular and extra-curricular activities. It is the sum total of all the educational experiences provided to the child by the school through instruction either within the four walls or outside the four walls.

What is Academic Monitoring ? Academic Monitoring is a periodic review of curricular, co-curricular and extra-curricular activities carried on in the school as scheduled/ planned. It is a continuous process of knowing to what extent the objectives are realized, whether the objectives/targets/execution need any or change. It involves measuring, recording, collecting, processing and communicating information to assist the management relating to the teaching-learning process. To bring about certain desirable changes in the behaviour of the child either at the thought level, perception level or psychomotor level is the ultimate objectives of the teaching process. To what extent these are achieved should be known and necessary steps should be taken either to change the strategy or the objectives to be realized. Whether there is any problem with regard to the teaching or problems with regard to learning are to be known and suitable measures are to be taken.

What is Academic Monitoring of Students ? Academic monitoring involves three important issues, viz. knowing, Identifying, and Assisting. Knowing involves-knowing whether the student is progressing in learning the academic as well as non-academic activities organized in the school, whether the expected learning outcomes are achieved or not, whether the desired behavioural changes have taken place in the child as a result of instruction? Identifying involves-identifying the strengths and weaknesses of the student, the deficiencies, the interests and attitudes etc., Assisting involves-suggesting steps to make good the deficiencies, implementing the programmes to make good the weaknesses, taking up remedial instructional programmes, taking up individual care and attention, arranging for special coaching etc.

Who is Responsible for Academic Monitoring of Students ? Since monitoring is a managerial function, all those who are involved in the project implementation should do monitoring. It is important to appreciate that monitoring is not an individuals' functions but it is a collective function. However to be more specific the responsibility needs to be taken by the following personnel. Teacher in the school situation, Prefect in the dormitory, Parent at home, Warden in the hostel and Supervisor/Administrator/Manager of the System.

How to Collect Information in Academic Monitoring? Through the following Programmes information for providing academic monitoring of students may be collected. Through the observation of classroom teaching-learning process-student participation in the process, interviews/putting questions, observing and checking the written work, class work and home work, attendance registers, performance in Unit Tests and Terminal Tests, assignments, pupils products, progress cards, cumulative record cards, pupils diaries, library work, laboratory work, project work, through peers, group work, through teachers, through parents, participation in debates, discussion, quiz, programmes, celebrations, participation in co-curricular activities, review meetings and analysis of answer scripts of unit tests and terminal tests, etc.

What are to be Identified ? After collecting the data for Academic Monitoring, the next step is identification of strengths, and weaknesses. Some students may be academically sound in some subjects and some others may not. In which areas they are sound and in which areas they are weak is to be identified. Identify outstanding performance and identify deficiencies-in academic subjects, in activity subjects and personality traits.

The current practice of academic planning for school education is largely a 'top down' annual exercise. Its focus is on how teaching time should be allocated for teaching of subject content over the year, and stipulating other activities that will be conducted in schools. This is done by SCERTs or the Directorates! Departments of Education, and prescribed uniformly for all schools in the State. The importance of school level planning was emphasized by the Kothari Commission when it underscored the need for each school to prepare an 'institutional plan' and evolve a 'development programme spread over a period of time.'

To be meaningful academic planning has to be done in a participative manner by heads and teachers. One component of planning will include augmentation and improvement of physical resources of the school. The second is to address the diverse needs of students and to identify the inputs and academic support that the school needs in order to response to these needs. The planning exercise is an important process through which schools can enlist the involvement and support of the larger community in the education of the children. This includes the village education committees and other statutory bodies. Micro planning, which includes village level mapping of school participation (non-enrolled children, attendance patterns, children with special needs, etc.) as well as identification of human resources allows the school to plan on a more realistic basis for every child.

The potential role of Headmasters in providing academic leadership to their schools is yet to be adequately realized. At present they are seen largely as the administrative authority within the school, though they lack the necessary control to exercise this authority, or even to ensure regular school functioning. Often they are equipped with neither the capacity for authority to exercise choice and judgement relating to school curriculum. Headmasters and teachers need to be able to identify specific supports they require for their schools, articulate their expectations regarding the content of trainings and school visits from the cluster and block personnel and participate in the process of monitoring and supervision. Currently they are not differentiated enough from teachers with regard to their academic roles. The role that the Headmasters can play within a cluster of schools must be highlighted.

Schools are now the focus of an increasing number of programmes to enhance quality, spread awareness about societal concerns relating to the environment, health and so on. Headmasters are often besieged by the numerous programmes they are called upon to conduct and participate. Programmes often lack clarity regarding their objectives and methodology and their activities tend to overlap. It is important that as part of the process of school level planning, they should be able to participate in decisions about programmes they need and how they should be integrated into regular school activities. These programmes could then be coordinated at the cluster and block level.

Conventionally, monitoring of schools has been through the Inspectorate system. This system has served largely to exercise authority and control rather than provide academic support to teachers. The School inspectors perform a number of functions, one of which one is to visit schools under their purview. Their visits are usually few and far between, during which the students and teachers tend to present positive picture of the school, regardless of ground realities, due to fear of punishment. This reduces monitoring to a 'policing' function. Monitoring for quality must be seen as a process that enables and provides constructive feedback in relation to the teaching and learning processes within specific classroom contexts. The monitoring system put in place must be carefully analysed in relation to its objectives, and the norms and practices that are to be institutionalized to achieve the objectives. It must provide for sustained interaction with individual schools in terms of teaching-learning processes within the classroom context.

How to Provide Assistance ? After identifying the strengths and weaknesses the next step is to provide assistance. The following are the ways through which assistance can be provided: suggest more and higher type assignments to gifted or outstanding students to progress further, give multilevel assignments based on individual differences, arrange for special coaching in time, arrange for remedial teaching, meeting the school officials/ parents/wardens, discussions with school education committees, examination of progress cards, organization of activities like debates, discussions, quiz programmes, working out the questions given in unit tests and terminals, regular laboratory and library work, adoption of primary education project pedagogy, correction of scripts before students, regular habit of studying, frequent testing, arranging extension lectures, timely supply of text books, writing materials, clothing, timely release of scholarships, supply of nutritious food, health checkups, frequent visits, organization of co-curricular activities more in number, updation of syllabus, conduct of pre-final examination and correction of answer scripts before the students, working out the question papers of the last three years public examination and questions from question banks, adoption of students by staff, working out the exercises given at the end of the lessons in the textbooks, by-hearting the materials given in the boxes in the textbook, drawing science figures, extra drill, map pointing in social sciences, organization of supervised study programme, organization of brains trust, training in letter writing and comprehension exercises and emphasizing on co-operative learning, etc.

What are the Hints for Administrators in Academic Monitoring of Students ? The following are the hints for Administrators: Maintain a register with names of students, their personal details and school details. Record their academic progress during personal visits. Interviews, discussions with teachers, progress cards, classroom visits, putting questions etc. Suggest measures for making good the deficiencies noticed based on the visits, putting questions etc. Follow up. Visit at lest once a month the school and hostel and observe the academic progress of the students. Have direct interaction with students. Go through the school inspection reports. Hold review meetings. Maintain contacts with parents. Attend the review meetings organized by Education Department on academic issues. Attend the Headmasters conference organized in the District either at the District level or Regional Level, etc.

REFERENCES

1. A Study on Problem of Tribal Children with Respect to Enrolment, Retention and Quality (A World Bank Sponsored), TCTRI, Hyderabad, June 1999, p. 3.
2. Action Plan ITDA, Vizianagaram District, Andhra Pradesh, p. 10.
3. Aggarawal, J.G., *Education Policy in India, Retrospect and Prospect,* Shipra Publications, New Delhi, 1992.
4. At the level of monitoring and supervision due emphasis is given in the tribal schools of Andhra

Pradesh. Special efforts were made for effective monitoring and academic supervision of schools at the local level by decentralizing the centers. Cluster Resource Centres have been responsible for this function. The Education Officers are being created by the Government, to discharge monitoring and supervisory responsibilities. At the Community level, Village Level Committees (VEC) are vested with power to look after the academic and monitoring of the tribal schools to improve the quality of teaching and regular presence of teachers. The concept of 'school complex' has come into existence as means to improve the quality of teaching and break the isolation of teachers. Supervision was improved at the institutional level by empowering the VECs and ensuring community participation and involvement in the educational development of the tribal areas. The VEC members have been given training in monitoring, supervision and administration of schools. See K. Sujatha, *Education among Tribals, Year 2000 Assessment, Education for AU,* National Institute of Educational Planning and Administration; Ministry of Human Resource Development, Government of India, pp. 17-18.

5. Biligiri S.H., "Problems of Tribal Languages in India" in Language and Society in India, indian Institute of Advanced Study, Simla, Vol. 8, 1969, pp. 245-250.
6. Curriculum for Tribal (Gond) Students (Classes I to V), Department of Teacher Education, Special Education And. Extension Services, New Delhi, 1994, pp. 2-3.
7. Dewey's philosophical views on educational aims, curriculum and pedagogy exercised an influence on the educational imagination of pedagogues and several national systems of education from the late nineteenth century and into the early half of the twentieth century. In his pedagogic creed, the teacher assumes the functions of an enquirer in order to set a model for the child. Dewey's yardstick for judging authentic or meaningful education is that it must provide experimental learning for each child by introducing real life problems in the classrooms. Dewey's educational ideal is the problem-solving, self-reliant, articulate individual. See Krishna Kumar and Padma M. Sarangapani, "History of the Quality Debate, in *Contemporary Education Dialogue", Vol. 2*:1, *Monsoon 2004,* P. 34. Also see, Dewey, J., Democracy and Education: The Middle Works of John Dewey, Vol. 19, Carbondale: South Illinois University Press, 1996.
8. District Primary Education Programme Annual Work Planning and Budget 1998-98 Vizianagaram District, Andhra Pradesh, p. 40.
9. *DPEP Calling,* Strategies for Tribal Education, District Primary Education Programme, April 1996, pp. 256 to 276.
10. Government of India, *National Policy on Education,* 1986, Ministry of Human Resource Development, Department of Education, New Delhi, August 1986.
11. Haimendorf CVF, The Gonds of Andhra Pradesh—Tradition and Change in an Indian Tribe, Vikas Publication, New Delhi, 1979, p. 18.
12. Hubley John, British Council Division, British High Commission-A Report, Our Children-Our Future, A Strategy Paper on School Health in India, 1995, p. 18.
13. Krishna Kumar wrote "The examination system is actually cheating the masses by concealing the deep divisions that exist within the education system, where a poor mill worker's child from a neglected government school is made to compete with children from well-to-do public schools. The system submerges these ugly realities under a veneer of total parity among candidates. But it hardly needs probing to find that a majority of failures belong to the disadvantaged." See Probe team, *Public Report* on *Basic Education in India,* Oxford University Press, New Delhi, 1999, p. 81. Also see Krishna Kumar, "Schooling in Rural India", The Hindu, January 11, 2005, p. 8.
14. Lalitha. V, The Making of Criminal Tribes—Patterns and Transition, New Era Publications, Madras, 1995, p. 5.
15. Mazda Jenkin, Jeff Jones, Sue Lord, *Monitoring and Evaluation for School Improvement,* Heinemann Educational Publishers, Oxford, 2000, p. 5.
16. Midatala Rani, Tribal Language and Tribal Education Social Action, Vol. 50, No. 4, October-December 2000, p. 414.

17. Mohan Rao. K, Tribal Profile of Andhra Pradesh, Tribal Culture Research and Training Institute, Hyderabad, 1969, p. 24.
18. NCERT, Tribal Education in India, Publication No. 20, Tribal Education Unit, Department of Adult Education, 1967, p.14.
19. See K. Sesidbara Rao, *"Academic Monitoring* of *Students in Tribal Areas"*, Paper presented at a training programme conducted at Regional Institute of Education, NCERT, Mysore, March 2004.
20. See Malli Gandhi, *Report on the Training Programme for TTI/DIET faculty* on *Monitoring* of *Learning Achievement, in Tribal Schools* of *Andhra Pradesh,* unpublished Report, submitted to NCERT, Regional Institute of Education, Mysore, March 2004.
21. See P. Venkata Rao, *"Monitoring* of *Community Participation Activities and School Education Committees"*, theme paper presented at a training programme conducted at Regional Institute of Education, NCERT, Mysore, March 2004.
22. See, *Draft National Curriculum Framework 2005,* National Council of Educational Research and Training, New Delhi, 2005, pp. 92-93.
23. *See,* K. Sesidhara Rao, *"Academic Monitoring* of *Students in Tribal Areas"* Paper presented at a Training Programme conducted at Regional Institute of Education, NCERT, Mysore, March 2004.
24. Selected Educational Statistics 1996-97, Commissioner and Director of School Education, Andhra Pradesh, Hyderabad, p. 5.
25. Seshadiri. C, "Education, Quality and Culture—An Analysis" Journal of Higher Education, Vol. 3 UGC, New Delhi, 1973, p. 71.
26. Sujatha K., "Education Among Scheduled Tribes" in R. Govinda; *A Profile* of *India Education Report,* Oxford University Press, New Delhi 2002.
27. The National Policy on Education 1986 (Programme of Action 1992) stated that: the monitoring of education in scheduled caste and scheduled tribe areas will be entrusted to the local community/Village Education Committee with adequate representation of SC/ST members especially women. The local community will take the total responsibility of planning the educational facilities in SC/ST areas. See Government of India, *The National Policy* on *Education,* 1986, *Programme of Action,* 1992, Government of India, Ministry of Human Resource Development, Department of Education, p.13.
28. The teacher, the child's window to learning and knowledge, has to play the, role model in generating creativity in the child. If parents and teachers show the required dedication to shape the lives of the young, India would get' a new, life. See A.P.J. Abdul Kalam, *Ignited Minds, unleashing the power within India,* Viking Penguin Book; India, 2002, pp. 25-26.
29. UNESCO, Multiple Class Teaching in Primary Schools: A Methodological Guide, APWID, UNESCO, Bangkok. 1988, p. 23.
30. Venkatarao. P., Personality Development of Tribal Children in Development of Culture Specific Co-Curricular Activities for Tribal Children in Residential Schools of Andhra Pradesh—A Paper Presented for the NCERT Project, Mysore, 2002, pp. 100-101.

3

Educational Scenario of Denotified Tribes in Andhra Pradesh

Introduction

Education of children of the DNT communities is a very important concern of our government. Although schools were provided in their colonies, attendance was made compulsory for the children of school-going age, the expenses on education were met by the governments, children were fed, yet desirable results have not been achieved in the standard of education. The educational problems concerning these DNT children should be tackled by the apex educational organisations as a part of their extension programmes. It is with this background that it has been decided to study the educational pattern available to these DNT children with a view to improving the achievement levels of DNT children in the present settlement schools. The main objective of the chapter is to study the academic/educational conditions of the children of the DNTs and to suggest the ways and means to improve their quality of education.

Profile of Education in Siddhapuram

For the education of the Waddar children, a school was established during the year 1915. Twenty-six boys and 26 girls were receiving instruction during the year 1916. Education was imparted in the 3Rs and no attempt had been made to give them industrial training. The attendance was fairly regular. The school was run by 2 masters and 1 mistress who were paid Rs. 15 and Rs. 12 and Rs. 10 respectively. Educational Department was inspecting the school now and then.

The average attendance during the year 1924 was 76. The boys were made to learn agricultural work in the fields during the season. Carpentry, weaving tapes, masonry and brick-making work were taught. The girls were taught sewing. They had the proficiency in making their own jackets. Taylor the then Labour Commissioner, said: "the children look well cared for and show satisfactory knowledge of their subjects." The settlement school was excellent in every way. Most of the boys used to read and write Telugu well. They were smart, clean and well drilled. The following Table shows the classwise distribution of children during the year 1927.

The scout troop of boys was started in 1923. The boy's scouts were prepared for the inspection of officers. The officers were pleased with their smart turnout. The educated Waddar settlers were sent to teachers' training at Kurnool and were later appointed as

Table–1
The Strength of Siddhapuram School, 1927

Standard	*Boys*	*Girls*	*Total*
Infant	8	7	15
1st Class	2	2	4
2nd Class	-	3	3
3rd Class	3	2	5
4th Class	5	-	5
5th Class	4	-	4

teachers in the school. The school worked for 252 days in a year. The school mistress, the wife of the compounder, took care of the girls in the lower classes. Elementary school boys were given practical lessons in agriculture on the government farm. The school was regularly inspected by the Deputy Inspector of Schools, the District Educational Officer and the Sub-Assistant Inspectors. Elderly boys were taught some agricultural theories in the class and then they were given manual work on the government farm. Some were sent to weaving. Some were trained as scouts. The best boys were presented with 8 goats as school prizes to promote interest in education.

The Headmaster was a secondary grade trained teacher. He possessed good teaching ability and organizing capacity. English was introduced as an additional subject in the IV and V standards during the year 1937, as suggested by the collectors. The Headmaster was the only person who was competent to handle that language. We can draw comparisons between Siddhapuram children to those students of advanced localities in the district. The Waddar children were brought under excellent discipline. They were trained to become self-reliant and useful members of society. The old boys of the school were encouraged to form into a drama troupe and enacted four street dramas. It served them as a diversion and moral instruction. *"The Animal Week"* was celebrated and the settlers were taught how to show sympathy towards their animals. Leaflets were read and explained to them. The supply of mid-day meals to the school children commenced in Siddhapuram from 13.3.1937.

Sometimes the settlement manager used the innocent Waddars in scandals. Since the manager was the incharge of the school, tuition work was given to the grown-up girls. Elderly girls in the school used to visit delinquent's houses for preparing lessons and learnt Banjara songs. Brutal assaults were made on school girls. It was very sad to know that, "In a school, especially of criminal settlers, a strict standard of discipline was absolutely essential and any chastisement by the Headmaster in the exercise and maintenance of such a discipline should not be criticized. Exercise of discipline must be measured with a different standard."

The school was developed into a first grade elementary school during the year 1938. Pupils who completed 5th standard joined in higher elementary school. The government sanctioned, to open the sixth standard in the school at Siddhapuram during 1947-48 and to convert one of the higher elementary grade teachers' post into a secondary grade post. The students who passed the sixth standard were sent to Velgode for further studies in the

Telugu lower secondary school. The settlers' girls who passed the sixth standard were sent for training in mid-wifery. The students of elementary school and secondary grade school were too slow to understand lessons due to lack of proper motivation. The children in each classes were more in number. This was not an easy task for a teacher to coach up more than a reasonable number. The parents of the children did not appreciate the value of education. They were constantly goaded to send the children to the school. The strength of the school during the year 1948-49 was as follows.

Table–2

The Strength of Siddhapuram School During the Year 1948-49

Standard	*Average Attendance Strength 1948-49*	
	Boys	*Girls*
1st Class	18	17
2nd Class	10	6
3rd Class	9	6
4th Class	10	2
5th Class	6	1
6th Class	4	11
Total	57	43

At present, the location and condition of the school at Siddhapuram is in a deplorable condition. A teacher with the secondary teacher training qualification (SGT) is running the school. It is not planned properly, since there is no syllabus or curricula prescribed for the school. The environment is not conducive for the children to study. There are only two graduates in the entire settlement and they too are still unemployed.

Profile of Education Stuartpuram

The SA thought that education was compulsory for the Yerukulas of this settlement and therefore, started an elementary school in 1916. Elementary education was made compulsory and those not attending the school were strictly punished. Out of 481 children in the settlement, 250 children were school going during the year 1916. 74 children attended the school regularly. The children in the school were very bright. The Governor of Madras was delighted with the school and took a photograph of the boys.

The school was run in a Palmyra shed of the size '60 x 20' which was leaky. In the elementary school, the children were taught three 'R's and general knowledge including rural science, gardening, nature study, English, physical training and the Bible. In the higher standards of the school, industrial education and moral training were introduced. Instruction in agriculture was made compulsory in school education. The school was a co-education school. There were 40 children in each section. Class books, maps, slates and slated pencils, pictures of animals and plants, a globe, Ananda Primer and Ananda Readers for Standards I, II and III, and garden implements for children were purchased by the manager. Night classes were conducted for adults. The teachers employed in the day school taught in the night schools also. The wives of the teachers evinced keen interest in girls' education. For this, the teachers were given extra salary of Rs. 8 to Headmaster and

Rs. 5 for assistant teachers. The subjects taught in the night school were reading, writing and Arithmetic. The strength and attendance of students in the elementary school on 29th October 1917 was as follows.

Table–3
Strength of Elementary School, Stuartpuram, 1917

Standards	*No. on Rolls*		*No. Present*		*Total*
	Boys	*Girls*	*Boys*	*Girls*	
Infants A	14	11	14	9	23
Infants B	22	14	13	11	24
Infants C	15	23	10	18	28
Infants D	30	34	25	27	52
1st Standard	8	3	6	2	8
2nd Standard	11	1	8	1	9
3rd Standard	7	3	7	3	10

The management of the school and the employment of teachers were left entirely to the SA. The government desired that the rules prevailing in the Educational Department should be adopted. An interesting feature of that time was that qualified teachers from the Yerukulas, both men and women, were appointed as teachers in the school. This was done with the intention of creating an atmosphere in the settlement primarily to promote the self-confidence of the whole tribe and, secondly to prove that those who were committed to do any work they were asked to do seriously. To strengthen this, periodical inspections were arranged by the educational officers of high mental caliber. The teachers were given better salaries and provided with free quarters in the settlement. *Ganji* (boiled rice water) was supplied at noon to the students who were present both in the morning and in the evening. The following Table describes the teachers in the school during the year 1918.

Table–4
Position of Teachers in Stuartpuram Elementary School

Name of the Teacher	*Qualifications*	*Scale of Pay*
K. Jacob	L.S.P.T.C. of 1915	25/-
Ch. Joseph	S.S.L.C. of 1915	20/-
Santhoshammal	L.S.P.T.C. of 1915	15/-
Soubhagyammal	L.S.P.T.C. of 1915	15/-
P. Simon	Unpassed	12/-
Lyssammal	Passed 4th Std.	12/-
B. Solomon	Unpassed	12/-

The newly established boarding school helped the settlers in withering away of the crime atmosphere. The boarding school was established for the sake of 1. orphan children, 2. children whose parents were in jail, 3. children of parents who were miserably poor, 4. children of parents just returned from jails, 5. children of parents from whom separation was made because of the bad character of parents or because of the suspected character of children and 6. children of absconding settlers.

The boarding school was very well managed and in a report the manager stated that the school was an asset to the settlement. In order to improve the sleeping conditions of the children of the settlers, the Commissioner of Labour constructed separate dormitories for boys and girls. Two matrons were appointed separately to take care of them. Another classification was the young children and the older ones. A separate building was arranged for recreation purpose.

The meeting of parents and children either at the school or at home added to the disturbance of the children's minds. It was felt that reformation was impossible in an atmosphere where the crime culture was not forgotten. The SA dissuaded the parents from meeting their children. But the influence of the parents on their separated children was very severe. The new generation was made up of honest people. The SA visualized the hours of work as to make use of timings in such a way that no time was left for them to visit their parents and hence no perpetuation of crime among the youth. Thus they segregated their children from their parents and arranged a boarding school in the settlement and permitted occasional visits of the parents.

The SA appointed peons for the reformation of the children of the ex-settlers. The peons for these schools were selected from the settlers themselves. Their duty was to go round and collect the children for the school. At the age of 5 years, the settlers' children were sent to schools. In the elementary school, instruction was given upto 5th standards. The Headmaster was with a certificate of higher grade training.

There was an increase in the number of children attending the school every year. During the year 1924 there were nearly 401 children on rolls and the average attendance was 261. Furthermore, the outside influences were felt by the children. The SA authorities considered that the solution to the problem was in sending girls to Nellore and boys to Perambur (Near Madras city). It would help them in reformatory process. Mackenzie, the SA official wanted to change the structure of the building to create a new atmosphere in the settlement. The availability of buildings at Nellore was a positive factor and this was congenial to the growth of children. The SA suddenly closed the boarding school in Stuartpuram and shifted some of the girls to Nellore girls' school. But the closing down of the Stuartpuram Boarding School (1926) had a severe blow on the settler's children.

A significant feature of the settlement school was that, the manager L.R.Gale, gave a Christian bias to the whole atmosphere of the school. When the first children batches of Yerukulas were brought into this settlement, school boys and girls were dirty looking and they involved in petty thefts and road robberies. It was not an easy task to teach CTs to be on the path of righteousness'. But much had been done towards this good end. The younger generation understood and responded well. The SA constructed a church in the year 1915, ostensibly to reform the Yerukulas by giving Bible education and thereby making them disciplined. All the settlers were gathered and brought into the church.

S.H. Slater, the Labour Commissioner, bestowed attention on the school children. Some students got through the SSLC (Secondary School Leaving Certificate) examination. Those who failed were also given utmost care. They were admitted either in Paddison hostel or in the Industrial School, Perambur, Madras. Some of the boys who passed through the five standards in the settlement school were admitted in the 4th and 6th forms of the high school at Bapatla. Dowson, the then Deputy Inspector General of Police, Madras, inspected the settlement school on 8.7.1931 and wrote "I knew this settlement in its earliest infancy. My visit today was peculiarly interesting. My first visit was in 1914. Today i.e. 8.7.1931, it is possible to see that the settlement has completely filled the purpose for which it was instituted." After inspecting the school, he said: "The kiddies looked fat and happy. Neither the manager nor the police had any controversies. The settlement is in a most flourishing condition."

The SA opened a new girls' school for the development of women's education. During the year 1921, there were nearly 100 girls in it. During the year 1926, few girls were transferred to Nellore Industrial School. Owing to the closure of the girls' reformatory school at Nellore, a number of girls were sent back to their parents. There were no classes above 5th standard. The girls who studied at Nellore in the higher classes were again sent to the higher elementary boarding school at Kavali. Nursing and sewing training were given to the girls. The manager of Stuartpuram settlement selected some women who were familiar with three 'R's and talented with the art of conversation and possessed with the ability to describe, explain them completely to have an idea of such topics. In addition to that, they were also trained in the proper maintenance of the house or the working place by sweeping, dusting and cooking. For extracting talent from them, they were encouraged. For example, on 10th March 1928 a modal was done by a girl for essay writing on 'Home Sanitation' during *Health Week Competition*.

The settlers had a brigade of scouts since 1923. Although the members were constantly changing owing to employment and other circumstances they had a creditable brigade. A small bugle band had been formed and equipment supplied. The Assistant Manager had taken a keen interest in the movement and himself went into camp with the scouts. The scouting activities in the schools were conducted by the school teachers who were trained as scout masters. All the adult-reformed settlers were expected to give importance to morality. Polygamy was prevalent and the traces of polyandry were rare among them. The SA thought that religious and moral instruction were the greatest factors for their improvement. They used to instruct the women folk of the settlement to take stern steps to control their crimes. But it happened to the contrary that even the wives were also involved in the culture of crime.

The supply of mid-day meals was started at Stuartpuram for the first time only from December 1947. Other settlements' school children were also supplied with mid-day meals at the government cost of Rs. 3. The introduction of mid-day meals to the school children was to encourage the children to attend the school regularly and make them fit to receive instruction. The school children were taken to excursions. The Government Authorities, the DIG of Police, CID and railways sanctioned the expenditure not exceeding Rs. 50 per year.

It is striking to note that among the Yerukula community of Stuartpuram already some secured good employment both in Central and State Governments. At present, more than 150 members even received University Education. This is obviously to some extent due to the efforts of the SA and the awareness among the youth. Separate hostels are also being maintained by the SA for these children. Consequently, there are nearly 155 students in these hostels today. In the hostels there are 101 boys and 54 girls studying in Class I to the S.S.C. (10th Class). It is providing scholarships, food, hostel facilities and clothes to the students. The SA had requested the Secretary, Government of Madras, to sanction a general library for children outside the premises of the school and it was conceded.

In the year 1958, the SA combined with the Inspector General of Police, opened a new high school for the children of the settlers. The school comprised of mainly Yerukula children and some converted Christians together with the children of upper castes. Later, it was converted into a middle school from the academic year 1958-59. It was run by the Social Welfare Department. The high school followed the syllabus prescribed by the Board of Secondary Education, Andhra Pradesh, Hyderabad. The strength of the high school as per the annual record of the year 2006 is 277. The division of boys and girls from Class VI to X was as follows.

Table–5
Strength of High School in Stuartpuram, 2005

Class	*Boys*	*Girls*	*Total*
VI	34	26	60
VII	29	18	47
VIII	26	17	43
IX	34	28	62
X	41	24	65
Total	164	113	277

After the repeal of the CTA Act in 1952, it was contemplated that all State Governments should undertake welfare schemes especially education. In the second Five Year Plan, funds were sanctioned by the government for the education of these tribal children. During the 3rd Five Year Plan, a plan provision of Rs. 375.00 lakhs was made for the purpose. An estimated expenditure of Rs. 55.36 lakhs was incurred during 1962-63. In the fifth Five Year Plan no separate provision has been made under centrally sponsored programmes for undertaking educational and other schemes for DNT communities.

Various societies such as Bharatiya Adimjati Sevak Sangh (New Delhi), Andhra Rastra Adimjati Sevak Sangh and Andhra Rashtra Yerukula Maha Sangam came forward to reform these people. The main aims and objectives of Andhra Rashtra Adimjati Sevak Sangh were 1. Education, 2. Literature, 3. Liberation, 4. Sadachar work, etc. Yerukulas, Yanadis and Banjaras were included in the list of Scheduled Tribes by the Parliament in 1956 owing to the efforts of the B.N. Datar, the then Minister of Home Affairs. The first school for Scheduled Tribes was started by the Sangh in 1934. The first Harijan Hostel was started in 1929. The first tribal hostel was started in 1939. Female education among tribals was taken up by the Sangh. Various types of books, magazines and articles were published in Telugu and English. The best examples are Kallumunta, Rama Rajyam, Yekalavya which are ballads. *Adivasi, Dalit Marg, Girijana Jyoti, Yekalavya Patrika and Harijanoddharana* were other important newspapers published by Andhra Rashtra Adimjati Sevak Sangh.

In addition to the SA and various social organizations, social workers namely Gora, Lavanam, Hemalatha Lavanam of Atheist centre Vijayawada and M.V. Thomas, the former Superintendent of Police, T. Gopala Rao, the former Collector of Guntur district, endeavoured hard to reform these people, through education. During the year 1983, DNT students who secured highest marks in public examinations in VII and X standards in the school at Stuartpuram were awarded prizes by Lavanam and Hemalatha Lavanam.

The welfare measures initiated for Yerukulas, Waddars, Yanadis and Sugalis bear a resemblance to the efforts to squeezing oil from sand. The development of scheduled tribes is a real challenge to the present government. The utterances of the government on the welfare measures are making much noise emanating from empty vessels. Policy formulation and its execution, most often, fall apart. Tribal children are required to pay special fee at the time of admission, though they are exempted from other fees. Poor tribal students are not in a position even to pay this. Added to this, tribal welfare scholarships are generally delayed and released at the end of the year. As a result, students are bound to face many problems. There is a lot of injustice being done to tribal children.

In the sphere of employment too, tribal children are facing serious problems. Though the public advertisements earmark a number of vacancies to these people, they appear so with a clause saying that the posts would be convertible to other castes in the absence of the eligible tribal candidates. In such a situation, the very policy of reservation loses its meaning and validity. It is suggested that the government takes appropriate measures to overcome these problems. The elected representatives from the tribal region should educate the government about these fundamental hardships of tribal children.

It is evident that in the quagmire of poverty, they prefer immediate gains to long term benefits that accrue to their children after a continuous schooling of ten to fifteen years. They are under the false impression that the schooling eats away their economic fruits. Therefore, need-based or job-oriented education is an effective alternative to the existing monotonous and unproductive education. In the interviews, we found from the settlers that their children could not reach higher echelons of society because of the psychological barriers they suffer from. For this, revamping the present school set up, on ashram or gurukula type, would make a considerable difference. Trained teachers and well-equipped schools would be a significant factor in moulding the personalities of children in these colonies. This is what we have observed in Siddhapuram settlement. There is no proper schooling for the children. Hence no advancement is found in that settlement.

There should be a major drive to eradicate illiteracy among these people. It goes without saying that any positive change in their attitude towards earning their livelihood, necessarily drives them towards a positive realization of the important aspect like education. The aim of social education can best be achieved only when feelings of deprivation, discrimination and aloofness are erased from their minds. A dynamic group of young volunteers and social workers will have to shoulder the responsibility of disseminating enlightened ideas among these people.

Today, there is a strong objection raised regarding the pathetic conditions of education and educational institutions prevailing in the settlement schools. The status of Andhra Pradesh in respect of these tribes stands in unique contrast to the rest of the country. There are social and behavioural changes taking place among the members of the denotified tribal settlement areas in Andhra Pradesh. The denotified tribal settlements such as Stuartpuram, Seethanagaram (Guntur district), Kaparallatippa and Bitragunta (Nellore district), Siddhapuram (Kurnool district) and Lingala (Mahabubnagar district) settlements constitute a major segment of the total schedule tribe population in Andhra Pradesh. In all these settlement areas Yerukulas, Waddars, Katheras, Chenchus, Sugalis, Yanadis and other nomadic tribes form a major part of population. Some of the settlers are still having some serious problems of crime and illiteracy. On the whole, the scenario in Andhra Pradesh offers contrast on any comparison.

One of the main problems identified by the field experiences and the field survey is about the social treatment meted out to the families of these tribes. For generations together, the families and their members have been labelled as criminals suffered dishonour and social negligence. The reasons are not far to seek given the background of the socially despicable avocation as practiced by some of the people belonging to these tribes. The children and women, in particular, have suffered ignominy from mainstream society. The stigma of criminality is still one of the major impediments in the smooth run of educational progress of children and youth. Children often faced a kind of social alienation in most of the walks of social life. Social alienation particularly in young age hampers the growth of psycho-social faculties of the children. Social practices of the mainstream society have denied opportunities for the children coming from the so-called criminal families residing in the settlement areas. The approaches of the government often times remain impersonal and lack human element and eye on social cohesiveness, in its approach. However, there can be education without even the formal modes and methods of schooling. But mere efforts on mainstream socialization do not open wide social canvas for the children because there is already a hostile attitude in the outside society. The school or the process of schooling in settlement areas or settlement schools may be used as instruments or tools to impart social culture, feelings of common fraternity, community approach, adjustment mentality, atmosphere of working and learning together and finally moral dynamics of social and cultural behaviour. The schools in settlement areas are to be treated or perceived from a different angle where they are expected to combine the role of an instructor, and change agent.

Profiles of Schools (Pen Pictures of Primary Schools) in Settlements

The following is the situational analysis of Primary School facilities and educational needs of DNT settlement schools of Andhra Pradesh:

Salvation Army Aided Primary School, Stuartpuram, Guntur District

This school was established by a missionary group viz. Salvation Army and later the Government of Andhra Pradesh provided aid and presently it is functioning as an aided primary school. It is a two teacher school. Both the teachers are not residing in the same school village but are residing in places upto a distance of 4 to 5 kilometres. The following are the details of roll of the school at present.

Table–6

Strength of Salvation Army Aided Primary School, Stuartpuram

	Boys	*Girls*	*Total*
I Class	10	10	20
II Class	10	05	15
III Class	11	06	16
IV Class	07	10	17
V Class	16	08	24
Total	54	39	93

The strength in each class is low, ranging from 15 to 24. On the whole, the number of male students is more than the number of female students except in Class IV. Multigrade teaching is going on in the school and the head teacher is taking Classes I to III and the assistant, teacher is taking Classes IV and V. Instead of subject teacher system, class teacher system is adopted. Children are provided free textbooks and mid-day meals. No other incentives are enjoyed by the pupils. Except for teachers, there is no furniture for students. The school and classrooms do not possess the minimum equipment. Teacher grant and school grants are provided and from the school grant a radio was purchased and the students are exposed to the radio lessons. Daily school assembly is organized and news is read. The children need to be exposed to moral education stories, wise sayings, etc. Further there is need to organize activities which develop honesty among the children. The school is situated in a place having railway line on one side and road on the other side. It is not accessible to children in the sense that parents are afraid of sending their children to school for fear of accidents. The school is being run in a tiled building having 5 rooms. Only two rooms are under use and the other three are vacant and used only for using the school furniture. The roof is leaky and needs immediate repairs. Neither the aided management, nor the government which is providing aid is looking after the repairs of the building. Because of craze towards English medium education, many parents are sending their children to nearby towns wherein conveyance facility by school bus or auto or riksha are available. There is no compound wall to the school and no garden and no demarked playground. Only open space is used as playground. Socially Useful Productive Work (SUPW) activities are also not given the required attention in the school.

Table–7

The Population Details of the Settlement (Colony)

Population	661	688	1349
School age	139	143	282
Enrolled	54	39	93
Remaining	85	104	189

Some well to do family children are studying elsewhere and very few children whose parents are very poor, are left out and they are to be enrolled. Limited play material is available with schools like skipping ropes, rings, etc. Last year (2005-06) about 20 students who have completed Class V were admitted into Class VI in the High School situated in the same village. Some of the problems faced by the teachers are as follows: *(i)* Repairs to school building, *(ii)* Lack of equipment like furniture to students, aids, etc., *(iii)* Lack of learning aids and play materials, *(iv)* Lack of sanitation facilities and compound wall, *(v)* Absence of students for long because of their parental harassment by police. The students are psychologically depressed by this and are not able to concentrate in their studies and attend the school, *(vi)* Lack of facilities for organization of SUPW activities, *(vii)* The social stigma is attached on the part of the community. Because of this, the educated children are neither employed nor able to have self support. Due to this, there is danger of reverting to the old practice of thefts and robberies. and *(viii)* Early child care education centre, (ECE) is not in the school campus. etc.

In view of the present conditions of education prevailing in the colony the following are some of the suggestions that can be made to improve condition of the school: *(i)* to provide for close supervision facilities by the Department of Education/Tribal Welfare to the teachers. *(ii)* to provide facilities for the organization of SUPW activities. *(iii)* to organize such activities which develop honesty among the students. *(iv)* arrange extension lecture by local educated youth and others who are employed. *(v)* In the broader interest of the village the solution lies with the voluntary organizations of the specific programmes. *(vi)* Formation of co-operatives for providing self support to the settlers (villagers) such as milk cows, mushroom growth, autos, piggery, cashew plantation growth, etc. *(vii)* establishment of industries by inviting the interested industrialists which provide employment opportunities to the settlers in the settlement itself, *(viii)* some of the NGOs (Samskar) should think of these programmes in the interest of the settlers, *(ix)* convert these settlement schools as Ashram schools and introduce vocational courses, *(x)* provide incentive facilities more in number like uniforms, writing materials, etc. and finally. *(xi)* lack of safety to girl students. Therefore, security measures should be adopted for the welfare of the girl children also.

Government Denotified Tribal Elementary School, Siddhapuram, Kurnool District

This school was established by the British Government during the year 1913 for the benefit of the DNT children and the following is the present strength of the school during the year 2006.

Table–8
Strength of the School in Siddhapuram

Class	*Boys*	*Girls*	*Total*
I	13	18	31
II	18	23	41
III	17	12	29
IV	16	06	22
V	10	10	20
Total	74	69	143

In lower classes, the strength of girls is more than that of the boys. The school age population (children 5–11 age group) of the village is 168. Yet 25 pupils are to be enrolled in the school during the year 2006. The population of the village is 571 males and 564 females with the total of 1135. The literacy rate of the village is 34 per cent. This is a four teacher school. Class teacher system is followed in the school in place of subject teacher system. Only one teacher is incharge of multiple class teaching; he is handling Classes III and IV. None of the teachers are residing in the school village. All are residing outside school village. Some are residing at a distance of 10 kms and some at a distance of 5 kms. The school is being run in three buildings (two RCC buildings and one tiled old building). The tiled old building needs immediate repairs wherein Class I is located. The two RCC buildings have a verandah and one room each in which two classes each are located. There is no furniture to pupils and it is available only to teachers. Playground is available to the school. No equipment is available to the school. Teacher grant and school grant are provided to the school. It is reported that the major occupation of the villagers is illegal preparation of arrack. Even the students are involved in the preparation and transportation of the same. The dire need of the village is to have an upper primary school. The girls are afraid of going to nearby upper primary schools because of eve teasing and lack of social security. The village needs area specific programmes. Some of the areas in which some industries can be established are sericulture, match stick industry, weaving gauge clothes, honey collection and preservation, beedi leaf collection, Bamboo work, etc. Some NGOs can come forward and help the local villagers in their development and self-support. S.U.P.W. scheme needs special care and attention in the school to train students to support themselves in life.

Bitragunta Salvation Army Government Upper Primary School, Kapparallathippa, Bogole Mandal, Nellore District

This is an upper primary school with seven classes as follows: The strength of the School during the year 2006 is

Table–9
Strength of the School

Class	*Boys*	*Girls*	*Total*
I	22	27	49
II	16	16	32
III	08	13	21
IV	03	11	14
V	09	17	26
VI	04	12	16
VII	08	09	17
Total	70	105	175

The population of the village is 640 men 660 women with a population 1300 people. There are about 10 children yet to be enrolled in the school. None of the teaching staff are residing in the school village. The HM and other teachers are coming from a distance of 20 km and others are residing at a distance of about 2 kms. The HM is incharge of Classes VI and VII and the others are teaching one class each. Class teacher system is in vogue in the school. The school is being run in three buildings a tiled one, an asbestos roofed one and an RCC building. All the three buildings need repairs. Upto 5th class furniture is available for students. The school needs equipment and aids. Teacher grants and school grants are also received for the school. The following are the problems of the school. Lack of equipment and A.V. Aids, Upgradation as High School, Girls afraid of eve-teasing, and social security is needed to girls in the colony.

Government Upper Primary School, Sitanagaram Colony, Tadepalli Mandal, Guntur District

The school was established by the erstwhile British Government during the year 1916. The Government of Andhra Pradesh provided the aid under Social Tribal Welfare Department. Presently the school is managed by Tribal Welfare Department, Government of Andhra Pradesh. The school has the strength of 9 teachers viz. two B.Ed. qualified teachers, five secondary grade teachers and two pandits. The following is the details of the enrolment of DNT children of the Colony during the year 2006.

Table–10
Strength of School Children

Class	*Boys*	*Girls*	*Total*
I	1	2	3
II	1	1	2
III	2	1	3
IV	2	2	4
V	1	3	4
VI	1	1	2
VII	0	0	0

Subject teacher system, class teacher system is going on. Children from other communities viz. such as Christians, Muslims and Hindu caste groups are undergoing instruction simultaneously with the DNT group children. The DNT (Tribal) children are not provided free textbooks, uniforms, notebooks, scholarships, mid-day meals, etc. Other incentives are also not provided by the Government to the school so far. The children are squatting on the floor. Furniture is not available to the students. The school building is collapsed and damaged very badly. The school does not possess the minimum equipment and aids. The settlement population are scattered in 3 areas-that is: Tadepalli 1st Ward, Tadepalli 2nd ward and Annapurna Devi Nagar. The well-to-do family settlers' children are sending their children to the nearby English medium schools. Some elderly girls who dropped out of the school were provided tailoring work in the school. The Headmaster is handling maths and science subjects for all classes. TLM grant though provided, still the grant is not utilized by the Headmaster.

Conclusion

The social conditions, living standards, income and educational level of the tribal people living in these settlements are much below than the conditions of non-tribal people living in Andhra Pradesh. This fact remains as a grim reminder to the more privileged people in spite of the efforts and huge amount of money allocated and spent by the government.

Over the years in spite of the efforts put in by missionary and Non-Governmental Organisations such as Salvation Army, American Baptist Telugu Mission, Canadian Mission and other Christian missionary groups and also several voluntary organisations/NGOs, etc.

Lack of census data, absence of Policy-level discussions on DNTs, treatment of DNT issues seems outside the purview of Planning Commission estimates (always Primitive Tribal Groups (PTG) other than DNTs are covered), weak community participation in the settlements or colonies and lack of need-based training (contextual) given to teachers teaching in settlement schools, are some of the gaps identified during the visit of the settlements which are seriously affecting the progress of the DNTs in their colonies.

A complete and comprehensive survey conducted in the five settlements hints at the establishment of separate schools with English as the medium of instruction. Many of the reformed parents in the selected settlements wish to send their wards to schools at a different places. For, they perceive English medium of instruction as one important tool of mainstream social integration. The NGOs working in the settlements look for a time bound tie-up between RIE/NCERT and wish to ground a separate school with an eye on social integration. NGOs also expressed their wish to shoulder the responsibility of land procurement, construction, recruitment, school infrastructure and admissions of students from settlements (also from non-settlement areas of the surrounding settlements). The NGOs are also looking at RIE/NCERT or similar apex educational bodies for help in training the teachers. The NGOs should be in a position to shoulder complete responsibility of the education of the DNT children. The future tie-up will be confined to teacher training and teaching aid support from RIE/NCERT or similar institution. A comprehensive census data collection may be undertaken in all the existing settlement areas by the NCERT as a part of educational survey reports, PAC/ERIC programmes. To undertake advocacy campaign and networking meets with Government Departments and NCERT so that issues and problems of these tribes in transition will be put on the agenda of general discussion on tribal welfare.

In view of the above analysis, few suggestions can be made to improve the educational scenario of the denotified tribes of Andhra Pradesh.

1. The government has to conduct sample surveys to know about their present position pertaining to the present state of literacy achievement levels of the DNT children in primary schools.
2. They should be provided with jobs which give them immediate remuneration and relief. Some of them who are minimum educated, may be recruited into the departments of police as constables, water boys and sweepers.
3. Educational facilities as they exist today are not adequate. A few more schools may be established and all these schools should be provided with necessary infrastructural facilities.
4. Rigid enforcement of the provisions of the compulsory primary education Act is highly essential. The Government should issue strict orders to the various school boards to enforce primary education in schools situated in areas where the members of DNTs are residing in considerable number.

5. Free coaching centers should be opened in these colonies for educated unemployed youth. Coaching facilities should be provided for the students of both technical and general courses.
6. Best sports persons are available among these denotified tribe children. Physical education should be improved and special training facilities should be provided to make them national and state level players etc.

REFERENCES

1. The teachers were supplied clothing, rations and all sorts of contingency grants. A special pay, unhealthy locality allowance of Rs. 5 per month was sanctioned to the assistant teachers in Siddhapuram elementary school. The higher elementary grade teachers were placed in the scale of Rs. 27-1-1-50 from 1.4.1932. Rs. 10 were paid as unhealthy locality allowance from 1.4.1932. See Public Works (Labour) Department, GO No.1675 dated 9.8.1932, pp.1-2, APSA.
2. Of the 76 children at the settlement 23 boys and 17 girls attended the school. The average attendance was 19 for the whole year 1924. See Note Showing The Progress Made in the Settlements of Criminal Tribes in the Madras Presidency upto January 1926, Madras, 1927, p. 30, AP State Gazetteers Office, Hyderabad.
3. Public Works (Labour) Department, GO No.137 dated 19.1.1927, p. 5, APSA. The children are kept away from their parents. The younger children are sent home at night. Others sleep in the school building. Also See Public Works (Labour) Department, GO No.1719, dated 9.8.1927, p. 2, APSA.

The Strength of the School During the Year 1930

Standard	*Boys*	*Girls*	*Total*
I	24	26	50
II	2	1	3
III	2	2	4
IV	3	-	3
V	5	-	5
Total	36	29	65

4. Home Department, GO No. 3557 dated 6.9.1937, pp.1-3, National Archives of India (NAI).
5. Public Works (Labour) Department, GO No. 2190 dated 28.7.1930, pp. 7-13, (APSA).
6. Public Works (Labour) Department, GO No. 2671 dated 6.12.1934, p. 5, Andhra Pradesh State Archives.
7. Home Department, GO No. 6170 dated 22.12.1938, p. 36, NAI.
8. Public Works (Labour) Department, GO No. 2671 dated 6.12.1934, p. 6, Andhra Pradesh state Archives.
9. Home Department, GO No. 6170 dated 22.12.1938, p. 3, NAI.
10. Home Department, GO No.149, dated 11.1.1947, pp. 1-2, NAI.
11. The strength of the school was improved after the internment of Golla Kuppam Dasarees. After passing Vth Standard, the children were sent to Kurnool for studies. See Administration Report on Kallar Reclamation, Korava Reclamation, Criminal Tribes Settlements and Yanadi Reclamation for the year 1947-48, Madras, 1949, p.13.
12. Home (Judicial) Department, GO No. 2074, 18th August 1916, p. 4, Tamil Nadu state Archives.
13. Home (Judicial) Department, GO No.1225, 20th May 1918, p. 6, TNA.
14. See, Mildred Mackenzie, The Mud Bank, Peensylvania, 1959, p.12.

15. Law (General) Department (Annual Report), GO No.3187, 14th November 1924, p. 3, APSA.
16. The two unpassed teachers were sent up for the sessional school. See Home (Judicial) Department, GO No.1225 dated 20th May 1918, p. 6.
17. Law (General) Department, GO No. 1714, 22nd October 1921, p. 4, APSA.
18. Settlers criticized that it was cruel to separate the children from their parents. The SA made the parents to understand that the separation was done to enable them to get in future an honest employment. The parents put forward no objections. However, we can note that both Mabe and Robilliard were strongly opposed to the separation of children from their parents. They did not object for the boarding schools in the settlement where the parents were allowed to see the children under supervision. See Home (Judicial) Department, GO No.1759, 5th August 1918, p.1, TNA.
19. Law (General) Department, GO No.2267, 16th June 1925, p. 2, APSA.
20. PWLD, GO No.2338, dt.19th August 1930, p. 2, APSA.
21. Law (General) Department, GO No.3187, 14th November 1924, p. 3, APSA.
22. Law (General) Department, GO No.1907, 15th June 1925, p. 1, APSA.
23. Law (General) Department, GO No. 2267, 16th July 1925, p. 2, APSA.
24. PWLD GO No. 1551, 20th July 1927, p. 6, APSA.
25. PWLD GO No. 2061, dated 21.8.1928, p. 1, APSA.
26. PWLD GO No. 1926, dated 30.7.1931, p. 2, APSA
27. PWLD GO No. 1313 dated 17.6.1932, p. 7, APSA.
28. Booth Tucker said that, "If a man wished to marry one of the girls in the settlement he had to come into the settlement and live there". Gillman pointed out that the proposed husband would in the majority of cases, be already a member of the tribe. See Home (Judicial) Department,GO No.1759, 5th August 1918, pp. 13–17, APSA.
29. Home (Judicial) Department, GO No. 1639, 8th August 1917, p. 2, TNA.
30. The Scouts went to the camp during the year 1931 for 5 days and enjoyed the outing. See PWLD GO No.1313, 17th June 1932, p.6, APSA.
31. Home Department, GO No. 1571, 21st April 1947, p. 1, NAI.
32. Home Department, GO No. 1508, 21st March 1938, p. 1, NAI.
33. Home Department, GO No. 1571, 21st April 1947, p. 1, NAI.
34. Home Department, GO No. 1571, 21st April 1946, p. 1; NAI.
35. Interview with the Headmistress, Stuartpuram High School dated 6.2.2006.
36. Interview with The Manager of Stuartpuram Settlement, Stuartpuram dated 2.2.2006.
37. Report of the Commissioner for Scheduled Castes and Scheduled Tribes for the year 1962-1974.
38. L.M. Sreekant Report of the Commissioner for Scheduled Castes and Scheduled Tribes for the year 1953, 3rd Report, New Delhi, 1954, p.200.
39. L.M. Sreekant, Report of the Commissioner for Scheduled castes and Scheduled Tribes for the year 1954, 4th Report, New Delhi, 26th February 1955, p. 232.
40. Adivasi, Issue No. 9 and 10 dated 15.12.1962 and 15.1.1963, p. 1.
41. Adivasi (Telugu monthly) Published by R. Nagaiah, Vol. 10, Nos. 9 and 10, Guntur dated 15.12.1962 and dated 15.1.19063, p. 1.
42. Kallumunta is a ballad. The authors of the work are Ponna Koteswara Rao and Ponna Satyanarayana. It was published in 1950. Rama Rajyam is another ballad on Yerukulas by Ponna Koteswara Rao. It was published by Jayanti Publications, Vijayawada during the year 1960. These two sources, through valuable, are out of print today. The two important sources give detailed information of the culture of Yerukulas, how they perform their marriages. They also provide information on the general conditions in the settlements. Adivasi Patrika is a Telugu monthly published by Rameswaram Nagaiah from Guntur in 1943. Each issue was priced at 1 anna and the annual subscription rate was Rs. 1. Yerukula Patrika was published by Kampa Punnaiah during the year 1943. Dalit Marg was another monthly by Ponna Koteswara Rao. Some other papers of the same kind were Girijana Jyoti and Yekalavya. Out of financial crisis, these publications were stopped from 1980 onwards.

4

Tribal Education in India: A Human Rights Perspective

Introduction

Human Rights are generally defined as the right which every human being is entitled to enjoy and to have protected. The struggle for the recognition of Human Rights and the struggle against political, economic, social and cultural oppression against injustice and inequality have been an integral part of the history of all human societies. Education is one of the crucial factor responsible for individual and social development. Article 26 of the Universal Declaration of Human Rights emphasises the right to education. In imparting sound education language as a medium and subject of education has a crucial role to play. India is a multilingual and multiplural country. Linguistic diversity is an integral part of our nation building activity. This poses a big challenge to our policy planners. The socio-economic development intervention has been a major task before the framers of the Constitution, National Planners and State Administrators in the post-independent period. The framers of the Constitution have assured the protection of linguistic, cultural and educational rights to the individuals and groups by providing and incorporating various constitutional safeguards. This chapter discusses tribal education from a Human Rights perspective.

Tribes and Tribal Languages

The Census of India (2001) shows that the Scheduled Tribes (STs) with a population of 84.3 million constitute 8.2 per cent of the total population (1028.6 million) of India. The Scheduled Castes (SCs) constitute 16.23 per cent of the population. The Anthropological Survey of India (ASI) in its People of India Project (Singh, 2002) listed 623 tribal communities out of which about 573 are notified as Scheduled. The People of India Project shows that the tribal groups speak 218 languages out of which 159 are exclusive to them. Most of the tribal groups are bilingual or multilingual at the community levels. According to People of India out of 623 tribal communities 500 are bilingual ones.

Even though education in India is multilingual many tribal languages are struggling to create a space for themselves in the field of education. The Sixth All India Educational Survey of National Council of Educational Research and Training (NCERT) shows that out of 41 languages used in schools (as medium of instruction and subjects) only 13 are tribal languages. Out of these 13 tribal languages in schools only 3 to 4 are used regularly as medium of instruction (Jingran, 2005). The rest are languages taught as school subjects or used as Mother Tongue in some special programmes not on a regular basis.

An analysis of the use of languages both as medium of instruction and as school subjects in Indian education shows that a large number of tribal languages are weakened and endangered by their exclusion in school education. The tribal communities which should have been served with more attention have become victims of deprivation and Human Rights violation.

The desirability of having early education through one's own mother tongue is a universally accepted dictum specially so when it applies to tribal children. The UNESCO Position Paper entitled, "Education in a Multilingual World" (2002) highlights that educationalists all over the World agree that the medium of instruction atleast in the initial stages should be the mother tongue of the learners. The UNESCO Asia Level Conference on Language Development, Language Revitalisation and Multilingual Education (2003) endorsed this view. Closer home, the content and process of the National Educational Policy, 1986 has an important bearing on education in Human Rights. The Focus Group Report on the teaching of Indian Languages (2005) by NCERT as part of the National Curriculum Framework reiterates that the initial teaching in tribal schools should be in tribal language.

Language and the Indian Constitution

Indian Constitution is based on four important ideals that is justice, liberty, equality and fraternity. As per 42nd Amendment Act the country is a Sovereign, Socialist, Secular, Democratic Republic. There are several important provisions relating to the protection of language. Article 29(1) of the Constitution states that citizens residing in any part of the country but having their own language, script and culture will have the right to maintain them. According to Article 30(1) all minorities based on religion or language will have the right to setup and administer institutions in their own interest. Article 350 states that every individual has the right to give representation to an officer in the State or the Centre in any of the languages used in the Union or in the State. Article 350(A) advises that education be imparted in the mother tongue, stating that it will be the endeavour of every State and every Local Official within the State, to provide suitable facilities for providing education to the children of linguistic minorities in their mother tongue at the primary stage.

Despite the above assurances, linguistic discrimination is rooted in the very process of political governance in the country. The recognition of only 22 languages as official languages clearly shows that most of the Indian languages are kept out of the power range. Out of the 22 languages only 2 tribal languages namely the Bodo and Santali were recognised as official languages and included in the VIII Schedule of the Constitution vide the 100th Constitution Amendment Act in December 2003. With the exclusion of Constitutionally recognised languages, the rest of the languages are dubbed as 'minor languages' or 'dialects' and thus are subjected to suppression in the educational and political spheres. The surprising development is the 1991 census lists only 216 languages as mother tongues with a cut off margin of minimum of 10,000 speakers. The mother tongues declared by less than 10,000 persons were grouped under the 'other mother tongues' category which included nearly 9 million speakers (Ajit K. Mohanty, 2005). Thus more than 900 mother tongues spoken by nearly 1 per cent of the population remained unlisted.

In the case of the tribals the Constitutional provisions clearly emphasised the fact that the interests of tribals in all spheres must be protected and promoted. This has been by and large violated in many parts of the tribal areas. Even though Education in one's own mother tongue is a basic Human Right it is being neglected in the case of tribal education leading to a big gap between the tribal mother tongue and school language.

Linguistic Rights

Language is not only a tool for communication and knowledge but also a fundamental attribute of cultural identity and empowerment both for the individual and the group. Claims for language are among the first rights that minorities have voiced when there have been situations of political change and evolution. Such claims of linguistic rights range from the official and legal status of the minority and indigenous language to language teaching and use in schools and other institutions as well as in the media. With regard to education, the linguistic rights that have been framed in International Agreements for minority and indigenous groups include the following:

(i) Schooling in their languages, if so desired.
(ii) Access to the language of the larger community and to that of national education systems.
(iii) Inter cultural education that promotes positive attitudes to minority and indigenous languages and cultures they express.
(iv) Access to International Languages.

Education and Human Rights

All Human Rights documents give a prominent position to education. Further they emphasise the importance of education in promoting and protecting human rights. As one of the fundamental standard setting instruments, the Universal Declaration of Human Rights proclaimed in 1948 lays down the basic principle against discrimination on the grounds of language. Article 2 states, "Everyone is entitled to all rights and freedoms set-forth in this declaration, without distinction of one kind such as language."

The rights of persons belonging to minorities are further more established by the 1966 International Covenant on Civil and Political Rights and the 1992 Declaration on the Rights of persons belonging to National or Ethnic, Religious and Linguistic Minorities. Whereas Article 27 of the International Covenant refers more generally to the right of persons belonging to minorities to use their own language in community with the other members of their group. The Declaration is of explicit relevance to the language issue in the field of education as it formulates in Article 4 that persons belonging to minorities should have adequate opportunities to learn their mother tongue and that measures should be taken in order to encourage knowledge of the language and culture of the minorities.

The educational rights of indigenous people are addressed by the 1989 ILO Convention 169 concerning Indigenous and Tribal Peoples in Independent Countries. Article 28 of the convention requires that children belonging to the people concerned shall wherever practicable, be taught to read and write in their own indigenous language or in the language most commonly used by the group to which they belong and that adequate measures shall be taken to ensure that these people have the opportunity to attain fluency in the National Language or in one of the Regional Languages of the country. The Article provides at the same time that measures shall be taken to preserve and promote the development and practice of the indigenous languages of the people concerned.

UNESCO Endeavours

UNESCO's mandate charges it to deal with language issues. In this sense Article 1 of the UNESCO Constitution sets forth the fundamental principle that language should not induce any kind of discrimination. The Human Rights and fundamental freedoms are affirmed for the people of the world, without distinction of race, sex, language or religion. There are certain basic guiding principles which have been common to all the documents, agreements and recommendations produced throughout the years of UNESCO's mandate for action in this field. They are divided into three basic principles:

1. UNESCO supports mother tongue instruction as a means upon the knowledge and experience of the learners and teachers.
2. UNESCO supports bilingual/multilingual education at all levels of education as a means of promoting both social and gender equality and as a key element of linguistically diverse societies.
3. UNESCO supports language as an essential component of intercultural education in order to encourage understanding between different political groups and ensure respect for fundamental rights.

Tribal Languages and Education

Multilingualism is a way of life in India and its complexity generates an enormous challenge for education. A uniform system may be easier to administer and manage, but as Shaeffer noted, "most formal systems are inappropriate for, or even hostile to indigenous minority groups," creating a barrier to learning achievement, access to further education, participation in national life as well as causing the death of linguistic and cultural diversity. In order to provide a quality education, which takes into consideration the needs of tribal children as learners and the social, cultural and political milieu, their rich linguistic and cultural heritage must be acknowledged and used (UNESCO, 2002).

The Constitution of India and the India Education Policy state that every child has the right to learn in his/her mother tongue. The National Curriculum Framework for School Education 2000 states that, "the medium of instruction ideally, ought to be the mother tongue at all the stages of school education. In the case of learners whose mother tongue and the regional languages are different, the regional language may be adopted as the medium of instruction from the third standard."

Article 46, Part IV of Directive Principles of State Policy under the Constitution speaks about the promotion of educational and economic interests of the SC, ST and other weaker sections. It reads, "the state shall promote with special care the educational and economic interests of the weaker sections of the people and in particular of the SCs and STs and shall protect them from social injustice and all forms of exploitation."

However in India Education is generally conducted in the major State languages as most tribal languages are not officially recognised and few have been scripted. Written literature and curricula in these languages have therefore never been developed. Where they have, they have generally been translations from the dominant cultural group. Tribal children, who are not familiar with the language of instruction or with the dominant culture, are at a disadvantage from the beginning. Teachers rarely speak the community language, or appreciate the children's traditional culture and therefore cannot use translation. Added to this, teachers have no training in teaching minority language children (Seel, 2004; Pam Mackenzie, 2005).

Tribal languages and cultures, and thus children's identities are being sidelined in the present education system. As education becomes more widely accessible and the State (or national) language is imposed as the only language of instruction, tribal languages and cultures will rapidly lose ground and are likely to be lost within two or more generations (Fishman, 1990). While it is essential to know the State and National Languages, to do so at the exclusion of the mother tongue is not only causal in the demise of tribal languages and cultures, but also creates a crisis in tribal children's sense of identity and self worth (UNESCO, 2002).

Tribal Languages and their Exclusion in Education

There is a problem of non-comprehension of tribal child with a big gap between home language and school language. The monolingual tribal child faces cognitive and communicative problems where the instruction is in regional language. Exclusion of tribal mother tongues from early stage of education has serious consequences for tribal children in India. It clearly shows a violation of human rights by denying the tribal child to learn in his/her own mother tongue. The impact of this is reflected in the low literacy, high drop out rate and poor educational performance of the tribal children resulting in their capability deprivation and poverty. This is alarming since a number of classrooms throughout the country have good proportion of tribal children. Unfortunately less than one per cent of the tribal children get a fair chance to study in their mother tongue. As per the Database of the Ministry of Human Resource Development, Government of India there are 103,609 Primary Schools (grades I to V) with more than 50 per cent; 76,458 Schools with more than 75 per cent and 58,343 Schools with more than 90 per cent ST children who are taught in a majority language education are available. (Jhingran, 2005).

The enrolment ratio is relatively high in early stages due to the special Government facilities provided for the STs with a goal of universalisation of education upto 14 years of age. But more than 50 per cent of tribal children enrolled in Class I drop out before completing primary education. Apart from large scale educational failure, lack of educational attainment and poor literacy rates plague the tribals in India. This situation is mainly due to the neglect of tribal mother tongue for education and literacy instruction. Neglect of tribal mother tongue limits their academic success and curtails their chance of access to higher education. Due to this situation most of the tribals take to low quality employment. Thus denial of right to tribals to get education in their own mother tongue leads to a vicious circle of capability deprivation, economic under development, poverty and insecurity among the tribals (Ajit K. Mohanty, 2005).

Conclusion

Deprivation of linguistic human rights in the context of tribal education will perpetuate discrimination, inequality and curtails democratic participation. Education is one of the critical factor in human development. From the view point of schooling linguistic competence is more important for tribal children for understanding concepts and academic participation. Many Expert Commissions/Committees have suggested the need to use tribal mother tongue in the elementary stages of schooling to enable the tribal children to gain confidence. Many linguists suggest making unwritten language into a written one by using local dialect will ensure the proper use of tribal languages in the field of education. Exclusion of tribal languages in education will only mean denying opportunity to learn and develop, violation of linguistic human rights, Constitutional Provisions and the Government Policy. This will eventually contribute to perpetuating discrimination and inequality in the society. An integrative language policy and planning from the view point of protecting human rights in tribal education is the need of the hour in India. The tribal child will be lost if the aim of education remains making of citizens rather than making a man.

REFERENCES

1. Arjun Dev, Indira Arjun Dev and Supta Das Ed. (1996), *Human Rights – A Source Book*, New Delhi, NCERT.
2. Jingran D. (2005), *Language Disadvantage: The Learning Challenges in Primary Education*, New Delhi, APH Publishing Corporation.
3. Joshna Fishman (1990), What is Reversing Language Shift and How Can it Succeed ?, *Journal of Multilingualism and Multicultural Development, Vol. 11, No. 2*, pp. 5-36.
4. Malone S. (2003), Education for Multilingualism and Multiliteracy: Linking Basic Education to Life Long Learning in Minority Language Communities, *Conference on Language Development, Language Revitalisation and Multilingual Education*, Bangkok, 6-8 November, 2003.
5. National Council of Educational Research and Training (2005), *National Curriculum Framework, Position Paper on National Focus Group on the Teaching of Indian Languages*, NCERT, 2005.
6. National Council of Educational Research and Training (2005), *National Curriculum Framework, Position Paper on National Focus Group on Problems of Scheduled Caste and Scheduled Tribe* Children, NCERT, 2005.
7. *National Policy on Education (1986)*, NCERT, New Delhi.
8. Pamilla Mackenzie (2005), Multilingual Education for Tribal Minorities in India, *India Workshop in Multilingual Education*, CIIL, Mysore, 25-27 October, 2005.
9. Schaeffer, S. (2003), Language Development and Language Revitalisation—An Educational Imperative in Asia, *Conference on Language Development, Language Revitalisation and Multilingual Education*, Bangkok, 6-8 November 2003.
10. Seel, A. (2004), *Language and the Right to Quality Education: An Overview of Issues in Andhra Pradesh and Orissa States*, India, Save The Children Fund, U.K.
11. Singh, K.S. (2002). *The People of India, Vol. 3*, Delhi: Oxford University Press.
12. St. Clair Robert N. (2002), Review of "Managing Multilingualism in India" by Annamalai in *Language Problems and Language Planning, Vol. 26, No. 3*.
13. UNESCO Position Paper (2002), *Education in a Multilingual World.*

5

Ignored Claims of Forgotten Communities: Human Rights and Tribal Education in India

Introduction

The challenge for education systems in many countries is to adapt to complex realities and provide quality education which takes into consideration learner's needs whilst balancing these at the same time with social, cultural and political demands. The status and the role of languages in various domains have been the subject of numerous international declarations, recommendations and agreements. The Constitution of India has various provisions for the educational advancement of the Scheduled Castes, Scheduled Tribes and other weaker sections. Unfortunately the successive Governments in India have failed in adopting an Affirmative Policy coupled with suitable action to translate the Constitutional Provisions into actual reality. Education is the complete development of individuality so that one can make an original contribution to human life according to one's best capacity. To spread the education among the marginalised sections of the society especially in the case of tribal people has been a formidable task in India. In this chapter an attempt has been made to discuss the educational rights of the Indigenous Communities in India; how the claims of the tribal communities are ignored in the field of education with multiple layers of the discrimination and the paradoxical situation in which these communities are placed today with exclusion and non-accommodation of tribal mother tongues in education. Specifically the chapter attempts to look at the violation of human rights in the context of imparting tribal education in India.

Social progress, political development, cultural achievement and transformation are possible only by the attainment of minimum standards of economic development. In any community where the poor people from the majority the possibility of spreading literacy and education becomes all the more difficult. Owing to absolute poverty members of such communities cannot utilise the educational opportunities.

Jean Dreze and Amartya Sen (2002) conceptualise poverty as "capability deprivation" and "unfreedom." Capability in their view "refers to the ultimate combination of functioning from which a person can choose" and freedom is "the range of options a person has in deciding what kind of life to lead." Thus curtailment of capabilities and lack of real social opportunity, rather than conventional indicators such as low income, impoverishment of life conditions are relevant to understanding the nature and causes of poverty. Sen stresses the cyclic nature of the relationship between social discrimination, lack of opportunities, lack of freedom, capability deprivation and poverty. In the opinion of both Dreze and Sen, "the crucial role of social opportunities is to expand the realm of human agency and freedom both as an end in itself and as a means of further expansion of freedom." Education plays a crucial enabling role in Sen's view of economic development. Illiteracy is 'unfreedom' imposing severe limitations to economic opportunities. Besides directly enhancing economic opportunities through easier access to jobs and income, school education adds to social and cultural freedom and empowers persons for adequate participation in the exercise of political rights. Inequality of opportunities is related to distributional aspects of freedom – inequalities in respect of freedom, participation and development. This is particularly crucial for Indian society where social divisions based on caste, class, culture, language, religion, etc., are pervasive. Dreze and Sen (2002) speak of the substantial problem of 'voicelessness' of the disadvantaged groups in India, particularly the Scheduled Tribes, arising out of large scale illiteracy and lack of education which is an important enabling factor for economic underdevelopment.

Thus, education is seen as the most crucial input necessary for development. Lack of education for the disadvantaged in India according to Dreze and Sen is not due to parental indifference or due to the so called large scale participation of children in the labour force (a claim which they show to be unsubstantiated). They attribute large scale non-attendance and school dropout to lack of interest (of parents as well as children) and to a host of 'discouragement effects' due to alienating curriculum, inactive classroom, indifferent teachers and social discrimination in the classroom.

Indigenous Communities of India are commonly referred to as tribal communities. Under the Constitution of India they are recognised as Scheduled Tribes. Although the Constitution does not define Scheduled Tribes it designates these communities in accordance with Article 342 of the Constitution. At present, 533 tribes in India have been notified under Article 342 of the Constitution.

As per 1991 census, the Scheduled Tribes account for 67.76 million representing 8.08 per cent of the country's population. Of this 1.32 million (1.95%) belong to Primitive Tribal Groups (PTG) who are more marginalised than the Scheduled Tribe population. The Scheduled Tribe population is estimated to have reached 88.8 million in 2001 which is 8.6 per cent of the country's total population in 2001. The Scheduled Tribes are spread across the country and reside mainly in forest and hilly regions. The proportion of Scheduled Tribes within general population varies across States/Union Territories and indicates heavy concentration in certain parts such as Madhya Pradesh (16.4 million), Orissa (7.03 million), Bihar (6.61 million), Mizoram (94.7%), Lakshadweep (93.2%), Meghalaya (85.5%), Nagaland (88%), Arunachal Pradesh (64%), Dadra and Nagar Haveli (79.9%). Kerala (1.1%), Tamil Nadu (1%) and Uttar Pradesh (0.2%) have a low percentage of Scheduled Tribe population in comparison to the general population. Since Independence the percentage of Scheduled Tribe population has increased following the growth in general population.

A number of Scheduled Tribes live below poverty line with very poor access to health services. Tribal children like several marginalised groups of children in the country are trapped in the vicious cycle of poverty, illiteracy and deprivation. This is evident in extremely poor adult literacy rates, which are reproduced as low education levels among the children from Scheduled Tribe communities. The literacy rate of Scheduled Tribes is abysmally low at around 29.60 per cent as against the national average of 52.21 per cent. So far as female literacy is concerned, more than three quarters of Scheduled Tribe women are illiterate and their involvement with the main stream society is seriously limited.

Educational Rights of the Tribal Children: Constitutional Safeguards

The Constitution of India was framed in 1950 with an objective to guarantee social, political and economic justice to all. It was well visualized that development in education along with other allied sector would play a vital role to bring about desirable changes in the country. These promises laid the foundation for the attempt of Universalization of primary education in India among the entire eligible category of children within the age group of 6-14 years of age within a span of 10 years.

The Constitution of India guarantees right to equality as the fundamental right under Articles 15, 16 and 17. Article 29 protects the interests of the minorities. Article 29(1) of the Constitution states that citizens residing in any part of the country but having their own language, script and culture shall have the right to maintain them. According to Article 30(1) all minorities based on religious or language shall have the right to set-up administer institutions in their own interest. Article 350 states that every individual has the right to give representation to an officer in the State or the Centre in any of the languages used in the Union or in the State. Article 350(A) advises that education be imparted in the mother tongue stating that it will be the endeavour of every State and every local official within the State, to provide suitable facilities for providing education to the children of linguistic minorities in their mother tongue at the primary stage. Article 46, Part IV of Directive Principles of State Policy speaks about the promotion of educational and economic interests of Scheduled Tribes and other weaker sections. Besides the National Policy of Education, 1986 gives special place to the education of the Scheduled Tribes. The policy has explicitly stated that there is a need to develop curriculum and instructional materials in tribal languages at the initial stages. It endorses the need for making education relevant to the community.

Even though the Constitution has provided for the socio-economic development and empowerment of Scheduled Tribes through several articles there has been no National Policy which could have helped translate the Constitutional Provisions into a reality. The Government of India formed Ministry of Tribal Affairs in October 1999 to accelerate tribal development.

The Education Rights of tribal children are closely linked to human rights and it is impractical to separate rights of tribal children from those of their families and communities. Children's Rights remain unfulfilled so long as the position of social group is not improved. In the case of India the problems faced by the tribal communities including displacement, alienation, migration, etc. make it extremely difficult for tribal children to gain entry and sustain within the mainstream education system.

Forgotten Communities and Ignored Claims: Tribal Education in India

Every social group have their own interests, claims and counter claims to make for educational rights. Assertion by tribes is indeed encouraging and they form an integral part of meaningful awakening in a Democratic country like India. A lot of attempts have been made to mainstream the tribal children in education process. Most importantly by providing access, reading writing materials, free textbooks and empowering village community to participate in management of school. Achievements are also quite significant in areas of provision of access by opening of new schools, hostels, enrolment of children and empowerment of teachers through mass teachers training on child centered approach. However there seem to be lack of achievement in retention and achievement of students (on the basis of completion rates) in schools. The dropout rate is still quite high and achievement sores in subjects need significant increase.

A tribal child is relatively less exposed to other languages at the age of his entry to the school, because of the tribals have their own Eco-zone where they inhabit in relative isolation and therefore have lesser exposure to the outside world. Since the tribal languages are different from the medium of instruction in schools (which is generally the State Language) tribal children find it very difficult to cope up with their studies. Lack of language skills acts as a serious impediment when a teacher is non-tribal. Aspirations among tribal children are also low considering that there are not many educational persons in tribal communities. The inability to secure jobs amongst tribals who have completed formal education have led some to get disillusioned with the education system and question the futility of spending several years struggling to get educated. Some consider school educated children as unfit to carry out their hereditary occupations, thereby rendering them 'useless' in their traditional lives.

The present system of language curriculum is one of the major reasons for low educational achievements of the tribal children. The dominant language of the State is presented as the norm or standard, value based, culturally superior, powerful and resourceful. It is also emphasized in so many ways that the tribal child must master this language in order to assimilate with the mainstream. This ultimately generates among the tribal children a feeling of inferiority towards themselves, their language, culture and their own parents and family. Lack of school related parental support, family pattern, gender roles, family insistence on the tribal child for active involvement as a labour force in the agricultural work also contributes to school drop out rate.

Tribal children who go to non-tribal schools face the language problem more severely as in most cases the non-tribal classmates and teachers make fun of their mother tongue and assign low status to it. The majority dominant State language becomes a threat to the tribal children's mother tongue. It runs the risk of being displaced or replaced. As a consequence it is not learned at all, sometimes it is forgotten and does not develop because the children are forbidden to use it or are made to feel ashamed of it. When this happens it becomes a worst form of violation of linguistic human rights of the tribal children. The tribal children in a tribal school feel unmotivated to learn new non-tribal languages primarily due to cultural differences in learning. Tribal ways of learning is through cooperation and not through modern concept of competition. Tribal culture is oral and not written.

The tribal child entering school for the first time sees a completely different environment. The teacher, his apparel and language unseen and incomprehensive creates a sense of suspicion and fear in him initially. It is often seen that teachers working in tribal areas have prejudices and biases towards tribal society and culture. They do not treat tribals as normal beings due to their blind beliefs and conservative ideas. To them the tribal language which has no written script does not qualify for a status of language and hence inferior. These senses of ethnocentrisim are expressed in their dealings with tribal students in the classroom. The teachers in tribal schools seldom inquire into the socio-cultural background of the tribal children.

The tribal child is no less competent than others. The tribal children acquire ability in learning songs at the age of five years. They learn beating of drums, dances, short stories, proverbs and riddles at the age of ten. The tribal child is close to his things, dreams, plays and interacts with infinite thing, words, jargons which are not taught to the tribal child in post primary education. So far as the scope of learning language, the tribal child gets plenty of contexts at home in an informal and friendly atmosphere and learning is spontaneous. But in school every thing is formal and structured and the language of the book is considered as the source of knowledge. The child has no scope to interact with friends while the teacher teaches on monologue basis. The tribal child cannot concentrate because of communication failure and instead beaten by the teacher for not being attentive and responsive in the class. The in-conducive and hostile school atmosphere leads to dropouts of most of the students from school. Above all the tribal children are the first generation academic learners and have least scope of support from parents and relatives who are illiterate.

Many tribal languages have no script. Preparation of suitable textbooks for such children is a challenging task. Often the language of the textbook is in standard state language for school students all over the State. It is believed that experts knowing tribal language and culture prepare these books. Generally these books have contents of subjects which are reflective of dominant society. The books have few local tribal specific contents and sometimes pictures and description of birds, animals, trees, etc. which are all alien to the tribal child and poses problem to comprehend.

The Mismatch

There is a mismatch between the Constitutional provisions and their actual implementation. Firstly as per the Constitutional provisions basic education to tribals must be provided in their own mother tongue which seems to be a Herculean task for any State Government. This is because the language and culture of the tribes differ a lot linguistically. Secondly, in case of multilingual situations in a classroom whereby students come from different tribal groups, the problem for the teachers is as to what should be the standard medium of instruction for all children. The teacher knowing one tribal language finds it impossible to teach students coming from different ethnic and language background. Thirdly, the teachers mostly non-tribals do not have adequate knowledge of tribal language. Lastly, the problem could have been reduced with the engagement of sufficient number of local teachers from the community. But unfortunately there is dearth of qualified tribals who can be appointed as teachers in schools. The problems and issues in language, textbooks and medium of instruction are very typical to multiethnic, multilingual indigenous tribal groups.

Educational development of the tribals is possible only when the above discussed key issues are addressed judiciously through strategic planning. Proper measures must be taken keeping in view the need and cultural orientation of the tribals. Suggestions which are offered in this respect include linguistic mapping to assess the category of tribals before planning their education, preparation of bilingual primers to use tribal mother tongue as medium of instruction, making school environment more attractive, defining the role of tribal teacher clearly, offering proper incentives for non-tribal teachers working in tribal areas, posting of tribal teachers to schools, using village community for classroom transactions, undertaking intensive and innovative research to identify the problems plaguing tribal education and to seek suitable solutions.

Conclusion

Considering the Constitutional Directives and actual implementation of educational schemes one would certainly identify a clear gap or mismatch between what should have been done and what has been done so far. Although the Constitution guarantees the tribals the right to preserve and develop their language such guarantees cannot become a reality until the tribal languages are used in education, administration and mass media. In order to protect their linguistic rights all the tribal languages of the State need to be developed. New planning is required to make the tribals well versed in their native language both orally and in written form while enabling them at the same time to learn the other languages, i.e. Regional Language, English and Hindi to be at par with the mainstream.

It is imperative to preserve and protect the indigenous tribal languages to prevent violation of human rights in tribal education in India. Tribal communities in India have been historically deprived of access to resources and opportunities including the opportunity to get educated. The present efforts of the Indian Government to bring these children into formal school fail at two levels. Firstly, because it is not able to enroll all tribal children and provide them access to good quality functional schools. In some States the Government has started providing alternate schools run by untrained local youth which is opposed by educational activists since it is a poor and substandard system given out to those who are already marginalised. Secondly, even when tribal children are enrolled into schools, the education system besides doling out some incentives does not do much to improve the school environment which will treat these first generation learners with respect and dignity.

Historically the tribals are ignored and deprived communities in the country. Providing access to education is simply not enough, the Government has to take a pro-active role in creating overall conditions and opportunities that will enable their transition and breaking of the intergenerational cycle of poverty and illiteracy. A sensitive cadre of teachers and bureaucrats are required to make the difference. At another level the educational deprivation from the human rights perspective must be seen in the context of overall deprivation of the community and hence emphasis must be placed on improving the situation of tribal communities in general. Restoring land and livelihood, empowering women, providing basic civic amenities are pre-conditions to the advancement of rights of tribal children. Unless the Government takes urgent steps to address these issues its proclamation on child rights would remain only empty rhetoric and its actions would continue to exclude those already sidelined. Respecting the ignored claims of the forgotten and marginalised communities should set the ball rolling in the right direction.

REFERENCES

1. Amartya Sen and Jean Dreze, *Omnibus (1995)*, New Delhi, Oxford University Press.
2. Ambast, N.K. (2001), *Tribal Education: Problems and Issues*, Delhi, Venkatesh Prakashan.
3. Biligiri, H.S. (1969), *"Problems of Tribal Languages in India"*, in N. Ray Ed, *Language and Society in India*, Simla, Institute of Advanced Study, pp. 245-50.
4. Capotorti, F. (1979), *Study of the Rights of Persons Belonging to Ethnic, Religious and Linguistic Minorities*, New York, United Nations.
5. Chalam, K.S. (1988), *Education and Weaker Sections*, New Delhi, Inter India Publications.
6. Das Gupta, Biman, K. and Danda, Ajit, K. (Ed.) (1984), *Tribal Education in India in Retrospect*, Calcutta, Anthropological Survey of India.
7. Devarennes, F. (1996), *Language, Minorities and Human Rights*, The Hague-Kluwer Law International.
8. Hemalatha, T. (1989), *Tribal Education*, Udaipur, Himanshu Publishers.
9. Jhingran, D. (2005), *Language Disadvantage: The Learning Challenges in Primary Education*, New Delhi, APH Publishing Corporation.
10. Kundu, M. (1994), *Tribal Education: New Perspectives*, New Delhi: Gyan Publishing House.
11. Mathur, N.N.G. (1994), *Tribal Education: Past, Present and Future*, Udaipur, Shiva Publications.
12. Ministry of Human Resource Development, Department of Education (1986), *National Policy on Education*, New Delhi.
13. NCERT (1991), *Minimum Levels of Learning*, New Delhi, NCERT.
14. NCERT (2005), *Position Paper on the Teaching of Indian Languages: National Focus Group Report on the Teaching of Indian Languages* (NFG, NCERT), New Delhi, NCERT.
15. Parvathamma (1984), *Scheduled Castes and Tribes*, New Delhi, Ashish Publishing House.
16. Patel, S. (1991), *Tribal Education in India*, New Delhi, Mittal Publications.
17. Singh, S.N. (1991), *Tribal Education in India*, New Delhi, Uppal Publishing House.
18. Skutnabb Kangas, T. (2000), *Linguistic Genocide in Education or Worldwide Diversity and Human Rights ?* Malwah New Jersey: Lawrence Erlbaum.
19. UNESCO Position Paper (2002), *Education in A Multilingual World*.

6

Language: Constitutional Provisions—Curriculum Transaction through Tribal Dialects

Ours is a multi party system of democratic Government, multi religious mixed society and mixed economy. India is a multilingual country. It is a mosaic of different languages and a multi coloured roof of different communities. It has been hospitable and open minded in assimilating within itself languages, cultural traditions, religious beliefs, etc.

Language is a vehicle of communication and a means of social transmission of cultural heritage from one generation to another. It is important for human growth. It is human, aural-oral and symbolically meaningful. Any given language is structured uniquely. The structure of a language can be discovered and usefully and systematically described. Languages are habits which are established by repetition and languages must be taught through repetition of some sort.

Every language has three constituents. They are sound, structure and vocabulary. The chief problem in learning a foreign language is to master its sound system i.e. to understand the stream of speech, to hear the distinctive sound features and to approximate their production. The second problem is to grasp the structure of the language i.e. the arrangement of words into sentences. The third problem is to learn the vocabulary, but it is a minor problem compared to the other too. It must be remembered that one cannot learn all the words of a language. We know only those words which fall within the range of our experience. Our main task in the initial stages is with the teaching of sounds and structures within a limited vocabulary. Having mastered them, the learner can expand his vocabulary to any extent he likes. The pupil is to be taught through oral practice. Speech is the language. The written report is only a secondary representation. It is through speech that a student is able to make the sentence pattern automatic habit. A pupil knows a language if he has mastered its basic speech and grammatical patterns and essential vocabulary through the basic skills viz. listening, speaking, reading and writing.

In ancient India Sanskrit was the medium of instruction. Later on Pali and Prakrit took place of Sanskrit. During the middle ages Arabic and Persian were the medium of instruction. During the reign of Akbar Hindi and Urdu were also given great importance. After the arrival of Britishers in India there was a fast change in the educational policy. In 1835 Lord Macaulay emphasized that English should be the medium of instruction for more than hundred years. After independence the controversy of the medium of instruction arose. Different scholars put forward different views regarding medium of instruction. Some of the scholars were of the opinion that English should remain the medium of teaching, while others were in favour of state language Hindi. Some pleaded for regional language. The Radhakrishnan Commission recommended that Indian languages should be the medium of instruction in place of English. Mudaliar Commission recommended that upto the secondary stage Mother Tongue or the Regional Language should be the medium of instruction. Kothari Commission was of the view that the regional languages should be the medium of instruction upto the primary and secondary stage. Even at the higher stage of study regional language should be the medium of instruction. The Kothari Commission recommended the study of three languages *(i)* Mother Tongue (Regional Language), *(ii)* State Language, Hindi and *(iii)* One of the Indian or European languages.

Prominent educationists and various reports on education have recommended that the Mother tongue of the child be made the medium of education. Mahatma Gandhiji stated, "I am convinced that children who receive education in a tongue other than their own commit suicide." The Wardha Committee (1937) recommended the use of mother tongue as the medium of instruction. Language Commission (1956) specifically mentioned the need to make Hindi the official language. Rabindranath Tagore was of the opinion that, "There is no joy, no expansion, no blossoming of our faculties without mother tongue."

The need for social integration also supports the claim of the mother tongue. The Emotional and the National Integration Committee have also supported that the regional language of the child should be made his medium of instruction. It is essential to make Mother Tongue as the medium of instruction because it facilitates learning and teaching, it is a more psychological and natural medium; it is helpful in the intellectual, mental and emotional growth of the child; it enables the children to understand and appreciate their cultural traditions; it will facilitate the promotion of emotional and national tradition; it will reduce the burden of cramming, barbarism in teaching and learning; it will give pleasure to the children and it enables the school to attract the children and sustain them in school. It has been rightly asserted by Dr. V.K.R.V. Rao that, "India would be as any other advanced country in the world in the next fifty years if medium of instruction in Schools and Universities is switched over to the mother tongue from now."

Education is essentially a social affair and the schools are charged with the responsibility of training and bringing up the youth so that they may be able to participate effectively in the life of the group to which they belong. The individual has to be trained with reference to and for the sake of the needs, demands and ideals of society which are always changing and modifying. But all this training of individual is possible if the medium of instruction is within his easy approach. The Secondary Education Commission recommended that the regional language or mother tongue should be made the medium of instruction throughout the secondary stage of education. The National Policy on Education 1979 recommended that the medium at all stages should be the regional language except at the primary stage when it will be mother tongue. The National Policy on Education reiterates that the policy of 1979 will be implemented more energetically and purposefully.

Our Constitution is based on four important ideals, that is, justice, liberty, equality and fraternity. As per 42nd Amendment Act our Country is a Sovereign, Socialist, Secular

Democratic Republic. The following are some of the provisions relating to protection of language.

Article 29(1): The Constitution states that citizens residing in any part of the country but having their own language, script and culture will have the right to maintain them.

Article 30(1): All Minorities based on religion or language will have the right to set up and administer institutions in their own interest.

Article 350: States that every individual has the right to give representation to an officer in the State or Central language.

Article 350(A): Advises that education be imparted in the mother tongue, stating that it will be the endeavour of every state and every local official within the state, to provide suitable facilities for providing education to the children of linguistic minorities in their mother tongue at the primary stage.

The Constitution has recognised eighteen languages. But there are almost 1652 dialects spoken in India without script. In the case of tribal communities there are only dialects.

It is an accepted fact that if the children are taught in school in their own language, then they feel homely and be attracted to it. At the primary stage the children are exposed to three academic subjects and five activity subjects. The academic subjects include Language, Mathematics and Environmental Studies I and II. The activity subjects include Health Education, Physical Education, Socially useful productive work, moral Education and Creative activities.

Specially at the primary stage of education the school should attract the children and retain them till the completion of the full school course. School should not become a day prison for the children. It should act as a school with a smile. This would be possible when the instruction is carried on in the school through the mother tongue of the children specially in tribal areas. In Classes I and II it is always desirable to teach the children in their mother tongue. The classroom teacher at the primary stage of education faces a number of problems in transacting with the curriculum by adopting the school language as the medium of instruction. Some of the problems include non-familiarity with local language; non-exposure to tribal culture and languages in training; lack of simple phrase books for teachers in tribal dialects; lack of supplementary instructional materials in tribal dialects; inadequate pre-service and in-service training; little understanding of the material they teach; lack of training in innovative programmes like joyful learning, school with a smile, child friendly classrooms, lack of instructional materials in tribal dialects, no support for school learning, home language is different from school language; problem of textbooks, textbooks do not reflect tribal culture; lack of documentation of folklore; lack of language training to teachers in tribal dialects and lack of bilingual textbooks and charts. These being the problems faced by the teachers, tribal students differ in certain qualities from the students of plain areas. The special qualities a tribal child enjoys are complete freedom, the opportunity to take, if provided, not a leader but a follower, slow learner because of lack of opportunities, he can also learn like others, disadvantaged because of lack of opportunities, posses inferiority complex, not a speaker of words but a doer of deeds, heads only those which are useful to him, very disciplined, more self respectful, very plain and comes to do anything or any activity if convinced, opportunities are not given due to vested interests, education through productive activities, needs vocation based education, requires activities to draw out innovate potentialities, lacks distributive justice, participates in physical activities.

Keeping the problems faced by the teachers of the tribal areas and the special qualities of a tribal child, the need of the hour is to assist the teachers of tribal areas in using the tribal dialect in their classroom transaction to make learning more effective and quicken the process. In this connection, there is need to develop glossaries in tribal dialects for the assistance of teachers working in tribal areas with tribal students as well. Glossary is a vocabulary of words requiring special explanation. It is a brief dictionary. Attempts must be made to bring glossaries in all tribal dialects. This will go a long way in enriching curriculum transaction through tribal dialects.

REFERENCES

1. Emeneau, M.B. (1955): *Kolami: A Dravidian Language*. Berkeley: University of California Press.
2. Furer-Haimendorf, Christoph Von. (1944): 'Aboriginal Education in Hyderabad', *Indian Journal of Social Work* 5(2),97-106.
3. Krishna Murthy, B.H. (1969): *Konda or Kubi*: A Dravidian Language, Hyderabad: Tribal Cultural Research and Training Institute.
4. Krishna Reddy, B. and Ramachandran Reddy, M. (1987): 'An Ethnographic Account of the Banjaras', *Vanjayati*, Vol. XXXV, No.2, 19-23.
5. Pratap, D.R. (1980): *The Naikapods and their Language*, ISRA, Bidisa.
6. Sitapathi, Gidugu (1943): 'The Saoras and their Country', *Journal of the Andhra Historical Research Society*.
7. Trivedi, G.M. 1978. *Linguistic Study of the Chenchus of Andhra Pradesh*, Calcutta: Anthropological Survey of India.

7

Literacy of Scheduled Tribe Children in the Tribal Schools

Introduction

Andhra Pradesh is a State with acute problems to be addressed in the field of tribal education. Sustainable efforts are being made by the Government of Andhra Pradesh for the educational development of the tribal communities, in order to provide education and improve literacy among the Scheduled Tribe children such as opening of the Grama Vidya Vikas Kendra Schools (GVVKS), Mabadi Schools, Ashram Schools are functioning in the State. But there is a feeling that these Schools are not functioning properly. According to the Department of Tribal Welfare, Government of Andhra Pradesh, there are many problems facing the tribal population including low access due to small scattered habitations, language problem, low motivation, sibling care, child labour and lack of awareness. The conditions of the five districts in Andhra Pradesh mainly Vizianagaram, Nellore, Kurnool, Karimnagar and Warangal gives a clear picture of the position of the tribal education in Andhra Pradesh. The Scheduled Tribe population in Vizianagaram district as per 1991 census is 1,90,185. The literacy rate among this group is 15.68 per cent. The female literacy is very poor and needs special attention. Jatapu, Kondadora, Mukadora and Mannedora are major tribal groups in this district and Savara and Gadaba communities are the primitive tribal groups. The enrolment percentage of the children at primary stage is 71 per cent and dropout is 68 per cent. There is a problem of access and high dropout in this district among the tribals.

The Scheduled Tribe population in Nellore district as per 1991 census is 2,14,062. The literacy rate among tribals is 16.36 per cent. Yerukula and Yanadi are the major tribal groups in this district. Yanadis are cultivators, doing fishing, scavenging work, watching the fields, etc. The enrolment and dropout rate among the tribal children in the district is 77 per cent and 79 per cent respectively. Access is a problem to the Yanadis and retention is a problem for the Yerukulas. The Yanadis (Challa Yanadis) are the most backward and needs special focus. The Scheduled Tribe population in Kurnool district as per 1991 census is 56,455. The literacy rate is 24.86 per cent. The male literacy is considerably higher than female literacy. Lambada, Yerukula, Chenchu and Yanadi are the tribal communities existing in the district. Chenchus are the primitive tribal group. The enrolment and dropout rates in this district, at 59 per cent and 52 per cent at primary stage. There are considerable number Lambada Thandas without schools. There are more unenrolled children in schools among the Chenchus. As per 1991 census the Scheduled Tribe population in Karimnagar district is 83,017. The literacy rate of this district among tribals is 12.31 per cent. The female literacy is very low. The district is inhabited by Gond, Koya, Lambada and Yerukula tribes. The enrolment and dropout rate among the tribal children of 6-11 years age group are 59 per cent and 80 per cent respectively. There is a problem of low enrolment and high dropout in this district. As per 1991 census the Scheduled Tribe population in Warangal district is 3,85,369. The literacy rate is 11.39 per cent. The female literacy is very poor. Lambada, Koya and Yerukula are the important tribal groups in this district. There are considerable number of school less habitations in this district. The enrolment and retention rates of this district are 46 per cent and 81 per cent respectively.

Education of Aboriginal Tribes

The subject of education for tribals (aboriginal tribes) received attention during the British and Nizams period. The Gond Education Scheme in Adilabad district, the Koya Development Scheme in Khammam district, the Chenchu Education Scheme in Kurnool district, etc. were taken up in early 1940s. Gandhians like Rebbapragada Mandeswara Sarma, Mallipeddi Krishna Murthy, S.S. Nanda, Vennelakanti Raghavaiah through organizations like Adimjati Sevak Sangh have started educational institutions in Srikakulam (Mandasa), Visakhapatam (Araku), West Godavari (Ramannagudem) and Nellore districts. These efforts formed the bass for psychological acceptance of Universal Primary Education. After the adoption of the Constitution of India the educational advancement of Scheduled Tribes became a mandate for the Central and State Governments. All though educational development of the tribals has been receiving its due priority, considerable progress has not been observed. In this direction the Government of Andhra Pradesh has opened non-residential single teacher primary schools in villages with more than 200 population and has also opened Ashram Schools for groups of small and scattered villages. Residential schools have been started to provide higher education.

Specific Problems

The problems of absenteeism, wastage, stagnation and attainment are responsible for the present conditions in the schools. The physical facilities available in the school and the teacher input are the other important factors that contribute to the performance of the schools and children. In most of the tribal areas pucca buildings, furniture, blackboard, teaching aids like charts, maps, kits, display material, drinking water facility, clean and green surroundings are not available. Most of the teachers are appointed from outside the mandal areas and mostly from a tribe other than the local tribe. Language and residence become a problem for these teachers. The syllabus for teacher training programme for general areas was adopted for tribal areas also. No tribal orientation in terms of tribal ecology, folklore, tribal child psychology, etc. formed part of the syllabus. Teachers are not trained in tribal language. Female teachers are less compared to male teachers. Also the commitment of the teachers towards their profession is not uniform. The teachers reside outside the school location. This is a big barrier for the functioning of the school. Teachers find it difficult to travel long distance and reach the school on time. They often come late. As most of the schools are single teacher schools, the absence or late coming of teacher means closure or non-functioning of the school. The tribal teachers are assigned with additional responsibilities like census operation, election duty, clerical jobs, etc. which increases their absenteeism from school. The curriculum designed and followed for the general population is also followed in tribal areas. Telugu language is the medium of instruction which is sometimes a barrier in initial stages as the tribes have their own language or follow a local dialect even where they speak Telugu as mother tongue. The contents of the textbooks do not reflect the rich forest and mineral wealth, variety of flora and fauna, local tribal festivals, culture and heroes. The child reading the book gets a feeling of "out of context" and students have to imagine situations with which they are not familiar. Using play methods, giving illustrations, observing students while teaching and ensuring their participation, reviewing previous learning, giving assignments in classrooms and home work, etc. are absent in the tribal schools. Regular supervision is a rare phenomenon for the tribal schools. Though the teachers work in difficult areas and strive to promote literacy, they are not given incentives in terms of reward or award. The tribal children in interior villages are malnourished and the nutrition deficiency diseases are prevalent.

Education of the PTGs

The primitive tribals in Andhra Pradesh who are living in the top hill tribal areas are far from the civilization. As long as the scourge of literacy exists among these tribals development among them is not possible. Therefore, it is the responsibility of both the State and Central Governments to encourage their language and bring them to the mainstream of society. The study shows that there is a need to develop the primitive groups of Andhra Pradesh.

Recommendations

The following suggestions can be made to improve the literacy of primitive tribal group children in Andhra Pradesh:

1. Alternative schooling facilities should be provided to solve the problem of access. To provide education to the children of these communities more educated teachers, residential schools are urgently needed. Further, these schools must be provided with well trained teachers.
2. Preparation of bilingual books, charts in tribal languages and school language for use by teachers to attract children are needed.
3. The teachers should apply activity based teaching-learning process. Joyful learning programme should be followed.
4. House to house enrolment drives should be conducted. More attention is needed to increase girl's enrolment and retention.
5. Teachers knowing tribal language should be appointed as far as possible in tribal schools.
6. The lessons taught in tribal schools must reflect the tribal culture in the textbooks. While preparing the textbooks tribal teachers must be involved.
7. The DPEP and ITDA schools are being established by the Government in the remote villages of the tribal areas. However, these schools must be provided with infrastructural facilities alongwith residential quarters for the teachers to stay with the tribals and improve education among the tribal children.

8. Officers must visit these schools periodically and study development of schools and offer suitable suggestions for improving the literacy rate of the tribal children.
9. The teachers and the tribal children should be provided with proper health care and medical facilities. More number of primary health care centres should be opened in the hill top areas.
10. The Government should curb the child labour in the tribal areas. Parents using their children as child labourers should be strictly punished.
11. Government must organize periodic jathas and campaigns to bring awareness among the tribals about the need and importance of literacy and education. These should convince the tribal parents and leaders that literacy and education will lead to all round development of the tribals.
12. The development of tribal languages and education calls for political will power politicians and language protagonists must support the Government in developing the tribal languages and their use in education through suitable policy decisions taken from time to time. It also calls for proper support from the bureaucrats and other agencies both Governmental and Non-Governmental Organisations.

REFERENCES

1. Buckman, Peter, 1975, *Education Without School*, Rupa and Co., in association with Souvenir Press, London.
2. Biligiri. H.S., 1969, "Problems of Tribal Languages in India", in *Language and Society in India*, Vol. 8, pp. 245-250.
3. *District Primary Education Programme – Annual Work Plan and Budget*, 1998-99, Vizianagaram District, Andhra Pradesh.
4. *District Census Handbook, Census of Andhra Pradesh*, Part XII, A&B, Vizianagaram District, Village and Townwise Primary Census Abstract.
5. Gupta, V. *et al.*, 1999, *Tribal Development – Appraisal and Alternatives, Indus Publishing Company*, New Delhi.
6. Government of India, Ministry of Education, 1966, *Education and National Development.*
7. Hemalatha Talesra, 1990, *Tribal Education*, Himanshu Publications, Udaipur.
8. Kailash, 1993, *Tribal Education and Occupation*, Manas Publications Pvt. Ltd., NIRD, Hyderabad.
9. Midatala Rani, 2000, 'Tribal Languages and Tribal Education', *Social Action, Vol. 50, No. 4, October-December 2000*, pp. 414-419.
10. Midatala Rani, *Tribal Language in India: Reflections on Some Issues*, (Paper presented at a Workshop), RIE, Mysore.
11. NCERT, 1995, *School Effectiveness and Learning Achievement at Primary Stage International Perspective.*
12. NCERT, 1967, *Tribal Education in India*, Publication No. 20, Tribal Education Unit, Department of Adult Education.
13. Panda, B.N., 1992, *Tribal Education*, APH Publishing House, New Delhi.
14. Ravi. N., 1997, *The Hindu Speaks on Education*, Kasturi and Sons Ltd., Chennai.
15. *Selected Educational Statistics*, 1996-97, Commissioner and Director of School Education, Andhra Pradesh, Hyderabad.
16. Seshadri, C., 1983, *Improving Access to Education of the Disadvantaged Groups*, Paper presented at the Operational Seminar, Islamabad.
17. Seshadri, C., 1973, *Education, Equality and Culture: An Analysis*, Journal of Education, Vol. 3, UGC, New Delhi.
18. Sudhir Shukla, "Aliens in Their Own Home", *The Hindu, 14th March, 1993.*

8

Education through Tribal Languages: Issues and Prospects

Introduction

Language has been defined as a system of arbitrary vocal symbols by which members of a social group cooperate and interact. By means of language, learning process of culture is effectuated and a given way of life achieves both continuity and change. Without language the accumulation and transmission of cultural knowledge that differentiates man from other animals could not have been possible. Thus there is a close link between culture and language.

Importance of Language in Tribal Education

The purpose of the formal education is to provide opportunities to the tribals and to bring psychological integration with the rest of the population. As a result, tribal languages and tribal cultures are ignored in teaching tribal children. In the context of schooling, language skills become a crucial variable for understanding concepts and academic participation. Linguistic competence is more important for tribal children as they find it difficult to follow academic instruction and communicate with teachers. They are already handicapped due to lack of enough support on the home front. This results in lack of interest ultimately leading to drop outs and failures. Experts have suggested the need to use home language in the elementary stages of schooling to enable tribal children to gain confidence. They also emphasised on importance of teachers relating the home language of the children to the school language i.e. teachers should use home language of children for explaining difficult concepts. As most tribal languages do not have a script, using regional language script can solve the problem. Many linguists suggest making unwritten language into a written one using local dialect. But this is stupendous task financially. Examples are available from former Soviet Union where State financed construction of tribal languages was undertaken. But the constraints involved in replicating such exercise in India are: 1. The cost factor, 2. Lack of language experts in tribal languages, 3. Regional and local variations in languages and dialects.

Government Policy on Tribal Education

The realization of the importance of instruction in mother tongue is reflected in Article 350A of the Constitution. It lays down that *adequate facility for instruction in mother tongue at the primary stage* of education shall be endeavoured to be provided. More than five decades later, the Draft National Policy on Tribals (2004) stated that the following are to be ensured to achieve the objective of reaching the benefit of education to tribals:

- Tribals are included in the national programme of Sarva Shiksha Abhiyan run by the Ministry of Human Resource Department.
- Schools and hostels are opened in areas where no such facilities exist.
- At least one model residential school is located in each tribal concentration area.
- Education is linked with provision of supplementary nutrition.
- Special incentives like financial assistance, pocket allowance, free distribution of textbooks and school uniforms are provided.
- Teaching is imparted in tribals' mother tongue at least up to the primary level. Educated tribal youth are given employment as teachers, wherever possible.
- Pedagogy is made relevant so that tribals do not find it as alien.
- Curriculum and co-curriculum include aspects of meta skill up gradation of tribal children.
- Curricula for meta skill up gradation are to include aspects of tribal games and sports, archery, identification of plants of medicinal value, crafts, art and culture, folk dance and folk songs, folk paintings, etc.
- Emphasis is laid on vocational/professional education. Polytechnics are set up for studies in subjects like forestry, horticulture, dairying, veterinary sciences, and polytechnics.

Thus, we can see that Constitution of India and Government Policies on tribals gave importance for teaching in mother tongue to tribal children in elementary stages.

Tribal Languages – Speech Areas in Andhra Pradesh

There are thirty-three scheduled tribes in Andhra Pradesh, apart from nomadic tribes and de-notified communities. In the north coastal districts of Andhra we can see four speech areas as far as tribal languages are concerned, viz., Savara, Kui, Kubi and Gadaba. The Savara language belongs to Mundari group of languages. Gidugu Rammurthy Panthulu and Gidugu Sitapati studied the language. Through their efforts, a Savara – English Dictionary was prepared and an attempt was made to evolve a script so that the language could be used as a medium of instruction. *Kui* is spoken by Khonds (Samanthas) and *Kubi* is spoken by Kondadoras. Gadaba sub-groups speak different Gadaba dialects. The Koyas speak a language called as *Koi*, which is very much influenced by Telugu. *Gondi* language which is similar to *Koi*, is the language of Raj Gonds. A large number of studies were made on the Gondi language. Kolami is a Dravidian language spoken by Kolams. Several authors have studied Kolami. Banjara is the only tribe in Andhra Pradesh speaking an Indo-Aryan language. Yerukala (*Kurru*) language is not concentrated in any belt. This dispersal makes it difficult to carve out a speech area. Majority of the tribal communities in the state speak Telugu, Bagata, Chenchu, Goudu, Konda Kammara, Konda Kapu, Konda Reddi, Koya Dora, Manne Dora, Mukha Dora, Nayak (Nayakapodu), Reddi Dora, Valmiki and Yanadi use Telugu. The Yanadis speak in the Telugu language, but those who live in the border areas of Tamil Nadu also speak a mixture of both Telugu and Tamil. Communities living in Andhra, Orissa border such as Kotiya, Mulia, Porja, Rona, Rena and Savara speak both Telugu and Oriya. Similarly, the communities like Pardhan, Gond and Andh speak Telugu and Marathi (Pardhans speak Gondi also).

There are also tribes, who use Telugu along with their tribal language. They are Gadaba (Gadaba), Gond (Gondi), Koya (Koya), Lambada (Lamani, Sugali or Lambani), Porja (Parji), Yerukala (Yerukula), Jatapu, Samantha and Khonda (Kuvi). According to Krishna Reddy and Ramachandra Reddy, the linguistic speculation as well as celebration of Holi festival by the Banjaras support the explanation which points out that the Banjaras are of North Indian origin. Their dialect shows connections with North Indian languages like Hindi, Rajasthani and Punjabi. However, the Banjara dialect in South India is mixed with the surrounding Dravidian languages. In all the tribal languages, script has not developed. The tribal dialects are slowly disappearing because of culture contact and the children being educated in schools where medium of instruction is Telugu. Apart from the above, there are also a large number of nomadic and denotified tribes. Languages and dialects of communities like Dommara, Peddinti Golla, or Budabukkala have not received much attention. The tribal communities of Andhra Pradesh mainly belong to three linguistic families are shown below.

	Family		*Examples*
1.	Dravidian language family	—	Gondi, Koya, Kolami, Erukula
2.	Mundari language family	—	Savara and Gadaba
3.	Indo-Aryan language family	—	Banjara

The following authors carried out studies on tribal languages. Sitaptai (1943) on Savara, Emeneau (1955) on Kolami, Krishna Murthi (1969) on Kubi (Kondadora), Trivedi (1978) on Chenchu, Pratap (1980) on Naikapods.

Language Problems of Tribal Students

Tribal children in Andhra Pradesh are taught in the schools in Telugu, the regional language. Being first generation learners, tribal children lag behind in vocabulary, spelling and reading speed and comprehension. School language is different from home language most of the time. Tribal children who come from homes where the mother tongue used is different from the medium of instruction in the school face problem of understanding and adjustment. Family dialect and peer group affect children's style as they imitate these styles. They learn language by listening from the language environment in the home and community. Thus, by the time they come to the school, they have a set language skills having distinctive usage of syntax, structure, forms and usage. The words and sentences spoken by teacher in the classroom and present in the textbooks create confusion in the minds of the children. They sound strange, difficult to pronounce, remember and understand. When children come to school, they bring with them communication habits different from those expected in the school. The non-tribal teachers not having understanding of tribal languages lack in first hand communication with young children and do not appreciate the difficulties of tribal children. This leads to a communication gap. Misunderstanding, mis-communication between students and teachers leads to negative evaluation of each other.

When the teachers and students do not share the same communication background, they differ in communication strategies and contextual meanings of utterances. To understand classroom lessons, both literary meaning and contextual cues are required, but the latter are culturally determined for tribal children. It is well known that teachers resort to categorization of the children into low and high achieving groups. The teacher does not expect the low group do better, spends less time teaching them, though they actually need more attention. Apart from their socio-cultural disabilities, students from low group are affected by inadequate attention paid by the teacher in teaching. Relationships develop between the teacher and those who have a greater chance to do well in studies. As a result, students lagging behind because of various reasons feel frustrated and tend to withdraw from schools. Language and communication discontinuities between home and school are crucial variable in the adjustment problems faced by children. Language thus becomes a major factor leading to drop outs. Realization of this factor made many psychologists and educationists to emphasize on teaching in mother tongue to young tribal children.

Attempts to Teach Tribal Children in Mother Tongue

In Andhra Pradesh, Haimendorf is one of the pioneers to attempt education of tribals in their mother tongue (Haimendorf, 1944). In Adilabad district, Haimendorf found that much of the land alienation was because the illiterate tribals are cheated in their credit transactions. Wherever present, schools were unattractive to tribals, as the Urdu and Marathi speaking teachers were unable to communicate effectively with tribal children. He started a school in 1943 for Gond youth who knew Urdu or Marathi, for training them as teachers. The teachers were trained to impart teaching in Gondi language using Devanagari script. The trainees were provided stipend during training period and after the completion of training, they were asked to open primary schools in the tribal villages. Readers and Premiers in Gondi, were prepared with the help of trainees. Lessons were mainly based on mythology, folklore and way of life of Gonds. On the pattern of the first training school started at Marlavai, training schools were later started at places like Sudimalla and Kamaram in Khammam district.

Teaching in tribal languages has started in tribal areas of North East India in fifties. Central Institute of Indian Languages (CIIL – Mysore), NCERT (New Delhi), and Tribal Cultural Research and Training Institutes, Integrated Tribal Development Agencies in different states are said to have made some contribution towards preparation of reading material in tribal languages and dialects. The role played by missionaries in different parts of the country also needs to be mentioned here. But, the reading material prepared by various agencies made no significant impact due to the policy of uniform syllabi for tribal students and non-tribal students.

Issues and Prospects

Education through local tribal dialects at least up to second standard is said to be desirable. Notwithstanding the Constitutional provision, teaching in tribal languages did not receive much attention. There are no clear instructions on policy guidelines. There are several issues involved in achieving this laudable objective. The linguistic diversity of tribal population does not allow one pattern of medium of instruction in tribal education. Presence of multi-lingual speech areas poses a problem in imparting education in mother tongue in tribal areas. Most of the tribal languages do not have a script. Instructional material is not available. Speakers of many languages are not a viable number. Non-availability of teachers knowing tribal languages is another constraint. Parents themselves are apprehensive if their children are taught in mother tongue. They will face problem in switching over to other languages at higher levels. Shift from tribal dialect to regional language from Class III onwards will create problems for tribal student whose vocabulary of regional language is not up to the mark. This shift from mother tongue to regional language is considered as over burdening of students. Some suggest the need to have supplementary premiers in state language for those studying elementary classes in tribal languages so that a smooth transition is ensured from tribal language to state language. Everywhere the trend is to go for English medium schools as it is considered prestigious and adds to prospects. Except for Convents, Public Schools, and a few selected Private Schools, the medium of instruction is regional language. How a separate system of primary education carried through their mother tongue prepares the tribal children for higher studies in Regional languages and English is an issue for debate. Many point out to the fact that Christian missionaries were able to achieve better literacy and education in the tribal areas of northeast, though the medium of instruction is English. One view is that, the teachers dealing with tribal children studying in a language other than home language need to be trained specially and to be provided with incentives for following a bilingual multilingual approach in teaching. They need to be provided with glossaries in tribal languages for technical terms. Here one of the problems that need to be overcome is lack of equivalent terms and concepts in tribal languages.

REFERENCES

1. Emeneau, M.B. 1955 *Kolami: A Dravidian Language*. Berkeley: University of California Press.
2. Furer-Haimendorf, Christoph Von. 1944. 'Aboriginal Education in Hyderabad', *Indian Journal of Social Work*. 5(2), 97-106.
3. Krishna Murthy, B.H. 1969. *Konda or Kubi: A Dravidian Language*, Hyderabad: Tribal Cultural Research and Training Institute.
4. Krishna Reddy, B. and Ramchandra Reddy M. 1987. 'An Ethnographic Account of the Banjaras', *Vanyajati*, Vol. XXXV, No. 2, 19-23.
5. Pratap, D.R. 1980. *The Naikapods and their Language*, ISRA, Bidisa.
6. Sitapathi, Gidugu, 1943. 'The Saoras and their Country', *Journal of the Andhra Historical Research Society*.
7. Trivedi, G.M., 1978. *Linguistic Study of the Chenchus of Andhra Pradesh*, Calcutta: Anthropological Survey of India.

Appendix

Language Development and Multilingual Education in Tribal Schools

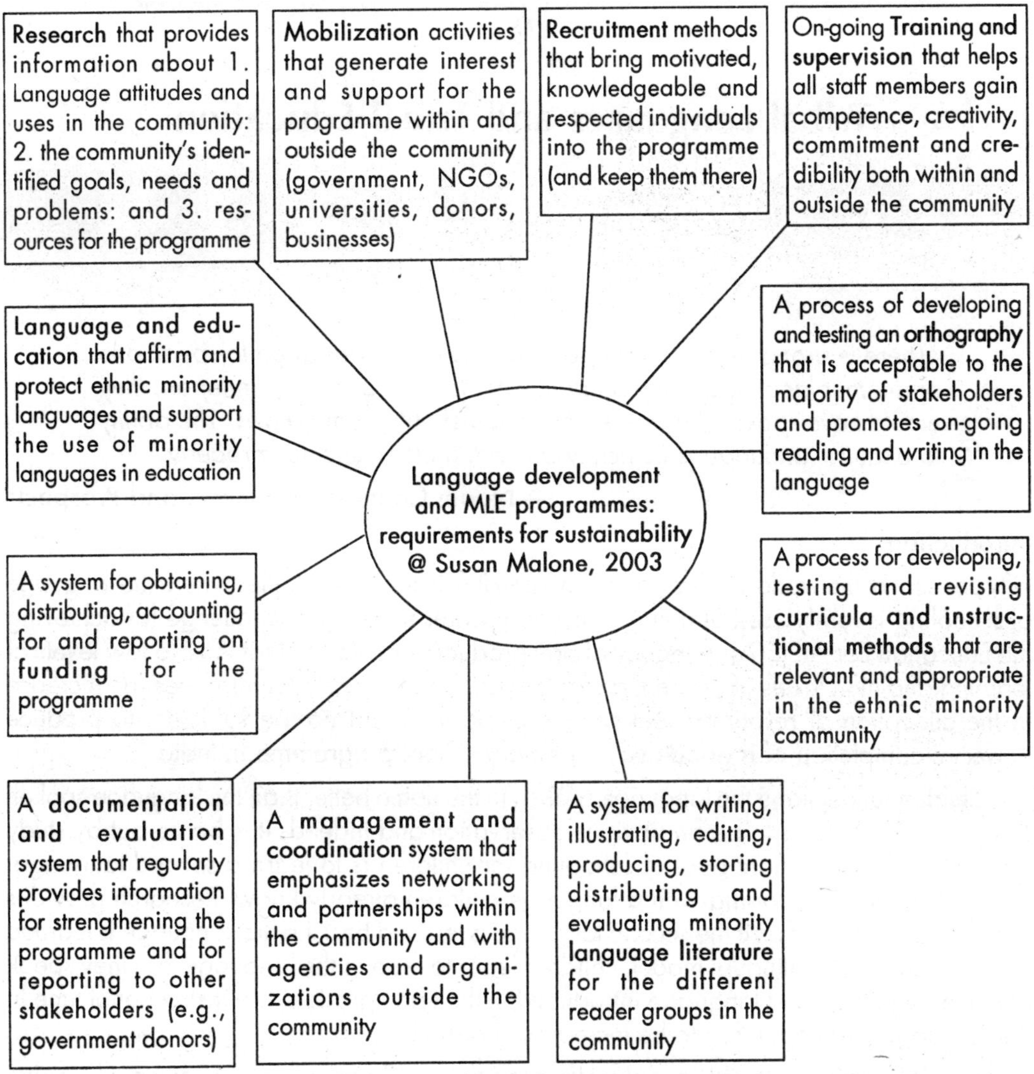

Language development and MLE programmes: requirements for sustainability @ Susan Malone, 2003

- **Research** that provides information about 1. Language attitudes and uses in the community: 2. the community's identified goals, needs and problems: and 3. resources for the programme
- **Mobilization** activities that generate interest and support for the programme within and outside the community (government, NGOs, universities, donors, businesses)
- **Recruitment** methods that bring motivated, knowledgeable and respected individuals into the programme (and keep them there)
- On-going **Training and supervision** that helps all staff members gain competence, creativity, commitment and credibility both within and outside the community
- **Language and education** that affirm and protect ethnic minority languages and support the use of minority languages in education
- A process of developing and testing an **orthography** that is acceptable to the majority of stakeholders and promotes on-going reading and writing in the language
- A system for obtaining, distributing, accounting for and reporting on **funding** for the programme
- A process for developing, testing and revising **curricula and instructional methods** that are relevant and appropriate in the ethnic minority community
- A **documentation and evaluation** system that regularly provides information for strengthening the programme and for reporting to other stakeholders (e.g., government donors)
- A **management and coordination** system that emphasizes networking and partnerships within the community and with agencies and organizations outside the community
- A system for writing, illustrating, editing, producing, storing distributing and evaluating minority **language literature** for the different reader groups in the community

Four Stages of Multilingual Education

Stage 1	Stage 2	Stage 3	Stage 4
Build oral fluency in L1 Begin literacy in L2 Use L1 as MOI	Build fluency in oral and written L1 Begin oral L2 Continue using L1 as MOI	Continue L1 literacy Bridge to literacy in L2 Use both languages as MOI	Use both/all languages for continuing education Add additional languages, as desired

9

Tribal Languages and Tribal Education

"There is strong reason to suppose that no one is designed to speak one or another language. If my children were to have grown up in Japan, they would have spoken Japanese, indistinguishably from natives. The ability to acquire language is basically a fixed, uniform species property."

—Noam Chomsky in Powers and Prospects

Introduction

Fifty per cent of the world's out-of-school children live in the communities where the language of schooling is rarely used at home. This underscores the biggest challenge for achieving the Education For All (EFA): a legacy of non-productive practices that lead to low levels of learning and high levels of dropout and retention. Under these circumstances, an increase in the allocation of resources, although necessary, would not be sufficient to produce universal completion of a good-quality primary school programme in India.

Children understand the language spoken in the home better than the language spoken in schools. This seems to be an obvious observation-and indeed, it is borne out by study after study. The important goal of schooling for children is to learn a second language. This is facilitated by starting with a language children already know. Research provides convincing evidence that if the second language is learned best the first language is learned well. In the existing bilingual model, children learn to read in the language that they speak at home, with a second language introduced in the early grades. The instructional time in the language learning needs to be increased gradually.

First language instruction naturally results in *(i)* increase of access and equity, *(ii)* improved learning outcomes, *(iii)* reduced repetition and dropout rates, *(iv)* socio-cultural benefits and *(v)* reduction of the overall costs. In many countries the bilingual programmes have generally been instituted in rural areas and among more marginalised populations. They have been widely shown to help the children stay in school longer, reach higher levels of education and increase their social mobility. In Male, for example at the end of the primary education level the pass percentage rates between 1994 and 2000 for children who transitioned gradually from a local language to French were on average 32 per cent higher than for children in French. The use of a language that children understand well allows teachers to use more active and more effective teaching-learning methods. Supporting mastery of the first language promotes the cognitive development. This helps to learn the second language easily. In Brazil, first language teaching has been linked to better acquisition of literacy skills. Several independent studies on the indigenous populations have demonstrated that the use of children's home language has been successful in raising the levels of literacy in the local language and the national language (Portuguese), as well as raising their achievement levels in a variety of academic subjects. In Burkina Faso, children with initial literacy in the Moore language before beginning instruction in French achieved better results in French and mathematics than the students who had only participated in French-language schooling. The use of local languages also ensures that the knowledge children bring to school is used as the basis for further learning.

In Male, where about 10 per cent of primary school children are in classrooms that use first languages as languages of instruction; these children are 5 times less likely to repeat the year and more than 3 times less likely to drop out of school. In bilingual schools in Guatemala, covering about 15 per cent of the population, grade repetition is about half that of traditional schools, while dropout rates are about 25 per cent lower. These results are all the more significant because children receiving instruction in first languages are often from more at risk populations. The use of local languages for instruction often leads to inclusion of more local content in the curriculum and greater participation of parents and community members as classroom resources. Parents are better positioned to become involved in the school and to feel that their knowledge and their culture are valued. The legitimisation of local languages that comes from their use in schooling can strengthen children's, families' and communities' sense of inclusion in schooling. The use of local languages in formal education has a positive impact on adult literacy as well. As parents see their children successfully learn to read and write in their own language, the parents are often motivated to attend literacy classes as well.

The financial benefits of the use of local languages in education derive largely from decreases in repetition and dropout. In the few cases where these benefits have been calculated, the savings have considerably outweighed the incremental costs of establishing and maintaining schooling in local languages (production of learning materials, teacher training, etc.). In Male, for instance, a World Bank study found that French-only programmes cost about 8 per cent less per year than mother-tongue schooling, but the total cost of educating a student through the six-year primary cycle is about 27 per cent more, largely because of the difference in repetition and dropout rates. Similar benefits have been found in Guatemala. Many developing countries have been reluctant to adopt a policy of delivering basic education in local languages. Donors have also not given high priority to such policies and in some cases have actively opposed them. Governments have cited goals such as the reduction of ethnic tensions and national unity as reasons to use foreign languages in education, although there is limited support in recent history for the unifying role of a single national language in a multilingual country. Other countries have decided to use several or even all of their national languages in order to avoid internal conflict. For example, after independence, the Government of Eritrea was committed in providing public education in all of its languages, to avoid internal disunity.

A more pressing obstacle to the use of local languages in schooling has to do with high development costs and weak implementation capacity. In many developing countries, materials in even one language are scarce, which leads to an understandable reluctance to try to publish books in several languages, where it is harder to achieve economies of scale. Yet technologies like desktop publishing are changing the situation. Papua New Guinea, for instance, has published materials in hundreds of languages by using a basic 'shell book' format. As of 2000, the country was using 380 languages in schooling. The Democratic Republic of the Congo has long published materials in the four languages which are regional lingua franca. Male is currently providing education in 11 languages with materials made available in each language.

A further challenge is that where there are many languages, formerly centralised approaches to teacher development and deployment will need to be modified. To address this challenge, countries can decentralise the recruitment of teacher candidates and pre- and in-service teacher training can also be managed regionally rather than centrally.

Another obstacle is that parents and teachers may resist the use of the mother tongue as a language of instruction. In Mexico, researchers have found that some parents who speak Triqui believe that Spanish is more important in schools because it is the "language of progress." Similarly, in Haiti, many parents resist the use of Creole as the language of instruction because the mother tongue is thought to be the language of the poor and the oppressed. A campaign to explain language policy and its benefits is an essential part of any solution but ultimately, resistance will continue unless the education system is designed to value what children themselves bring to the learning process. Further, parents who hesitate to send their children to a mother tongue-medium classroom are often convinced of its value when they see children in the bilingual programme outperforming their official-language counterparts by the end of the 4th grade-In the official language.

Resistance will continue unless the education system supports the use of local languages in several ways: ensuring a constant supply of appropriate textbooks and other materials, training teachers in the benefits of using local languages for instruction as well as in appropriate methods, and ensuring that high stakes examination systems reward the skills in which children instructed in local languages excel (i.e. redesigning exams to emphasize reading, writing and problem solving, not just extensive memorisation of second language texts). In Male, for instance, overcame some teacher resistance by designing the reform to include *(i)* teacher training in active and effective teaching methods, *(ii)* a transfer to the second language in the early grades and *(iii)* changing examination policies and ensuring 'quick wins' for teachers, students and parents. Literacy classes for adults can also reduce parental reluctance and provide legitimacy for local language.

The use of first languages as languages of instruction can contribute to the attainment of EFA goals 2nd should be a part of the World Bank's dialogue with educators and policy-makers. Particular attention should be paid to the following issues: Policy formulation around language of instruction issues and successful implementation require political commitment and the support of parents and community members. Bilingual programmes are most successful where the goal is to make children literate in their first language and also to acquire fluency in the second (usually the former colonial) language; these should not be either/or propositions. The policy environment of language reforms must be carefully managed, with significant training and planning, to include. Consensus building and awareness campaigns among teachers, parents and NGOs; Professional development for teachers; Curriculum and teaching materials development and consistent provision of high or equivalent quality materials at the classroom level; and Financial support, particularly for initial investment costs.

Language and the Indian Constitution

The Constituent Assembly of India faced a very delicate situation on the language issue. The idea at large was to evolve a common language to preserve the unity of the country. But the linguistic picture of India was highly heterogenous with none of the languages having majority of speakers. Even Hindustani was spoken only by 45 per cent of the population. In spite of this a strong emotional and political urge existed among the members to evolve a common language. When the Constituent Assembly started framing the various language provisions a number of dissensions and disagreements emerged. The Assembly split and thus the language issue became a very controversial aspect. The central points of language controversy centered around the issue of Hindi as National language, replacement of English and the time frame for it, status of regional languages and definition of Hindi.

With divergent views expressed on these issues, the controversy dragged on and ultimately it ended with a near unanimous acceptance of the K.M. Munshi Gopalaswamy Ayyanagar formula. It provided for Hindi in Devanagiri script as Official Language of Indian Union along with the continuation of English language for a period of fifteen years from the commencement of the Constitution. However, the Official Language Act of 1963 and its subsequent Amendment in 1967 has given a veto power to the State Governments regarding the displacement of English by Hindi as an Official and Link Language. The various language provisions of the Constitution are contained in part XVII from Article 343 to 351 ably supported by the 8th Schedule which recognizes eighteen languages as National Official Languages (Manipuri, Nepali and Konkani where included vide 71 Amendment to the Constitution in 1992). Out of the eighteen Schedule Languages, thirteen fall in Indo-Aryan branch, four in Dravidian family and one in Tibeto-Burmese family. Its quite surprising that out of 114 languages and 216 classified mother tongues in the country only 18 languages have been brought under the category of Schedule Languages.

By going through the deliberations in the Constituent Assembly and the Indian Parliament, it becomes clear that neither the Constituent Assembly nor the Indian Parliament debated the language question of the country as a whole. What has been debated is whether English or Hindi would be the National Official Languages and what role Sanskrit should play in the scheme of languages. Jawaharlal Nehru's recommendation for the use and protection of tribal languages fell on deaf ears.

After the linguistic re-organisation of the states in 1956, a number of minority language groups were left behind in several states. Most of these minority language groups are politically powerless tribal communities indigenous to the states, while others are speakers of major languages migrated from other states. In every State, the language of the majority is used for official transactions and as medium of instruction. Political importance attached to regional languages in states has enhanced their functional value. At the same time, this has exerted enormous socio-political pressure on the speakers of the minority tribal languages to learn the "regional languages for their socio-economic mobility and educational development."

In India, conflicting feelings exist about development. On one side national integration is confused with assimilation. On the other side protection is confused with isolationism. It is often forgotten that these two do not exhaust the possibility of contact. Structural incorporation of groups maintaining their languages and cultures forming a mosaic has been holding the country together since many years. Tribals are not an exception to this trend.

Tribal Language and Tribal Education

With the exclusion of constitutionally recognised languages, the rest of the Indian languages can be taken as minor languages. It may be pointed out that the notion "minor language" need not be based on the numerical strength of a language. Riders like socio-economic power, social prestige and pressure group tactics that their speakers carry in a multilingual society matter most. In this context most of the minor languages are spoken by the tribals. The dichotomy of major and minor languages is reflected in terms of the dominating and the dominated.

The dominating languages exhibit features like numerical majority, medium of education, communication and administration, vehicles of regional development and prestige. Speakers are monolingual. The dominated tribal language speakers are bilingual or multilingual depending on the local linguistic situation. They are invaded by outsiders in various spheres viz., socio-economic and cultural, though they are locally in numerical majority they are turned into a minority under the regional pressures, they are discriminated against by non-recognition of their languages and cultural traits. The attitude of dominant ethnic groups towards tribal languages consists of outright rejection of a tribal language in a bilingual context and ridiculing the tribals for using their mother tongue in a public place. The attitude of tribals towards the majority languages is total recognition and learning it for inter group communication and acceptance as a language of social mobility, economic emancipation and status. The tribals identify themselves with majority language of their area.

The tribal child is not unique or deficient. A tribal child is born into a culture which uses a language different from others. Like any other culture. The tribal child also uses language, grammar and dialect in the same manner as others do. Tribal education is not opposed to mainstream education.

The general notion is that the tribal child needs to be motivated to attend school. Both the parent and the child need to be convinced that schooling is learning. The tribal learner includes both the child at the school and the adult learner seeking literacy. The teacher is the focal point and a catalytic agent in the educational process of the tribal child. Unfortunately many teachers are non-tribals working in tribal schools. Unless they have knowledge of a tribal language or a language of wider communication prevailing among the tribals forming a school community, the teacher is at a great loss. In the interest of healthy classroom and community interaction, the teacher' must learn the language of tribal community.

The monolingual tribal child faces cognitive and communicative problems where the instruction is in the major regional language. For instance, the Kuvi and Santali children attending the Oriya or Bengali Medium schools in Orissa or West Bengal. In a situation like this, the content of the primers is also alien and new. Writing about "Aliens in their own home" Sudhir Shukla writes, On his first day in a remote village school in Madhya Pradesh, six year old Bishnoo asks his friend Surta to "Ingey Vaita" (Gondi for "Come here"). But what follows is a scream from the teacher. "Chup baith, janwar kahin ka" (Shut up, you village idiot). Shukla further writes, "cowed down, little Bishnoo does not know whether he was wrong in using Gondi in the classroom which has invited his teachers wrath. But within few months he learns that speaking his native tongue in the classroom in an offense. Though Bishnoo cannot understand the Hindi of the teacher or of the text books he realises that the only language he knows has no place in the school."

There are several Bishnoo's allover the country and tribal children suffer for speaking in their mother tongue and not being able to speak the school language. They either understand the language of the text nor the teacher. As the teacher does not know the language of the learner and the parents neither know the language of the text book nor the teacher, the break is almost complete. The education is therefore merely symbolic.

Very often the multiplicity of tribal languages and small members of learners in each class are cited as hurdlers for giving instruction. Language as a medium should not be mixed with language as a subject. Language as a subject can be taught at different levels drawing students from different classes into a single level. It requires will to instruct in tribal languages. Secondly the socio-linguistic setting is closely related to the strategies of instruction. For instance, the bilingual settings with respect to the Wagdi-Hindi in Rajasthan are more in number and the tribal children's exposure to the situation are also more. Taking advantage of this situation more number of lessons using both the tribal mother tongue and state language are included right from class one primer. In the case of tribal languages of Karnataka Jenu Kuruba and Soliga, are considered as dialects of Kannada, as they are genetically related. This has made the preparers of material to use both tribal mother tongue and standard Kannada lessons to bridge the gap between the two.

Remedial Measures Needed

Many impediments are to be removed if a clear perspective is to emerge in relation to tribal language and tribal education: Firstly, there is a need to explore the commonness in structure and culture in terms of material production and in reading and learning between tribal and non-tribal languages (vocabulary, grammar and pragmatics). Secondly, adult literacy among the tribals needs to be improved though bilingual instruction. The teaching manuals must include contents relevant to the socio, cultural, economic, political and communication needs of the tribes. Thirdly, there is an imperative need for introduction of bilingual education. Mother tongue should be the medium of instruction at primary school level. This should lead to a smooth switch over to bilingual instruction i.e., local contact language and general switch over to regional language and link language in a phased manner. Tribal languages must find their due place in the language formula. Fourthly, the content of the primers is very important. Environmental experience, perceptions, ethnicity needs and value systems are to be accommodated in instructional materials. Lastly, oral literature must form part and parcel of instruction materials. Tribal children's own words and stories are to be used as the basis for primers. Further the language teachers are to be trained and acquainted with tribal languages. The tribal child will be lost if the aim of education remains making of citizens rather than making a man.

Conclusion

There is religion, culture and tradition but mother tongue has its own importance. In India there is an urgent need for the introduction of local languages in the school academic curriculum for the preservation of indigenous languages. At the same time there is also an important need for the importance of English in today's world of globalisation for the connectivity. Language is needed for the enrichment of the mind and building up of the personality. 'Education is something that opens up our mind to comprehend and then to analyse what one comprehends. The next step is to retain what one has analysed to articulate else the idea behind education is lost'. Connectivity is language, culture, literature, history, mythology, science, information technology, etc. to lead our children to the next millennium. There is an urgent need to be an extensive research on languages and cultures of different tribes in states so that the society will have a solid scrip of whom we are and not based on our society through mythology and chronicles. The State Governments should prepare a blueprint for preserving and starting local languages in the schools. State Governments also should take active steps to preserve the culture and the identity of the various tribes in the respective states. The extinction of any language in the states will pave the way for the group to succumb to the domination of the others. It was stated that 'since the coming of Globalisation, the world has turned into a small village and this very fact has become a big question as to whether our culture will be able to survive and sustain this change'. The society should move towards development without affecting danger to our cultural identity. People in India should safeguard their traditional language that is being directly or indirectly invaded by others. The Government should encourage to the cultural script of the indigenous population in the country. The State Governments also should advocate for the introduction of local languages in schools as enrichment programmes. The Education Departments in the states must act as catalysts in the development preservation of tribal languages. Most of the tribal children are not accustomed to their mother tongue due to the negligence on the part of the parents and schools. Working parents generally keep their children in residential hostels and Ashram school teachers who are not well versed in tribal languages. As a result, the tribal children are deprived from learning of their own mother tongue. Therefore, there is an urgent need to document the tribal languages for the future generations. The development of tribal languages and tribal education is two dimensional– first the preservation of rich indigenous culture and tradition of the state and second the adherence to the national fervour in the education system. Without the use of any of the indigenous languages as regional or state language and consequently as the medium of instruction in schools in the States would put additional pressure on students of learning more than required languages besides mother tongue of the students. It is also important to note that it will be difficult for the students to learn their subjects in the language other than their own, which ultimately leads to insurmountable contents deficiency over the years in every succeeding classes primary or elementary level to discontinuation of studies.

REFERENCES

1. Annamalai, E. "A Programme for Bilingual Education in India", *Proceedings of the IV All India Conference of Linguists*, Agra.

2. Annamalai, E. Linguistic Dominance and Cultural Dominance: A Study of Tribal Bilingualism in India", *Presidential Address, XVII All India Conference of Dravidian Linguists*, Kanyakumari.
3. Mohanty, A.K. 1990. "Language of Literacy Education for the Linguistic Minorities in India", *Indian Journal of Adult Education, Vol. 51*, pp. 78-88.
4. Pattanayak, D.P. 1981. *Multilingulaism and Mother Tongue Education*, Delhi: Oxford University Press.
5. Pattanayak, D.P. 1990. "Orality and Literacy: An Indian Perspective", *Indian Journal of Adult Education, Vol. 51*, pp. 14-20.
6. Shukla, Sudhir. "Aliens in Their Own Home", *The Hindu, 14 March 1993.*
7. Srivastava, R.N. 1984. "Literacy Education for Minorities: A Case Study from India", in F. Columes ed., *Linguistic Minorities and Literacy: Language Policy Issues in Developing Countries*, Berlin: Monton Publishers.
8. *The Bilingual-Education for Tribal Children: The CIIL Experiment*, Mysore, CIIL, Unpublished typescript.
9. Toppo, Sita. 1979. *Dynamics of Educational Development in Tribal India*, New Delhi: Classical Publications.
10. Wagner, Daniel A. 1993. *Literacy, Culture and Development*, Cambridge: Cambridge University Press.

10

Bilingual Education in Tribal Schools

Introduction

Imparting early education through one's own mother tongue is a universally accepted dictum. In India education at the primary school level including tribal education is generally imparted through official languages of the states. This creates a gap between the official language of the state and the tribal mother tongue. Owing to this there is slow progress, lack of interest and high drop out rate among the tribal children at the primary school level. Teaching tribal children in an "unknown" language ultimately demotivates them. However in recent years educationists have realised the importance of giving early education to tribal children through their own mother tongue. In this context "Bilingual Education Model" assumes importance. This chapter attempts to look into the Bilingual Education framework in tribal schools of Andhra Pradesh, important aspects of Bilingual Education, curriculum needs of tribal children, expected outcome of Bilingual Education and stages for the conduct of Bilingual Education.

Universalisation of primary education and provision of free and compulsory education to all children upto the age of 14 years are two cherished mandatory goals of the Indian Constitution. Early education through one's own mother tongue is an accepted pedagogical dictum. Education at the primary school level, in our country generally is imparted through the Official Languages of the States. The same situation prevails in the case of tribal education. The gap between the official language of the state which is used as a school language and the home language of the tribal children i.e. the tribal mother tongue happens to be major cause for tribal children's slow progress, lack of interest and achievement which ultimately lead to the high rate of drop outs among the children especially at the primary school level. This situation prevails even today in some of the tribal areas. In such situations the tribal children have to learn all subjects through a language which is not their "mother tongue" and "unknown" which ultimately demotivates them.

In recent years educationists have realised the importance of giving early education to tribal children through their own tribal mother tongue. In this context 'Bilingual Education Model' (transfer bilingual education model) assumes importance. In this model two languages namely the tribal mother tongue and the dominant official language of the state which is used as a school language are used as medium of instruction. Tribal mother tongue and school language are taught as language subjects. Initially the instructions will be in the tribal mother tongue and through programmed and graded instructions, the tribal children will be transferred from the tribal mother tongue to the main stream school language (which is the official language of the state). The transfer will be completed over a period of 3 to 5 years at the primary school level depending upon the tribal situation.

Bilingual Education Framework in Tribal Schools of Andhra Pradesh

Any educational programme which uses two languages as medium of instruction either simultaneously or subsequently may be called a programme of bilingual education. There are many types of bilingual education programmes depending upon how and when the two languages are used as medium of instruction. The "Bilingual Education" is therefore a broad framework within which variation is possible depending upon the particular tribal situation. The tribal situation may be classified on the following parameters: (1) Exposure to and competence in the state official language before the children go to school. (2) The genetic relationship between the tribal language and the state language. (3) Relationship due to contact and shared cultural traits between the tribal community and the majority community of the state. As a general principle when the competence, relatedness, convergence and shared traits are more switch over to the sole medium of the state language can be sooner.

The minimum and the maximum points in terms of classes at the primary stage for the use of tribal language and the state language as medium however is fixed. The tribal language must be used as medium right from Class I and it must also be taught as a language subject from that class. The state language may be used as a medium in any class in the primary stage but it may be taught as a language subject at the oral level from Class I. The tribal language may cease to be a medium and the state language will be the sole medium by the end of the primary stage. The tribal language may be continued to be taught as a language subject after the primary stage. The choice of the variety of the tribal language to be used in school may be chosen by following usual criteria such as the size of the population, derivability of other dialects, intelligibility for other dialect speakers, etc.

Regarding the instructional materials in the state language for the tribal children it will be necessary to prepare special material until the end of bilingual education. The teaching principles and content to tribal children must relate to the cultural values and life experience of the tribal community. The existing state language material is designed for mother tongue children and in most cases cannot be used in the case of tribal children. The content may shift towards the major language community as one goes to higher classes.

As far as non-language subjects like sciences are concerned, the concepts evolved at the national level to be used in textbooks for different classes may be used in the textbook of bilingual education also. But illustrations of these concepts may be drawn from and pertinent to the tribal experience and environment. For instance, safety as a concept may not be illustrated with doors and locks of a house in a tribal community which do not have them. They may instead be illustrated through collective vigil, fire as a protective device, etc. which are prevailing practice in a particular tribal community. The technical terms to write the science subjects in the tribal language, choice may be allowed to borrow them from the state language or to create word through derivation and compounding in the tribal language itself.

In the case of tribal languages of Andhra Pradesh namely Savara, Gadaba, Koya, Chenchu and Banjara are considered as 'dialects' of Telugu, as they are genetically related. This will enable the material preparers to use both the tribal mother tongue and the standard Telugu in the lesson with ample number of conversion exercises to bridge the gap between the tribal mother tongue and the state language, i.e. the standard Telugu.

Bilingualism among the tribal children in Andhra Pradesh is comparatively low. Taking this into consideration different kinds of materials have been prepared by Tribal Cultural Research and Training Institute, The District Primary Education Programme and Sarvashiksha Abyan and The Integrated Tribal Development Agencies. To teach the tribal mother tongue and school language, i.e. Telugu language separate primers are prepared. Tribal primers are introduced in the first year using the same content of Class I textbooks. With the help of "known content", "learner content" unknown tribal language primers are taught to tribal children.

Important Aspects of Bilingual Education

The important aspects in Bilingual Education are as follows: (1) Bilingual education attempts to teach the mother tongue using the script of the state language so that the reading and writing skills are established by the use of a known language. Script of the state language with modifications are used because of educational advantages and social benefits. (2) The acquired skills namely reading and writing skills in the mother tongue situation are used for the smooth transfer from the mother tongue of the children to school language, i.e. state language through specially prepared materials. (3) Two languages namely tribal mother tongue and state language are used as a medium of instruction to teach non-language subjects such as Environmental Studies, Arithmetic, etc. (4) As far as Orthographic and spelling are concerned, the conventions of the state language is to be followed. (5) Primary education must be in bilingual and each tribal child must get an opportunity to learn his/her own mother tongue in addition to state language.

Expected Outcome of Bilingual Education

The expected outcome of bilingual education are:

1. The parents in particular and community in general will have greater involvement in the education of the tribal children.
2. The attendance of the tribal children in the school will be regular and the dropout rate will reduce.
3. Interaction between the teacher and tribal students will increase.
4. The tribal child will develop basic literacy skills faster in the mother tongue/home language.
5. The tribal child will develop a sense of cultural rootedness.
6. The tribal child will transfer the skills acquired in one language to another.
7. The competence of the child in the school language/state language will increase to match the competence of the children whose mother tongue is also the school language.
8. Bilingualism will develop in the tribal child non-unitary perception and an analytical approach to the problems of life.

Curriculum Needs of Tribal Children

PHASE 1: FIRST YEAR

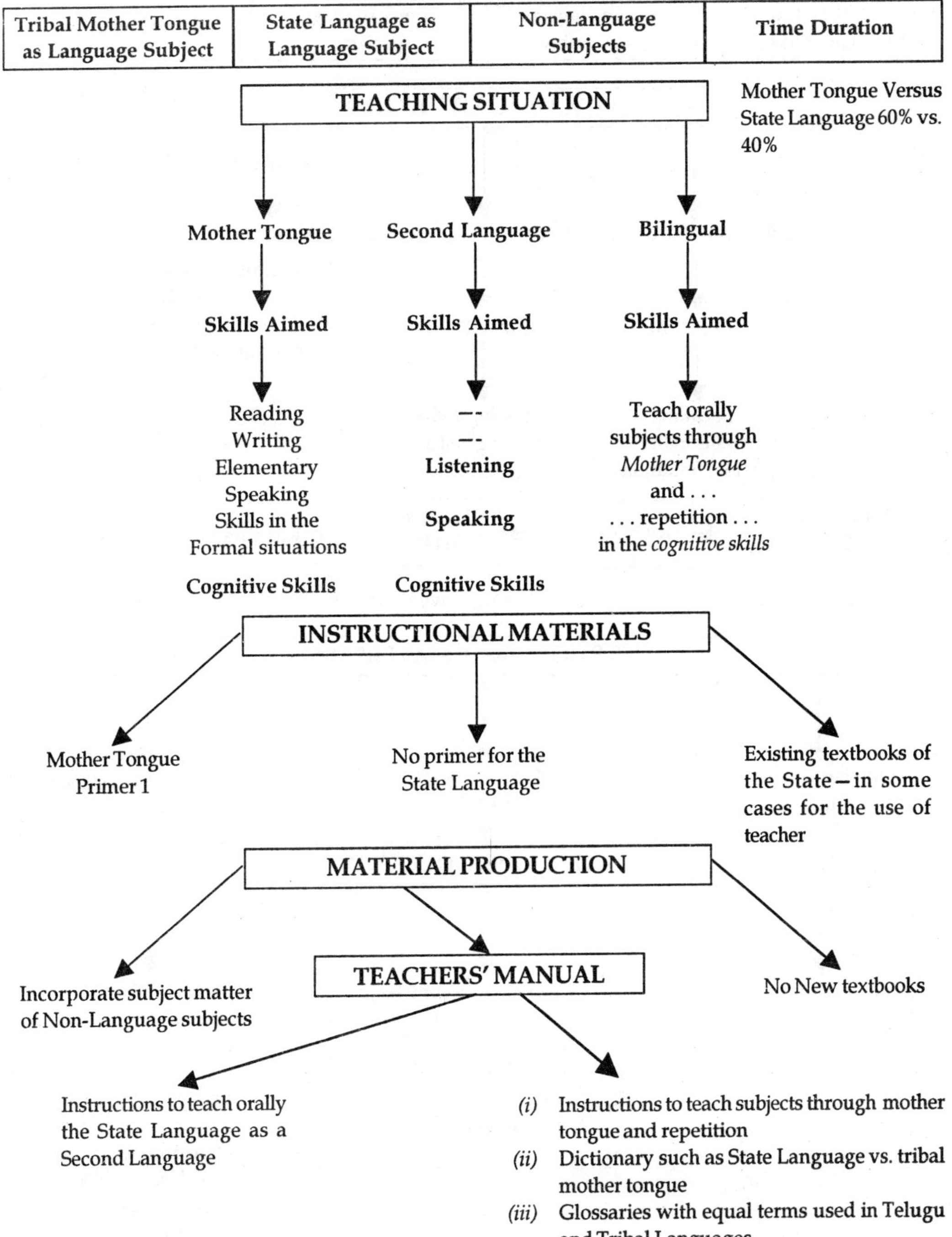

PHASE 2: SECOND YEAR

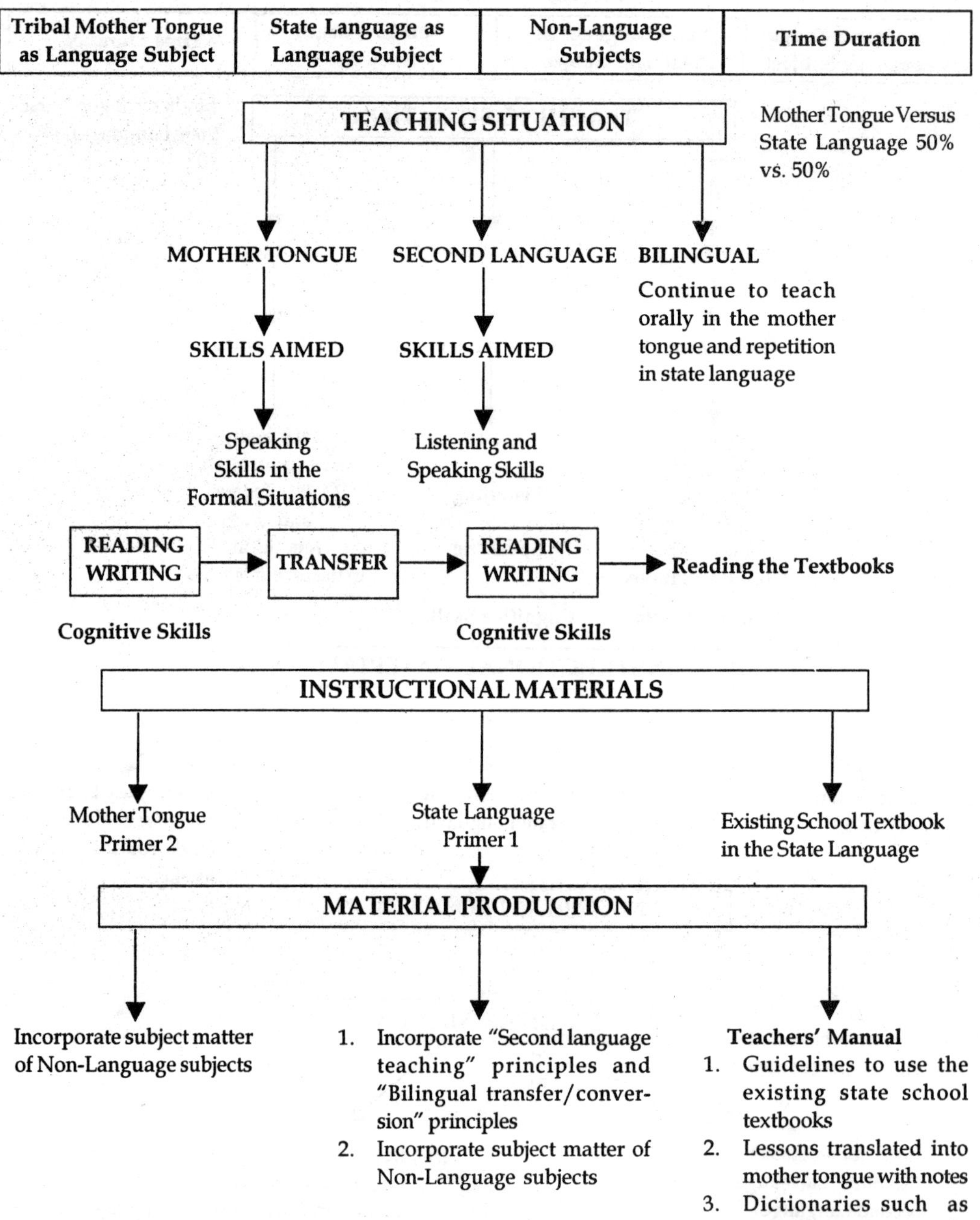

PHASE 3: THIRD YEAR

Tribal Mother Tongue as Language Subject	State Language as Language Subject	Non-Language Subjects	Time Duration

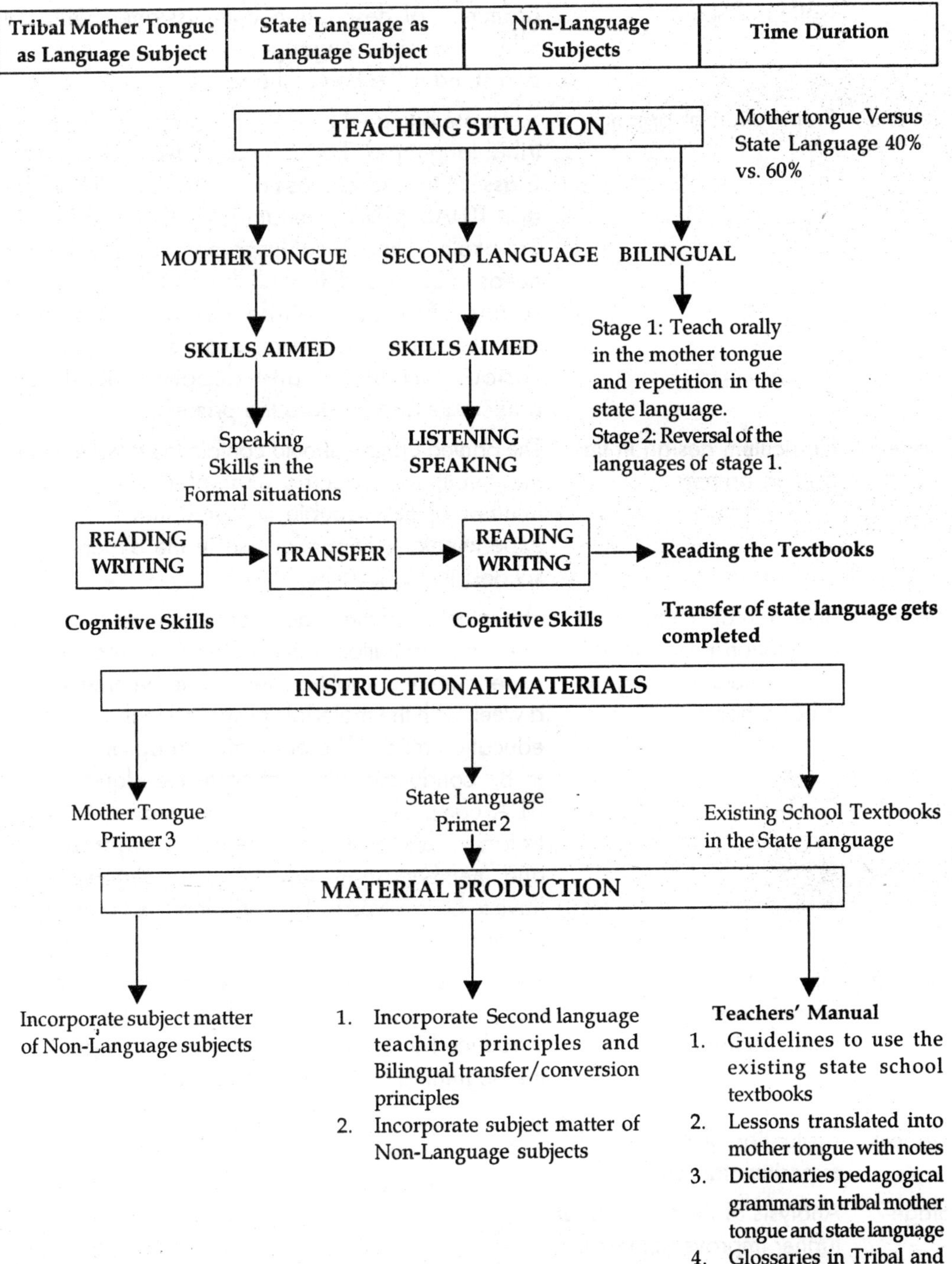

Stages for the Conduct of Bilingual Education

Stage	Activity	Description
Stage-1	Creation and Standardisation of script	The linguistic study of the language includes grammatical description commissioned with the school and state language. It includes the creation and standardization of the script.
Stage-2	Preparation of primers	Separate bilingual primers are prepared for some tribal languages. For example Savara Bharati for Class I in the workshops conducted by DPEP, TCTRI and ITDAS (ITDA, Seetampeta, ITDA Paderu in Srikakulam and Visakhapatnam districts). This needs to be extended to all the 33 tribal groups in Andhra Pradesh. While conducting similar workshops tribal teachers, experts, scholars from various institutions and departments should participate and prepare the primers.
Stage-3	Curriculum design in the printed primers	The printed primers should contain the tribal environment, culture, specific examples with a good number of new double colour visuals. They are experimental editions for use in the experimental schools in tribal areas.
Stage-4	Selection of schools and orientation programme for teachers working in tribal schools	The selection of the experimental schools should be done in consultation with the State Government. The experimental school teachers has to be oriented for a week with the materials prepared in the bilingual education mode. The orientation programmes has to be conducted either at State Headquarters or ITDA complexes. The State Educational Administrators, SCERTS, TCR&TI, research organizations and members from new voluntary organisations have to be involved in the workshops and orientation programmes.
Stage-5	Introduction of the primers in the experimental schools	The academic year in the tribal school starts from June/July months. Therefore the primers should be introduced in the experimental schools right from the beginning of the academic year onwards.
Stage-6	Evaluation of the experimental schools	
Stage-7	Analysis of the findings for further improvement and feedback	

Conclusion

Effective tribal education at the primary level may be imparted by adopting suitable Bilingual Education model. This helps in preserving the diversity in a multilingual country like ours and links each individual to the mainstream society. Even though a good beginning has been made by apex educational institutions like NCERT RIEs, DPEP, TCTRI, SSA and others in Andhra Pradesh in preparation of dictionaries, Bharaties, glossaries, bilingual charts, bridge inventories and training programmes a comprehensive Bilingual Education model is required for the improvement of tribal education and curriculum needs of tribal students in Andhra Pradesh.

REFERENCES

1. Annamalai, B. 1983. "A national framework for bilingual education for tribal children", *Vartha Vaha, No. 3, CIIL, Mysore*, pp. 11-12.
2. Annamalai, B. 1990. "Dimensions of bilingual education in India", New Language Planning, *Newsletter, Vol. 4, No. 4*, pp. 1-3.
3. Gnanasundaram, V. "*Language use in tribal education: perspectives and problems*", CIIL, Mysore.
4. Gnanasundaram, V. "*Writing systems for tribal languages*", CIIL, Mysore.
5. Government of India, Ministry of Education, 1966. *Education and National Development*, p. 157.
6. NCERT, 1967. *Tribal Education in India, Publication No. 20, Tribal Education Unit, Department of Adult Education*, NCERT.
7. Pattanayak, D.P. 1974. *Language Curriculum*, CIIL, Mysore.
8. Pattanayak, D.P. 1991. *Language Education and Culture*, CIIL, Mysore, p. 170.
9. Wunn, Stephen, A. 1993. "Information Document. The red book of languages in danger of disappearing", *UNESCO*.

11

Tribal Education: Preponderance, Problems and Prospects

Introduction

Today education is considered as the most important tool not only for the development of individual but also for the onward march of the society. The purpose of education is to promote the development of a 'well integrated person capable of exercising such responsibilities in the society as his powers allow. Education is the key to progress. All the countries of the World are giving importance to education and emphasising on providing basic education to all the members of the society, young and old. As literacy holds the key to progress, education, is being given top priority for the development of all sections of the society. The scheduled caste, scheduled tribe and other backward sections constitute the majority of the disadvantaged population in the state of Andhra Pradesh. The Government has been striving hard to improve their social, economic and educational status.

Tribal Education Scenario in Andhra Pradesh

Jatapu, Kondadora, Mukadora, Mannedora, Lambada, Yerukala, Koya, Gond, Pardhan, Yanadi are some of the major tribal groups and Savara, Gadaba, Thoti, Chenchu, Kolam, Kanda Reddy, Porja and Khond are some of the Primitive Tribal Groups (PTGs) existing in the state of Andhra Pradesh. So far as the percentage of literacy among these tribes is concerned, it is very low and below the national average. The literacy among women is very poor. Illiteracy, ignorance and superstition are the evils that are dominant in these societies. After independence sustained efforts were being made for the educational development of the tribal communities to bring them on par with the other communities of the society. Schools are being opened in tribal areas to provide access for the tribal child and considerable efforts are being made to retain the children to complete the full school course and also to improve the quality of education.

Problems of Tribal Education

Often both physically and socially isolated from majority communities, scheduled tribes have lower enrolment and achievement rates and higher dropout rates than the general population. A recent study of 60 schools in two tribal districts in Andhra Pradesh found high absenteeism among tribal children who were enrolled (Sujatha, 1995). The personal experience of the writer confirms the fact, that in Utnoor tribal area of Adilabad district the enrolment is only 57 per cent. Absenteeism is higher in Grades I and IV than in Grades II and III. Sujatha points out that very young children and those old enough to help with the household work are less likely to attend regularly. Dropout rates are also high among ST children. The important cause for this situation is household welfare.

Gaps in the Field of Tribal Education

The major causes for the gap in the education field of tribal education, to mention a few, are cultural discontinuity between family and school, the language of instruction and the quality of schools. Family, community and school factors play a part in limiting enrolment, retention and achievement among tribal children. Traditional pollution, laws of the tribal communities restrict their interaction with other communities. Limited acceptability of regional schools which serve more than one community. In tribal communities, most of the children are first generation students. There is no support for school learning. Behaviour required of children at school may be unfamiliar to tribal families. Their traditional methods differ from what is taught in schools. Tribal communities are not aware of the benefits to which they are entitled. One-third of the children do not attend the school instead prefer to spend their time moving around, swimming in ponds and streams, catching fish, climbing trees, hunting birds, collecting berries, riding on buffaloes, etc. 'The day prison model of the schooling', i.e. in school the children are expected to, be highly disciplined and to follow the rigid timings and be confined to a classroom. The socialisation in tribal society presents children with a lot of freedom and free nature. Very rarely are the children punished. The conflict between the norms of the school and socialisation at home results in resistance and unwillingness among children to attend the school.

Factors Affecting the Response of Tribal People to Formal Education

Language of instruction is another most important factor affecting the response of tribal people to formal education. The textbook language is different from the home language. The third important factor is the school quality. A few pucca buildings, less furniture and equipment, few teachers educated to Grade 10 or above, few teachers with recent inservice training, teacher's absenteeism, poor teaching-learning methods, poor achievement levels are the great hindrances for the tribal children in their present educational setup.

Reasons for Low Attendance of Tribal Children in Schools

In its study on tribal education made in 7 SSA states, the NCERT mentioned many reasons for low attendance of tribal children in schools. The reasons are as follows: financial problems, house work, health problems, agricultural work, school atmosphere, teachers behaviour, children's failure in examination and unwillingness of parents. In his publication, '*Primary schooling in India*', Amarjeet Sinha felt that tribal remote locations posed a serious problem in providing for school buildings, teachers and other minimal facilities.

Strategies Suggested to Overcome the Problems in Tribal Education

To overcome these problems and achieve better results the strategies suggested are: rationalisation of teachers posts, opening of full time alternate schools, change of working hours and holidays in tune with local needs, use of bilingual charts, developing teaching-learning materials in tribal dialects, the use of bridge text that use words in the tribal dialect, training in multigrade teaching, empowerment of community, school complex programmes, convergence services of various departments at school level, school readiness programmes, activity based teaching-learning process, community mobilisation programmes, timely supply of incentives, effective teacher training and research.

Programmes taken up in Different States

Various programmes were taken up in different states for tribal education. In the Utnoor Agency area of Adilabad district, with the problem of access, enrolment, retention and quality of education at primary state. However, the Government of Andhra Pradesh implemented the following programmes and gained some fruitful results. With regard to access, rationalization of teachers posts, opening of community schools/maabadi schools in school less habitations, encouraging voluntary organizations to open schools were planned and implemented likewise. With regard to enrolment, retention and quality, the programmes implemented by the State Government were as follows: opening of Village Census Registers, door-to-door survey, incentives of school committees which achieved a cent per cent enrolment and retention, construction of two roomed sheds and teacher doctor programme, etc. With regard to retention, the programmes implemented are: activity-based instruction, mid-day meal programme, constitution of Awal Committees, supply of minimum educational material as a package of incentive, residence of teacher in the school village and contacts with parents about the progress of the children. With regard to quality the programmes implemented were: improving the competence of teachers, training the minimum levels of training, training in activity approach, preparation and supply of instructional modules, supply of instructional kits, preparation and supply of 116 instructional charts, filling up of vacant posts by locals, strengthening of supervision through project Education Counsellors, payment of teachers salaries through banks, Awal Committees to watch the regularity of the school teachers, monthly review of academic work at cluster level, teaching through bilingual charts, daily schedule of academic work in the form of a calendar, frequent orientation in activity method, adoption of APPEP pedagogy and incentives to those who do good work.

Tribal Education Interventions in Different States

The interventions taken by the Government of Kerala was opening of new schools, multigrade learning centres, non formal education centres preparation of link language materials child friendly textbooks, two day summer camps for tribal mothers in tribal hamlets conduct of processions, one additional batch of TIC, appointment of tribal volunteers in selected panchayats Organisation of Griha Sadasu, Mother PTAs. The initiatives taken by the Government of Orissa state is: motivation meetings and involvement of NGOs, use of tribal and fork media for mass mobilisation, gitkadia Sabha, meeting in weekly tribal markets, school community interaction during tribal festivals in the village, meeting with tribal leaders and village headman (gomango) in primary, education, language training to teachers (non-tribal), publication of book lets on communicative conversation in tribal languages, publication of savra primer for Class I, commissioning of a study i.e., linguistic survey and mapping, the aim is to know the level of understanding of the tribal language and state language by the teachers, children and parents and also to focus on common words used by tribal and non-tribal children, parents and teachers, organisation of a workshop on the "use of folklore in primary education", informal learning process present in tribal society, the cognitive aspects present in tribal folklore, understand how the birthplace and local environment help develop the cognitive aspects of children, importance of experiential learning from the environment of the child, the potential for education and learning present in the village use by teachers, integrated knowledge on language, arithmetic and evs already present in the minds of the children prior to coming to school, the oral tradition, art, craft and social life present among children prior to coming to school, how teachers knowledge on the local culture and language can help bridge the gap between school and home and how a cordial relationship between school and community can be developed. The initiatives taken by the Government of Maharashtra was the development of a tribal dialect dictionary. In the state of Tamil Nadu the initiatives were: teams of college girls conducted awareness camps in tribal areas at nights in the month of January, alternative schools in the form of NFE centres, and special training programme for teachers posted in tribal areas. In the state of Assam: study network with anthropology departments of universities and others, utilise NFEs as AS, literacy activities through traditional mechanisms, opening of ECEs, organisation of Kalajathas, documentation of tribal forklore and orient teachers posted in tribal areas by developing training materials. In the state of Karnataka the initiatives were: workshop to develop MLL textbook for Class I soliga dialect, handbook for teachers in forming them of social and cultural norms of the tribals and develop a training module for teachers posted in tribal areas. In Madhya Pradesh the efforts were opening of Ashram schools, opening of ECEs, assessment of learning difficulties and identification of informal learning patterns, bridge language inventory. Finally, NCERT also has done some efforts in this field. They are: undertake research, preparation of textbooks in tribal dialects and training of key functionaries and teachers working in SC/ST areas, etc.

REFERENCES

1. Alexander, R., 2000, *Culture and Pedagogy: International Comparisons in Primary Education*, Oxford: Blackwell.
2. Amar Kumar Singh, "Status of the Tribals in India", *Social Change, Vol. 23, No. 2&3*, 1993.
3. Ambasht, N.K., "Universalisation of Elementary Education, Constitution and Right to Education", *Journal of Indian Education, Vol. 19, No. 6, March 1994*, NCERT.
4. Ambast, N.K., 1970, *A Critical Study of Tribal Education*, New Delhi, S. Chand and Company.
5. Ambast, N.K., 1970, *Reducing Educational Wastage in Tribal Areas*, New Delhi, NCERT.
6. Ambast, N.K., 1986, *An Indepth Analysis of Ashram Schools*, New Delhi, NIEPA.
7. Anand, G., 1998, *Ashram Schools*, New Delhi, Concept Publishers.
8. Ananda G., 1994, *Ashram Schools in Andhra Pradesh—A Case Study of Chenchus of Nallamalai Hills*, New Delhi, Commonwealth Publishers.
9. Annamalai, E., "Tribal Development and Education", http://www.google.com.
10. Annowitz, Stanley and Henry Giroux, 1987, *Education Under Seize: The Conservative, Liberal and Radical Debate over Schooling*, London, Routledge & Kegan Paul.
11. Apple, Michael, W., 1979, *Ideology and Curriculum*, London, Routledge & Kegan Paul.
12. Apte, J.S., 1960, "Talwada Ashram School – An Experiment in Tribal Education, *Vanyajati, Vol. VIII, No. 52.*
13. Artis, E., C. Doobay and K. Lyons, 2003, Economic, Social and Cultural Rights for Dalits in India: Case Study on Primary Education in Gujarat, Paper presented at the workshop on Human Rights: From Grassroots courage to international influence, Princeton University, January 2003.
14. Arya Shachi, 1998, *Tribal Activism*, Jaipur, Rawat Publications.
15. Ashok Kumar, 1991, *Current Trends in Indian Education*, New Delhi, Ashish Publishing House.

12

Functioning of Ashram Schools: Some Preliminary Observations

"Education is a right which enables individuals and communities to act on reflection"

—Rabindranath Tagore, 1908

Introduction

The present chapter examines the Ashram School Education in India in general and Karnataka State in particular. The study is based on the field work undertaken in some selected Ashram Schools in Hunsur and Hegdevena Kote (H.D. Kote) taluks in Mysore District. Apart from tracing of the origins of Ashram Schools in India and Karnataka, the profile of the functioning of the selected Ashram schools in Karnataka have been discussed in this chapter. Major issues in tribal education have been highlighted in this chapter. A critical analysis of the problems of Ashram schools and tribal education have been discussed.

The chapter mainly focuses on the major constraints that act as impediments in the all round development of students who are studying in these schools. Finally the chapter offers a fruitful discussion on the innovations and special initiatives that has to be implemented sincerely in all the tribal areas and also the issues that confront the planners and policy makers in ensuring quality education for the tribal students in the present Ashram school system in the country.

Education has an acculturating role. It refines sensitiveness, activities and perceptions that contribute to national cohesion, scientific temper and independence of mind and spirit thus furthering the goals of socialism, secularism and democracy enshrined in our Constitution. Education is a basic need and requirement of all Indian citizens. It is also important for the economic growth of the country. Education enhances the individuals well being. Widespread education helps to resolve social problems like poverty, ignorance, illiteracy, disease, population growth and environmental degradation. To march towards a bright future, the only hope rests with the children. The Kothari Education Commission Report has observed, "The destiny of India is now being shaped in the classrooms."

India has a long history of educational disparities. Social inequalities is based on class, caste and gender. Literacy and Education are important tools of self-defence. The powerlessness is associated with illiteracy in modern society. Education is a panacea for all individual and social ills. Mahatma Gandhi was of the opinion that education is, 'the basic tool for the development of consciousness and reconstruction of the society'.

Indian Constitution identifies for special consideration for certain ethnic minority groups traditionally referred to as adivasis, tribes or tribals as Scheduled Tribes who constitute around 8 per cent of the total population of the country. There are 573 Scheduled Tribes living in different parts of the country having their own languages which are different from the one mostly spoken in the State where they live. There are more than 270 such languages in India. The tribal languages in India belong to all major language families among which the Austric, the Dravidian, Tibeto-Chinese and Indo-European families are the dominant ones. According to 2001 census the tribal population in India is 74.6 million.

The framers of the Indian Constitution have assured the protection of linguistic, cultural and educational interests to the individuals and the groups by incorporating various Constitutional safeguards. The Constitution Seventh Amendment Act, 1956 introduced Articles 350A and 350B exclusively to protect the linguistic minorities apart from the statutory safeguards kept in Articles 29, 30, 347 and 350 of the Indian Constitution.

The main objectives of the Ashram Schools as envisaged by the various Committees and Commissions are: *(i)* to wean the children away from an atmosphere which is generally not conducive for the development of their personality and outlook. *(ii)* to impart general formal education. *(iii)* to impart socially useful vocational/crafts along with the general education. *(iv)* to encourage tribal traditions like folk songs and dances so that the schools are not only mere learning places but also centres of cultural activities. *(v)* to provide close interaction between the teacher and taught through individual attention and *(vi)* to reduce the dropout rate and to improve the retention capacity of the school.

Ashram Schools are in general residential and the inmates are provided with facilities of boarding and lodging. The broad policy guidelines for the Ashram Schools as envisaged by various Committees and study groups on tribal welfare programmes are: *(i)* Ashram Schools should be intervillage schools. *(ii)* Ashram Schools should be opened in such areas where normal schools cannot be opened. *(iii)* Most backward tribal groups should be covered.

An evaluation of the functioning of Ashram schools in tribal areas of Gujarat, Karnataka, Maharashtra, Andhra Pradesh and Madhya Pradesh reveals the fact that the Ashram schools did not function to the extent to which with the aims, objectives and with the reasons these schools were established. There are serious lapses in planning and execution of the educational programmes in these schools. The Ashram schools combines both functional and literary aspects based on education relieving the tribal parent off the burden of feeling, clothing his school-going children, providing a congenital school environment. However this aspiration of the tribal parents and the government has not fulfilled so far. The structure, functioning and objectives of the Ashram schools varied widely in many states to the extent that it is really difficult to find similarities in their working pattern or in the resource allocation. Vocational or craft education though strongly advocated to be implemented, has not taken its roots yet. In some of the states like Andhra Pradesh and Madhya Pradesh there is no relation between tribal literacy levels and the provisions of Ashram schools or vice-versa. The reasons for disparities in the distribution of Ashram schools in Karnataka can be attributed to political and administrative factors. In the Ashram schools the enrolment of girl children among the tribals is not encouraging as they have more domestic responsibilities than boys and the parents are not interested in the girl children's education. The Government has not taken any action to improve the girls enrolment in the Ashram schools in Karnataka. The Government has spent lakhs of rupees for the improvement of Ashram schools and to carryout various educational schemes. However, these schemes need to be implemented seriously to see the benefits of the establishment of the Ashram schools.

The Government of Karnataka has been allocating resources to improve the tribal education through Ashram schools. There are serious lapses in the implementation of welfare programmes, prescribing syllabus, teaching, conduct of examinations, selection of teachers, instructional planning, curriculum design, teaching schedule, monitoring, supervision, maintenance of records, providing quality food, maintenance of schools, hostels, office rooms, maintenance of office and school records, etc. The Headmasters do not supervise the teaching staff in the schools. The Headmaster and the teachers have the utmost responsibility to increase the enrolment of students in Ashram schools. The wardens have to supervise hostel activities including serving of food. The supply of material and their quality like soaps, oil, food in Ashram schools are very poor.

The records are not properly maintained in Ashram schools. There are gaps between actual attendance and attendance on records in Ashram school hostels. Less qualified tribal teachers in Ashram schools are made into hostel wardens. These teachers/wardens are not able to prepare hostel bills and maintain records properly. There is absence of monitoring mechanism in these Ashram schools. Administration of incentives needs to be streamlined. Tribal community members must be involved in the monitoring of the Ashram schools. Teacher competency building is an important intervention in the development of Ashram schools. Institutional support needs to be established with regular in-service training and orientation of tribal teachers working in the Ashram schools. The role of the school complexes needs to be strengthened. Both education and the maintenance of hostel should be under the management of sincere Administrative Officers.

Though the enrolment figures available indicate satisfactory performance, the real situation differs with the field level realities. Inspite of good networking of schools, package incentives the enrolment of tribal children is discouraging. The Government should take steps to intensify the universalisation of primary education through Ashram schools. Necessary infrastructure needs to be provided. Boarding, lodging facilities, medical kits, teaching aids, play material, furniture and contingencies needs to be supplied to all the Ashram schools regularly. Residential quarters for Ashram school teachers needs to be provided. The personal hygiene among the tribal children are very poor. The inputs such as clothes, uniform, bedding materials should be supplied regularly. Ashram schools should follow a prescribed menu.

The Government should take measures to recruit qualified teachers for the Ashram schools. Tribal community and non-tribal community teachers, who are genuinely interested to work in tribal schools only to be recruited in these schools. Efforts must be made to provide good results in the Ashram schools. Sufficient women teachers must be recruited. Payment and other benefits to the teachers should be paid without delay. The higher qualifications in recruitment of Ashram schools must be maintained. Salary structure of the teachers working in these schools must be higher. Teacher training courses for the Ashram school teachers must be made compulsory. Teacher is the backbone in the education system. If the teacher is sincere and committed, he/she can educate children successfully even without infrastructure. The teachers occupy the key position in the Ashram school system. Teacher education programmes must be more prescriptive and realistic.

Wide disparity in educational levels prevailed among the tribals in various districts in Karnataka. Education of parents is a major contributive factor in their children's education. Illiterates dominate in the tribal villages. Village education committees needs to be strengthened. The village education committees should take more responsibility in supporting the Ashram schools and mother's committees should be given the responsibility of managing the mid-day meals and ensure the regular attendance of the children. Parent-teacher associations need to be streamlined. Periodic meetings must be organised. The distribution of students according to age, class and sex in Ashram schools reveals the truth that some of the children with average are admitted in the Ashram schools. Some of the interior schools have bogus enrolment to get the benefit of incentives provided by the Government. The world view of the tribal children in the Ashram schools is limited due to isolation and lack of exposure. More number of dropouts were found at the primary level itself in the Ashram schools in Karnataka.

Origin and Development of Ashram Schools

The concept of Ashram Schools for tribal children has been derived from the traditional Indian Gurukulas and the Gandhian Philosophy of basic education, in which the teacher and the taught live together and have close interaction. This type of closeness helps the students not only in sharpening the capacities but also in full personality development. It stems from the objective of providing an atmosphere in which the inmates are offered full opportunities for total personality development due to the closeness between the teacher and the students. Ashram schools are residential schools for tribal children from a cluster of habitations. One of the major thrusts of the Ashram school is imparting skills in crafts, vocations apart from providing general education. Based on the Gandhian Philosophy of self reliance, the concept of Ashram school was first experimented way back in 1922 by Thakkar Bapa a Gandhian and social worker, who was influenced by the Gandhian Movement and he initiated an experiment of Ashram schools in the Panchamahal district of Gujarat during the pre-independence days for the tribal children. His efforts proved successful in imparting education to tribal children along with training in Vocation Craft education. Later he replicated the same system in Maharashtra and Bihar. Soon after India got Independence, as part of the developmental work various voluntary organisations in the states of Maharashtra, Gujarat and Orissa took immense interest in educating tribals by establishing Ashram schools. During the First Five Year Plan there was an attempt by the Government of India to open such schools. However, the momentum in opening Ashram schools started increasing from the Third Five Year Plan onwards. In Karnataka the Ashram schools were started during the year 1961-62.

Ashram schools were found effective as it was not feasible to open full fledged schools in very small and scattered habitations. It created congenial atmosphere for teaching and learning as it is assumed that the tribal households do not have such an environment. It helped to develop the total personality of the child and impart vocational skills to improve employment opportunities. In 1960-61 there were 189 Ashram schools in the country enrolling 10,890 students and the number of Ashram schools in the year 1980-81 was 1,609 enrolling 83,049 students. Majority of the Ashram schools in the country are concentrated in six States namely Andhra Pradesh, Madhya Pradesh, Maharashtra, Gujarat, Orissa and Rajasthan. Even though the concept of Ashram schools is common to all States, the levels of education, norms of establishing schools and working pattern differ from State to State. The financial and administrative part of Ashram schools is looked after by the Director of Tribal Welfare Departments, whereas the academic inspection and supervision are the responsibilities of Education Department. In some of the States like Maharashtra and Gujarat they are mostly run by Voluntary Organisations as private aided schools, whereas in Andhra Pradesh, Orissa, Madhya Pradesh and Rajasthan Ashram schools are exclusively under the Tribal Welfare Departments of the respective State Governments.

Several Committees and Commissions like the Renuka Ray Committee (1959), Elwin Committee (1960) and Dhebar Commission (1962) have gone into the question of improving the quality of education in scheduled areas and suggested Ashram schools as an improvement strategy over the existing pattern of education. Ashram schools are residential schools in which free boarding and lodging along with other facilities and incentives are offered to the inmates. The National Policy on Education (1986) has strongly advocated that the new policy will lay special emphasis on the removal of disparities and equalise educational opportunities by attending to the specific needs of those who have been deprived equality so far. Therefore Residential schools including Ashram schools were established on large scale. Although the concept and objectives of Ashram schools are basically common in all States, their planning, administration and management varies in different States. Many scholars have studied different aspects of Ashram schools and tribal education and suggested several measures for the promotion of education and improvement of the Ashram schools in different states among the tribals. This chapter attempts to discuss the functioning of Ashram schools in Karnataka and comes out with some preliminary observations based on the field survey of a few selected Ashram schools in Karnataka.

Karnataka State inhabited primarily by Kannada speaking people occupies a significant place in the middle of the Western half of Southern India. The State is located between 11° 31″ and 18° 45″ North Latitudes and 74° 12″ and 78° 40″ East Longitudes. Its maximum length from North to South is about 700 kms and from East to West 400 kms. According to 2001 census Karnataka has a population of 5,27,33,958 and a literacy rate of 67 per cent. It accounts for 5.83 per cent of the total area of the country. The State occupies the eighth position both in terms of area and population among the States in India. The State is bounded by Maharashtra in the North, Goa in the Northwest, in the East by Andhra Pradesh, in the South and Southeast by Tamil Nadu, in the Southeast by Kerala and in the West by the Arabian Sea. The State is divided into four geographic regions including the coastal region, Karnataka Plateau, Northern Plateau and Southern Plateau. The State in its present form was formed on 1st November 1956 under the State's

Re-Organisation Act and acquired the present name on 1st November 1973. The State has 27 districts and covers an area of 1,91,791 sq kms with a forest area of 38,284 sq kms. It accounts for 5.83 per cent of total area of the country and ranks eighth among major states of the country in terms of size. The population of the State according to 2001 census is 5,28,50,562. The literacy rate of the State is 67 per cent.

Government Programmes for the Development of Scheduled Tribes in Karnataka

There are 50 Scheduled Tribes (STs) in Karnataka as per the Scheduled Castes (SCs) and Scheduled Tribes Order (Amendment) Act, 1976 and by the Act of 39 of 1991. The Government of Karnataka established the Directorate of Tribal Welfare on 30.8.1994 for the welfare of the STs. A senior Karnataka Administrative Service Officer heads the Directorate. He is assisted by two Deputy Directors, one Assistant Director, one Research Officer, seven First Division Assistants, seven Second Division Assistants, two Typists, two Stenos, two Drivers and two Peons in the Directorate. All the State Sector Schemes will be monitored and implemented by the Chief Executive Officer of Zilla Panchayat at the District level. The developmental programmes at the District level are implemented by the District Social Welfare Officers who are working under the control of the Chief Executive Officers of the Zilla Panchayats. Apart from this five districts in Karnataka have Integrated Tribal Development Programmes or Project Coordinators are working. They include – Mysore, Kodagu, Chamarajanagar, Dakshina Kannada, Udupi and Chickmagalur Districts. At the Taluk level the welfare programmes are being implemented by the Taluk Social Welfare Officer along with the supporting staff. The population of STs in the State as per 2001 census is 34,63,986 amounting to 6.55 per cent of the total population of the State. The percentage of literacy among STs in the State as per 2001 census is 46.3 per cent. In order to inculcate school going habits at an early age, 70 Women Welfare Centers benefiting 3288 ST children are functioning. In addition to pre-primary education, the children in these Centers are provided with mid-day meals and two sets of dresses annually.

There are 122 Ashram Schools benefiting 9,125 ST children run by the Directorate. Primary education from I to IV standard is being given to these students. The Directorate is maintaining 67 Pre-matric hostels providing boarding and lodging facilities to ST students studying from V to X standard. Besides there are 19 Grant-in-aid hostels in the State covering 1061 ST students. Pre-matric scholarship ranging from Rs. 75 to Rs. 100 per annum is being sanctioned to the ST students studying from V to X standards.

Tribal Sub-Plan is a significant step in the direction of all round development of STs. The Tribal Sub-Plan is being implemented in the State from 1977-78. Five Integrated Tribal Development Projects are functioning in the districts of Mysore, Madikere, Chickmagalur, Dakshina Kannada and Udupi districts. The objectives of Tribal Sub-Plan are: *(i)* to lay down policies which will protect tribal culture and promote tribal welfare. *(ii)* to provide the tribal habitates with the minimum infrastructure required and *(iii)* to accelerate social and economic progress and to remove the obstacles in tribal development. In addition to the main economic benefits, the Public Works Department is constructing roads to approach the tribal colonies. Under the Zilla Parishad Sector drinking water facilities in the tribal colonies are being provided. Electricity is being provided to ST houses under the Bhagya Jyothi Scheme. Primary Health Centers and Mobile Health Units are also functioning in the tribal areas to take care of the health problems of the children of the STs.

Mysore district occupies an important place in the state with an area of 6,269 sq kms with a population of 26,41,027 as per the 2001 census report. Out of the total population the tribal population is 27,13,51. Jenu Kurubas, Kadu Kurubas, Soligas, Eravas and Hakkipikki tribes are predominantly found in Mysore district. There are 20 Ashram Schools functioning in Mysore District (9 schools in H.D. Kote, 5 schools in Hunsur, 3 schools in Nanjangud and 3 schools in Periyapatna). For the present study Hegdedevana Kote and Hunsur taluk schools are selected. Five schools from each of these taluks were randomly selected.

Major Issues in Tribal Education: Policies and Programmes

Recognising that Scheduled Tribes constitute the most deprived and marginalised sections of the Indian society, a host of welfare and developmental measures have been initiated for their social and economic development. In this regard particular reference has to be made to the Tribal Sub-Plan Approach which came into existence as the main strategy from the Fifth Five Year Plan. Along with core economic sectors elementary education has been accorded priority in Tribal Sub-Plan Approach. In Karnataka various programmes for the all-round development of the STs have been undertaken including providing pre- and post-matric scholarships, various incentives, training for educated unemployed youth, providing free hostels, stipend, mid-day meals for school going children, distribution of free textbooks, uniforms, providing housing facilities, electricity, drinking water, tribal colonies, etc. The tribal sub-plan is being implemented in the state from 1976-77 onwards.

Despite all these measures disparity in educational level is not only between States but it also exists at District Level within the States. In Karnataka out of total 27 Districts only 13 Districts have a tribal literacy rate of 40 to 50 per cent. While 7 Districts have literacy between 50 to 60 per cent, 5 Districts have above 60 per cent and only 2 Districts are having a tribal literacy rate of above 70 per cent.

Gender Disparity

In a highly stratified society like India there are numerous layers of differentiation apart from caste and class. Gender is now recognised as a more pervasive and distinct category of social stratification. In the context of literacy gender is an important factor. The literacy rate among the tribals is not only low but also show a high level of gender disparity. In Karnataka data reveals that the female tribal literacy rate is only 36.6 per cent.

Primary Education: Access and Participation

As mentioned already, tribal communities normally reside in interior, under developed and inaccessible areas. Demographically tribal habitations are small in size, scattered and sparsely populated. Because of these problems most of the villages lack basic facilities like transport, communication and basic amenities. With the introduction of Tribal Sub-Plan Approach efforts are made to expand educational facilities and this got a major boost with the formulation of National Policy on Education in 1986.

Still in view of the difficult terrain geographical and ecological barriers in tribal areas the school distance of more than half a kilometer is a difficult proposition for young children to attend school. The distance of one kilometer and above between the school and habitation means that practically these habitations and inhabitants lack access to primary schools given the tribal context. More than one-fifth of tribal population are constrained by this problem.

Enrollment

Enrollment is dependent on factors such as availability of school, its regular functioning, regularity of teachers and willingness of parents, their perception of the value of education and their capacity. When compared to others the participation of tribal children in education is very low. However some of the recent interventions and initiatives like mid-day meal scheme, self-help women groups, developing partnership between school and village communities in school management have helped in raising awareness levels among tribals to realise the importance of education.

Retention

Enrollment has no meaning unless students are retained in the system for prescribed number of years to complete the primary level of education. However in tribal areas high levels of absenteeism, large scale failure in year end assessment and high drop out rate contribute to slow progress of education among tribals.

Problems of Tribal Education

Inspite of Constitutional guarantees and continuous efforts tribal communities continue to lag behind the general population. The reasons for this can be categorised as external, internal, socio-economic and psychological.

External Constraints

In formulating policies and programmes for tribal education it is essential to understand the complex realities of the tribal life and the expectation of tribals from the system and this has never been done either by the tribal welfare department or by the education department. Consequently no worthwhile policy for tribal education has been formed. One of the major constraints of tribal education at planning level is the adoption of dual system of administration. The tribal welfare department deals with tribal life and culture and administers the development work at the local level including education. On the other hand, the education department is the sole authority for planning of education development at the State level. They formulate implementation guidelines and instructions regarding curriculum, textbook, teacher recruitment, transfer policies and so on. In this, the education department tends to form uniform educational policies for the whole State with little consideration for local context and festivals of the tribals. This lack of sensitivity to the problems and the failure in understanding the tribal social reality coupled with the faulty selection and appointment of tribal teachers in tribal areas have resulted in poor performance and teacher absenteeism among tribal schools and has stunted educational development among the tribals.

Internal Constraints

The internal problems of tribal education refer to the quality of school provision, suitable teachers, relevance of content and curriculum, medium of instruction, pedagogy and special supervision. A majority of school in tribal areas are without basic infrastructure facilities. Normally the school buildings in tribal areas are with thatched roofs, dilapidated wall and non-plastered floors. Research evidences shows that a large number of tribal schools do not have teaching learning materials and even blackboards. In tribal areas the opening of a school is equated with the posting of a teacher and same is the case with the Ashram Schools. In most Ashram Schools which are residential in nature there is not enough space for children to sleep. Consequently, the classroom turns into the dormitory and vice-versa. Due to lack of minimum sanitary provisions it is not uncommon to find that many children studying in Ashram Schools are affected by contagious diseases.

Content and Curriculum

Though the demand for changing the content and curricula to suit the tribal context has been an old one, no serious effort has been made in this direction in any State except for some sporadic pilot projects. The uniform structure and transaction of curriculum has put the tribal children at a disadvantage. Also the rigid system of formal schooling which emphasize discipline, routine norms, teacher-centered instruction have made tribal children wary of the school. This goes against the culture of free interaction, absence of force as embedded in tribal ethos and culture prevalent at home. This has led to sharp division between home and school leading to lack of interest among the children towards school and research findings have shown this as a major factor behind non-enrollment.

Another area is the inherent fear of tribal children toward the teacher and their inability to establish a communication link with the teacher and this is reflected in low attendance and high dropout. The Constitution of India allows the use of tribal mother tongue as the medium of instruction in case the population of the said tribe is more than one lakh. But this has not been adopted on the pretext of feasibility and viability of introducing and sustaining such a change.

Socio-Economic and Cultural Constraints

In a broad sense the socio-economic and cultural factors can be outlined as poverty and poor economic conditions, social customs, cultural ethos, lack of awareness and understanding of the value of formal education, conflict and gap between the home and school. Studies on educational deprivation of tribals have inevitably linked it to their poor economic condition and poverty. The main occupation of the tribals is agriculture practiced through shifting cultivation. Consequently children play an important role contributing directly or indirectly to family income in participating in family occupation and household work like cattle grazing, fuel and fodder collection, etc.

Poor health is another hinderance in the promotion and participation of tribal children in education. Contagious diseases are common in tribal areas which too affect the children's attendance at school. Further some tribal communities are seasonal migrants and their absence in a particular place for a year lead to absenteeism among their children and makes it difficult for them to effectively benefit from schooling.

Perspectives for the Future

Education of the tribals cannot be left merely to short term plan strategies. It is important that planners take a long term view which is embedded in a meaningful policy framework. Following are some important points emerging from the review of Ashram School education in Karnataka.

1. Emphasis should be on quality and equity rather than quantity. The primary focus should be on provision of quality education that makes the tribal communities economically effective and independent.
2. Looking at the tribal context it is of absolute necessity that the school schedule be prepared as per the local requirement rather than following a directive from the State. It has been found that vacations and holidays are planned without taking into cognizance local contexts and thereby unnecessarily antagonizing tribal communities and keeping them out of school.
3. Though it has been highlighted time and again no concrete step has been taken to provide locally relevant materials to tribal students. Availability of locally relevant materials will not only facilitate faster learning but also help the children to develop a sense of affiliation to the school.
4. In order to make education effective and sustainable building partnership between community and the Government not only augments state expenditure on education but also guarantees supervision and monitoring thus addressing an intractable problem for the State.
5. Environment building is of immense importance in the context of educational development among tribal communities. Community awareness and community mobilization which are the core elements should receive adequate importance and attention.
6. Decentralisation of education management is another aspect that needs special consideration in the context of tribal areas. It is crucial to restructure the existing system of educational management, adaptation of structure such as school complexes and vocational education centres to the tribal areas need careful consideration.
7. Skill development, competency building and motivating the teachers also need to be strengthened for sustaining educational development. Teacher should be made the center of educational transformation and therefore must remain as the primary facilitator.

Tribal Education in Karnataka

The Directorate of Tribal Welfare is implementing several schemes for the progress and development of the STs in the State. The extent of infrastructure facilities like physical space, equipment, teaching aids and teacher-pupil ratio available in the schools are some of the indicators for the quality of education provided in Ashram schools. In terms of enrolment pattern, Ashram schools widely differ. The syllabi, text books and examination system in Ashram schools are the same as in non-Ashram schools which are prescribed by the State Government. Though the Ashram schools are the best means of educating the tribals, the outcome of these in some of the areas is not upto the mark due to various factors. Basically the tribal child suffers from social, psychological and emotional deprivation, isolation, unawareness of situation outside his community and shyness. The infrastructure and the study materials provided by the Government of Karnataka are not suitable to local culture. Further socio-cultural and economic conditions of the tribals may not permit them to succeed even at primary level of education. It is commonly accepted that socio-cultural and economic aspects of the family greatly influence the educability of the children in all societies.

Literacy Rate Among ST Children

The literacy rate of STs in Karnataka is a cause for concern, as it, has consistently been lower than that of the total population. The literacy rate among STs which was 36.0 per cent in 1991 increased to 46.3 per cent in 2001. The State average moved up from 56.04 to 66.64 per cent. The decennial literacy rate of the ST population has increased at a faster pace (12.3%) than the rate for the total population (10.6%). The literacy rate of urban STs (64.6%) is higher than the overall literacy rate of STs and compares favourably with the State average.

The female literacy rate among STs in 1991 was 23.6 per cent and it increased to 36.6 per cent in 2001. While it has increased at a faster pace than the male literacy rate, the gap between the ST male and female literacy rate declined only marginally from 24.3 in 1991 to 23.1 in 2001, which is slightly higher than the gap between the male and female literacy rates for the total population (22.92 in 1991 and 19.22 in 2001). The literacy rate for ST women is the lowest in the State in comparison with all women as well as Scheduled Caste women. The literacy rate for rural ST women is 33.3 per cent compared with 56.9 per cent for men. Overall the STs in the State have markedly lower literacy rates than other groups. The fact that they are above the all India average in respect of men and women is of course an indicator that Karnataka has performed better than many other States in this respect.

Enrolment, Retention and Dropouts

Many schools in tribal areas suffer from high dropout rates. Children either never enroll or attend for the first three to four years of primary school. This leads to lapse into illiteracy later. The attrition rate is quite strong at various levels of the educational system. The first step in the education ladder is enrolment, where performance is high for most social groups, except STs. For instance the Gross Enrolment Ratio (GER) in 2001 for STs for Classes I-VIII (90.12) was significantly lower than the gross enrolment ratio for all students (98.81) and SCs (104.57). This inequality is heightened even more by the gap between the gross enrolment ratio for South Karnataka (110.62) and North Karnataka (74.21). Gross enrolment ratio for girls (103.64) is also much better in the southern districts than in North Karnataka (70.22). In that respect, the GER of the Scheduled Tribes in South Karnataka more closely approximates the overall GER of other social groups. The Northern districts are caught up in a cycle of deprivation. They have the higher levels of ST population and also have poor human development indicators.

ST children also constitute the highest percentage of out of school children (2.42) compared with the State average of 1.54 per cent. The percentage of out of school ST girls (2.67) is the highest across all categories. The Sample Survey of ST households conducted by the Department of Economics and Statistics in 2004, which elicited responses from persons in the age group of 9-35 years found that the primary reason for females dropping out of school were *(i)* to work at home and *(ii)* their parents could not afford to pay for their education. The reasons are identical to the ones attributed to SC girls and indicate that the poor cannot afford the high opportunity costs of education.

Girls are the first to be pulled out of school to work at home and take care of siblings to enable their parents to work. In such cases, families do not find the many incentives offered by the Government such as free uniforms, textbooks and even scholarships, an adequate compensation for lost wages. For boys, agricultural labour, cooli work and family work is the main reason for dropping out. 'Akshara Dasoha', the recently introduced mid-day meals programme (Bissivuta) for school children showed a more sustained impact on ensuring the enrolment and retention of the tribal children in the schools.

Unequal access to schooling is further exacerbated by the fact that ST children stay in school for the least amount of time, as indicated by the mean years of schooling. In 2003-04, STs constituted 4.46 per cent of students in Government schools and 2.80 per cent in private aided schools. There is a marked disparity in the enrolment of boys (3,209) and girls (1,652) in Tribal Ashram schools in Karnataka. Traditionally the tribal economy was based on subsistence agriculture and hunting and gathering. However, since the tribal people treated land as a common resource, they rarely had land titles, and thus, lost their lands to outsiders when exploitation of forest resources began to take place on a significant scale. This ensured that a majority ended up as small and marginal landholders. The 2001 Census data reveals that around half of the ST population is in the workforce. Women constitute about 41.7 per cent of the workforce. More than 85 per cent of the working population is in rural areas. Out of 76.4 per cent male workers 51.5 per cent is concentrated in the rural parts of the state. Bellary has the highest percentage of male workers (11.5%) followed by Raichur (7.8%). The highest percentage of ST marginal workers lives in Raichur (11.7), which also has the highest proportion of the ST population to the total population. This clearly indicates the highly precarious livelihood conditions of STs in Karnataka bearing the serious consequences on the education of the tribal children. The children joined in the Ashram schools also had serious impact on them with these conditions.

The National Curriculum Framework 2005 Position Paper, National Focus Group on the Problems of Scheduled Caste and Scheduled Tribe children has clearly stated that: Despite the fact that the vast majority of tribal children study in government day schools, Ashram schools were instituted to provide residential facility for those living in remote areas without schooling facilities in their vicinity. Various SC/ST Commissioner's reports and research studies provide insights into the functioning of these schools. Serious problems of inefficiency, mismanagement, nepotism and corruption besiege Ashram schools. Reports have commented upon shortcomings of the Ashram schools run by both Government and voluntary agencies. They draw attention to the sub-standard levels of education and facilities provided and prevalence of malpractices, including the use of inmates as unpaid, forced labour. We have some detailed accounts of the appalling living and educational conditions prevalent in Ashram schools in Gujarat, Karnataka, Maharashtra and Andhra Pradesh. The problems highlighted include poor construction, overcrowding, alienating environment, inadequate numbers and quality of teaching staff, lack of regular inspection, and lack of basic facilities of the children such as toiletries, uniforms and fans. For girls, lack of personal safety services as a major deterrent. Clear vested interests have developed in the sanctioning and management of Ashram schools leading to many malpractices and much corruption. On the whole, schools have reached out to limited proportions of SC/ST children. (National Curriculum Framework 2005: Position Paper on Problems of SC/ST Children, p. 17).

Disparities in the Existing Ashram Schools in Karnataka

Compared to the other major tribals of the state the primitive tribal groups are a more disadvantaged population. As for as non-existing facilities within a habitation is concerned, one can find that other major tribes of the State are placed in a favourable situation relative to their total population. Looking at the disparity condition in terms of deprivation, more children of primitive tribal group school age children are deprived of a primary school within their habitations. Children belonging to the other major tribes like *Soligas, Betta Kurubas, Malae Kudiya* and *Lambanis* are in a better position than the PTGs. These tribal groups habitations did not have atleast one Ashram school within their habitations. However, so for as the number of habitations without a school is concerned the PTG children are highly in a disadvantaged position. In general the primitive tribal children should have to commute more than 5 kms distance to attend a school. In some case it is even more. Distance is one of the major drawbacks in case of providing education to the people who are still away from the modern world. Many of the parents don't like to send their children especially their girl children to school, which is quite far away from their original habitation. A large number of ST population of the country school age children are still facing the disadvantage of distance between their own habitation and the location of a primary school. The more disturbing situation is this disadvantage is, high in case of PTGs habitations in the tribal belt of Karnataka. The Ashram schools in the PTG Tribal Areas are not established so far.

Language and Medium of Instruction in Ashram Schools

The tribal situation in India presents a varied and complex picture and poses peculiar problems of social and economic development. Demographically speaking, there are more than 244 scheduled tribes with many sub-groups speaking some 100 languages/ dialects. Most unfortunate thing is that major portion of Government's resources is diverted to provide concessions and little is left for the development of tribal education, language and culture of the PTGs. The striking aspect that emerges from the scanty data on languages in primary education is almost total absence of the use of tribal languages in schools. The attitude of our policy planners towards these tribal people appears to be one of assimilation. Little is being done to preserve their culture. Almost all major and minor tribes suffer with this kind of negligence. Not much work has been done to find out minimum and maximum resistance into their culture. Linguistic experts have made no attempt to standardise tribal languages by developing scripts, elaborating lexis and writing grammars and dictionaries in tribal languages. Till today there has not been any serious efforts to provide basic education in their respective mother tongues. No proper curriculum have also been framed based on tribal culture and tradition. Present education system does not orient the tribal children towards perusing their own mode of life. In phonology and syntax, the tribal languages are quite different from the medium of instruction like Kannada except in certain mutually borrowed lexical items due to their close contacts over a long period of time. This is one of the vital reasons responsible for these PTGs poor literacy conditions and dropout problem among tribal children.

Attitude of non-tribal teachers towards tribal children and tribal language is stereotyped. The social distance is high. Teachers impose their own culture. Teachers from tribal comminutes have detribalised to the extent that they don't understand the role of mother tongue in teaching in primary stage. No teacher either from tribal or non-trial comminutes have raised the issue of how the tribal children face difficulties in understanding school language and how the language gap hampers the construction of knowledge. The teachers working in the Ashram schools need to be oriented to use tribal languages in their respective schools.

Urban Biased

The success of one's education largely depends on the motivation. Basically, the PTGs are living with low socio-economic status. Obviously the level of motivation and self-esteem will be comparatively low among tribal children. The main reason for this problem is current education system is more or less urban based, non-tribal and absence of culture specific. Even though these tribals are emotionally attached to their local cultural norms Government has no interest in providing education which is more suited to the tribal children. Modern teaching methodologies, content of the text, appointment of non-tribal teachers and suitable parameters for evaluation have become *Grains of Iron* to the low motivated tribal children. Implementation of uniform textbooks both for urban and tribal children is another hindrance to them. The theory, concepts, values alien to tribal people is generally contained in the textbooks which generates negative attitude and a big blow to the learners' self-confidence. There is no attempt to take stock of the existing situation regarding instructional materials in tribal languages. Education policy documents also have not dealt with the magnitude of tasks that are involved in the preparation of primers and textbooks for the PTG tribal children and have not outlined the concrete steps that has to take place in this direction. The increasing tendency for tribal people to retain the regional language as their mother tongue is only one indicator of their growing vulnerability in the face of the larger social processes.

The problem of dropout persists among all categories of children in both urban and rural India. However, in the context of children studying in Classes I-X the gap between the ST and total population of dropouts has widened from 1990-91 to 1998-99. The reduction in the dropout rates could be because of various incentive schemes offered by the State Government for ST children such as providing free textbooks, uniforms and scholarships in Government Ashram schools. But schemes such as those providing for hostels for ST boys and girls are not implemented fully by the State owing to lack of financial resources and therefore fewer ST children pursue high school education and very few up to the college level. The policy of reserving seats for ST students at higher education levels is not widely availed since a large number of ST students do not even reach those levels and dropout at lower levels of school education. Even the Ashram schools run by both Government and NGOs are poorly maintained and sometimes lack the basic facilities. Given the low level of literacy among the ST population, several children from these comminutes happen to be 'first generation learns' and in the absence of State support for helping them to cope with studies, many children drop out of the schools. This disproportionately low representation of ST children at higher level of education compounds the existing disparities among Indian society. Lack of proactive Government in favour of the STs is not linked only to lack of resources. Government indifference and lack of political will are largely responsible for the state of affairs. The facilities provided in the Ashram schools are so meager and poor that it is very difficult for the ST children to stay and continue their studies in the State run Ashram schools.

Inaction of Teachers

Teachers are the real directors of every tribal school. There was a time in India where teachers were equal to the God. The major problem is that Government is recruiting teachers from the urban area to teach tribal children. A report says that only 0.56 per cent of teachers are basically from either Anthropology or Sociology discipline. Majority of the teachers are from non-tribal community. Many of them have studied only in English medium schools and they even don't know the regional language properly. In this situation how one can expect to teach the relatively disadvantaged tribal children down to their level. More unfortunate thing is that many schools don't have teachers for all the subjects. Even though many NGOs are hiring teachers to teach at tribal schools many of them don't even have any basic degrees in education like B.Ed./DEd/TCH. Some of the teachers are prejudicious about the performance of the tribal children. As they are the only literate persons having some political connections in the tribal areas, they neither fulfill their duties properly nor the concerned higher officers dare to take any action against them for dereliction of their duties. The teachers in the Ashram schools are not recruited on permanent basis. They are working on contract basis in the schools. The Government should take serious action on those teachers who do not work sincerely in these schools.

What Ashram School Teachers Say

Many of the teachers are of the opinion that tribal children cannot understand the modern Kannada language. Content of the text is too high standard to their level. Few of them will complain about the ignorance of the parents. Moreover, teachers are facing many problems in the tribal areas. Proper residential and medical facilities are a nightmare for them. Higher education for their children some times will not be possible. Since many primitive tribal hamlets live deep in the forests some time it will be humanely impossible to reach the school due to the lack of appropriate transport. More over feed back from the students is completely absent. No proper laboratory facilities to teach Science and Mathematical subjects effectively. Teachers raised and brought up in a more sophisticated urbanized society would find it difficult to adjust themselves to the cultural shock that generates communication gap.

Parent's Apathy

Tribal community feels childhood or adulthood largely depends not on the physical age but on the degree of responsibility that children could successfully fulfill. Apart from that children's responsibilities towards the family and the contributions they make are significant and much important while conceptualising the above mentioned terms. In tribal society, children from the early age will be engaged in cooking food, fetching water, siblings care, support in the field, collection minor forest food, grazing, etc. Decision to give a chance to a child to spend happy childhood is not isolated from other aspects of household decision making nor are they purely household based. They reflect the norms and values of the wider community within which the tribal household is located and the social and economic possibilities which local contexts offer to different categories of households. Hence, parents may think sending their children to school means dislocation of traditional pattern of earning livelihood and of division of labour in their societies. Most vital problem of low literacy among tribal children is that children are considered by parents as economic assets to the family. The education of tribal girl children is more neglected because of deep-rooted beliefs, traditions and mind sets. Educational philosophers use the concept of false consciousness to refer to the existence of beliefs and values that individuals socialise into and operate upon. It can be argued from the universalist perspective that the parents believe that girls need to be socialized into their adult roles as children and the formal education has no meaning for them. In Karnataka many of the girl children are not enrolled in the Ashram schools due to parental apathy. The Government should take action in this regard to join more girl children in the Ashram schools.

Universal Primary Education

The question of how elementary education can be made universal has not received the attention it deserves. It needs to be highlighted. Recent studies has shown that an alarmingly large number of children do not become literate even after four years of primary education especially in both rural and tribal areas. Hence, total school effectiveness and actual learning have to be the central theme rather than secondary concern for universal education. Further, more important is that how effective schools are and successive learning basically depends not only on school level inputs but also on many vital factors outside the school. Basic infrastructures of Ashram Schools in tribal areas are worst than anything in many southern districts of Karnataka. Many schools even don't have hard roofs. Hostels are ruining. Unavailability of playground, lab and library and separate toilets are most common things that can be identified in many of the tribal Ashram schools. Absence of extra curricular activities makes children learning as a kind of unavoidable burden. Since tribal children are completely different from urban children or atleast from rural children learning should be a joyful experience for them otherwise simply they may be dropouts. For genuine universal elementary education the impact of the wider context on schooling has to be understood in a better way.

Absence of Central Monitoring Unit

Absence of effective monitoring unit on the tribal schools is one of the major drawbacks in case of development of tribal education. Concerned inspecting staff hardly visit to the tribal Ashram schools. Some time even only one time in a year inspections were conducted. This makes teacher to lack commitment to their profession. Some people reported that teacher's visit one or two times in a week only to the Ashram schools. This is also due to low level of motivation, inspiration and commitment among the inspecting staff, which are again matched by the low level of motivation and interest among the head teachers and teachers. It is high time that Government should think to establish a Centralised Monitoring Unit especially for Tribal Ashram Schools.

In the light of above discussion it can be inferred that on one hand, economic backwardness is responsible for the low percentage of literacy in the younger generation and on the other social backwardness and lack of social consciousness are responsible for low percentage of children attending the Ashram schools. When the school going children are few it can be well understood that higher education will be a rare phenomena among the tribals. Hence, along with other development it is also necessary that we should create some awareness about the significance of education among the tribals. Also proper facilities must be made available to them for their education. The internal problems of tribal education refer to the quality of Ashram schools, availability of suitable teachers, relevance of content and curriculum, medium of instruction, pedagogy and special supervision. A majority of the Ashram schools in tribal areas are without basic infrastructure facilities. Normally, the school buildings in tribal areas are with thatched roofs, dilapidated walls and non-plastered floors. Research evidences shows that a large number of tribal schools do not have teaching learning materials and even blackboards. In tribal areas the opening of an Ashram school is equated with the posting of teachers and same is the case with the other Ashram schools. It is found that in most of the Ashram schools which are residential in nature there is not enough space for the children to sleep. Consequently, the classroom turns into the dormitory and vice-versa. Due to lack of minimum sanitary provisions it is not uncommon to find that many children studying in Ashram schools are afflicted by contagious diseases like scabies, diarrhea, etc. leading to high dropout rate. The schools in tribal areas just function with bare minimum facilities.

Policy Suggestions

1. There are many basic differences that can be seen between major tribals and primitive tribals in case of India. Hence, the Government should bring a new educational policy especially for primitive tribals. It must be culturally and geographically specific. Moreover educational experts should be very sensitive while framing the policies which should not destroy the social solidarity of the tribes and kill their zest for life.
2. It is a well revealed fact that modern education cannot cater to the basic needs of the tribes. Modern education system cannot deem to have held much relevance for them since they are from the outer world. During the field work it has been revealed that tribals consider 'culture as their first educator'. Hence there is a need to identify the areas of minimum and maximum resistance to innovations in their culture and vital linkage to their cultural fabric. Once we identify enough space we can imbibe education into their culture.
3. It is the high time to have special education programme made for tribal children in consonance with the privileged cultural pattern and also in keeping with the needs and resources of the area concerned in order to secure the maximum amount of tribal children participation. Moreover new education programmes should be in the position to assert the existing perception, behaviour and action in education seeking process and culturally determined attitude towards use of different systems of education.
4. The State Government should construct a Textbook Commission especially for tribal education development. While framing the textbooks experts should focus on three important prospectives: 1. Linguistic, 2. Instrumental and 3. Culture. From the primary level itself all text materials should be in their respective mother tongue. There is need to evolve scripts, grammar and as well as appropriate vocabulary to communicate 'school knowledge'. Proper training should be given in tribal language, culture and society to the non-tribal teachers working in the tribal areas.
5. Lack of good quality teachers in sufficient numbers resulting in high pupil teacher

ratio may be an important factor in explaining the variations of educational status in tribal education. Given the inaccuracies in enrolments and the attendance/ absence of teachers, probably pupil teacher ratio may not be efficient and meaningful variable representing the quality of tribal education.

6. Ashram Schools should have a multi-purpose complex. If possible there should be a provision for selling and buying of consumer goods and minor forest products. Further Ashram Schools initially must emphasis on the service rendered to the primitive tribals than on costly building. In the initial stage provision should be made for a Kacha thatched Ashram type building rather than a pucca building.
7. The socio-economic context along with the development dimension is an integral part of school effectiveness. It is difficult to ensure good school quality in less developed tribal areas. On the other hand, it is found that area type affects learning directly by influencing poverty levels and also opportunities and motivation for learning. The impact of the area type on schools and learning is such that no description or analysis of schools can be meaningful without a parallel understanding of the area type (rural, hamlet of major tribals or primitive tribals).

Conclusion

Education cannot change in any fundamental way unless we change our basic patterns of thinking and interacting so that learning can become a way of life. Teachers, parents, administrators, district resource persons and community people are coming together to learn how to revitalise their schools with a process known as "Tribes". Evaluation of Tribes Learning Community (TLC) Schools has examined the impact of the Tribes process on student behaviour, academic performance, school culture, and teacher collegiality. Studies have shown that Tribes Learning Community (TLC) has a positive impact on classroom environment. Teachers report that they are spending less time managing student behaviour. Students are significantly less likely to be referred for disciplinary problems. The Tribes process helps teachers address performance and content standards, students in well-implemented classrooms score significantly higher on standardised tests than students from comparison groups. Teachers report increased staff collegiality and planning. "Responsive Education" is an essential pedagogy for academic achievement and school reform. It is the synthesis of artful teaching practices. It is based on understanding the critical development needs of a student age and cultural group. The Goal is to engage all teachers, administrators, students and families in working together as a learning community that is dedicated to caring and support, active participation and positive expectations for all students. In spite of sixty years of independence and more than fifty-five years of planned development and social provision for accelerated socio-economic development of weaker sections, the gap in literacy levels among the general population and the socially disadvantaged sections in persisting and in some cases this gap is further widening.

REFERENCES

1. Amarnath R. Das, R. Vijaya Krishna Naidu and N. Sreedhar, (2003), 'Ashram Schools and Education of Tribal Children', *Man and Life, 29(1-2):83-94.*
2. Ambasht, N.K., (1970), *'A Critical Study of Tribal Education'*, New Delhi: S. Chand & Co.
3. Anand, G., *Ashram Schools in Andhra Pradesh (A Case Study of Chenchus of Nallamalai Hills)*, New Delhi, Commonwealth Publishers, 1994.

4. Bhanage, N.P., *Tribal Commissions and Committees in India*, Bombay, Himalaya Publishing House, 1993.
5. Biman K. Dasgupta and Ajit K. Danda, *Tribal Education in India*, Calcutta, Anthropological Survey of India, 1984.
6. Chatterjee, S.K. (2000), *'Educational Development of Scheduled Castes: Looking Ahead'*, New Delhi: Gyan Publishing House.
7. Desh Mukh, B.A. (2004), *'Tribal Education'*, New Delhi: Sonali Publications.
8. *Details of ST Haadis in Mysore District*, Directorate of ST Welfare, Mysore District.
9. Geetha B. Nambissan, "Language and Schooling of Tribal Children – Issues Related to Medium of Instruction", *Economic and Political Weekly, 15 October 1994*, pp. 2747-2754.
10. Government of India, 1998, *National Commission for Scheduled Castes and Scheduled Tribes, 4th Report, 1996-97 and 1997-98*, Vol. 1, New Delhi.
11. Government of Karnataka, *Details of Ashram Schools*, Directorate of ST Welfare.
12. Government of Karnataka, *Details of Population and Literacy Among STs in Karnataka, 2001*, Statistical Institute, Bangalore.
13. Government of Karnataka, *Hand Book on the Programmes for the Development of STs, Bangalore*, Directorate of ST Welfare.
14. Gupta, Danda (1984), *'Tribal Education in India'*, Anthropological Survey of India, Calcutta.
15. Kabeer, Naila, Geetha G. Nambissan and Ramya Subrahmanian (eds.) (2003), *'Tribals and the Right to Education in South Asia: Needs Versus Rights ?'*, New Delhi: Sage Publications.
16. Kailash, G. (1993), *'Tribal Education and Occupation: Dynamics of Impact and Change'*, New Delhi: Nanak Publication.
17. Kamat, A.R., (1985), *Education and Social Change in India*, Mumbai: Somaiya Publications.
18. Malhotra, O.P. (1998), *'Tribal Education: Impact of Education on Tribal Life and Adjustment'*, New Delhi: Cosmo Publications.
19. Malli Gandhi, *An Investigation into the Problems Associated with the Literacy of ST Children in Tribal Schools of Vizayanagaram District of Andhra Pradesh* (Unpublished) Project Report, NCERT.
20. Mamatha (1994), *'Tribal Education: New Perspectives'*, New Delhi: Gyan Publishing House.
21. Manmatha Kundu, *Tribal Education – New Perspectives*, New Delhi, Gyan Publishing House, 1994.
22. Midatala Rani, "Bilingual Education in Tribal Schools of Andhra Pradesh", *ISDA – Studies in Development and Administration, Vol. 16, Nos. 1 & 2, January-March, April-June 2006*, pp. 133-144.
23. Midatala Rani, "Tribal Languages and Tribal Education", *Social Action, Vol. 50, No. 4, October-December 2000*, pp. 414-419.
24. Midatala Rani, "Tribal Languages in Andhra Pradesh: Issues and Prospects", *Journal of Political Science, Vol. 2, No. 2, November 2006*, pp. 37-44.
25. *National Curriculum Framework, National Focus Groups Position Papers, Vol. I, II and III*, Position Paper on Problems of Scheduled Caste and Scheduled Tribe Children (3.1), New Delhi, NCERT, 2005.
26. Pushpa Mandal (2000), *'Ashram Schools in Action'*, New Delhi: Rajat Publications.
27. Pushpa Mandal, *Ashram Schools In Action*, New Delhi, Raj Publications, 2000.
28. Rath, R.N., "Impact of Education in Modernising The Tribals", *New Frontiers in Education, Vol. XXXIII (1), 2003*, pp. 58-62.
29. Rathnaiah, E.V., *Structural Constraints in Tribal Education*, New Delhi, Sterling Publishers, 1977.
30. Roy Burman, B.K., (1964), *A Preliminary Appraisal of the Scheduled Tribes of India*, New Delhi: Registrar General.
31. Roy Burman, B.K., (1994), *Tribes in Perspective*, New Delhi: Mittal Publications.

32. Sachidananda and Ramesh P. Sinha, *Education and the Disadvantaged*, New Delhi, Uppal Publishing House, 1989.
33. Sharma S. Ram (1996), '*Education of Women of Scheduled Castes and Scheduled Tribes*', New Delhi: Discovery Publishing House.
34. Shukla (1998), '*Education of Indigenous People*', www.google search.
35. Shyamalal, *Education Among Tribals*, Jaipur, Printwell Publications, 1987.
36. Singh Bhupinder and Mahanti Neeti (1995), '*Tribal Education in India*', New Delhi: Inter-India Publications.
37. Singh, K.S. (Ed.), *People of India, Karnataka Series, Part I, Vol. XXVI, Part II, Vol. XXVI, Part III, Vol. XXVI*. New Delhi, Affiliated Fast West Press Pvt. Ltd., 2003.
38. Sita Toppo, *Dynamics of Educational Development in Tribal India*, New Delhi, Classical Publications, 1978.
39. Sridhar, N., *Tribal Education—A Study of Ashram Schools in Karnataka (Unpublished PhD Dissertation)*, Sri Krishnadevaraya University, Ananthapur, 2000.
40. Sujatha (1994), '*Quality Education: Educational Development among Tribes*', New Delhi: South Asian Publishers.
41. Sujatha, K., *Education Among Scheduled Tribes in India, NCERT.*
42. Sujatha, K., *Education in Ashram Schools—A Case of Andhra Pradesh, NIEPA* Occasional Paper, 1990.
43. Talesra Hemlatha, *Tribal Education*, Udaipur, Himanshu Publications, 1989.
44. Vinoba Gautam (2003), '*Education of Tribal Children in India and the Issue of Medium of Instruction: A Janshala Experience*'.

Appendix

Table–1
Enrollment of ST Students (2006-07)

Sl.No.	*Schools*	*Scheduled Tribes (Numbers in Lakh)*			*% of STs to General Enrollment*		
		Boys	*Girls*	*Total*	*Boys*	*Girls*	*Total*
1.	Primary school	0.47	0.41	0.88	2.68	1.56	4.24
2.	Middle school	0.21	0.11	0.29	2.01	1.26	3.27
3.	High school	0.11	0.06	0.17	1.45	0.44	1.89
4.	Higher sec. school	0.08	0.02	0.10	0.89	0.18	1.07
	Total	0.87	0.60	1.44	7.03	3.44	10.47

Source: Department of Education, Bangalore.

Table–2
Enrollment in Ashram Schools (2006-07)

Sl.No.	*Schools*	*Number of Schools*	*Total No. of Enrollment*
1.	Primary schools	97	33506
2.	Middle schools	18	14466
3.	High schools	8	4674
4.	Higher secondary schools	3	3846
	Total	126	56492

Source: SC/ST Development Corporation, Bangalore.

Table–3
Standard wise Enrollment of ST Children (2006-07)

District	*Standard*				
	1	*2*	*3*	*4*	*5*
Mysore	56.23	44.77	44.67	52.45	47.55
Kodagu	56.71	44.29	34.78	54.45	45.52
Chamarajanagar	55.54	45.46	54.70	56.23	43.77
Bangalore (urban)	54.29	44.71	57.90	59.76	40.34
Bangalore (rural)	55.67	58.90	54.90	58.89	41.21
Hassan	43.60	44.87	55.78	57.87	45.90
Mandya	46.70	49.90	44.90	44.40	54.90

Source: SC/ST Development Corporation, Bangalore.

Table–4
Ashram Schools in Karnataka (2006-07)

Sl.No.	*Name of the District*	*Total No. of Ashram Schools Visited*	*Total No. of Students (2007)*	*Boys*	*Girls*	*Total No. of Teachers*	*Total No. of Regular Teachers*	*Drop Outs*	*Fundamental Facilities Provided*
1.	Mysore	20	732	465	267	61	16	204	Only for 11 schools
2.	Kodagu	12	452	254	198	45	11	125	Only for 4 schools
3.	Chickmangalore	11	411	328	183	47	9	117	Only for 5 schools
4.	Dakshina Kannada	11	398	302	96	41	1	98	Only for 7 schools
5.	Udupi	7	328	216	112	23	5	87	Only for 5 schools
6.	Chitradurga	2	93	54	39	6	1	12	Only for 1 school
7.	Belgaum	4	187	109	78	5	1	56	Only for 2 schools
8.	Raichur	2	46	29	17	—	—	34	—
9.	Chamarajanagar,	19	662	485	177	58	16	143	Only for 13 schools
10.	Bellary	3	121	69	52	9	2	24	Only for 1 school
11.	Davangere	2	72	55	17	5	1	12	—
12.	Bangalore	6	296	119	76	13	4	35	Only for 4 schools
13.	Bidar	1	56	29	27	3	—	9	Moderate
14.	Bijapur	1	51	32	19	5	—	12	—
15.	Dharwad	1	58	31	27	3	—	6	—
16.	Gadag	1	63	29	32	3	—	9	—
17.	Gulbarga	1	89	41	38	3	—	11	No
18.	Hassan	1	38	21	17	2	—	7	No
19.	Haveri	2	88	53	35	8	2	18	Satisfactory
20.	Kolar	3	118	87	31	5	1	21	Only for 1 school
21.	Koppal	2	125	78	0	6	1	24	Only for 1 school
22.	Mandya	1	53	13	0	4	1	8	—
23.	Shimoga	3	214	112	0	7	1	41	Only for 1 school
24.	Tumkur	3	113	65	0	9	1	37	Only for 1 school
25.	Karwar	1	28	17	0	5	1	2	—
26.	Uttara Kannada	—	—	—	—	—	—	—	—

Source: Field Survey of Ashram Schools during July 2006 to January 2008.

Table–5
Dropout Rate of Scheduled Tribes (Class I-V) in Various Districts of Karnataka 2006-07

Sl.No.	*Districts*	*Boys*	*Girls*	*Total*
1.	Mysore	64.23	73.95	68.64
2.	Kodagu	60.16	81.81	71.26
3.	Chickmangalore	53.18	66.11	59.39
4.	Dakshina Kannada	31.30	52.27	38.59
5.	Udupi	56.04	63.78	59.38
6.	Chitradurga	78.03	74.24	76.81
7.	Belgaum	73.01	84.20	75.72
8.	Raichur	62.27	69.78	65.17
9.	Chamarajanagar	62.21	58.19	60.71
10.	Bellary	65.13	67.10	66.00
11.	Davangere	68.00	67.95	67.99
12.	Bangalore	57.91	58.37	58.13
13.	Bidar	45.83	49.23	47.42
14.	Bijapur	46.67	49.00	47.90
15.	Dharwad	39.78	30.87	33.78
16.	Gadag	N/A	N/A	—
17.	Gulbarga	54.67	58.90	56.80
18.	Hassan	59.70	61.70	59.00
19.	Haveri	56.80	59.00	58.80
20.	Kolar	34.60	37.70	36.70
21.	Koppal	N/A	N/A	—
22.	Mandya	43.12	48.90	47.89
23.	Shimoga	56.71	59.11	58.00
24.	Tumkur	64.23	66.80	66.91

Source: Field Survey of Ashram Schools during July 2006 to January 2008.

Table–6
Achievement Levels (Class I-V) of Scheduled Tribe Students in Districts

Sl.No.	*Districts*	*Subjects*		
		Mathematics	*Language*	*Environmental Sciences*
1.	Mysore	4.55	6.18	4.12
2.	Kodagu	4.08	5.58	8.51
3.	Chamarajanagar	4.44	5.35	5.04
4.	Bangalore (urban)	3.23	7.70	7.12
5.	Bangalore (rural)	3.19	6.15	4.29
6.	Hassan	2.87	4.60	4.84
7.	Mandya	5.11	5.24	7.35
8.	Tumkur	3.09	5.72	3.02

Source: Mid-Term Assessment Survey, Karnataka.

Table–7
Co-curricular Activities Organised in the Ashram Schools

Sl.No.	*Districts*	*School Parliament*	*Debate*	*Drama*	*Essay*	*Cultural Pro-gramme*	*School Day*	*All National Festivals*	*Social Service*
1.	Mysore	7%	—	13%	11%	—	65%	78%	—
2.	Kodagu	2%	23%	—	—	—	56%	67%	2%
3.	Chamarajanagar	4%	18%	44%	—	27%	77%	89%	—
4.	Bangalore (urban)	—	—	67%	—	21%	85%	91%	—
5.	Bangalore (rural)	—	—	65%	2%	—	44%	89%	—
6.	Hassan	—	11%	31%	—	—	—	56%	—
7.	Mandya	—	3%	38%	—	—	—	66%	2%
8.	Tumkur	—	9%	—	—	24%	—	87%	—

Source: Mid-Term Assessment Survey Report, Karnataka.

Table–8
Ex-Students of Ashram Schools (2000-07)

Sl.No.	*Districts*	*Graduate*	*PG*	*Ph.D.*	*IAS/IPS*	*Class I*	*Other Govern-ment Job*	*Private Job*	*Own Busi-ness*
1.	Mysore	118	33	9	1	14	19	14	9
2.	Kodagu	56	9	—	—	7	11	7	4
3.	Chamarajanagar	102	17	7	1	4	21	14	11
4.	Bangalore (urban)	63	21	3	—	8	17	4	3
5.	Bangalore (rural)	11	6	—	—	3	2	11	3
6.	Hassan	18	9	3	—	—	1	8	—
7.	Mandya	25	7	1	—	—	1	4	2
8.	Tumkur	33	5	2	—	2	7	6	—

Source: Mid-Term Assessment Survey Report, Bangalore, Karnataka.

13

Natives Education in India: An Unsolicited Agenda

Introduction

Indian Constitution identifies special consideration for certain ethnic minority groups, traditionally referred to as tribes or tribals, as Scheduled Tribes who constitute around 10 per cent of the total population of the country.

In Karnataka State, the 50 Scheduled Tribes are living in different parts of the state. Most of the tribal communities have their own languages different from what is spoken in the State where they are located. There are more than 70 such languages. The tribal languages in India belong to all major language families among which the Austric, the Dravidian, Tibeto-Chinese, Indo European families are the dominant ones. One of the distinguishing features is that majority of them live in scattered habitations located in interior, remote and inaccessible, hilly and forest areas of the country. Nearly 5-6 per cent of tribal habitations have less than one hundred population and more than 10 per cent have 100 to less than 200 population, while others have less than 300 people.

Who are STs ?

The term tribe or tribal or adivasis is not defined anywhere in the Constitution although according to the Article 342, ST represents the tribe or tribal communities that are notified by the President. STs in India are more like the "indigenous" or "native people" in other parts of the world. Generally the Schedule Tribes are defined as people who *(i)* claim themselves as indigenous to the soil; *(ii)* inhabit forest and hilly regions; *(iii)* largely pursue a subsistence level economy; *(iv)* have great regard for traditional religious and cultural practices; *(v)* believe in common ancestry and *(vi)* have strong group ties. However all characteristics do not apply to all tribal communities. Tribals are not homogenous groups. There are at least four groups of STs – hunting-gathering group, agricultural group, irrigation-agricultural group and industrial wage earning group.

The Scheduled Tribes are tribes notified under Article 342 of the Constitution, which makes special provision for 'tribes, tribal communities; parts of, or groups within which the President may so notify'. There is no definition of a tribe in the Constitution but one may distinguish some characteristics that are generally accepted. They include self-identification, language, distinctive social and cultural organisation, economic under-development, geographic location and initially isolation which has been steadily and in some cases traumatically eroded. Many tribes still live in hilly or forested areas somewhat remote from settlements. Many stereotypes flourish about the tribal person and tribal society. Many of the tribal people are undeniably economically under-developed and the process of their marginalisation can be traced to the intrusion of British colonialism which quickly detected in the forest that was home to tribals great potential for appropriation of resources. Exploitation of forest-lands by both the British and the zamindars resulted in the clearing of huge tracts for commercial crops such as tea, coffee, rubber and allowing contractors to fell trees in the very heart of the forest. These actions deprived the tribal people of their livelihoods because many of them were hunters and gatherers of forest produce. The interaction with the outside world brought the tribal people face to face with problems they were not equipped to cope with such as alcoholism and diseases. In the post-Independence period, while the Constitution protected the rights of the Scheduled Tribes and accorded them reservation in the Legislature, Educational Institutions and Government jobs, other, 'development' activities, such as the construction of large dams or the sale of timber led to the further marginalisation of some tribes. The scenario is therefore a mixed one. It may be necessary to use natural resources to improve the living conditions of the people of the state, but it must be done in a manner that is sensitive to ensuring the protection of the environment, which provides a livelihood to tribal people. Apart from the Scheduled Tribes there are 75 indigenous groups in India known' as 'Primitive Tribal Groups'. The Tenth Plan of the Central Government observes that these vulnerable communities have experienced a 'decline in their sustenance base and the resultant food insecurity, malnutrition and ill-health has forced them to live in the most fragile living conditions and some of them are even under the threat of getting extinct'. In Karnataka, the Koragas of Dakshina Kannada district and the Jenu Kurubas of Mysore, Chamarajanagar and Kodagu districts have been classified as 'primitive tribals'. The tribal population of Karnataka increased to 34.64 lakh in 2001 from 19.16 lakh in 1991. The decadal growth rate during this period is a high 80.8 per cent, caused not by a spurt in fertility rates but by the addition of several new tribes to the Scheduled Tribes (ST) category. The decadal growth rate is higher for females (81.9%) than for males (79.8%). The highest decadal growth rate occurred in Mysore district (around 328.0%), Bagalkot (261.6%), Dharwad (201.1%) and Belgaum (193.0%).The decadal growth rate is negative in Dakshina Kannada (-2.9%). Raichur (18.1%) has the highest percentage of ST population followed by Bellary (18.0%), while Chitradurga (17.5%), which had the highest percentage of ST population in 1991 came down to third place in 2001 on account of its bifurcation. The reverse is true of Raichur. Bellary has the highest population of Scheduled Tribes as a percentage of the ST population in the state (10.6).

The Government of India have taken-up in right earnest the duty of educating the 25 million Adibasis of the country with the object of helping them to become absorbed in the larger Indian society. This is a very difficult but a very necessary task. The difficulty is partly due to the differences in the cultural levels of the various tribes, and partly due to the intra tribal social solidarity which can be an obstacle to the integration of the Adibasis with the Indian society. The Adibasis cannot therefore be expected to rise to the full stature of citizenship immediately. Neither would any large scale and sweeping legislation bring about the desired end. It can be done only by a gradual process of adjustment for which a suitable type of education has to be planned and carried out.

National Policy on Education has specified the following points regarding education of tribal children.

- Priority will be accorded to opening of primary schools in tribal areas.
- There is a need to develop curricula and devise instructional material in tribal languages at the initial stages with an arrangement to switch over to regional languages.
- Tribal youths will be encouraged to take up teaching in tribal areas.
- Ashram schools, residential schools will be established on a large scale in tribal areas.

Educational Programmes and Provisions

Though the educational programme for tribal people is looked after by the education department some other agencies and NGO's are also trying hard to improve the educational facilities of the tribal people. The National Programme of Sarva Shiksha Abhiyan (SSA) which aims at achieving universal elementary education has taken special interest in the education of tribal group. The tribal children are the special focus group under SSA. As the tribal group is the heterogeneous group, SSA recognized the internal, socio-economic and psychological issues and challenges in tribal education. SSA provides for Rs. 1.5 million per district per year for the education of SC/ST children. It provides free textbooks for SC/ST children arid girls. It also provides for a range of interventions for working children and out of school children. This includes summer camps, bridge courses, residential camps, remedial teaching centers etc.

"Working group" on elementary and adult education for 10th Five Year Plan (2002-07) stressed the need to improve the quality of education of tribal children and ensuring equity, besides further improving the access. The 'manual of appraisal of plans' brought out by the ministry of Human Resource Development has outlined the appraisal issues with respect to the education of tribal children. Another special educational input for tribal education is residential schools known as 'Ashram schools' which are based on Gandhian philosophy of self reliance in India. It was first experimented in Gujarat. Ashram schools were found effective as they are feasible to open full pledged schools in small habitations, created healthy atmosphere for teaching and learning and they also helped to develop the total personality of the child and to impart vocational skills.

Some states like Andhra Pradesh and Karnataka have lowered the population size norm, especially for tribal areas. Schools cannot be established even with 15 children. The community mobilization and awareness on issues of enrolment, retention of children in schools, school involvement, education of girl children are carried out in tribal areas. The specific characteristics of such programmes in tribal areas are as follows.

- Family meetings and involvement of tribal youth.
- Use of tribal art forms.
- Charts, posters, film shows, Kala jathas in tribal languages.
- Involvement of tribal organizations and community.

Challenges for Tribal Education

Under the Directive Principles of State Policy, compulsory education is to be provided for all children upto the age of 14, but even today many a tribal folk in our country are illiterates despite of many schemes offered by the Government in the form of incentives such as mid-day meals, free books and uniforms. Despite this there are various barriers for the growth of education. Some of them as economical, cultural, ecological and social. One of the challenges in providing education to tribal children is with respect to setting up schooling facilities in small, scattered and remote tribal habitations. The majority of the tribal people live in inferior, inaccessible hilly and forest areas of the country. Setting up school specially for tribal children is practically impossible.

As per the latest report (2003-04), there are about 81,000 unreserved habitations in the country. The states of Bihar, West Bengal, Andhra Pradesh, Orissa, Assam have the largest number of habitations without primary schools. Even though the formal schools are accessible to some tribal groups they do not make good use of the content and processes of socialization of the tribal people. Tribal children face the disadvantages arising out of social and location factor. Uniform plans of education, emphasizing the same sort of schools, books, materials, teachers, curricular and methods are provided for the tribals without a consideration to the cultural variations of the tribals.

Some other major constraints of planning for tribal education are small size habitation, lack of facilities of transport and communication, content, curriculum and textbooks not relevant to their culture and environment, medium of instruction, non-availability of teachers who have the knowledge of tribal culture. Most teachers do not have any specialized training for teaching tribal children and their handling of the tribal child, his culture and education are generally slipped. The study conducted by Biswal G.C. (1991) in Orissa reveals that girl's enrolment is very low while compared to the boys and most of the teachers were found to be non-tribals and less qualified. This is the real picture of tribal education in our country.

With respect to the achievements of tribal children at primary classes, research reveals that they have low levels of achievement as compared to non-tribals. Even though the tribal children do possess the basic cognitive abilities and psychological disposition for successful participation in schools, some of the factors like low level of parental education, occupation, income and deprivation are responsible for poor performance of tribal children in schools. Poverty, deprivation, poor economic condition, struggle for survival, dependence on forest products, seasonal migration are some of the barriers in the way of the education of tribal people. Children helping their parents in their work is a social norm in many tribal communities. Tribal children help their parents in cattle grazing. Collection of forest produce, agricultural activities etc. devoid them of getting education in the formal system. Various studies have shown that the main reasons for high dropout rate of tribal children are work at home, ill health, poverty and lack of interest. The other major drawbacks are the negative attitude of parents towards education, less parental support in school work, low level of motivation and poor self-esteem of children. Bringing them into the formal system of education is a very big challenge to the country.

Achievements in Tribal Education

Even though there are many constraints to the education of tribal children, the Government, NGOs and other agencies are continuously trying to improve the level of education for these groups. Because of their endeavours same achievement in the field of education is evidenced. According to All India Educational Survey 1993, 56 per cent of tribal habitations and 78 per cent of tribal population have been provided primary schools near to their place. The schemes like Education Guarantee Scheme and Alternative and Innovative Education, Sarva Shiksha Abhiyan and DPEP are responsible for this improvement. According to new enrolment rate of 2001-02, more than 14 million tribal children in the age group of 6-14 years are attending schools out of 16 million. The enrolment of this group is considerably increased from 1996 to 2001. There is a positive trend with respect to participation of tribal girls in education.

Enrolment of Tribal Children from 1995 to 2001

Year	*Enrolment in the Elementary Stage (millions)*
1995-96	11.7
1996-97	11.3
1997-98	11.4
1998-99	11.9
1999-00	13.5
2000-01	14.1

Source: Department of Education, Government of Karnataka, 2002.

In support to the view of introducing tribal dialect in the initial stages of education many states have attempted to improve the quality of education for tribal children. Assam is the first state to prepare teacher training modules and separate teaching learning materials for the Bodo tribal language in 1995. Orissa has developed a comprehensive strategy for education of tribal children in 1997. It has initiated a number of activities to improve the quality of education. In Madhya Pradesh teacher's handbooks called Bridge Language inventories have been prepared in tribal languages, i.e., Gondi, Bhili and Kuduk. Four hundred and fifty (450) teachers have been trained to use this material. The bilingual dictionaries were developed in Andhra Pradesh, Kerala, Maharashtra and Gujarat. A Bridge Language inventory has been introduced in Ho and Wandavi languages in Bihar. In Karnataka Textbooks for Class I and II have been developed for Soligas. The achievements of Dr. Sudharshan for the welfare of this group of Biligirirangana Betta in Karnataka should be appreciated in this context. A residential school has been set up and free facilities are provided for Soliga children here.

Conclusion

After the detailed study of the provisions, achievements and challenges of tribal education, it can be concluded that the formal education system has certainly not helped the tribal people to the full extent in getting education and employment. It has failed to remove the sense of alienation, inferiority and pessimism from their hearts. It has not been able to integrate them fully with the general population. There is a need to adopt non-formal education and to have suitable teachers who can devotedly handle the specially designed educational programme for the tribal people.

While planning for education in tribal areas, attention should be paid to provide extra facilities in the form of various inputs for education of tribal children with a view to reduce existing disparities in educational access and to influence retention and achievement of tribal children. The high drop out rate has to be tackled through attractive schemes beneficial for them. At the primary school level, the assistance can be given by school uniform, text books, note books and mid-day meals. Where there are schools in the neighbourhood the tribal children may be encouraged to join them. The tribal groups have to be prepared mentally so that they are able to withstand the degradation among them of external agencies. It is possible only through providing education to them, which indirectly instill in them a sense of confidence, self esteem, identity with distinct personality and cultural individuality.

REFERENCES

1. Ambasht, 1970, *A Critical Study of Tribal Education*, New Delhi, Chand and Co.
2. Mamtha Kundu, *Tribal Education – New Perspectives*, 1994, New Delhi, Gyan Publishing House.
3. Midatala Rani, 2000, "Tribal Languages and Tribal Education", *Social Action, Vol. 50, No. 4*, pp. 414-419.
4. Rathnaiah E.V., 1977, *Structural Constraints in Tribal Education*, New Delhi, Sterling Publishers.
5. Sachidananda and Ramesh P. Sinha, *Education and the Disadvantaged*, 1989, New Delhi, Uppal Publishing House.
6. Shyamalal, 1987, *Education among Tribals*, Jaipur, Printwell Publications.
7. Sridhar Naidu, 2001, "Educational Problem of Scheduled Tribes", *Economic and Political Weekly, Vol. IX*, pp. 1231-1239.
8. Talesra Hemlatha, 1989, *Tribal Education*, Udaipur, Himanshu Publications.

14

Problems in Educating Indigenous Children: A Case Study of Paniya Tribe

Introduction

Strength of a society lies in the role of education in training, development and allocation of its manpower resources. Education has been conceived as training for better life and better social adjustment in a community or group. It is a phase of the social process which is fostered by society for life in group. It can be said that education is the complete development of individuality so that one can make original contribution to human life according to one's best capacity. Experts are of the opinion that the schooling facility must be provided on demand of community and community in turn must be mobilised enough to spontaneously come forward to run and manage the school. In this chapter an attempt has been made to explore the present educational status in case of Paniyas of Karnataka. Further this chapter will look for such avenues where some of the suggested policy implications can play a significant role in improving tribal education in general. The aims and objectives of the present chapter is to focus on the educational conditions prevailing among the Paniyas in the Kodagu hill ranges in Karnataka. The chapter also deals with the socio-cultural aspects of the Paniyas and the intimate relationship of their cultural matrix and the educational system available in the tribal schools in Karnataka. The specific problems faced by the Paniya tribal children in their schools are also highlighted. Finally, the required initiatives that needs to be taken for the educational development of the Paniya tribal children in Karnataka by the State Government are also discussed.

It is clear that in an under developed tribal community, where the poor people form the majority, owing to sheer poverty, they cannot avail of the educational opportunities. Thus, the educational development of the marginalised people is interlinked with their socio-economic condition. Hence prior to solving the problems associated with the educational backwardness of the tribals the problem of bread must be satisfied. Among these people who hardly get meal twice a day, education is a tall talk, taking into account the predominant role played by socio-economic factors in determining the utilization of facilities by the STs and SCs (Das and Naidu, 2003).

No community can achieve development without the spread of education. Development means all-round development, i.e., in the field of social, economic, cultural and above all the quality of life of human being. Whenever man uses the modem scientific devices for their progress then the spread of education is badly needed. Education and development are correlated. That is why the developed countries give too much attention for the growth of education with a view to achieve quick development in all aspects. Thus, any micro or macro level study on education is very much relevant for the development studies of any country. Again, it has been found that in a country which is more advanced in the field of science and education the rate of growth is much higher. So to understand the nature and extent of development of a particular community, the study of the state of education of that community is very significant and important (Guptha, 2001).

As a welfare state the Government of our country has taken a lot of developmental programmes with a view to make the all round development of the people. For the purpose of the overall development of the people the Central as well as State Governments have set up both macro and micro projects, development cells etc. Special emphasis is given to the grassroot people and more particularly to the tribal people of the country.

The spread of education among the weaker sections of our society is vital as education is a primary requirement for socio-economic development. The policy to promote educational interests of the weaker sections of the people, especially the Scheduled Castes and Scheduled Tribes, has been enshrined in our Constitution as a Directive Principle of State Policy. In the days of yore tribal people had a well organised system of education. The child learnt at home and at 'dormitories' and this training related to various activities of tribal life. But with the advent of Christian missionaries modem schools came up in tribal areas.

Homogeneity is the main characteristic of a tribe, but this characteristic has been sidelined due to the impact of modernity. An implicit stratification system is emerging within the tribal society on the basis of education, income, status and power. On the one hand a few privileged people are reaping all the benefits and on the other the vast bulk of tribals are struggling from poverty and deprivation. Moreover the educated elite, instead of improving the lot of the underprivileged are trying to exploit them. This has led to a situation where the majority of the tribals look upon these educated 'babus' with distaste and distrust. This has evoked a negative attitude towards education. With modem education have come modern values, which in turn have clashed with the age-old traditional values of tribal society. Also this has led the tribals being antagonistic to modern education.

Retarding Factors

Lack of social mobility and the problem of inter-cultural communication are major retarding factors in tribal education. As the teacher and the taught in the tribal areas belong to different cultures the communication barrier becomes almost insurmountable. The late Humayun Kabir had rightly remarked that even the best system of education is bound to fail without an efficient and resourceful teacher. Most of the teachers appointed in tribal areas are a disinterested lot due to various problems faced by them such as lack of proper residential facility, good salary, communication facility and social distance from the tribal people.

Thus the teacher feels isolated and unhappy. Such a teacher certainly cannot be the best communicator of modern ideas and messages to tribal children. Even though the Government has come up in recent times with various plans and programmes to improve the educational lot of the tribals, there is not much result to show as there is lack of sincerity on the part of the officials charged with the implementation of these programmes. In fact a credibility gap has emerged between such officials and the tribal people. If all these problems are to be tackled successfully, the Government has to bring about a change in the basic orientation in tribal education.

The Government in its zeal to provide facilities to the tribals has constructed hostels for the tribal students, supplied textbooks, provided different types of scholarship, etc. But instead of bridging the gap it has widened the rift. The tribal students staying in separate hostels, availing themselves of separate scholarships, feel naturally ostracized. This should change and instead there can be some percentage of reserved seats for tribals in a general hostel and tribal students should be encouraged to take an active part in various college as well as hostel activities. Only then they could be brought into the mainstream.

It has also been proved that when a tribal child begins his education he starts with no linguistic information and conceptualisation whereas a non-tribal child starts with a few familiar concepts and linguistic associations. So pre-school training programme for the tribal child is a primary requirement and the Government should undertake such programmes if it wants to put the tribal students on an equal footing with the non-tribal students (Ambasht, 1990).

As regards appointment of teachers, more and more appointments should be made from among the tribal population so that the teachers become 'accepted' and they deal with the tribal students by using more motivational approach. The existing teachers should be provided with adequate facilities and they should be properly oriented. It should be a must for the teachers to learn the tribal language and there can also be attempts at writing textbooks in tribal languages.

Moreover the education of children has little functional importance to them. Even after secondary education there can be no gainful employment. Thus there is no incentive for education. So the existing curricula should be related to socio-economic and cultural life of the tribals. Emphasis must be on imparting skills and modern information such as agriculture, poultry, forestry, carpentry, etc. Only by providing better communication facilities, sanitary programmes, teaching materials and methods the Government can hope to bring about an attitudinal change in the tribal population towards education. Otherwise with the present state of affairs the dream of our Constitution makers about tribal education would remain unfulfilled (Sujatha, 2001).

After India attained its Independence and Constitution framed in 1950, the Universalisation of Primary Education has become one of the priorities of development. Huge amount of money has been earmarked and spent on undertaking many schemes and programmes but with little success in areas of educational development. Analysis of the educational scenario of the country reveals that there is a huge gap between rural and urban literacy. Further going down the ladder, the educational attainment and literacy of Scheduled Castes and Scheduled tribes is much lower and abnormal. Development practitioners and academia relate poverty and underdevelopment to lack of spread of education as the foremost reasons. The Government at the Center is always in pressure to revise policies and devise new strategies to curb the regional disparity that exists in educational development in the country.

The Paniya Tribe in Karnataka

Karnataka is the homeland to 50 tribal communities who reside in different parts of the State. Only 2 tribal communities have been declared as primitive, based on their low educational achievement and economic practices. However, the "Paniyan" is declared as major tribe. They reside mostly in the Southern part of the State and known for their infamous human sacrifice during British colonisation in India and even before that. They are mainly concentrated in the Kodagu hill ranges. They live in hill slopes surrounded by dense forests. They have a subsistence economy based mainly on shifting cultivation, hunting and food gathering. Now they have become skilled horticulturists. The Paniyan once infamous for their pernicious practice of human sacrifice and female infanticide was identified as early as August 1836 by Mr. Russell, a British Official under Madras Presidency during British Colonisation in India. It was of deep concern for the British Government to stamp out the barbarous practices to restore peace and order in the territory (Sridhar, 2001).

The Paniyan is a marginal indigenous tribal community in the State concentrated in the plateau of Malnadu hill range, which covers two blocks of Kodagu District. They live in hill ranges situated at a height of 1000-4970 feet above sea level. Two Micro projects have been undertaken by Government of Karnataka on the overall development of the Paniya tribe. They cover 45 villages and hamlets and 678 families with a total population of 6085 as per the latest survey. The male and female ratio stands as 1000:898. There has been no enumeration of population by the State Government on individual tribal communities since 1981.

The Paniyan villages and habitations are located in a tangle of thickly wood hill ranges, which is determined by availability of perennial streams and sufficient land for shifting cultivation. The houses are generally mud-built and straw-thatched, although nowadays, some brick-built straw-thatched houses are made by the Paniyan. The road communication network has not been developed much even after 50 years of independence of India. The dress and ornaments, which adore the Paniyan, are distinguishable from other sections of the tribe. Paniyan males put a narrow scarf wrapped around the waist will be seen tucked in the hair-knot at the back. Invariably all of them carry on axe on the shoulder and a knife is kept hanging from the waist belt. The women wear sarees. They cover their chest with a small, band of cotton cloth tied at the back. All the male and female members wear hair-clips on their head and often pierce their ears and love to wear as many earrings as they can. The women folk wear big neck rings made up of aluminium and iron.

Paniyan have a distinct skill of horticulture, which separates them from all other tribals in the state. They know their soil condition and grow many fruits of high commercial value. They grow pineapple, banana, jack-fruit, and *papaya* in plenty. They also grow high quality turmeric and ginger that has the highest demand in the state. Paniyan practise shifting or *podu* cultivation as it is called. They produce varieties of crops like maize, *ganja*, *ragi*, grams, etc. They also practice hunting and gathering. Some time they work as daily labourers in the coffee estates.

Gathering of variety forest produce are made for daily domestic requirements. Folks drink liquor very often prepared from bark of some trees. Paniya rear pig, cattle, buffalo and goat. These animals and birds meet their nutritional protein requirement. But most importantly these animals and birds are sacrificed before the spirits and ghosts on the occasion of propitiation when family members fall sick. Sickness of any sort is attributed as the effect of wrath of spirits, ghosts due to breach of norms, known or unknown. The Paniya family is normally simple nuclear family consisting of father, mother and their unmarried children. Extended families are rare due to the fact that it needs big houses to accommodate all members which is a rare probability and often dangerous on a hill top with rugged level. The Paniya family is patrilocal and patrilineal.

Education of the Paniya Tribe

The Paniya have their own dialect which has no script. Their culture is as strengthened as anyone's with songs, riddles, proverbs, myths, legends, dances and full of literacy works which are generally transmitted orally from one generation to another. These literacy pieces are often based on and linked to trees, animals, birds, streams, etc. in the forest which form the part of their ecology and environment. Therefore forest and tribals are in separable and forest plays the pivotal role in shaping their society and culture.

The tribal people are highly religious as their society and culture is totally governed by religious beliefs and practices. They see their world full of mysteries governed by deities, spirits, and ghosts; both benevolent and malevolent. Each and every natural object animate or inanimate is attributed to be the abode of some sort of deities, spirits, ghosts which are worshipped and propitiated with prescribed norms. Deviation of any such norm by any member of society is dealt with impurity. The Paniya family is nuclear and polygynous. The woman is more diligent and hard working in comparison to their male counterparts. She does all sorts of household work ranging from fetching water from distant streams to preparing food for family members, taking care of brothers and sisters, working along with other male members in the field. Therefore, she is treated as an economic asset to the family. Due to this reason girl child is preferred to over boy child in Paniya community. Further the prevailing marriage practice among the Paniya go in favour of women. The Paniya being conservative and educationally backward live in relative isolation from other people of the area. However due to various state development interventions like development in the field of communication, construction of Roads and Bridges, opening of offices for launching of various welfare schemes and programmes by Government, they are relatively exposed to the outside world. These interventions effected in thinning down of forest base and deforestation due to indiscriminate cutting of trees. While the spread deforestation has led to shrinking of their subsistence base, poverty and unemployment have left their society exposed to widespread discrimination and exploitation by other people of the area (Rathniah, 2000).

Modem education does not seem to be the priority of Paniya community because of lack of awareness and cultural orientation. Studies on their view of a happy life reveal that they certainly prefer to have more of forest lands where shifting cultivation can be practiced, fruit bearing trees for collection and consumption, wild animals and birds to hunt and more number of children to work for the household and run their progeny. It is worth describing their system of education here. In Paniya, the dormitory system is there to orient boys and girls to acquire skills and knowledge that is required to be a full phased member of their society. There are separate dormitories for boys and girls in each village. After returning from fields, they stay together in the dormitory and in an informal way i.e. through songs, dance, riddles, proverbs, gossip etc. which are transmitted orally from generation to generation. The whole night is spent amidst dancing and singing, traveling to other dormitories and interacting with boys and girls over there. When they turn to adulthood they master their arts, traditions and customs and command respect as a bonafide member of their community. Therefore sending children to school is considered as useless investment for parents. This is because not only he/she is deprived of helping their parents in sibling care and household works and learning basic skills of their society but also the family loses an able hand from the household and thus a lot of income.

If we consider the teacher and taught relationship, the teacher or instructor (most often non-tribal) is like a foreigner and looked suspiciously by the students and the community. His language, etiquette and manners are regarded as unusual and quite different from the tribal ways of life. The ethnocentric attitude of the teacher towards tribal society and culture also aggravates and worsen the situation. He does hot have meetings and interactions with people around him to gain their confidence. He often creates fear psychosis among pupils by castigating and punishing them in classroom. That fear and inferiority complex created among students cause large scale dropouts among Paniya students, specially the girls who are enrolled at an over-aged stage. Therefore at one end the school environment and attitude of teachers pushes them out of schools and on the other their love for freedom and forest based life pulls them out of the formal schooling environment (Singh, 2003).

The situation is not better of or different where even a tribal teacher having a positive out look and dedicated approach is working. The tribal children have a year round season of forest based collection and festivals. Accompanying parents at tender age to forest yield more forest collection of fruits, roots, tubers arid leaves, which in turn gives better economic property to family rather than sending children to school which has no tangible immediate gains for parents. There are few parents who have been mobilised and have got the conviction to educate their children. But in school the children find language as the greatest problem hence other curricular transactions meaningless. The standard language text book, its unfamiliar contents, contexts and picturisation depicts a whole range of unfamiliarity for which the students lack interest. The teacher centered monologue classroom transaction throws the pupils into absolute poor achievement in tests. Failure in examination is another most important reason for dropouts from school among Paniya children. Above all, the students find the subjects, contents and contexts not linked to their real life experiences extremely monotonous and boring. The reasons are so strong that, even in residential schools run by Department of Tribal Welfare, Government of Karnataka, with all sorts of facilities like free food, free reading-writing materials and other basic requirements like sitting mat, uniform, blankets, beds, etc., the enrollment, attendance and achievement of students are far from satisfactory (Ganesh, 2006).

The irony is that there is no supervision or monitoring of the work of teachers and school management by the personnel who are supposed to be the decision-makers in the system. The lack of performance of the schooling system is always attributed to the lack of interest due to poverty of the community for their children's education rather than the whole range of faulty planning and implementation by the Government.

Conclusion

The schooling facility must be provided on demand of community and community must be mobilised enough to spontaneously come forward to run and manage the school. The children should be provided text books in their own language in initial stages of their schooling and gradually they should be exposed to standard textbooks in state language at a later stage. The textbooks should contain local specific contents, contexts and narration by which the children can relate their learning to their real life situation. The timing of the school should be as per the availability of children and the holiday calendar should be as per the holiday pattern of the locality. The teacher belonging to the community should be posted if not a teacher having a positive attitude and some understanding about tribal community should be employed in the area. Moreover the education administrators should be more responsive and responsible to the education of the children with special needs. Close and continuous monitoring of schools (academic and administrative) would definitely render insights to the problem and its solutions at the earliest.

REFERENCES

1. Ambasht (1970). "*A Critical Study of Tribal Education*", New Delhi: Chand and Co.
2. Das and Naidu (2003). "*Development of Primitive Tribal Groups in India*", New Delhi: Kanishka Publication.
3. Ganesh (1998). "*Education of Indigenous People*", www.google search.
4. Guptha (2001). "*An Introduction to Indian Anthropology*", New Delhi: Vikas Publishing House.
5. Singh, B. (1977). "*Tribal Development at Cross Road*", *Man in India. 57(3):229-247.*
6. Sridhar Naidu (2001). "Educational Problem of Scheduled Tribes, *Economic and Political Weekly", Vol., IX,* pp. 1231-1239.
7. Sujatha (2001). "*Quality Education Development Among Tribes*", New Delhi: South Asian Publishers.

15

Educational Status of Indigenous People: A Moment of Truth

Introduction

The tribals have been the missing link in the development process of the country for generation's due to various factors. As such, their socio-economic development has always been at a low ebb in comparison to other Indian communities. Tribal education in India has reached a threshold point. The spread of education in the vast tribal belt of the country is still a challenging one. Many Governments have in the recent past followed the path of the trial and error method of education. But the result is not an encouraging one. This chapter examines the present educational status among STs, reasons for low educational development and policy implications. The study is based on the fieldwork in the selected districts of Karnataka State and documentary evidences. Since education for tribal children is quite different from other cultural groups of the Nation a culturally sensitive, ecologically valid and economically viable programmes of education will have to be evolved and implemented soon.

India has the second largest tribal population in the world. Large proportion of tribal population are living in rural areas. The tribal people have remained economically and socially backward because of many historical, economic and social reasons. There are a large number of tribes, which have stayed away from the mainstream society. The literacy rate among the tribals is very low.

Education is a pre-requisite for development. Our planners and administrators have emphasised on this fact, particularly, regarding tribal people. The post independent efforts have resulted in steady growth of literacy level among tribal groups. However the efficacy of efforts are not in tune with the desired goal. Regarding education, the tribal pockets are suffering from guiding and goading factors. Political organisations of tribals, though lost its original strength and applicability, still can act as a guiding factor, provided that certain encouragement is shown by tribal leadership, and if the latter receives attention from our planers and administrators.

To spread education in case of highly marginalised sections of the society it has been a gigantic task to any Government. Among tribals education is the indigenous learning process which is the systematic influence of senior member of the family to junior member in dormitory where all young kids gather to get oral education from elders of the community. The educational backwardness of STs has its roots in the socio-economic and cultural setting in which the tribal people live. In India they remained isolated for a long time and were confined to their traditional economic activities such as food gathering, shifting cultivation etc. The very primitive conditions of the tribal life, their vulnerability to exploitation and the existing socio psychological barriers developed through prolonged isolation, has a clear manifestation in the life they lead.

Since independence of the nation, quite a large number of anthropological studies have been conducted on the socio-cultural and economic aspects of the different tribes of Karnataka. But very few studies have been dealth with exclusively on the educational aspect of different tribes so far. Some of the anthropologists while studying the different aspects of a tribe concentrated only to study the tribal society, kinship pattern, etc. But these concerned studies don't deal with the educational aspects. Reports, symposia and surveys conducted from time to time, relating to welfare activities of the tribals includes the overall problems of tribals in general. Modernisation, Privatisation and globalisation have had enormous positive and negative effect on the education of tribals. Hence education to the indigenous people has undergone a different phase. In spite of tall claim of Globalisation and its success in relation to boost up the economy, very few attempts are made to analyse the adverse outcome with regard to the tribals.

Traditional Education

Many tribes had their indigenous system of education and some of the tribals are still following them. The tribal societies in the past have been mostly closed societies as far as contacts or communication with distinct groups are concerned. Hence most of them did not develop any script for their languages. This means that they had distinct grammar and language structure without a written from. To fulfill their educational needs many tribal communities in Karnataka had their traditional dormitories and Institutions. These Institutions prepared the young to take up socially useful work as members of the community. Further, these Institutions and dormitories also imparted traditional education to boys and girls of adolescent age. Children were supposed to spend their nights in these dormitories. They learn legends, folk songs, mythic tales, music and dances. Group life was its main character.

Modern Education

Missionaries were first to introduce the tribals to modern education. Some of the missionaries have tried their level best to educate some of the tribals like Jenukuruba, Kaadu Kuruba, Soliga and Koraga tribes of Karnataka. They also opened many informal learning centers for these tribals. Also these missionaries studied their language and prepared dictionaries and literature in a number of tribal dialects. The Indian Education Commission examined the problem in 1882 and found that the missionaries were the most significant agents in spreading education among the STs along with convertions.

In the Directive Principles of State Policy also a number of schemes and programmes have been stipulated. Some of these schemes are incentives, financial assistance, establishment of Ashram schools, hostels, etc. The education of tribal children has been engaging the attention of the educational planners, as it is providing to be a hard task in achieving universal elementary education. The problem all the more is acute in the case of girls among the Tribes.

Methodology of the Study

This study is limited to selected major and minor tribals spread across the Karnataka State. A few districts were selected giving weightage for the presence of patches of tribals to represent regional variations for analysis. For collection of data on the communities, standard anthropological technique of intensive participant observation among selected tribals has been made use of. Case study, closed interview, statistics are the other methods used on the basis of a broad research guidelines on Tribal Development. The Secondary data is based on the various Government records and academic reports.

How is the Situation in Karnataka with Regard to Tribal Education?

Karnataka is one of the major states in India having significant percentage of tribal people. Out of the 50 different tribes in the State, the Jenukurubas and Koragas are considered as primitive tribes. Soliga, Kuruba, Siddi and Nayka are major tribes living in different parts of the State. The major portion of the tribals are living in plain land while notable percentage of tribals are living in hilly areas like Coorg district. The literacy rate of primitive tribals is very pathetic.

Enrolment of ST Students in Tribal Schools

Enrolment of ST Students During 2004-05 (Numbers in Lakhs)

Sl.No.	*Schools*	*Scheduled Tribes*			*% of STs for General Enrolment*		
		Boys	*Girls*	*Total*	*Boys*	*Girls*	*Total*
1.	Primary Schools	0.37	0.31	0.68	2.68	1.56	4.24
2.	Middle Schools	0.18	0.11	0.29	2.01	1.26	3.27
3.	High Schools	0.11	0.06	0.17	1.45	0.44	1.89
4.	Higher Secondary Schools	0.08	0.02	0.10	0.89	0.18	1.07
	Total	0.74	0.50	1.24	7.03	3.44	10.47

Source: Government of Karnataka, Department of Education and Department of Labour, Bangalore.

It is found that enrollment of students for primary education during 2004-05 is 145.73 lakh. Out of this total enrollment only 1.24 (0.95%) lakh children belong to the Scheduled Tribe. Out of this total only 0.37 lakh are boys and 0.31 lakh are girls. Out of total 0.29 lakh enrollment at Middle school level 0.18 lakh are boys and 0.11 lakh are girls. In case of High schools out of 0.17 lakh total enrollment 0.11 lakh are boys and 0.06 lakh are girls. Situation is still worst incase of Higher secondary schools whereas 0.08 lakhs are boys and 0.06 lakh are girls. From this data it is clear that negligible percentage of ST children have been enrolled to the education at different levels.

Educational Advancement and STs

This table gives a clear picture about enrolment of students in Ashram schools. Out of 122 Ashram schools which are functioning in Karnataka, more than 92 per cent are primary schools in deep and remote areas of the tribal belt. Government has established only 8 High schools for tribal children. An interesting point here is why Government is not showing any interest in higher education of the tribal children? Since many high schools are quite

Enrolment in Ashram Schools (2003-04)

Sl.No.	Schools	Number of Schools	Total Number of Enrolment
1.	Primary Schools	96	28506
2.	Middle Schools	15	11456
3.	High Schools	8	3974
4.	Higher Secondary Schools	3	2874
	Total	122	46810

Source: SC/ST Development Corporation, Bangalore.

far away from their hamlets majority of the parents don't send their children to schools. It is very intensive in case of girls. This kind of disparity of schools will further deteriorate the educational status of tribal children. More pathetic fact is that more than 98 per cent schools don't have any permanent faculties and basic facilities.

Discussion

The progress of STs in India is closely linked up with their educational advancement, more so in today's changing world in which education plays an increasing role in everyday life apart from equipping a person with the necessary skills or more effective participation in different spheres of economic activity. Even after five decades of planned efforts and special provisions in the Constitution tribals in Karnataka lag much behind others in all fields. Our study has revealed about focusing attention on tracing the socio-economic constraints, and poverty as a major reason for slow progress of education. However, there are hardly any studies on internal aspects of schools, quality of facilities and the impact of education or occupational mobility of these tribals. Our study has shown that this kind of occupational mobility has an increased affect on the Supreme Court verdict on imposing a ban on collecting minor forest product. Also for all these years the tribals have been traced as a homogenous group in the macro level planning with uniform policies and programmes, though in reality the tribes and tribal areas are quite heterogeneous in terms of development due to their geographical locations, exposure to modernity and religious conversion. The effectiveness of formal education in bringing about a change in the life of tribes, particularly in terms of occupational mobility, therefore may not be uniform across different areas and different groups in the state.

Education in tribal areas, despite being promoted on a war footing manner by the various Governments, still struggles to survive. There is an increase in drop out rate and the decrease in the enrolment rate. Lack of infra structural facilities, indifferent attitudes of teachers towards students and vague understanding of the benefits of education among the parents of tribal children are some of the major ills plaguing educational scenario in tribal areas. More vital fact is that there are trends showing decline in sex ratio particularly in prosperous tribal belts where most children go to the primary schools. These are some of the major problems in case of Tribal education in Karnataka State. There is still much to do to actualize the goal of universal education in Karnataka. More over one of the vital problem facing in spread of education in remote areas is lack of transport and timely release of money from the State/Central Government. By this study it is realized that the hamlet based education programme can sustain for larger period of time if the village community is able to take over its running. Participation of local community in educational programmes in the tribal areas not only ensures physical and human facilities at schools but also motivates the teachers to achieve quality education. Also integrating an income generation component into the education programme may also help in a great manner.

There is an imperative need to create special opportunities to respond to the educational needs of tribal girl children. Consequences of the development process are not neutral. They militate more against girl children than boys and hence end to result in greater negative effects in girl child education. Loss of access and control of resources in tribal areas tend to push women out of productive activities. This also affects adversely their status in the family and community as their participation in the economy decreases. The major strategy to address this issue is to educate and elect more women representatives at Local Self-Government.

The demand for education varies widely across the tribal households due to difference in religion, income, location and parental education. Only few tribes in the State who are living in semi-urban areas are aware of the value of education and the available facilities and they send their children to schools. The cultural factors like polygamy also hinder the education of children. Drought, forest degradation, migration, displacement also hinder the education of these tribal children. Further, in case of many Ashram schools the mid-day meal programmes is not being implemented properly and corruption is rampant in managing the food items by non-tribal urban teachers. It seems that few qualitative changes are required in the functioning of the Ashram Schools to make them truly functional.

Tribal Institutions of both primary and secondary level education though functional are not succeeding in educating the children even after spending four years in schools. Probably the basic reason is that the content of textbooks does not take into account their traditional knowledge system. More over in these schools the syllabus is far away from teaching about control of natural resources and recognition of their own identity as tribal communities. Also there is no scope in the present methodology of teaching to enhance their inherent learning capacities. Mainstream educational Institutions tend to create an alienated group of youngsters with few opportunities to use their capacities. More specifically we need to campaign for a policy, which takes into consideration the learning needs of tribal youth, dropouts at the school and high school levels. Problems of drop-outs have to be viewed with great concern because the tribal people in the area are unaware about the initial wastage of years in education and consider it of no consequence. The incidence of high dropouts among ST students can be attributable to many factors.

In the context of multiplicity of languages in India where the tribal children have to learn 2-3 languages in the schools, it is needed to study the extent to which the concept of learning is affected, if learning in a language other than that of mother tongue. Further the long-range effects of bilingualism and multi-lingualism needs to be investigated. The effect of linguistic structure, where language of different complexity exists, will be an exciting study. Unfortunately no studies have been undertaken so far to study the effect of mental retardation among disadvantaged tribal children. Similarly very little has been attempted to see the relationship between cultural traits and cognitive development among tribal children.

Conclusion

Several Governments at the Centre have in past initiated various efforts to meet the challenges of education particularly primary education in tribal areas. However, the present Government showed its seriousness to give the primary education a massive thrust is discernible in its imposing a 2 per cent cess on all the Central taxes to mop up to least 7000 crore rupees to be used in universalisation of education. In India the educational efforts have to be contiguously meaningful and innovative to sustain over a long period of time. In our country where the society is facing various social and economic problems and indifferent attitude towards indigenous people and their education no uniform strategy can effectively work. If we are really committed about elimination of prevailing non-schooling and living up to the Constitutional Directives of Universal Elementary Education, our policies and programmes have to invest more resources while simultaneously staying open to multiple, context specific modes of meeting their objectives.

After the detailed study of the provisions, achievements and challenges of tribal education, it can be concluded that the formal education system has certainly not helped the tribal people to the full extent in getting education and employment. It has failed to remove the sense of alienation, inferiority and pessimism from their hearts. It has not been able to integrate them fully with the mainstream. There is a need to adopt non-formal education with utmost care.

However even at the State level they cannot be treated as a homogenous group in planning for their education. Among the tribes different approaches and treatment need to be adopted based on their socio-cultural and geographical situation. The unique problem of those who inhibit the plains need to be understood. In order to have balance in education within the tribes female education has to be given special attention as soon as possible. Further, various studies have shown that tribal children do possess the basic cognitive abilities and psychological disposition for successful participation in schools. Yet the evidences suggest very low level of participation and success of tribal children in the programme of school education. It points to our failure in evolving a sensitive model of tribal education rooted in the psychological strength of tribal children.

Proper location of educational facility merits high consideration. Instead of establishing Ashram schools in most interior tribal tracts, it is highly desirable to locate this facility at the places which have road points. ST children belonging to interior villages may be given preferences in the admission into Ashram schools. Supply of provisions and other necessary material to the interior tribal areas must be effectively supervised. Delay in the management affects the normal functioning of an Institution. Ashram schools should not rest as the feeding centers of tribal children. They have to develop to the level of offering proper orientation. The teacher has to exert more to supplement the parental care towards the tribal students.

REFERENCES

1. Kailash, "Education and Development", *Anthropologist, Vol. 12, No. 3, 1993.*
2. Maish, Education of Indian Tribes, *Adivasi, Vol. 13, No. 2,* 1998.
3. Mallik, Development Planning for Tribals, *Report of Planning Commission*, New Delhi, Government of India, 1997.
4. Rao, "Educational Status of Disadvantage Groups" in Guptur Ed., *Educational Development in India*, New Delhi, Kanishka Publication, 2001.
5. Verghese, 'Gender Issue and Education', *Journal of Social Science, Vol. 3, No. 12, 1993.*

16

Educational Deprivation in Primitive Tribal Groups: Some Preliminary Observations

Introduction

India is one of the major countries having larger concentration of tribal groups in the world. Among the tribals, Primitive Tribal Groups (PTGs) are highly vulnerable. These groups are still isolated from the main stream of civilized society. They are small in number and still having pre-agricultural technology. The rate of literacy among them is extremely low. Different people are exploiting these primitive tribal groups in different ways. Both Government and NGOs have implemented several policies and programmes for the upliftment of these tribals. It was thoughtful of the Government of India to have constituted several Committees to suggest measures for the welfare and development of the Tribes during different plan periods. But the result is not very significant and encouraging because of rigid traditional aspects of these tribals. Some time their dwelling places would be beyond reachable. Further the implementation machinery was faulty and development programmes could not be implemented properly. In this chapter an attempt has been made to explore the present educational status and understand the reasons for low rate of literacy in two identified primitive tribal groups of Karnataka State i.e. *Jenu Kuruba* and *Koraga*.

Tribal development has been given one of the major attention by all the Governments in India during all Five Year Plans on account of the socio-economic backwardness of the tribals. Also a number of provisions have been brought into the Constitution to safeguard their basic interests. Planning Commission (1991) has remarked that, "tribal welfare should aim at the advancement of the social and economic life of the tribes within a reasonable time with a view to gradually integrate them with the rest of the country on an equal footing." It is noted that the total number of Scheduled Tribe population as per the 2001 census constitute about 10.08 per cent of the total population in India. Out of this about 6.3 per cent tribes are spread only in five states of the country. Recent study shows that the total number of Scheduled Tribes (STs) in 643 in India (Singh, 1992). All Scheduled Tribe groups are entitled to have many benefits directly from the Government, with reservations for them in many sectors of development. Moreover the Constitution enshrines a number of important provisions for safeguarding and promoting the interests of Scheduled Tribes in the country. Though number of efforts have been made for overall development of Scheduled Tribes it was noticed that some administrative restrictions having been imposed on collection or utilization of forest land resources that the tribals traditionally depend upon. The major objective of this chapter is to prepare a background for discussion understanding for diminishing tribal education. Further the chapter will look for such avenues where some of the suggested policy implications can play a significant role in improving tribal education in general.

Who are the Primitive Tribal Groups (PTGs) ?

The first attempt to identify the PTG in the country was made in 1931. The group of tribals who have the following characteristic features have been classified into primitive tribal groups: *(i)* tribes still practicing pre-agricultural level of technology, *(ii)* extremely low level of literacy, *(iii)* near stagnant or diminishing population. Till today 75 groups have been identified as PTGs in 16 States and Union Territories. The problems of Indian tribals can be classified into two types: *(i)* problems of major tribes and *(ii)* problems of primitive tribes. But in India both of them are mixed up together and that's why no significant achievement could be made in solving the problems of primitive tribes. In recent years they are facing some serious problems like lack of basic facilities including poverty, illiteracy, lack of medical facilities, unreachable to NGOs, lack of essential agricultural technology, etc. In the recent past Planning Commission had issued some guidelines to the States that tribal development plan should emphasise on the following aspects: *(i)* elimination of exploitation of all forms *(ii)* rapid social and economic development, *(iii)* improving their organisational capabilities and narrowing down the gap between the levels of development of the tribals and others by providing proper education. Also the Commission suggested that the Integrated Tribal Area Development Plan focusing on the specific problems of the tribal people must be implemented vigorously emphasising on the cultural fabric of the respective tribes.

Profiles of Primitive Tribals of Karnataka

Jenu Kuruba and Koraga tribals have been identified as PTGs in Karnataka State. Jenu Kuruba tribe is concentrated in Mysore, Chamarajanagar and Kodagu districts of the State. The total population of this tribe is around 24654 (2001 census). Literacy rate is extremely low. Usually they are living in hamlets made out of bamboo and huts with their own judicial system. They believe in magic, sorcery and witchcraft. Neither polygamy nor polyandry is practiced. Besides working with raton and bamboo, collection of minor forest products like herb, honey, roots and fruits are their major occupations. Poverty exists more in this group.

Koraga is a very primitive tribal group in the Karnataka State. They are concentrated in Dakshina Kannada and some parts of the Udupi districts of the State. They also live in some patches of Kerala and Karnataka border. The Koragas live mostly in rural areas. Sussman has rightly said, 'they were compelled to lead a segregated life from the immediate multi ethnic, multi religious neighbourhood till few decades back owing to the severe untouchability prevailing in the region'. To a great extent they very much believe in magic and witchcraft and local medicine men. Their total population is around 19784 (2001 census). Neither polygamy nor polyandry is observed. The Koragas remain extremely backward socially, economically and educationally. They have their own rich culture and traditional heritage. Their traditional occupation is basket making. Few percentage of the population live in semi urban areas.

Education – A Tool for Development

Opening of the tribal areas in the wake of modern developmental process have brought in juxtaposition two distinct value systems – one based on inherent tradition and the other on technology and innovations. Harmonious synchronisation of the two systems is highly essential for rapid development of tribals (Jha, 1995). In this crucial moment education plays a vital role. Education is a backbone of every society. It is a tool for social change. In the past education was one of the main consideration for hierarchical classification in the Hindu society. Rapid population growth impedes educational development in several ways. Most obviously it produces a rapid increase in the school age population. To spread the education among marginalised sections of society has been a formidable task in India. However with the advent of modernization, the education of tribals has undergone a different phase. Globalisation has tremendously influenced tribal education and culture. The uniqueness of the tribal culture which enriches the country's cultural mosaic is fast disappearing and even getting distorted under powerful influences of the dominant urban culture. While dealing with the poor educational attainment of tribal children to formal schooling, researchers tend to emphasise the economic marginalization of these communities, their illiterate home environment, inadequate facilities for education and culturally the alien nature of the school system. Lack of education is largely responsible for the exploitation and pitiable plight of the tribals. Due to this, the tribals have not been able to take advantage of new development. The above mentioned factors explain the low level of education among the tribal children. Another important factor is school process. This is most crucial because heavy drop outs and almost stagnation of tribal children within a year of admitting to primary school has been reported since last decade. A large proportion of the poorer tribal children, on account of raising cost of the schooling and economic burden cannot afford to benefit from education. Most of the tribals tend to use their children for ancillary service that would bring in some added income for their starving families (Nagda, 1998).

According to the 2001 census the average literacy rate of these two PTGs are 28.6 per cent. It is very painful to note that the literacy among these two tribals increased to only 7.45 per cent during the period 1961-1971. More unfortunate is that during the same period female literacy grew by less than 3 per cent. As per the table given below Jenu Kuruba tribe has very low literacy rate when compared to the Koraga. Even though Jenu Kuruba tribe is in a more advantageous situation, its literacy rate is comparatively low than Koragas. In both the cases female literacy rate is little bit higher than males.

Table–1

Literacy Status of PTGs of Karnataka

PTG	*Total Population*	*Total Literates*	*Male Literates*	*Female Literates*	*Male*	*Female*	*Total*
Jenu Kurubas	27597	4033	3172	2161	15.10	19.29	17.09
Koraga	11566	3543	1678	1865	27.82	29.38	28.06

Source: Mohanty, 2002.

Reasons for Low Literacy Rate

(a) Disparity in the Existence of the Schools

Compared to the other major tribals of the State these primitive tribal groups are a more disadvantaged population. As far as non-existing facility within a habitation is concerned, one can find that other major tribes of the state are placed in a favourable situation relative to their total population. Looking at the disparity condition in terms of deprivation more children of primitive tribal group are deprived of a primary school within their habitation. Children belonging to the other major tribes like Soligas, Betta Kuruba and Malae Kudiya are in a better position than the PTGs for they have atleast one Ashram School within their habitation (Shukla, 1998). However so far as the number of habitations without a school is concerned the PTGs children are highly in a disadvantaged position. In general, primitive tribal children should have to commute more than 3 kms distance to attend a school. In some cases it is even more. Distance is also one of the major drawbacks in case of providing education to the people who are still away from modern world. Many of the parents don't like to send their children especially their girl children to school which is quite far away from their original habitation. Finally while a large population of school age children in the country still face the disadvantage of distance between their own habitation and the location of a primary school, the more disturbing situation is this disadvantage is high in case of PTGs habitations in the tribal belt of Karnataka.

(b) Language – A Medium of Instruction

The choice of the language is a recurrent challenge in the development of quality education. Speakers of mother tongues which are not the same as the national or local language are often at a considerable disadvantage in the educational system (UNESCO, 2002).

The tribal situation in India presents a varied and complex picture and poses peculiar problems of social and economic development. Demographically speaking, there are more than 244 Scheduled Tribes with many sub-groups speaking some 100 languages/ dialects. Most unfortunate thing is that major portion of Government's resources is diverted towards providing concessions and little is left for the development of tribal education, language and culture of these two PTGs. The striking aspect that emerges from the scanty data on languages in primary education is the almost total absence of tribal language in schools. The attitude of our policy planners towards these tribal people appears to be one of assimilation. Little is being done to preserve their culture. All major and minor tribes suffer with this kind of negligence. Linguistic experts have made no attempt to standardise tribal languages by developing scripts, elaborating lexis, writing grammar and dictionaries in tribal languages. Till today there has not been any serious efforts to provide basic education in their respective mother tongues. No proper curriculum has been framed based on tribal culture and tradition. Present education system does not orient the tribal children towards pursuing their own mode of life. In phonology and syntax the tribal languages are quite different from the medium of instruction like Kannada except in certain mutually borrowed lexical items due to their close contacts over a long period of time. This is one of the vital reason responsible for these PTGs poor literacy and dropout problem among tribal children (Pasayat, 1995).

Table–2
Primary Schools According to Different Languages used as Medium of Instruction -1986

Languages	*Rural*	*Urban*	*Total*
Official Languages	5,48,372	72,025	6,20,397
(Listed in Eighth Schedule)	(96.9)*	—	—
Other Indian Languages	13,936	1,147	15,083
(Not Listed in Eighth Schedule)	(2.5)	(1.5)	(2.3)
English	3,797	4,303	8,100
	(0.6)	(5.6)	(1.3)
Total	5,66,105	77,475	6,43,580
	(100)	(100)	(100)

Note: Figure in parenthesis is percentage of schools with different medium of instruction.
Source: Fifth All India Education Survey, Vol. 1, NCERT, 1996.

(c) Urban Biased

The success of one's education largely depends on the motivation. Basically tribals are living with low socio-economic status. Obviously the level of motivation and self esteem will be comparatively low among tribal children. The main reason for this problem is current education system is more or less urban biased, non-tribal and absence of culture specific. Even though these tribals are emotionally attached to their local cultural norms Government has no interest in providing education which is more suited to the tribal children. Modern teaching methodologies, content of text, appointment of non-tribal teachers and parameters for evaluation have become 'Grains of Iron' to the low motivated tribal children. Implementation of uniform textbooks both for urban and tribal children are one more hit to them. The theory, concepts, values alien to tribal people is generally contained in the textbooks which generates negative attitude and a big blow to the learners self confidence. There is no attempt to take stock of the existing situation regarding instructional material in tribal languages. Education policy documents also have not dwelt on the magnitude of tasks that are involved in the preparation of primers and textbooks for tribal children and have not outlined the concrete steps that have to be taken in this direction. The increasing tendency for tribal people to retain the regional language as their mother tongue is only one indicator of their growing vulnerability in the face of these larger social processes (Verma, 1995).

The problem of dropout persists among all categories of children in both urban and rural India. However in the context of children studying in classes 1-10 the gap between the ST and total population of dropouts has reduced from 1990-91 to 1998-99. The reduction in the dropout rates could be because of various incentive schemes run by the State Government for the ST children such as providing free textbooks, uniforms and scholarships in Government schools. But schemes such as those providing for hostels for ST boys and girls are not implemented fully by the State owing to lack of financial resources and therefore fewer ST children pursue high school education and very few up to the college level. The policy of reserving seats for ST students at higher education levels is not widely availed since a large number of ST students do not even reach those levels and dropout at lower levels of school education. Even the Ashram schools run by both Government and NGOs are poorly maintained and sometimes lack even the basic facilities. Given the low level of literacy among the ST population several children for these communities happen to be 'first generation learners' and in the absence of State support for helping them to cope. With studies, many children drop out of the schools. This disproportionately low representation of ST children at higher level of education compounds the existing disparities among Indian society. Lack of proactive Government in favour of the STs is not linked only to lack of resources. Government indifference and lack of political will are largely responsible for the state of affairs (Mahendale, 2001).

(d) Inaction of Teachers

Teachers are the real directors of every tribal school. There was a time in India where teachers were equal to God. Major problem is that Government is recruiting teachers from the urban area to teach tribal children. A report says that only 0.56 per cent of teachers are from non-tribal community. Many of them have studied only in English medium schools and even don't know the regional language properly. In this situation how can one expect to teach the relatively disadvantaged tribal children down to their level. More unfortunate thing is that many schools don't have teachers for all the subjects. Even though many NGOs are hiring teachers to teach in tribal schools many of them don't even have basic degrees in education like B.Ed./TCH. Some of the teachers are prejudious about the performance of the tribal children.

As they are the only literate persons having some political connections in the tribal areas, they neither fulfill their duties properly nor the concerned higher officers dare to take any action against them for dereliction of their duties.

(e) Teacher's Opinion

Many of the teachers are of the opinion that tribal children cannot understand the modern Kannada language. Content of the text is too standard to their level. Few of them will complain about the ignorance of the parents. Moreover teachers are facing many problems in tribal areas. Proper residential and medical facilities are a nightmare. Higher education for their children is not possible. Since many primitive tribal hamlets are deep in the forest it will be humanly impossible to reach the school due to the lack of appropriate transport. Moreover feedback from the students is completely absent. No proper laboratory facilities to teach Science effectively. Teachers raised and brought up in a more sophisticated urbanized society would find it difficult to adjust themselves to the tribal culture. This generates a communication gap.

(f) Parent's Apathy

Tribal community feels childhood or adulthood largely depends not on the physical age but on the degree of responsibility that children could successfully fulfill. Apart from that children's responsibilities towards the family and the contributions they make are significant and more important. In tribal society children from the early age will be engaged in cooking food, fetching water, sibling care, support in the field, collection of minor forest food, grazing, etc. Decision to give a chance to a child to spend happy childhood is not isolated from other aspects of household decision making nor are they purely household based. They reflect the norms and values of the wider community within which the tribal household is located and the social and economic possibilities which local contexts offer to different categories of households. Hence parents may think sending child to school means dislocation of traditional pattern of earning livelihood and of division of labour in their societies. Most vital problem for low literacy among tribal children is that children are considered by parents as economic assets to the family.

The education of tribal girl child is more neglected because of deep rooted beliefs, traditions and mind sets. Education psychologists use the concept of false consciousness to refer to the existence of beliefs and values that individuals socialize into and operate upon.

(g) Universal Elementary Education (UEE) for Tribal Children

The question of how elementary education can and be made universal has not received the attention it deserves. Recent study has shown that an alarmingly large number of children do not become literate even after four years of primary education especially in both rural and tribal areas (Sharma, 2002). Hence total school effectiveness and actual learning have to be the central theme rather than secondary concern for universal education. Further more important is that how effective schools are and successive learning basically depend not only on school level inputs but also on many vital factors outside the school. Basic infrastructure of Ashram schools in tribal areas are worst than anything in many southern districts of Karnataka. Many schools don't even have hard roofs, hostels are ruining. Unavailability of playground, lab, library and separate toilets are most common in many tribal schools where children of these two PTGs are learning. Absence of extra curricular activities makes children learning as a kind of unavoidable burden. Since tribal children are completely different from urban children or atleast from rural children learning should be a joyful experience for them otherwise simply they may be dropouts. For genuine universal elementary education the impact of the wider context on schooling has to be understood in a better way.

(h) Absence of Central Monitoring Unit

Absence of effective monitoring unit on the tribal schools is one of the major drawbacks in case of development of tribal education. Concerned inspecting staff hardly visit to the tribal schools. Some time even only once in a year. This makes teacher to lack commitment to their profession. It is even reported that teacher's visit one or two times in a week to the schools. This is due to low level of motivation, inspiration and commitment among the inspecting staff which are again matched by the low level of motivation and interest among the teachers. It is high time that Government should think to strengthen or establish Centralized Monitoring Unit especially for Tribal Schools headed by a chief having Anthropology or Sociology background.

In the light of the above discussion we may conclude that on one hand economic backwardness is responsible for the low percentage of literacy in the younger generation and on the other social backwardness and lack of social consciousness are responsible for low percentage of children attending schools. When the school going children are few it can be well understood that higher education will be a rare phenomena in these PTGs. Hence, along with other development it is also necessary that we should create some awareness about significance of education among tribes, the facilities available to them for education and the role of education in the upliftment of social, economic and political condition of the tribal community.

(i) Policy Implications

Some suggestions to handle the educational problems of Primitive Tribal groups are made based on the fieldwork and review of previous literature. These are brought out in this section.

1. Many basic differences can be seen between major tribals and primitive tribals in case of India. Hence the Government should bring a new educational policy especially for primitive tribals. It must be culturally and geographically specific. Moreover educational experts should be very sensitive while framing the policies, which should not destroy the social solidarity of the tribes and stifle their zest for life.
2. It is well revealed fact that modern education cannot cater to the basic needs of the tribes. Modern education system cannot deem to have held much relevance for them since they are from the outer world. During our field work it has been revealed that tribals consider 'culture as their first educator'. Hence there is need to identify the areas of minimum and maximum resistance to innovations in their culture. Once we identify enough space we can imbibe education into their culture.
3. It is high time to have special education programme made for tribal children in consonance with their privileged cultural pattern and also in keeping with the needs and resources of the area concerned in order to secure the maximum amount of tribal children participation. Moreover new education programme should be in a position to assert the existing perception, behaviour and action in education seeking process and culturally determined attitude towards use of different system of education.
4. The State Government should construct a Textbook Commission especially for tribal education development. While framing the textbooks experts should focus on three important perspectives: *(i)* Linguistic, *(ii)* Instrumental and *(iii)* Culture. From the primary level itself all text materials should be in their respective mother tongue. There is need to evolve scripts, grammar as well as appropriate vocabulary to communicate 'school knowledge'. Proper training should be given in tribal language, culture and society to the non-tribal teachers working in the tribal areas.
5. Lack of good quality teachers in sufficient numbers resulting in high pupil teacher ratio may be an important factor in explaining the variations of educational status in these two PTGs in education. Given the inaccuracies in enrolments and the absence of teachers probably pupil teacher ratio may not be efficient and meaningful variable representing the quality of tribal education.

Conclusion

If we go through from the other angle, the problem of dropout is still persisting among tribal students. The next question is once they become dropouts what will be their next plan? What will be their day-to-day context? How do their parents react for this? In our fieldwork it is revealed that many dropout children have become child workers. Many of them are working with their parents in the field and in some big estates. Of course there are many reasons for children dropouts even from the primary stage. Suppose if Government is ready to overcome all these problems and modernize the tribal education system will parents send their children to school? The Anthropological study on dynamic model of tribal child labour suggests that their decision to send to work today depends not only on current consideration such as the marginal productivity but also on expected returns to work compared with alternatives such as school attendance. The finding that increase in dropout suggest that at given levels of household income, the return to work relative to he return to school is significant determinant in sending their children to school. A natural policy implication is therefore to invest in raising the return to education. In addition to general investment in improving schools other measures including reducing labour market discrimination against tribal women and raising awareness to reduce inhibiting social norms are necessary. Policies that improve the labour market in rural and tribal areas may reduce the dropouts especially that of girls given the recent expansion of micro credit programmes, it is pertinent to note that developing tribal financial market may have positive spill over effects encouraging development of land and labour market. The growth of tribal action market will not only counter the substation effect highlighted here, it may also generate overall income growth and reduce tribal inequalities. If so parents may not mind in sending their children to school.

While implementing the tribal development plans especially in case of education care should be taken to see that the cultural traits of primitive tribes are not disturbed within the process of their interaction with the mainstream of nation life. Moreover a careful watch on the trends set in motion which should not destroy the social solidarity of the tribes and hinder their zest for life should be the part and parcel of every tribal development policy. Further there should be lot of scope for prioritizing their needs, solving their own problems and raising their own resources to meet their urgent needs in all schemes by using their knowledge got from schools. Finally it can be said that educational activities will have to be simultaneous with economic development.

REFERENCES

1. Makhan, Jha, 1995. *An Introduction to Indian Anthropology*, New Delhi: Vikas Publishing House.
2. Midatala Rani, 2000. "Tribal Languages and Tribal Education", *Social Action. 50(4)*:414-419.
3. Mohanty, P.K., 2003. *Development of Primitive Tribal Groups in India*, New Delhi: Kalpaz Publication.
4. Nagda, 1998. "Educational Problems of Scheduled Tribes", *Economic and Political Weekly. Vol. IX, pp. 1231-1239.*
5. Pasayat, 1994. *Development and Dualism of Primitive Tribes*, New Delhi: M.D. Publications.
6. Sharma, S., 2002. *Tribal Welfare and Development*, New Delhi: Sarup and Sons.
7. Shukla, 1998. "Education of Indigenous People", www.google search.
8. Singh, B., 1977. "Tribal Development at Cross Road", *Man in India. 57(3):229-247.*
9. Verma, R., 1995. *Indian Tribes Through the Ages*, New Delhi: Publication Division, Ministry of Information and Broadcasting, Government of India.

17

Problems of School Absenteeism Among Tribal Children

Introduction

The spread of education among the weaker sections of our society is vital as education is a primary requirement for socio-economic development. The policy to promote educational interests of the weaker sections of the people, especially the Scheduled Castes and Scheduled Tribes, has been enshrined in our Constitution as a Directive Principle of State Policy. Therefore, the main thrust continues to be on education. The general level of literacy is very low and is lower still in the case of Backward Classes. All over the world, Education is a powerful avenue for advancement of socio-economic status and social change. India has a sizable proportion of tribes who lag behind their non-tribal counterparts in many respects. Recognizing the importance of education, Government of India is giving much attention to their education but education has made little progress among the tribals. The poor socio-economic situation, illiteracy of the tribes plays a major role in high rate of non-attendance of students in tribal schools as well as drop outs from these schools. The tribal students do not get any motivation, inspiration, encouragement and guidance from their parents. They are made to work in the fields, look after the siblings and help in the household activities. Many villages do not have primary and high schools. Transportation is the biggest problem. Since there is insufficiency of teachers, classrooms and poor attendance of the students, the teacher faces lot of problems. This chapter discusses about school absenteeism among the tribal children with special reference to Karnataka.

Educational Deprivation Among STs in Karnataka

India is one of the few countries in the world having the largest tribal concentration. The tribals of this country are having fascinating rich cultural heritage and are playing a significant role in enriching our composite culture. The objective and comparative studies of pre-literate societies and their contribution to great indigenous culture of India is essential before they are totally eclipsed in the fast changing cultural canvass of India. Such indepth, comparative and analytical studies may throw light and provide missing cultural links in understanding complex Indian heritage.

The spread of education among the weaker sections of our society is vital as education is a primary requirement for socio-economic development. The policy to promote educational interests of the weaker sections of the people, especially the Scheduled Castes and Scheduled Tribes, has been enshrined in our Constitution as a Directive Principle of

State Policy. Therefore, the main thrust continues to be on education. The general level of literacy is very low and is still lower in the case of Backward Classes. According to Swami Vivekananda, "The Real India lives in the Villages. Unless we are able to uplift the Tribal and the backward classes, India faces dark future. Along with their economic improvement they have to be raised culturally and spiritually."

Education of Scheduled Tribe children is considered important, not only because of the Constitutional obligation, but also as a crucial input for total development of tribal communities. So long as there is a gap between the literacy levels, the position of Scheduled Tribes will remain backward. Lack of education may lead to child exploitation, child labour, gender discrimination and population explosion, etc. So the need of the hour is to bring quality education through 100 per cent school enrolment and retention with more emphasis on the girl child's education.

The Scheduled Tribes represents one of the most economically impoverished and marginalized groups in India. Karnataka has a high proportion of the tribal population. Education of tribal women is recognized as indispensable for their growth and development. As long as there is disparity between male and female in education levels the difference between the position of men and women would continue to exist. The tribal women's access to education in the country is inadequate and discriminating because of ignorance, lack of motivation, etc. Thus education is the key catalyst to the development of human resources. Lack of education is largely responsible for the exploitation and pitiable plight of the tribal women. For the tribals education disseminates knowledge which in turn gives inner strength and hence very essential for the tribals for attaining freedom from exploitation and poverty. But due to ignorance arising out of illiteracy, the tribals have not been able to take advantage of new economic opportunities. Empowerment of women covers aspects such as education, economic status etc. Abolition of gender based discrimination in all institutions and structures of society and participation of women in policy and decision process at domestic and public level are few dimensions of women empowerment.

Despite the significant progress that has been made in the past 15 years in achieving Universal Primary Education, approximately 115 million children still do not go to school. Especially in South Asia figures are alarming. Children who do not go to school in South Asia constitute more than one third of all children who are not enrolled in school around the world. If we look at the net primary school enrolment ratio (1998-2002) we see that in India only 91 per cent of the boys in the 6-10 age group were enrolled, for girls this figure was 76 per cent. It is important to keep in mind that these figures relate to children who are officially enrolled in school, but who are not necessarily attending. Looking at the net primary school attendance these numbers go down to 80 per cent for boys, and 73 per cent for girls. However, the attendance lists kept by teachers are not always accurate, and the actual attendance figures might be even lower. When we then look at UNICEF's gross Secondary School enrolment ratio (including all children, regardless of age) the figure is 56 per cent for boys, and only 40 per cent for girls. Only a segment of the total number of children which are not enrolled in school, can be found in the statistics of working children. There are thus a number of children that are excluded from these figures. These children can be classified as 'nowhere children' a term coined by D.P. Chaudhri (1997). According to the Planning Commission of the Government of India deriving their figures from the

Census of India, incidence of tribals was 5.4 per cent while incidence of nowhere children was 45.2 per cent in 1991. There has been a shift from the research focus on tribals alone to the out of school segment as a whole, which thus includes nowhere children. In order to design policy to get these children also to school, it is important to learn how they are spending their time. For this purpose IREWOC initiated a project on nowhere children in four Indian States including Andhra Pradesh, Bihar, Chhattisgarh and Karnataka. The results presented in this chapter are derived from qualitative research that was conducted in three tribal areas in Karnataka between September and December 2006.

Educational Status of STs in Karnataka

Karnataka, the largest state of India, with a total population that constitutes only 8.65 per cent of India's population as a whole, is one of the most sparsely populated states. It is a predominantly rural state, with agriculture and animal husbandry as the most important sources of income. Karnataka is one of the least performing states in terms of tribal literacy. The state also has a tremendous gender gap in terms of both school enrolment and literacy. Several factors are identified as the reasons for absence of children in school. The demand factors such as livelihood strategies, poverty, gender, caste and family crises are crucial. Looking at livelihood strategies it appears that during seasons with a great demand for agricultural labour, such as the crop-cutting season, the attendance of children, especially girls, decreases. These children are not found in the field, but are required to stay home to take over household duties such as caring for siblings, so that the mother is able to go to the field to do wage work. Like the 10-year-old Rangi, oldest daughter of parents who are out in the field all day during the crop-cutting season, says, "I have to be here to take care of my brothers, because who else is here to do this?" However, we cannot simply argue that children do not go to school only because parents have to do agricultural work. Similarly, where as many children can be found in the field looking after cattle, it is not the case that these children do not go to school, because they have to look after cattle. Often other factors are operational. In some cases parents might be aware of the importance to educate their children and try to send their children to school, but if the children are reluctant, the parents might lack the determination to make sure their children are indeed going to school. Here it is important to recognise the social capital that if a child is surrounded by one or more educated relative who encourages him to go to school, it leads to increased motivation for the child to learn and to go to school regularly. The 12-year-old Syama explains: "My uncle is literate, and he always encourages me to go to school. I want to continue the tradition of being literate in the family. I want to continue studying in the future and go outside the village to be a doctor." Likewise, if a child is not blessed with a learning environment at home, he or she is prone to fail and eventually drops out of school.

Migration occurs in various forms in the tribal areas. It can have both negative and positive consequences for the education of children. In some cases, especially with temporary migration of the whole household, the effects on the education of a child are negative, especially when the household leaves the village for a couple of months every year, and the child needs to leave school, and falls behind. However, temporary migration of only the father to the city in search of work could be positive, as it can also lead to increasing awareness about education for both boys and girls. Economical problems within the household do lead to absence of children in school. These may be a result of a crisis in the family, for example the illness or even death of a parent. This often results in the burden of working, in order to feed the household, falling on the shoulders of the child. Son, the "man of the household", are required to tend animals, either their own or those of others in order to make money, and girls, especially the oldest daughter, have to stay home doing household chores, or are sent to the field to do agricultural work, especially during crop-cutting season. The 13-year-old Manchavva had to dropout of school when his father fell ill. His father complains: "I do not want this for my child, but if I die, Manchavva needs to know how to be the man of the household. He is the oldest, and thus the only one who can do this work." Caste also influences whether children are sent to school in societies in Karnataka. The sub caste system is still of significant importance among Karnataka tribes, especially in the northern areas. The traditional perception that tribals do not recognise the importance of education does not hold true anymore. Yet, there are still certain castes that, because of traditional work arrangements, do not send their children to school, and these include upper castes as well. For example, we found Soliga boys and girls expected to help out in the household of a socially higher ranking family member.

Gender also plays a role. In general, there are more boys than girls attending school regularly. Of the total number of children enrolled in any school up to Class V in the three tribal areas, 55 per cent are boys. The difference is especially apparent on upper-primary level, where only 32 per cent are girls. For this there are various explanations. For example, it is often considered not safe for a girl, once she is a teenager and thus sexually vulnerable, to go outside the village for her education. Another reason given for keeping girls at home is related to household chores. In some cases it is a necessity for girls to stay home and take care of their younger siblings. This is often a result of economical crisis. In other cases household chores are looked upon as a good preparation for a girl's married life. Marriage then is another important reason behind gender discrimination. To quote the seventeen-year-old Macha, "Education is useless for girls, because they are just living in our houses doing female chores. But for boys it is useful, as we can get a job." Some parents do not recognise how education can help their daughter in her future life, while others are reluctant to invest in her, since she is going to her husband's house after her marriage, like a father expresses: "I cannot afford a good education for all my children, and in the future, the girls will be married off to another house, while the boys stay in my house." Thus, when a family has money for only one child's education, they will prefer to spend it on the boy. However, within some castes more and more people are interested in the amount of education the potential spouse of their child has received. Therefore, there is often an overlap between the factors of gender and caste mentality.

So far as the supply factors, the quality of education offered is crucial for parents to decide between sending their children to school, or keeping them at home. In all sample tribal areas, all children, disregarding caste, have access to the same educational facilities. These facilities are within reach of the children. Government school buildings are often built just outside the village, whereas private school owners have been able to open their schools in buildings in the middle of the village. The location of the school influences the parents when deciding to which school they should send their children. Especially small children are more likely to be sent to a school that is nearby the house. The number of children attending the school located within the village varies with the children who are attending a school outside the village. Attendance in the school along a busy road which has to be crossed by many people in order to reach the Government school, a father wants to postpone sending his two youngest sons to school, "since they are too young and scared to cross the main road." In the three tribal areas that were included in the study, the general perception of villagers on the quality of education offered by the Government is negative.

Most of the villagers prefer to send their children to the private school rather than to Government schools. But they complain that they cannot bear the costs of private education. They believe that teachers are more committed and that children learn much more than children who are enrolled in a Government school. In some schools, there are too few teachers appointed for too many children. Appointed teachers are usually present, and thus teacher absenteeism, a problem regularly mentioned in the literature, did not occur during the present research, apart from the absence of teachers due to other Government programmes, which they are required to attend. The fact that teachers reside outside the village and leave as soon as the school hours are over (or even earlier) makes communication between parents and teachers difficult. It thus would be better if teachers were appointed in their own village. Another issue is the lack of female teachers. There were only a few female teachers in the schools. This is unfortunate since female teachers often serve as a role model for girls, as one of the teachers explained. The presence of female teachers could positively influence the enrolment and attendance of girls. The ten-year-old Radha said that she aspired to be a "madam in school."

Among the children in all tribal areas, there is a fear of punishment by the teachers for skipping school, for not knowing the right answers or for not being clean or properly dressed. But children as well as their parents and other villagers also complained about the limited knowledge they actually gain after finishing a number of classes. When a parent asked a boy who studies in class ten to speak English, he replied (in Marwari, their local language), "If the Headmaster does not even know how to speak English then why should I ?" A twenty year old from another village States, "If you ask someone here who is enrolled in Class V to read or write, he will not be able to do so, because he does not learn this in school." However, some parents did not blame the school. "My youngest daughter Sannavva is in Class III, but cannot count until twenty. Radha is in Class IV, and cannot even read a book properly. But my oldest daughter Pinki could do all these things when she was of their age. As opposed to the other two girls, Pinki was very studious and always did her homework. She studied in the same school as Radha and Kabita, and she is doing fine. So I do not blame the teachers."

Both children and their parents mentioned the financial aspect of education as an obstacle. While primary education is supposed to be free, in all schools children were expected to pay fees. The fee structure however, is not transparent. Fees differ according to gender, caste, and class-level, and also per village. Furthermore, teachers and parents give different accounts on the exact amount that has to be paid for "admission" or "building maintenance." Boys of a general caste in Class IV and V for example were expected to pay a yearly fee of Rs. 60 some households complained about having to pay the Government school an yearly fee of Rs. 151 in addition to the school fees, there are also the expenses for school uniforms (to have a uniform made is Rs. 150-200) and stationary, which constitute a huge burden on the household's finances. Government schools were, however, still cheaper than private schools. These charged the children a monthly fee of Rs. 30-70. In the three tribal areas an average wage is Rs. 50 for one day of agricultural work or labour in a stone factory.

The Problems of Absenteeism Among ST Children

The problem of absence of children can unfortunately not be solved just by raising the quality of the offered education. Quality of education is not a sole reason for not sending children to school. But when the performance of school is inadequate children may only be sent when their duties are not required elsewhere; for example, in the household or herding the cattle. For some, school attendance then becomes a residual activity. In other cases, when parents decide the money required for a child's education can better be spent on other basic requirements, children might drop out altogether. Dropping out might also be a result of failure in standards. And once dropped out, it is unlikely the child will find its way back into the education system. Explanations for this might be the reluctance to go over the same curriculum again, and often they find that they just get used to working.

When children are out of school, for whatever reasons they can be found roaming around their house or in the village and we might then consider them as nowhere children. It goes without saying, that these nowhere children also do some work to help their parents in the household. But this work is not the reason that keeps them out of school. It is clear that the issue discussed here is a complex one. Overall, the awareness of the importance of education is present among all villagers, regardless of caste. We have seen that many factors can lead to the non-attendance of children in school, and more than often there is overlap. Both parents and children also seem to be convinced that the child will do the same work as their parents. Thus, the absence of a (Government) job-perspective for children also leads to a preference to keep them at home and to prepare them for their future occupation as animal-herder, agricultural labourer, or in some cases shopkeeper.

Programmes like community mobilisation, strengthening of Village Education Committees and involving NGOs to reach out of school tribal children would need to be re-visualised in a more tribal specific context. Keeping in mind the poor socio-economic background of tribal children, a re-assessment is required on how free the primary education is for the tribal child and what further measures are required to be taken to make their education totally free. Capacity Building at all levels as expressed by the experts is necessary. Further there is a need for training and orientation to administrators, resource persons, teacher-trainers on different aspects of tribal education. However it would be wrong to say that there is a dearth of experts at State/District level. Rather, what is required at present is that the State resource persons should be identified and trained by the national core group in developing separate training modules for administrators, teacher-trainers and teachers.

It was recognised that the teachers working in tribal areas are required to have special pedagogical training to tackle the special needs and problems of tribal children, especially as the present pre-service and the in-service training modules are found to be devoid of any special component of tribal education. The State nodal persons lack directives regarding how to make Village Education Committees more powerful. All the State strategies have included community awareness campaign. But the community awareness modules developed by the State or District components were not found effective. A fundamental error was pointed out in conceptualizing the awareness campaign. It was assumed that the tribal parents are not aware of the free primary education being provided by the Government. But as revealed by the State nodal persons, the tribal parents are aware of it but they are not convinced of the relevance of this education for their children. Thus emphasis should be placed on convincing the parents about the relevance of primary education for their children. However pedagogical revolution, backed by adequate compensation of the tribal parents for their labour loss, and a suitable academic calendar would convince the parents of the utility of primary education for their children. Although it was decided long back to have adequate representation of tribal parents in Village Education Committees as well as not much has been achieved in this regard. Besides many of the tribal villages do not have Village Education Committees.

The debate around quantity verses quality of education still is on. Before this, policymakers should note that quality and quantity are intertwined and cannot be separated. It is a real sense of urgency. Differences expressed pertained to the placement of priorities for the achievement of universal education, and are in turn related to the broader views held on the nature of the challenges. If State is really interested in the eradication of tribal illiteracy or at least mind to minimize the problem it must and should seriously think about the quality of primary education at present. Probably a new population policy may help in this regard. Resources need to be targeted at expanding provisions, if the Government wants to provide alternative income generation programmes to the poor parents who would like to send children to work.

Resources will have to be diverted to make the curriculum relevant and of high quality. Given the manifest failure of the standard schooling system to reach children, special efforts need to be made in this area and particular attention should be given to first generation learners. Some noted that high rates could put off many aspiring to secondary and higher levels of education, thus eroding the incentive to send children regularly and consistently to school. Without providing of universal coverage and equivalent standards in terms of quality, it is not feasible or just to penalize parents who do not send children to school. Clearly meaningful and genuine universal elementary education is associated not only with universal access to well-functioning schools but also with certain out of school initiatives. Children have varying capacities, apart from individual intelligence depending on factors such as adequate nutrition, good health and freedom to attend school regularly. It follows that the prerequisites have to be ensured for effective and genuine universal education.

Conclusion

To conclude, how elementary education should be made universal is central to the concern for making it universal. It is necessary to make sure that such education is effective. Apart from the need to scrutinize the education system, non-educational measures that prepare children for education and facilities for learning process are also needed. India is one of the countries having largest number of tribals in the world. Also a country having highest percentage of dropouts at higher primary level. Poverty and over population are intertwined with this problem (Sharma, 1998). At the same time, it has pioneered a number of different educational models for addressing the problems of children, models which reflect a shared value given to the welfare of children and the need to ensure their right to education, but with different philosophies and modalities. We should seriously try with these models with some addition or subtraction suiting our culture and traditions which are more effective. Under these circumstances, the experience of India will have made a major contribution to a long standing problem beyond boundaries.

India is one of the few countries in the world having the largest tribal concentration. The tribals of this country are having fascinating rich cultural heritage and played a significant role in enrichment of composite culture. The objective and comparative studies of pre-literate societies and their contribution to great indigenous culture of India is essential before they are totally eclipsed in the fast changing cultural canvass of India. Such indepth, comparative and analytical studies may throw light and provide missing cultural links in understanding complex Indian heritage.

REFERENCES

1. Bellamy, Carol (2004), *The State of the World's Children 2005, Childhood under Threat,* New York: UNICEF.
2. Chaudhri, D.P. (1997), 'Female Tribals and Gender Bias in Tribal Education in Indian States: 1961-1991.' *The Indian Journal of Labour Economics,* Volume 40, No. 3, pp. 493-505.
3. Government of India (2002), *National Tribal Development Report 2001*, New Delhi: Planning Commission.
4. Kabeer, Naila, Geetha B., Nambissan and Ramya Subrahmanian (eds.) (2003), *Tribals and the Right to Education in South Asia, Needs versus Rights ?,* New Delhi: Sage Publications.
5. Lieten, G.K., A.K. Karan and A.K. Satpathy (2005), *Children, School and Work: Glimpses from India,* New Delhi.
6. Mathur, Kanchan, Shobhita Rajagopal and Pradeep Bhargava (2004), *Childhood Poverty in Delhi: A Review of Literature,* Institute for Human Development, London.
7. Wazir, Rekha (ed.) (2000), *The Gender Gap in Basic Education, NGOs as Change Agents,* New Delhi: Sage Publications.
8. Weiner, Myron (1991), *The Child and the State in India*, New Delhi, Oxford University Press.

18

Government Policy Towards Development of Tribal Language and Tribal Education

Introduction

"History has indeed been extremely unkind to the characteristics of the tribal people. The tribal communities have not been viewed with any degree of respect by the alienated middle classes and intellectuals. None of the brave fights of the tribals against the British has ever been treated as part of the National struggle for freedom. Today, it is necessary to think of a genuinely pro-active policy, which is aimed at helping the tribals by creating a favourable climate for the general tribalisation of Indian communities." (Devy G.N. in "Rethinking Tribals", The Hindu, 16th July 2000).

The tribal people of Karnataka live in an unenviable situation. The tribal groups are socially and educationally backward. The progress achieved in the field of tribal education is decimally low. The enrolment and retention ratio among the tribals is low. There are several reasons for the high dropout rate among the tribal children. The Government of Karnataka is implementing various schemes for all round development of Scheduled Tribes in the State. But the progress is not satisfactory. Education in the tribal world poses a special problem. There is an imperative need to identity the problems associated with the education of the tribals. This chapter is an attempt to assess the Karnataka Government Policy towards the development of tribal language and tribal education in the tribal areas of Karnataka.

Acquisition of Education

Acquisition of education is imperative for proper enjoyment of basic human rights guaranteed under the Constitution and to discharge one's duty towards society. Without adequate knowledge of education an individual remains at severe disadvantage in democratic Government and earning a living. The right to education itself is a fundamental right in a civilised State and needs to be ensured to every individual. The framers of the Indian Constitution have ensured the protection of linguistic, cultural and educational interest to the individuals and the groups by incorporating various constitutional safeguards. The Constitution Seventh Amendment Act, 1956 introduced Articles 350A and 350B exclusively to protect the linguistic minorities, apart from the satisfactory safeguards kept in Articles 29, 30, 347 and 350 of the Constitution.

In addition to the social justice provided to the minorities in the Constitution many Expert Committees and Commissions including the Secondary Education Commission

(1952), the Central Advisory Board of Education (1956), the Education Commission (1964) gave importance to mother tongue as medium of instruction. The recommendations of these Committees and Commissions were endorsed at the Conference of Chief Ministers held at New Delhi in 1961. The All India Educational Survey on Medium of Instruction in Indian Schools conducted in 1981 and the All India Conference on Indian Languages as medium of instruction held at New Delhi in 1983 also expressed similar views.

Despite providing various safeguards to the minorities, the Constitution did not define more precisely the term "Linguistic Minority", but took it for granted as any section of the citizens residing in the territory of India or any part thereof having a distinct language, script or culture (Article 29). The Second Report of the Commission for Linguistic Minorities defined the term as follows: "The language of the minority group need not be one of the fifteen languages mentioned in the 8th Schedule of the Constitution. In other words, a 'Linguistic Minority' at the State level means any group of people whose mother tongue is different from the principle language of the State, the District or the Taluk levels. Thus tribal languages also come under the purview of linguistic minorities.

Early Education Among STs

The desirability of having early education through one's mother tongue is a universally accepted dictum, especially so when it applies to tribal children. The National Educational Policy, 1986 has clearly spelled out the importance of using the tribal mother tongue at the initial stages of education with arrangements for a gradual switching over to regional language of the State. The tribal child is not unique or deficient. A tribal child is born into a culture, which uses a language different from others. Like any other language, the tribal languages are repository of values of tribal culture. The tribal child also uses language, grammar, and dialect in the same manner as others do. Tribal education is not opposed to mainstream education. The tribal learner includes both the child at the school and the adult learner seeking literacy. The teacher is a focal point and a catalytic agent in the educational process of the tribal child.

Educational Policy in Tribal Areas

Apart from the general policy relating to the development of the Scheduled Tribes, the Government of Karnataka has not come up with any specific policy decision relating to the use of Tribal languages in tribal education in the Ashram Schools. The general policy of using regional medium at the Primary stage of education, which is applicable to the entire State, is also being used in the case of the Ashram Schools. On the other hand the Government of Karnataka in the field of Primary education is implementing a number of schemes and programmes for the tribals. They include the following: 1. Free text books, uniforms, school bags and note books are supplied to Scheduled Tribe children from Classes I to IV. 2. Children studying in Government Schools up to V standard with 80 per cent attendance are provided with 3 kgs of rice per child every month under mid-day meals. 3. *Keli Kali* (hear and learn) programme especially for the children of Class I to IV through *Akashavani* broadcasting. 4. Under the *Samudayadatta Shale* Programme people themselves are made to involve actively bringing back the dropout children back to School. 5. School Adoption Programme is another novel exercise wherein Government Schools, which are in slums or backward areas and not so developed, are entrusted to the care benefactors who voluntarily come forward to improve school education. 6. *Chinnaraangala* a bridge course programme was started during 2001-02 to bring back the drop out and non-enrolled school age children into the mainstream and to have access, retention and achievement. 7. *Shaishika Samkirna* is initiated by the Government of Karnataka to provide education for the poor among tribal girls only. 8. *Nali Kali* (a process of joyful learning) was launched in October 1995. The curriculum is learnable by the child in a manner with minimum levels of learning expected to be achieved. The teacher encourages responsibility among children and the learner learns at his/her own pace. 9. *Chaitanya*, the content-based training programme was launched in 2001 to bring about a gradual transformation of newly recruited teachers in developing professional competencies and commitments. 10. In order to achieve Universal Elementary Education the Sarva Shiksha Abhiyan (SSA) was launched in 2001 covering the whole country. The SSA Programme is an attempt to provide an opportunity for improving human capabilities to all children through provision of community owned quality education in mission mode.

Problems in Tribal Education

There are a number of problems in Tribal Education. They include the following: 1. Lack of specific Government Policy towards development of tribal languages and tribal education. As per the general policy of the Government of Karnataka, Kannada is used as medium of instruction in all the Ashram Schools. As a result use of tribal mother tongue in teaching is being totally ignored. Students feel shy to converse in their mother tongue at school with teachers as they do not use tribal language while teaching. 2. The main reasons for low enrolment and high drop out rate among the tribal children are child labour, sibling care, illiteracy of the parents, lack of encouragement and motivation from parents to send their children to school. Education of the tribal girl child is neglected due to several reasons. 3. The teachers teaching in tribal schools are non-tribals. They are not trained in tribal languages. They find it difficult to teach in tribal language. The commitment of teachers towards their profession is not uniform. 4. The textbooks supplied to teachers in tribal schools are printed in Kannada language. These books do not focus on tribal culture customs and environment. Most of the Ashram Schools lack teaching materials and teaching aids. 5. The teachers working in tribal schools are non residential. They have to walk a long distance to reach the tribal schools which are located in interior forest areas which lack proper facilities like roads, transportation, housing, electricity and medical facilities. 6. The teacher's absenteeism is more in the schools due to lack of interest and motivation among teachers to work in remote areas. Sometimes it is also due to assignment of additional responsibilities to the teachers. 7. The educational gap during summer and other seasonal holidays have a serious effect on the tribal students.

Implications and Suggestions

The tribals live in forest areas far away from the civil society. They are illiterates and less developed. Even though the Directorate of Social Welfare under the aegis of Government of Karnataka has under taken several programmes for tribal education, the results are not very fruitful. Tribal language and education needs more focus and attention by the Government. The following suggestions can be made to improve tribal language and tribal education in Karnataka: 1. Government of Karnataka should come up with a specific policy for developing tribal language and the use of tribal mother tongue in education. 2. While prescribing textbooks Government should give proper attention to the language and content of the texts. At the Primary level, language of the textbooks should be in the dialect of tribal languages in Kannada script and the content of the text should reflect tribal life style, culture and environment. At a later stage tribal students may switch over from the tribal dialect to Kannada gradually. Adoption of bilingual transfer model will attract the tribal children to school. The Government can use the services of Language Institutes, Research Centers and Tribal Teachers in the preparation of bilingual books, charts, glossaries, reading materials etc. 3. Government must appoint tribal teachers to Ashram Schools. If tribal teachers are not available the Government must conduct orientation and training programmes to the teachers belonging to non-tribal communities to acquaint themselves about tribal language, education, culture and environment, Government has to make it mandatory for the teachers to work in tribal areas. 4. Government should improve the facilities for teachers working in Ashram Schools by providing them with quarters, medical facilities, incentives, etc. 5. Recruitment of more tribal women teachers will help in motivating the tribal girl child to go to school. 6. To reduce the dropout rate and making school going more attractive educating the tribal parents, guidance and encouragement by Government, more developmental programmes to improve their economic position are necessary. 7. Opening of more Anganvadis will solve the problem of using tribal children for sibling care. This will also improve attendance in schools. 8. Government should open more Residential and Ashram Schools away from tribal "HAADIS". These schools are of immense help for proper development of tribal education. 9. Government must organize periodic jathas and campaigns to bring awareness among the tribals about the need and importance of education. These should convince the tribal parents and leaders that education would lead to all round development of the tribals. 10. The development of tribal languages and education calls for political will power. Politicians and Kannada protagonists must support the Government in developing the tribal languages and their use in education through suitable policy decisions taken from time to time. It also calls for proper support from the bureaucrats and other agencies both Governmental and Non-Governmental.

Conclusion

Development of tribal languages and their use in education are not receiving proper support from the Government. The Constitutional Provisions clearly emphasise the fact that the interests of the tribals in all spheres have to be implemented. However this has been largely violated in many parts of the tribal areas. The facilities in tribal schools must be improved to make it convenient for the teachers to teach and students to learn. Tribal languages can find a proper place in education only with a suitable language policy decision providing for the use of tribal language in tribal education in Karnataka.

REFERENCES

1. Government of Karnataka, *Abyudya – Manual of Welfare Programme for the Development of Scheduled Castes and Scheduled Tribes*, Bangalore, 1996 (Kannada).
2. Government of Karnataka, *Annual Report, 2000-01*, Social Welfare Directorate, Bangalore (Kannada).

3. Biligiri, H.S., "Problems of Tribal Languages in India", in *Language and Society in India, Indian Institute of Advanced Study, Simla, Vol. 8, 1969*, pp. 245-250.
4. Edgar Turston, *Castes and Tribes of Southern India*, Cosmo Publications, Madras, 1909, Vol. 1 to 7.
5. Gnanasundaram, V., *Use of Tribal Languages in Education – Some Issues and Problems* (Seminar Paper), CIIL, Mysore.
6. Midatala Rani, Curriculum at the Primary Stage in the Tribal Schools of Andhra Pradesh.
7. Midatala Rani, Tribal Languages and Tribal Education, *Social Action, Vol. 50, No. 4, October-December 2000*, pp. 414-419.
8. Midatala Rani, *Tribal Languages in India: Reflections on Some Issues*, Paper presented at a Workshop.
9. Government of Karnataka, *Nali – Kali, District Primary Education Programme*, Mysore, ND.
10. Government of India, *National Policy on Education*, New Delhi, 1986.
11. Government of Karnataka, *Neravu – Nirdeeshana, Information and Publicity Department*, 1995 (Kannada).
12. Government of Karnataka, *Perspectives for Education Sector – Policy Paper for VIII Five Year Plan*, Department of Education, Bangalore, 1989.
13. Government of India, *25th Report of The Commission for Linguistic Minorities*, New Delhi, 1985.
14. Government of Karnataka, *Report of the Directorate of Tribal Welfare*, Bangalore, ND.
15. Roy Burman, B.K., "Languages of the Tribal Communities of India and their use in Primary Education" in *Language and Society in India, Indian Institute of Advanced Study, Simla, Vol. 8, 1969*, pp. 251-259.
16. Sarvashiksha Abhiyan—*Perspective Plan 2002-10*, Office of the District Project Coordinator, DPEP, Mysore, ND.
17. Government of Karnataka, *Social Welfare Department Programmes 1991-92*, Bangalore (Kannada), ND.
18. Sudhir Shukla, "Aliens in their Own Home", *The Hindu, 14th March, 1993.*
19. Tribal Education in India. *Publication No. 20, Tribal Education Unit.* Department of Adult Education, NCERT, 1967.
20. Government of Karnataka, *Welfare Programmes for Scheduled Tribes, Directorate of Social Welfare*, (Kannada), ND.

19

Tribal Education and Tribal Development in India

Introduction

Tribal people who account for about 8 per cent of the Population must have their rightful share of development and should be facilitated to play their role in the country's progress. Education could be a major instrument for achieving these objectives. The golden Jubilee year of our Independence should provide an occasion for deep introspection review and for seeking remedial measures in the area of education for tribals. Article 46 of the Constitution states that the State shall promote with special care the educational and economic interests of the weaker sections of the people, and in particular of Scheduled Castes and Schedule Tribes, and shall protect them from social injustice and all forms of social exploitation. Articles 330, 332, 335, 338 to 342 and the entire Fifth and Sixth Schedules of the Constitution deal with special provisions for implementation of the objectives set forth in Article 46. These provisions need to be fully operationalised for the benefit of the weaker sections of our society. Education of weaker sections would greatly facilitate their empowerment and for the realisation of the provisions of the Constitution.

After Independence, the Government of India have taken a number of steps to strengthen the educational base of Scheduled Castes and Scheduled Tribes. Establishing of educational institutions on priority basis in the areas predominantly inhabited by these communities, provision of incentives like scholarships, mid-day meals, uniforms, books and stationery, reservation of seats in educational institutions, relaxation of standards for admission to institutions of higher learning, providing coaching classes for competitive examinations, remedial coaching, and provision of hostels are some of the steps which have contributed a great deal in raising the educational levels of Scheduled Castes and Scheduled Tribes. But these communities still have to go a long way to raise to the level of other communities in the filed of educational development. Apart from other disparities, there are some special problems involved in the educational development of Scheduled Tribes, which are mostly socio-economic. Although the educational facilities have been extended to most of the habitations of these communities, they are still not able to utilise the facilities fully on account of their socio-economic backwardness. With the introduction of Tribal Sub-plan for Scheduled Tribes, it was expected that their socio-economic status would improve further and this normally should have a positive impact on educational development of these communities. It is generally observed that in the education sector, the present quantum of incentives provided to the Scheduled Tribes for improving their participation and retention has been inadequate in achieving the objectives. It is evident that Tribal education needs a different approach for its success.

General Review

The population of Scheduled Tribes, as per the 1991 census is 6.77 crores accounting for 8.01 per cent of the country's total population. Out of the total Schedule Tribe population, males are 3.4 crores and females are 3.3 crores. There are no Scheduled Tribes in the States of Haryana, Punjab, Chandigarh, Delhi and Pondicherry. The 1991 Census could not be held in Jammu and Kashmir. The scheduled tribe population in Goa is less than 10,000. In Madhya Pradesh Scheduled Tribe population is more than one crore. The Scheduled Tribe population in the states of Arunachal Pradesh, Meghalaya, Mizoram, Nagaland, Dadra and Nagar Haveli and Lakshadweep is more than 50 per cent of the total population. The percentage of scheduled tribe population is highest in Mizoram accounting for 94.75 per cent of the total population of the State.

Literacy Status

There has been an increase in the literacy rates of SCs/STs since independence, but the position is far from satisfaction. The following figures show the comparative picture of literacy rates in the last four decades (1961 to 1991).

Table–1
Literacy Rate of SCs and STs Compared to General Population

Year	*SC*	*ST*	*Non SC/ST*
1961	10.27	8.54	27.86
1971	14.67	11.30	33.80
1981	21.38	16.35	41.30
1991	37.41	29.60	52.11

The following Table and figures provide us the Statewise general literacy rates (1991) and Statewise literacy rates for Scheduled Castes and Scheduled Tribes according to the 1991 census.

Table–2
Literacy Rate of SCs and STs

	1981			*1991*		
	Persons	*Male*	*Female*	*Persons*	*Male*	*Female*
SC	21.38	31.12	10.93	37.41	49.21	23.76
ST	16.35	21.52	8.04	29.60	40.65	18.19

Enrolment: Primary, Middle and High School Stages (Classes 1 to 10)

Enrolment of Scheduled Tribes increased substantially at high school level from 2.66 lakhs in 1980-81 to 6.41 lakhs in 1991-92 accounting for 3.73 per cent and 4.26 per cent respectively. The percentage enrolment of Scheduled Tribe boys and girls in their respective groups at high school level increased from 3.90 lakhs and 3.36 lakhs in 1980-81 to

4.41 lakhs and 3.98 lakhs respectively in 1991-92. The enrolment of Scheduled Tribes at middle stage (classes 6 to 7) increased from 7.42 lakhs in 1980-81 to 17.94 lakhs in 1991-92 accounting for 3.74 per cent in 1980-81 and 5.21 per cent in 1991-92 of the total enrolment. Enrolment of Scheduled Tribes at high school level (Classes 9 to 10) increased substantially from 2.66 lakhs in 1980-81 to 6.41 lakhs in 1991-92 accounting for 3.73 per cent and 4.26 per cent respectively. The percentage of enrolment of Scheduled Tribe boys and girls in their respective groups at high school level increased from 3.90 lakhs and 3.36 lakhs in 1980-81 to 4.41 lakhs and 3.98 lakhs respectively in 1991-92. The enrolment of Scheduled Tribe children at Senior Secondary level which includes the enrolment at Higher Secondary level (10+2 pattern), Pre-university (one year course), Pre-degree/Pre-university (two year course) and intermediate/Junior College level. Scheduled Tribes enrolment at Senior Secondary level increased sharply. It increased from 63 thousands accounting for 1.52 per cent of the total enrolment in 1980-81 to 2.02 lakhs accounting for 3.26 per cent in 1991-92. The Scheduled Tribe girls enrolment which was less than 1 per cent in 1980-81 increased upto the level of 2.61 per cent in 1991-92. The enrolment of Scheduled Tribe boys increased upto 3.57 per cent in 1991-92 which was 1.73 per cent in 1980-81.

Dropout Rates

The dropout rates for the year 1988-89 amongst general, SC and ST categories are given below.

Table–3
Dropout Rates (1988-89)

Classes	*SC*	*ST*	*General*
1-5	49.62	64.53	47.93
1 to 8	67.78	78.08	65.40
1 to 10	79.88	86.72	75.36

Table 4 depicts the dropout rates among scheduled tribes and general categories at primary, middle and high school levels. Like scheduled castes, scheduled tribes also record considerable reduction in dropouts at various levels. At primary level, the dropout among scheduled tribes in 1960 was 75.66 per cent which reduced upto 64.53 per cent in 1988-89. At middle school level the dropout rate which was 86.71 per cent in 1980-81 reduced to 78.08 in 1988-89 while at high school level it came down to 86.72 per cent in 1988-89 from 91.18 in 1980-81.

Educational Development

General Scenario

Education is the most important element in the development of any community. The role of education as an investment in human resources has been increasingly recognised in all the countries. For the all-round development of the Indian Society the importance of educational development of the general mass, and particularly of the Scheduled Castes and Scheduled Tribes is well known. Education has special significance for the weaker sections of the society which are facing a new situation in the developmental process to

Table–4
Dropout Rates of Scheduled Tribes

Year	*Dropout Rates of STs*			*Dropout Rates of all Communities*		
	Primary	*Middle*	*Secondary*	*Primary*	*Middle*	*Secondary*
1980-81	75.66	86.71	91.18	58.70	72.20	82.46
1981-82	74.00	84.99	91.65	53.50	72.10	82.33
1982-83	72.44	83.35	90.42	52.10	69.57	81.37
1983-84	70.63	83.74	89.59	50.26	69.76	79.71
1984-85	69.40	82.86	88.37	47.93	65.39	78.13
1985-86	65.56	81.86	88.82	47.61	64.42	77.62
1986-87	66.12	80.19	87.26	48.60	64.90	76.44
1987-88	65.21	80.01	87.62	46.97	62.29	75.30
1988-89	64.53	78.08	86.72	47.93	65.40	75.36

adjust themselves properly to the changing circumstances. For them, education is an input not only for their economic development and for promoting in them self-confidence and inner strength to face the new changes and challenges. The SCs and STs have been the targets of economic exploitation, harassment, atrocities and social disabilities mainly due to their illiteracy. Likewise, the ST have fallen victims to the exploitation of the middlemen, merchants and moneylenders on account of their illiteracy and ignorance. The need for their educational development, therefore, assumes prime importance to save them from economic exploitation and to help them in their all-round development.

Although the spread of education in the country has been quite fast during the past five decades, the progress in respect of SC and STs has not been quite proportionate. The All India literacy rate in the country during 1971, being 29.4 per cent the corresponding rate of literacy for SC and STs are 14.7 per cent and 11.3 per cent respectively. In other words, the literacy rate of SCs accounts for 50 per cent of the All India level of literacy rate while in case of ST it works out to be 38.4 per cent. Even the level of educational development of the SC and STs is not the same in all the States/Union Territories (UTs) and in all the regions within the same State/UT. The educational programmes for the SC and STs have not succeeded in achieving the desired impact on account of various socio-economic problems faced by them. The SC/STs are not very much aware and convinced of the practical utility of education and need their children to help them in economic pursuits even from an early age. In view of the above, efforts for educational development for the SC/STs have to be tackled differently than for the general masses where the demand for education is already there and opening of a school is sufficient to attract them for education.

Incentive Schemes to Check the Problem of Dropouts

Besides providing dress, study materials, mid-day meals and pre-matric stipends, some of the State Governments/UT Administrations have taken up incentive schemes to check the problem of dropouts and encourage increased enrolment of SC/ST students at the pre-matric classes. Government of Gujarat have been implementing a scheme to provide economic aid to SC/ST/OBC girl students in 185 Taluks as to increase the enrolment of the girls. Each girl student is granted an amount of Rs. 100 per annum under this scheme. As a drive to increase enrolment in tribal areas, each-family of Kolgi, Kotwalia, and Kathali whose children are admitted in the school is given special incentives in kind i.e. grains worth Rs. 12 and Janata Saree and Dhoti worth Rs. 12 for ten months. In Haryana, the SC girls studying in primary classes are given attendance prize at the rate of Rs. 50 per student per annum. Incentive prizes in shape of clothing are given to SC students in Tamil Nadu who attend schools regularly. The Headmasters/Head Mistresses at the district level are also awarded prizes in the shape of silver medals for maintenance of best attendance. To check the incidence of dropouts, the Chandigarh Administration have a scheme to award attendance scholarships to SC students. Each student studying in Classes I to V gets Rs. 4 per month and the rate of award per student studying in Classes VI-VIII is Rs. 5 per month. It is also learnt that the Government of Kerala provide monetary relief to the parents for enrolment of more ST students in the primary and middle classes and to check the problem of dropouts.

The Problem of Stagnation

The extent of the problem of stagnation in different stages of pre-matric education is not known, but the problem is quite alarming in post-matric courses of study, where the performance of the SC/ST students is poor and the failure rate is quite high. As an illustration the following old studies may be quoted as we could not lay our hand on the latest data as it is not readily available. A study conducted by the Madras Office of the National Commission for SCs/STs in 12 colleges of Trivandrum and Ernakulam districts of Kerala during 1976-77 indicates that out of 396 SC/ST students on roll in pre-degree, degree and post graduate classes during 1976-77; 333 students constituting 85.55 per cent of the total pupil appeared in their final examination. Only 99 students passed and the extent of failure was as high as 74.36 per cent.

A study report of the Madras Office of the National Commission for SCs/STs on the assessment of the performance of SC/ST students in Tamil Nadu during 1975-76 also throws much light on the problem of stagnation in post-matric classes. The results of 7 colleges indicate that in non-professional courses, the percentage of passing was 17.00 per cent as against the failure rate of 83 per cent. The failures was more pronounced in P.U.C., B.A., B.Sc., B.Com, and M.Sc., courses which were estimated to be 86.9 per cent, 81.7 per cent, 90.8 per cent and 100.00 per cent respectively, while in M.A. final examination the failure rate was 29.2 per cent.

In professional courses, out of the total 109 SC students studying in Medical college during 1974-75, only 6 passed, the percentage of passing being 5.5 per cent. During 1975-76 the percentage of passing increased to 12 as 9 out of 75 SC students passed during the said year. In Engineering courses, out of the total, 28 SC/ST students passed during 1971-72. During the corresponding years of 1972-73 and 1973-74, the percentage pass of the SC/ST students were, however, reported to be 71.4 and 66.6, respectively.

Reasons for Stagnation

Reasons of frequent failures of SC/ST students in a particular class of study leading to stagnation are well known. Lack of proper family orientation for studies, non-adaptability to the school atmosphere, frequent absence of teachers in remote areas and especially in single teacher schools, absence of students in the classes on account of the school going children being utilised by the poor parents for looking after the young children during their out door work, grazing cattle and helping in other economic pursuits are some of the important reasons for high rate of stagnation of SC/ST students at the pre-matric level of study. The problem is more acute in interior and inaccessible pockets where the SC and ST parents are not much convinced about the need of the School education. Single teacher schools are run in many villages, where the teacher remains absent frequently and the schools are closed during their leave period or unauthorised absence.

The problems of education in tribal areas are manyfold. Many tribal communities speak a dialect of their own, and the medium of instruction in primary classes being the State language, the tribal students fail to understand the courses taught to them by the teachers in the language other than the one spoken by the tribal children. They also got disinterested in their studies being unable to read the text books written in the language quite unfamiliar to them. The quality and standard of education in tribal areas also suffer due to lack of efficient and good teachers who have least inclination to serve in tribal areas devoid of amenities of modern life. The teachers posted in tribal areas are also drawn mostly from non-tribal areas and they do not have any knowledge of the local tribal dialect and the proper aptitude to serve the downtrodden.

Other hurdles for educational development among tribal communities include their type of socio-economic pursuit and their traditional ethos of life. Some of the tribal communities practicing shifting cultivation and they have to shift their settlement from time to time to different sites situated close to their field selected for cultivation. Likewise there are many nomadic tribes and food gatherers who have no definite place of abode and move from one part of the jungle to other in search of collection of food and other forest products. The tribes like Toda having large herds, move from one area to the other in search of grazing ground for their cattle. Locating schools for such communities becomes a problem and the only solution for this would be to open pre-school centres and Ashram type of schools with residential facilities for the tribal children from pre-primary to middle and high school stages of education.

Cultural factors also act as barriers of educational development. Among the Binjhaias, a ST of Kalahandi district in Orissa, the girls are given in ceremonial marriage to a boy and after attaining puberty they are not allowed to take food and water outside their family. Such customs retards educational advancement of girls. It is also a general apprehension among the tribal people that their boys will become insolent and rebellious and the girls will go astray if they go to school. They have also a fear that the educated tribal youths do not respect their traditional norms and values of life and look down upon their own people. These social barriers, fears and psychological complexes of the tribal people have to be overcome for carrying forward the educational programme in tribal areas.

Schemes for Minimising the Extent of Stagnation

The problem of stagnation can be tackled by improving the educational standards of the students. The schemes like providing special coaching to failed students and poor students to improve their performance in the class, award of incentive prizes to the meritorious SC/ST students, and awards for the school for achieving better results in school final examination aim at minimising the stagnation rate in pre-matric classes.

Three schemes are implemented in Andhra Pradesh for providing Incentives for the meritorious ST students. The first and second rank ST students of SSC examination in each district are granted a scholarship of Rs. 100 each per month for 12 months. All the ST students securing 60 per cent or more marks in SSC examination are sanctioned a lumpsum award, students in VII Class in each district are also awarded Rs. 50 each per month for 12 months by the Government of Andhra Pradesh. The State Government proposes to admit 200 bright SC students of Classes V to XI in reputed institutions for availing better standard of education. Similar scheme is also implemented to benefit the ST and Denotified Tribe students also.

In Tamil Nadu, first and second prizes in the shape of National Savings Certificates are awarded to SC students in each district who secure highest marks in S.S.L.C. public examination and VIII standard examination' to inculcate a spirit of competition in their studies. A silver shield of a value of Rs. 200 is also awarded to the Adi-Dravidar Welfare Schools securing, the highest percentage of marks in the public S.S.L.C. examination. Part-time tutors are appointed for all the hostels to provide coaching to the boarders. In order to improve the educational standard of the failed SC/ST students in Classes IX to XI, the Government of Tamil Nadu have sanctioned a scheme in 25 Adi-Dravidar Welfare High Schools for giving Coaching in Mathematics, English and Science. A cash award of Rs. 200 to each Warden/Matron of the Government Welfare Hostels in each district is also given for securing better results in the public S.S.L.C. examination.

For improving the educational standards of the SC and ST students in post-matric classes the Government of Tamil Nadu have taken up four schemes. The "Gandhi Memorial Scholarship Scheme" was introduced in 1970-71 for the SC students who secure the highest marks in pre-university classes in each district. One boy and one girl of each district are awarded this scholarship. Under this scheme, a lumpsum grant of Rs. 500 is sanctioned to each student at the time of admission in college, and a recurring scholarship of Rs. 100 per month is given per student for 10 months in a year. The scholarship is sanctioned for a period of six years and in addition to any other scholarship to which the student is entitled..

Under the "Loan Scholarships Scheme" financial assistance is given by way of interest free loan to such SC/ST students who are not eligible for award of either the State Government or Government of India post-matric scholarship and whose pecuniary circumstances are such that they are not able to meet the full expenditure for pursuing professional post graduate degree courses. The loan ranges from Rs. 900 to Rs. 1,750 per annum per student.

For providing free tuition and special coaching to the SC/ST students studying in PUC and Degree Courses, the State Government have sanctioned a scheme during 1974-75 by opening 2 centres in Madras, Coimbatore, Tiruchirapalli and a scheme for giving special coaching to meritorious SC/ST college students is also taken up by the State Government. Students securing 60 per cent and more marks are selected by the Director of Collegiate Education, and are given coaching in Madras city for 400 students. In Haryana the SC students of Classes IX, X and XI are given special coaching in English, Science and Mathematics from November to February, every year. During 1978-79, the Government of Kerala have sanctioned a scheme for providing special coaching to SC/ST students of pre-degree courses. The coaching is provided in 10 colleges, one in each of the 10 districts of Trivandrum Quilon, Kottayam, Ernakulam, Alleppey, Trichur, Palghat, Malapuram, Kozhikode and Cannanore. Each centre gives the coaching to 60 students in Physics, Chemistry, Mathematics, Botany and Zoology and SC/ST students from other educational institutions are also allowed to attend the special coaching classes.

No schemes for providing incentives to the meritorious students and special coaching appear to have been implemented in Punjab, Rajasthan, Bihar and Gujarat where special coaching is provided only for the SC/ST boarders in Government Hostels. No special coaching scheme or scheme for giving incentives to meritorious SC/ST candidates is being implemented in Madhya Pradesh and Uttar Pradesh. The position in respect of other States is not known.

According to the information available, the schemes for improving the educational standard of the SC/ST students are implemented in the Union Territory (UT) of Goa, Daman and Diu and Pondicherry. In Goa, Daman and Diu, the scheme only benefits the SC/ST girls. Merit scholarships of Rs. 20 per month are paid to each of the girls' students studying in Class IX who secure 55 per cent and more marks. The rate of scholarships for each such girl student in Classes X and XI is Rs. 25 and Rs. 30, respectively. In Pondicherry, 97 tutorial centres are run to provide coaching facilities to the SC students studying in Class VI to X.

Higher Education

The University Grants Commission (UGC) has been contributing towards social equity and upliftment of the under-privileged sections of society through special schemes as well as specific provisions within regular schemes in higher education. The following are the provisions made and schemes implemented: (1) Relaxation of upto 10 per cent in the cut off marks in the results of National Eligibility Test (NET) Junior Research Fellowship (JRF) is given to SC/ST candidates and all the qualified candidates are awarded JRF. In case no vacancy is available, UGC provides supernumerary positions of JRF to the universities. (2) In addition, fifty Junior Research Fellowships are awarded every year, in Science and Humanities and Social Sciences, to SC/ST candidates who appear in NET and qualify the eligibility test for lecturership. (3) With a view to provide opportunities to teachers belonging to SC/ST categories in affiliated colleges, 50 Teacher Fellowships (20 for Ph.D and 30 for M.Phil) have been instituted under the scheme of Direct Award to Teachers belonging to SC/ST categories and were awarded to as many teachers during 1994-95. (4) Forty Research Associateships have been set aside for the Schedule Caste/Tribe candidates every year. (5) The UGC has prescribed relaxation in criteria for financial assistance to colleges having SC/ST enrolment and to those located in backward regions. (6) Special Cells in various universities/institutions have been set up with a view to ensure effective implementation of the various schemes for the Scheduled Caste/Tribe students. The total number of such Cells was 9788 on 31.3.1995. The Commission provides assistance to the universities for the appointments.

Reservation for Scheduled Caste/Scheduled Tribes

The UGC has brought to the notice of the universities the orders issued from time to time by the Government of India for 15 per cent and 7.5 per cent reservations for SC/STs, respectively in admissions to various courses, in appointments to the posts of lecturers and non-teaching posts and in the allocation of seats in students hostels and in staff quarters and teachers hostels. The UGC has also made a provision that all the universities which receive grants for construction of hostels should reserve 20 per cent of the seats in these hostels for SC/ST students.

Remedial Coaching for Scheduled Caste/Scheduled Tribes

The Commission has introduced a scheme entitled Remedial Coaching for Scheduled Caste and Scheduled Tribes in the universities and colleges. The main purpose of the scheme is to: improve the academic skills and linguistic proficiency of these students in various subjects and to raise the level of comprehension of students in such subjects, where quantitative techniques and laboratory work, skills are involved. Under the scheme, a University/College would be eligible to receive rant on 100 per cent basis as follows: at the College level Rs. 75,000 per annum and at the University level Rs. 1,50,000 per annum. The UGC assistance will be available for a period of 3 years, in the first instance, which could be extended for a further period of 3 years if the programme is performed satisfactorily by the institutions, determined on the basis of pass percentage of SC/ST students. During the year 1994-95, the Commission accepted the proposals of 102 affiliated colleges and 7 universities for conducting remedial coaching for the Scheduled Caste/Scheduled Tribes.

Education of Scheduled Tribes

Enrolment: Enrolment by Type of Institutions

Table 5 below depicts the All India picture of the total enrolment of Scheduled Tribes in various types of educational institutions during the year 1978-79 and 1988-89.

Table–5
Enrolment of Scheduled Tribes by Type of Institutions

Type of Institutions	*Number of Scheduled Tribes Enrolled*			
	1978-79		*1988-89*	
	Total	*Girls*	*Total*	*Girls*
1. Pre-primary schools	58176	24666	108260	52821
2. Primary/Jr. Basic schools	3397938	1124348	3365770	1322383
3. Middle/Sr. Basic schools	1278806	401266	3298556	1188567
4. High/Hr. Sec. Schools (Classes IX and above)	560549	153582	1456648	434473
5. Vocational, Professional, Special and others schools of education	131984	44236	993755	443863
Total	5427453	1748098	9222989	3442107

It will be seen from the above Table that the total enrolment of children belonging to STs increased from 54.27 lakhs in 1978-79 to 92.23 lakhs in 1988-89 registering an increase of 69.95 per cent. Girls' enrolment increased from 17.48 lakhs in 1978-79 to 34.42 lakhs in 1988-89. The percentage of STs enrolment out of all communities was 5.4 per cent during 1978-79, which increased to 7.19 in 1988-89. A comparative review of the progress of enrolment of Scheduled Tribes as percentage to the corresponding enrolment of all communities for the years 1978-79 and 1988-89 in various types of educational institutions is given in the following paragraphs:

(i) Pre-Primary Schools

Enrolment of Scheduled Tribes children in pre-primary schools increased from 58,176 (11.3% of all communities) in 1978-79 to 108260 (11,03% of all communities) in 1988-89. Similarly enrolment of ST girls children showed an increase from 24,666 in 1978-79 to 52821 in 1988-89.

(ii) Primary Schools

Total enrolment in primary schools in the country as a whole increased from 483.99 lakhs in the year 1978-79 to 644.97 lakhs in 1988-89. The corresponding enrolment of STs was 33.98 lakhs in 1978-79 and 33.66 lakhs in 1988-89. The percentage enrolment of STs to the enrolment of all communities was 7.0 per cent in 1978-79 and 5.17 in 1988-89.

(iii) Middle Schools

The total enrolment in Middle Schools in the country as a whole increased from 265.59 lakhs in 1978-79 to 372.52 lakhs in 1988-89 showing an increase of 40.26 per cent. The enrolment of Scheduled Tribes increased from 12.79 lakhs to 32.99 lakhs, thus registering an increase of 157.93 per cent during this period. The percentage enrolment of Scheduled Tribes to the total enrolment of all communities in this type of schools was 4.8 per cent in 1978-79 and 8.86 in 1988-89.

(iv) Higher Secondary Schools

While the total number of students belonging to all communities enrolled in higher in secondary schools increased from 210.93 lakhs in 1978-79 to 370.86 lakhs in 1988-89, the corresponding enrolment of Scheduled Tribes increased from 5.60 lakhs to 14.57 lakhs during this period. The case of the former was 75.82 per cent. It was 160.18 per cent in the later case. The coverage of enrolment of Scheduled Tribe students as percentage of corresponding enrolment of all communities increased from 2.7 per cent in 1976-79 to 3.93 per cent in 1988-89.

(v) Schools for Vocational, Professional and Other Education

The total number of all community students enrolled in schools for special education in the country as a whole increased from 13.30 lakhs in 1978-79 to 87.90 lakhs in 1988-89. The enrolment of Scheduled Tribe students increased from 1.32 lakhs in 1978-79 to 9.94 lakhs in 1988-89. This resulted in increase in the percentage of STs enrolment from 1.31 per cent in 1978-79 to 9.92 per cent in 1988-89.

Enrolment by Stages of Education

So far, the progress in enrolment of ST students by above type of institutions has been discussed and comparative picture of enrolment for the years 1978-79 and 1988-89 has been shown for different categories of institutions. However, a better picture of enrolment of ST students can be had from the stage-wise position of enrolment as discussed in the following paragraph. Table 6 indicates the enrolment of all communities as well as of STs by different stages of education for the year1988-89. Enrolment of STs as a percentage of the corresponding enrolment of all communities for different stages of education has also been indicated for the year 1988-89.

Table–6
Enrolment – Percentage of Scheduled Tribes by Stages of Education

(in lakhs)

Stages	*Enrolment of all Communities*	*ST Enrolment*	*% of ST Enrolment*
I. General Education (School Stage)			
1. Pre-Primary	24.36	3.20	13.14
2. Primary (Classes 1 to 5)	912.71	60.46	6.62
3. Middle (Classes 6 to 8)	311.05	12.81	4.12
4. Higher Sec. (Classes 9 & above)	205.12	5.82	2.84
Total	**1453.24**	**82.29**	**26.72**
II. Vocational, Professional, Special and Other Education (School Stage)	87.90	9.94	1.13
Grand Total	1541.14	92.23	27.85

Teachers: Scheduled Tribe Teachers

Table 7 below depicts the all-India comparative picture of the total number of ST teachers in various types of educational institutions and percentage of Women teachers to total number of Scheduled Tribe Teachers for the years 1978-79 and 1988-89.

Table–7
Distribution of Scheduled Tribes Teachers by Type of Institution

Type of Institutions	*Total Number of ST Teachers*				*% of Women Teachers to Total Teachers*	
	1978-79		*1988-89*		*1978-79*	*1988-89*
	Total	*Women*	*Total*	*Women*		
1. Pre-primary schools	1404	480	1815	1583	34.2	87.22
2. Pry/Jr. Basic Schools	62750	10466	55166	13916	17.0	25.23
3. Middle/Sr. Basic Schools	28801	6906	58733	12180	24.0	20.74
4. High/Higher Sec. Schools	10236	2518	25376	6120	24.6	24.12
5. Vocational, Professional Spl. & Other Edn. Schools	2308	528	18926	6266	22.88	33.11
Total	105499	20898	160016	40065		

It will be seen from Table 7 that the total number of Scheduled Tribe Teachers increased from 1.05 lakhs in 1978-79 to 1.6 lakhs in 1988-89. The women Scheduled Tribe Teachers included in the total increased from 0.21 lakhs in 1978-79 to 0.40 lakhs in 1988-89. During this period 0.54 lakhs teachers have been added which includes 0.19 lakhs women teachers.

Table 8 gives the percentage of Scheduled Tribe Teachers to total number of teachers for various types of educational Institutions.

Table–8

Percentage of ST Teachers by Type of Institutions

Type of Institutions	*% of Scheduled Tribe Teachers*	
	1978-79	*1988-89*
1. Pre-primary schools	10.9	8.32
2. Pry/Jr. Basic Schools	4.9	3.55
3. Middle/Sr. Basic Schools	3.5	5.69
4. High/Higher Sec. Schools	1.3	2.10
5. Vocational, Professional Spl. & Other Edn. Schools	5.71	6.44

The above Table shows that the percentage of Scheduled Tribe teachers to the corresponding number of all community teachers rose from 3.5 per cent in 1978-79 to 3.88 per cent in 1988-89.

Trained and Untrained SC and ST Teachers

Another aspect for which information about Scheduled Caste and Scheduled Tribe Teachers has been collected relates to the number of trained teachers belonging to these communities working in schools. Since all school teachers are required to be trained, the number of trained teachers among Scheduled Castes and Scheduled Tribes has been compared with, the number of trained teachers of all communities.

Table 9 gives percentage of Scheduled Caste and Scheduled Tribe trained teachers working in various types of schools in comparison to the corresponding percentage of total trained teachers belonging to all communities.

Table–9

Percentage of Trained Teachers by Type of Schools

Type of Schools	*All Communities*	*Scheduled Castes*	*Scheduled Tribes*
	1988-89	*1988-89*	*1988-89*
1. Pre-primary schools	59.0	39.5	10.8
2. Primary Schools	87.1	86.1	66.1
3. Middle Schools	87.4	87.7	71.1
4. Higher Sec. Schools	86.4	85.4	57.1

From the above Table, it will be seen that the training competence of Scheduled Caste Teachers is almost at par with their other counter parts in general but it is quite low in case of ST teachers. The percentage of SC trained teachers in schools for general education was 86.3 per cent in 1988-89. However, Scheduled Tribe trained teachers were 65.8 per cent only. The percentage of SC trained teachers in all types of Schools for general education have shown an increase over the previous years.

Suggestions/Recommendations for Educational Development Among SCs/STs

The magnitude of the problem of wastage and stagnation among the SC/ST students, the factors and forces responsible for large scale wastage and stagnation of Scheduled Caste and Scheduled Tribe students, and the steps taken by the Government of India and the State Governments/Union Territory Administrations in tackling the problem have been discussed at length in the foregoing paras. In the light of the above discussion, it is necessary that the following steps may be taken to improve the education of tribal people.

While implementing the scheme proposed by the Government of India for giving financial assistance to 8 educationally backward States to enroll all the children of 6-11 age group and 57 per cent of 11-14 age group children and for improving their educational standard during the Sixth Plan period it is desirable that the State Governments should ensure covering all the eligible Scheduled Caste and Scheduled Tribe children in the target group.

For imparting pre-school training to the SC/ST students and to acquaint them with the school atmosphere, balwadis and creches should be opened in all the States/Union Territories for admitting the children of 0-3 and 3-6 years of age. This would not only help in achieving the national target of 100 per cent enrolment at the primary level of education, but also would create an urge in the young children for the studies and to improve their standard of learning. It is, therefore, necessary that such pre-school centres may be opened in sufficient numbers with qualified teachers to cover the pre-school going children of the target group.

The system of single-teacher schools weakens the elementary education system and defeats the purpose for which the schools are opened. The Government of Gujarat have proposed to do away with the single teacher schools in tribal areas during 1981-82. It is desirable that other State Governments/Union Territory Administrations take similar steps in this regard and provide at least two teachers for each of such schools so that in the absence of one of the teachers, the school need not be closed down.

It is unfortunate that only few States/Union Territories have taken steps to tackle the alarming problem of drop-outs among the SC/ST students by providing incentive schemes. Considering the magnitude of the problems, it is desirable that all the State Governments/ Union Territory Administrations take early steps in providing such schemes for the award of attendance prize to the Schedule Caste/Scheduled Tribe students and granting monetary relief to the parents of the Scheduled Caste/Scheduled Tribe students' so that they are not put to financial hardship on account of sending their children to school. This would encourage regular attendance in the class in early stages of education and promote improvement of educational standard of Scheduled Caste and Scheduled Tribe students.

With a view to checking the increasing trend of stagnation and to encourage the Scheduled Caste/Scheduled Tribe students to do well in their studies it is necessary that all the States and Union Territories draw up schemes to award prizes to Scheduled Caste/ Scheduled Tribe students securing 60 per cent and more marks in their VIII and XI standard public examination, in each district. To take special interest for improving the educational standards of the SC/ST students the Headmasters/Headmistresses of the schools and Wardens/Matrons of the welfare hostels which report better performance of the SC/ST students may also be awarded certificates and cash prizes. The scheme of importing special coaching may not be confined only to the welfare hostels, but also may be implemented for the SC/ST day-scholars studying in Classes VI to X and for the failed SC/ ST students. The Government of Tamil Nadu have already taken pioneering steps in this regard and other States/Union Territories should follow Tamil Nadu in implementing the scheme aiming at the improvement of educational standards of the SC/ST students.

Schemes to improve the educational standards of the SC/ST students in postmatric courses of studies appear to have been implemented only in Tamil Nadu and Kerala. The steps taken by the Government of Tamil Nadu for educational advancement of the Scheduled Caste/Scheduled Tribe students in post-matric classes deserve commendation and it is desirable that other State Governments/Union Territory Administrations take similar steps to accelerate the progress of education of SC/ST students and help in arresting the problem of drop-out and stagnation at the post-matric level of study.

The children of the tribal communities speaking their own dialect face difficulty during the early stages of their school education, where the text books and the medium of education are in the languages adopted by the State/Union Territory. So far no State Government/ Union Territory have printed textbooks in tribal dialects upto Class 5. (Only Andhra Pradesh and Karnataka Governments have printed bilingual textbooks upto Classes 2 only.) In Orissa, an attempt was made during 1966 to prepare primers in Juang dialect (spoken by the Tuang, a backward hill tribe of Keonhar district of Orissa) for the primary classes. The primers were prepared by a Research Officer of the State Tribal Research Bureau, who had learnt the tribal dialect. The State Text Book Committee reviewed the primers and acclaimed their technical standard, but did not favour for introduction as textbooks as it would go against the national policy of the general education. Since the medium of instruction at higher classes would only be in the State language, at the initial stages would only do harm to the tribal students who would not be able to pick-up the studies at higher classes where textbooks and teaching would be in Oriya Medium. Lack of teachers knowing Juang dialect was also viewed to be another problem. This is also the same case with other states.

The National Commission for SC/ST are in full agreement with the view expressed by the Orissa Text Book Committee and feel the adoption of tribal dialect as medium of instruction at primary stages of education. It would create further problems for the tribal children at subsequent higher stages of their education where it will be extremely difficult for them to again shift to the medium of the State language. However, the textbooks should include topics reflecting the culture and tradition of the tribal communities. It would rather be desirable to encourage preparation of books in tribal dialects, which could be used as supplementary books. Besides, the teachers employed in tribal areas may be encouraged to learn the local tribal dialect and may be suitably rewarded for that since the teachers play a vital role in spreading education in tribal areas, talented teachers knowing the local tribal dialect may be appointed with higher scale of pay and other incentives may be provided for serving in tribal areas. As far as possible, the local educated tribals should be appointed as teachers in their respective areas. If suitable tribal candidates with the requisite educational qualifications are available, other qualifications may be relaxed while selecting tribal candidates as teachers to serve in their own areas.

To promote regular attendance of the Scheduled Caste/Scheduled Tribe students in their classes it would be desirable to adopt the working hours of the schools keeping in view the local conditions. Likewise, during certain agricultural seasons, the SC/ST students go to the field to help their parents in agricultural operations and thereby remain absent in their classes. The proper solution for this would be to follow the vacations and other holidays according to the local requirements.

Among some of the tribal communities whose economy is based on shifting cultivation, food gathering and nomadic way of life, their place of habitation change frequently in connection with their economic pursuits. The only solution for this would be to open pre-school centres and Ashram type of schools with residential facilities for the tribal children from pre-primary to middle and high school stage of education.

Cultural factors also work as barriers for educational advancement of STs. It is desirable that adult literacy campaign and the publicity and propaganda on the utility of education for the all-round development of the tribal people may be intensified for overcoming these hurdles.

It is unfortunate that the extent of the problem of wastage and stagnation of SC/ST students is not known in respect of many States/Union Territories. To asses the magnitude of the problem and take remedial measures it is necessary that studies on this problem are conducted in all the States/Union Territories by the Tribal Research Institutes, Universities, Educational Departments and other educational bodies for formulation of suitable strategy in checking the problem.

Ashram Schools

Ashram schools are opened in tribal areas providing free education and boarding and lodging facilities to the tribals who inhabit in the inaccessible hills and forests without proper communication facilities. The tribal villages are also usually small and sparsely populated and the tribal children do not like to walk long distance to go to schools. With a view to attracting the tribal children to continue their studies, Ashram schools were opened in States with siseable tribal population to impart education for the tribal boys and girls at the primary and middle stages of education. In Orissa, the residential schools for girls are called Kanyashrams while the Ashram Schools are meant for boys. Besides general education, the Ashram Schools also impart training in agriculture, crafts like blacksmithy, carpentry and weaving for boys and tailoring for girls. In some States, Ashram Schools have also been opened to cater to the educational needs of the Scheduled Castes. To open new Ashram Schools in tribal areas, the scheme of establishment and maintenance of Ashram Schools has been included in the Tribal sub-plans.

The problems of the SC/STs in their pre-matric studies, reasons leading to high rate of wastage and stagnation and the apathy of the Scheduled Caste/Scheduled Tribe children towards the formal education have already been discussed in detail. To attract more SC/STs towards education and to achieve increased enrolment of these students in primary and middle level of education it is necessary to open residential schools and attract SC/ST students for study by providing them free lodging, boarding, dress and study materials. The State Governments/Union Territory Administrations may, therefore, provide sufficient funds for opening of adequate number of Ashram type of schools for the SC and the ST students for achieving the desired enrolment of these students and improving their standard of education under proper study atmosphere.

Hostels

Hostels play an important role in spreading of education among the SCs and STs. Provision of hostels helps in arresting the problem of dropouts resulting in increasing enrolment of SC/ST students. It is the general experience that many of the SC/ST students become disinterested in their studies and discontinue in the middle of the course on account of poverty. In tribal areas, the schools are located in distant places and the children find it difficult to attend the school. The hostels provide study atmosphere for the students. A study conducted by the Directorate of Social Welfare, Karnataka State on performance of the hostellers in S.S.L.C. examination held in 1978 revealed that the general percentage of passing being 50.8 per cent, for SC and ST it was 36.5 and 38.4 respectively. As against the above figures, the percentage of passing for the hostellers recorded 56.8 per cent for general (including SC and ST students), 53.5 per cent for SC and 68.0 per cent for STs. The fact that hostels help in the educational progress of SC and ST students, both quantitatively and qualitatively is very clear from the above survey. Hostels for the SC/ST boys and girls are constructed under the Backward Classes Sector of the State Plan and Tribal sub-plans. Non-official organisations running hostels for SC/STs also receive grants-in-aid from State Governments/Union Territory Administrations, and also from the Government of India.

The number of Government Hostels for SC/STs is not adequate in many State/Union Territories. In his Twenty Sixth Report (1978-79), the Commissioner for SC and STs observed that the number of such hostels continued to be inadequate in States like Bihar, Gujarat, Himachal Pradesh, Kerala, Rajasthan and Uttar Pradesh and reiterated that urgent action should be taken to meet the deficiency by opening sufficient number of such hostels in those States. The Third All India Educational Survey of Hostel Facilities for Scheduled Castes conducted by the National Council of Educational Research and Training (NCERT), during December, 1973 also throws light on this problem. From the statistics received from 13 States (Andhra Pradesh, Bihar, Gujarat, Haryana, Karnataka, Kerala, Madhya Pradesh, Maharashtra, Rajasthan, West Bengal) and two Union Territories (Dadra and Nagar Haveli and Pondicherry), the report has highlighted the inadequacy of hostel facilities in different States. According to the survey, Uttar Pradesh with the highest SC population did not have the highest percentage of hostels. With only 3.2 per cent of the total number of hostels Uttar Pradesh ranked only eighth in the country in numerical strength of hostels, while Maharashtra having the lowest percentage of SC population (6%) had the second highest number of hostels among all the States/Union Territories. Andhra Pradesh with

14.51 per cent SC population had the maximum number of hostels i.e. 1036 hostels constituting 26.46 per cent of the total hostels. Surprisingly enough, Haryana having as high as 18.88 per cent of SC population had only 2 hostels in the State for SCs.

The findings of the above study are quite revealing and it would be desirable for all the State Governments/Union Territory Administrations to take immediate steps in providing hostel facilities for the SC/ST students in both pre-matric and post-matric classes. This would help in arresting the problem of drop-outs of SC/ST day-scholars to a greater extent and help in continuing their studies as boarders. In States like Tamil Nadu, only SC/ST students whose native place is more than 8 kms. away are considered eligible for admission in hostels. This criterion has been adopted to eliminate a section of the students as sufficient number of hostels are not available to accommodate all these students. Since the SC/ST parents are poor and hostels provide better study atmosphere it is desirable that all the Scheduled Caste/Scheduled Tribe students irrespective of the distance from their homes are provided with hostel facilities for improving their educational standards.

The shortage of hostel facilities is met by construction of new hostels, expansion of the existing hostel buildings to accommodate more boarders, opening of new hostel in rented buildings, and providing alternate accommodation facilities to the SC/ST students to run their own mess. Since the construction of new hostels involved huge financial expenditure, the State Governments/Union Territory Administrations have taken up construction of new hostel buildings in a phased manner. In Tamil Nadu, new hostels buildings are constructed by the Tamil Nadu Adi-Dravidar Housing and Development Corporation (TAHDCO), providing sufficient accommodation to meet the requirement of the SC/ST boarders in future. A majority of the hostels in all the States/UTs are run in rented private buildings till sufficient number of hostels are constructed. In Tamil Nadu, out of the 631 hostels for SC/STs, only 115 are in Government buildings and the remaining are run in private rented houses. In Andhra Pradesh, majority of the hostels are housed in rented buildings. Out of the 1,392 pre-matric hostels and 68 college hostels run by the Social Welfare Department, only 268 are in Government buildings, and out of 335 girls hostels 297 are located in private buildings. To meet the growing demand of SC/ST students of post-matric classes for hostel facilities the Government of Andhra Pradesh have been sanctioning funds for running of students' managed hostels. In addition to the hostel charges as per the Government of India post-matric scholarships, each of the SC/ST students managing a common mess is sanctioned Rs. 180 per annum towards the rent of the building, water and electricity charges, salary of cook and other contingent expenses. In Orissa, each of the SC/ST student is paid Rs. 20 per month in addition to the usual scholarship for running a common mess during the post-matric studies. Admitting the fact that the existing 12 welfare hostels are not sufficient to extend the boarding and lodging facilities for all the SC students and some of the students coming from distant villages are denied of hostel facilities. The Pondicherry Administration have reported that they have sanctioned a scheme for granting bus fare to such students to attend their classes as day scholars. Though the students have to undergo such strain in coming to their classes from distant places, the scheme compensates the financial loss suffered by them on account of journey by bus.

Scholarships

The quantum of pre-metric and post-metric scholarships to SC/ST students was fixed as per the Cost of Price Index (CPI) prevalent some decades ago. Since the CPI has gone up several folds it is very essential to raise the scholarship commensurate with the existing CPI. Further, it is desirable to review the quantum of amount to be payable towards pre- and post-metric scholarships periodically, say annually. To make the increase more meaningful, payment of scholarships should be linked to dearness allowance paid to the Government servants and pensioners.

Reservation in Teaching Faculty

Implementation of the government policy of reservation in the matter of appointment and admission of students in institutions of higher learning and professional institutions such as IIMs, IITs etc., needs to be ensured.

Conclusion

During the past fifty years a number of programmes and projects have been under taken by the State and Central Governments to improve the lot of the Scheduled Tribes. Considerable efforts were also made towards education of tribals but complete success is evading. A comprehensive view of all aspects of planning, administration and socio-economic life of tribals and their cultural ethos and beliefs needs to be taken. In the ultimate analysis it leads to the conclusion, tribal education needs an innovation and different approach for its success.

REFERENCES

1. *A Report of Elementary Education in Rajasthan*, Department of Education, Government of Rajasthan.
2. *Annual Plan 1992-93*, Planning Commission, Government of India.
3. *Annual Report 1991-92 and 1992-93*, Department of Education, MHRD, Government of India.
4. *Background paper on tribal development*, Ministry of Welfare, Government of India.
5. *Background Papers (National Conference on Problems of Scheduled Tribes)* 31st March 1990; Tribal Development Division, Ministry of Tribal Welfare, Government of India.
6. *Status paper on Socio-economic conditions of SC/ST for 1989* in respect of Rajasthan, Office of the Director for Scheduled Castes and Scheduled Tribes, Government of India, Jaipur (Rajasthan).
7. *Education for all by 2000*, Indian perspective by NIEPA, March 1990.
8. *Education of Scheduled Castes and Scheduled Tribes 1988-89*, Department of Education, MHRD, Government of India.
9. *Education of SCs and STs 1988-89*, Department of Education, Ministry of Human Resource Development, Government of India.
10. *Educational Development in Rajasthan*, Department of Education, Government of Rajasthan.
11. *Educational Facilities for SCs/STs*, Department of Education, Ministry of HRD, 1986.
12. *Eighth Five Year Plan (1992-97)*, Planning Commission, Government of India.
13. *Elementary Education in India* (Enrolment trends during 1978-79 to 1988-89), School Education, MHRD, Government of India.
14. *Fifth All-India Educational Survey*, NCERT Publication.
15. *Internal discussion of the Education Division of the Planning Commission, 1996.*
16. Moonis Raza, Aokaziddom Amjad and Sheel C. Nuna, *School Education in India*, (the Regional Dimension), NIEPA, New Delhi.

17. *National Policy on Education 1986* (with modifications undertaken in 1992), Department of Education, Ministry of Human Resource Development, Government of India.
18. *National Policy on Education 1986 and Programme of Action 1992*, Department of Education, MHRD, Government of India.
19. Punalekar, S.P. and Jyoti Ranadive, *Tribal Education an Inter-State study-based on the survey of Maharashtra, Gujarat and Rajasthan*, Centre for Social Studies, University Campus, Surat.
20. *Report of the Committee on Special Multi-Purpose Tribal Blocks*, Ministry of Home Affairs, New Delhi.
21. *Report of the Sub-committee on Planning and Programme of National Committee on Centenary Celebrations of Dr. B.R. Ambedkar*, January 1991, Ministry of Welfare, Government of India.
22. *Report of the Working Group on development and welfare of SCs during Eighth Five Year Plan, Ministry of Welfare, Government of India.*
23. *Report of the working group on development and welfare on ST during Eighth Five Year Plan*, Ministry of Welfare, Government of India.
24. *Report of the Working Group on the Development of SCs.*
25. Ruhela, S.P., *Educational challenges in socialist India.*
26. *Second Report of the SCs and STs Commission* (April 1979-March 1980) Government of India.
27. *Selected Educational Statistics 1988-89; 1989-90; 1990-91; 1991-92 and 1992-93*, Department of Education, MHRD, Government of India.
28. *Selected Educational Statistics as on 30th September, 1993*, Department of Education, Ministry of Human Resource Development, Government of India.
29. Shyam Lal, *Education Among Tribes*, (Research project on Tribal Education in Rajasthan), 1984-86.
30. Tyagi, P.N., *Education for all a graphic presentation*, NIEPA, New Delhi.
31. Varshney, H.K., *Socio-Economic Inequalities in Education, Part I, Frame work for disparity*, IAMR, New Delhi.
32. Verma, R.C., *Indian Tribes Through The Ages*, Publication Division, Ministry of Information and Broadcasting, Government of India.

Appendix–1
Scheduled Tribes Population of 1991

State/Union Territory	Total Population			ST Population			% of Population		
	Male	Female	Total	Male	Female	Total	Male	Female	Total
1	2	3	4	5	6	7	8	9	10
Andhra Pradesh	33724581	32783427	66508008	2142817	2056664	4199481	6.35	6.27	6.31
Arunachal Pradesh	465004	399554	864558	275397	274954	550351	59.22	68.82	64.02
Assam	11657989	10756333	22414322	1461560	1412881	2874441	12.54	13.14	12.84
Bihar	45202091	41172374	86374465	3357563	3259351	6616914	7.43	7.92	7.675
Goa	594790	575003	1169793	199	177	376	0.03	0.03	0.03
Gujarat	21355209	19954373	41309582	3131947	3029828	6161775	14.67	15.18	14.925
Haryana	8827474	7636174	16463648	-	-	0	0	0	0
Himachal Pradesh	2617467	2553410	5170877	110240	108109	218349	4.21	4.23	4.22
Jammu & Kashmir	4014100*	3704600*	7718700*	-	-	0	0	0	0
Karnataka	22951917	22025284	44977201	976744	938947	1915691	4.26	4.26	4.26
Kerala	14288995	14809523	29098518	160812	1601558	1762370	1.13	1.08	1.105
Madhya Pradesh	34267293	31913877	66181170	7758174	7640860	15399034	22.64	23.94	23.29
Maharashtra	40825618	38111569	78937187	3717783	3600498	7318281	9.11	9.45	9.28
Manipur	938359	898790	1837149	322720	309453	632173	34.39	34.43	34.41
Meghalaya	907687	867091	1774778	760234	757693	1517927	83.76	87.38	85.57
Mizoram	358978	330778	689756	329819	323746	653565	91.88	97.87	94.875
Nagaland	641282	568264	1209546	545156	515666	1060822	85.01	90.74	87.875
Orissa	16064146	15595590	31659736	3512891	3519323	7032214	21.87	22.57	22.22
Punjab	10778034	9503935	20281969	-	-	0	0	0	0
Rajasthan	23042780	20963210	44005990	2837014	2637867	5474881	12.31	12.58	12.445
Sikkim	216427	190030	406457	47504	43397	90901	21.95	22.84	22.395
Tamil Nadu	28298975	27559971	55858946	293012	281182	574194	1.04	1.02	1.03
Tripura	1417930	1339275	2757205	434225	419120	853345	30.62	31.29	30.955
U.P.	74036957	65075330	139112287	150420	137481	287901	0.2	0.21	0.205
W.B.	35510633	32567332	68077965	1938955	1869805	3808760	5.46	5.74	5.6
A & N Island	154369	126292	280661	13750	13020	26770	8.91	10.31	9.61
Chandigarh	358614	283401	642015	-	-	0	0	0	0
D & N Haveli	70953	67524	138477	54102	55278	109380	76.25	81.86	79.055
Daman & Diu	51595	49991	101586	6037	5651	11724	11.77	11.3	11.535

Contd...

1	2	3	4	5	6	7	8	9	10
Delhi	5155512	4265132	9429644	—	—	0	0	0	0
Lakshad-weep	26618	25098	51707	24160	24003	48163	90.77	95.67	93.22
Pondicherry	408081	399704	807785	—	—	0	0	0	0
Total	43923048#	407072230#	846303688#	34363271	33395109	67758380	7.82	8.20	8.01

* Project Population of Jammu & Kashmir.
# Including Projected population of Jammu & Kashmir. In Jammu & Kashmir, 1991 census was not conducted.

Appendix–2
Literacy Rates–1981 Scheduled Casts, Scheduled Tribes and All Communities

States	All Communities	SC	ST	All Communities Excluding SC/ST
India	36.23	21.28	16.35	41.3
Andhra Pradesh	29.94	17.65	7.82	33.91
Assam	-	-	-	-
Bihar	26.2	10.4	16.99	30.17
Gujarat	43.7	39.79	21.14	48.14
Haryana	36.14	20.15	-	30.9
Himachal Pradesh	42.48	31.5	25.93	47.37
Jammu & Kashmir	26.27	22.44	-	27.05
Karnataka	38.46	20.59	20.14	42.95
Kerala	70.42	55.96	31.79	75.32
Madhya Pradesh	27.87	18.97	10.68	36.15
Maharashtra	47.18	35.55	22.29	51.65
Manipur	41.35	33.63	39.74	42.11
Meghalaya	34.08	25.78	31.55	44.97
Nagaland	42.57	-	40.31	54.39
Orissa	34.23	22.41	13.96	44.22
Punjab	40.86	23.86	-	47.11
Rajasthan	24.38	14.04	10.27	29.31
Sikkim	34.05	28.06	33.13	34.84
Tamil Nadu	46.76	20.67	20.87	51.01
Tripura	42.12	33.89	23.07	53.93
Uttar Pradesh	27.16	14.96	20.45	30.45
West Bengal	40.94	24.37	13.21	43.12
A & N Island	51.56	-	31.11	54.31
Arunachal Pradesh	20.79	37.14	10.04	36.39
Chandigarh	64.78	37.07	-	69.33
D & N Haveli	26.67	51.2	18.86	64.41
Goa Daman & Diu	56.66	38.38	26.48	57.38
Delhi	61.54	39.3	-	66.44
Lakshadweep	55.07	-	53.13	84.57
Mizoram	59.88	84.44	59.63	63.53
Pondicherry	55.85	32.36	-	60.32

Appendix–3
Literacy Rates (Age 7 Years and Above)–Census 1991

States	*1991*		
	Persons	*Males*	*Females*
India	52.11	63.86	39.42
Andhra Pradesh	45.11	56.24	33.71
Arunachal Pradesh	41.22	51.1	29.37
Assam	53.42	62.34	43.7
Bihar	38.54	52.63	23.1
Goa	76.95	85.48	68.2
Gujarat	60.91	72.54	48.5
Haryana	55.33	67.85	40.94
Himachal Pradesh	63.54	74.57	52.46
Jammu & Kashmir	N.A	N.A	N.A
Karnataka	55.98	67.25	44.34
Kerala	90.59	94.45	86.93
Madhya Pradesh	43.45	57.43	28.39
Maharashtra	63.05	74.84	50.51
Manipur	60.96	72.98	48.64
Meghalaya	48.26	51.57	44.78
Mizoram	81.23	84.06	78.09
Nagaland	61.3	66.09	55.72
Orissa	48.55	62.37	34.4
Punjab	57.14	63.68	49.72
Rajasthan	38.81	55.07	28.84
Sikkim	56.53	64.34	47.23
Tamil Nadu	63.72	74.88	52.29
Tripura	60.39	70.08	50.01
Uttar Pradesh	41.71	55.35	26.02
West Bengal	57.72	67.24	47.15
Union Territory			
A & N Island	73.74	79.68	66.22
Chandigarh	78.73	82.67	73.61
D & N Haveli	39.45	52.07	26.1
Daman & Diu	73.58	85.67	61.38
Delhi	76.09	82.63	68.01
Lakshadweep	79.23	87.06	70.88
Pondicherry	74.91	83.91	65.79

Source: The 1991 Census has not yet been conducted in Jammu and Kashmir.
The figures are as per projections prepared by the Standing Committee of Experts on population Projections, October 1989.
N.A.: Stands for not available.

Appendix–4
Literacy Rates of Scheduled Castes and Scheduled Tribes–1991 Census

State Union Territory	*Scheduled Caste*			*Scheduled Tribes*		
	Persons	*Male*	*Female*	*Persons*	*Male*	*Female*
India	37.41	49.41	23.76	29.6	40.65	18.19
Andhra Pradesh	3.59	41.88	20.92	17.16	25.25	8.68
Arunachal Pradesh	57.27	66.25	41.42	34.45	44.00	24.94
Assam	53.94	63.88	42.99	49.16	58.93	38.98
Bihar	19.49	30.64	7.07	26.78	38.4	14.75
Goa	58.73	69.55	47.51	42.91	54.43	29.01
Gujarat	61.07	75.47	45.54	36.45	48.25	24.2
Haryana	39.22	52.06	24.15	0	0	0
Himachal Pradesh	53.2	64.9	41.02	47.09	62.74	31.18
Jammu & Kashmir	0	0	0	0	0	0
Karnataka	38.06	49.69	25.95	36.01	47.95	23.57
Kerala	79.66	85.22	74.31	57.22	63.38	51.07
Madhya Pradesh	35.08	50.51	18.11	21.54	32.16	10.73
Maharashtra	56.46	70.45	41.59	36.79	49.09	24.03
Manipur	56.44	65.28	47.41	53.63	62.39	44.48
Meghalaya	44.27	54.56	31.19	46.71	49.78	43.63
Mizoram	77.92	77.54	81.25	82.71	86.66	70.7
Nagaland	0	0	0	60.59	66.27	54.51
Orissa	36.78	52.42	20.74	22.31	34.44	10.21
Punjab	41.09	49.82	30.03	0	0	0
Rajasthan	26.29	42.38	8.31	19.44	33.29	4.42
Sikkim	51.03	58.69	42.77	59.01	66.8	50.37
Tamil Nadu	46.74	58.36	34.89	27.89	35.25	20.23
Tripura	56.66	67.25	45.45	40.37	52.88	27.34
Uttar Pradesh	26.85	40.8	10.69	35.7	49.95	19.86
West Bengal	26.85	40.8	10.69	35.7	49.95	19.86
A & N Island	0	0	0	56.62	64.16	48.74
Chandigarh	55.44	64.74	43.54	0	0	0
D & N Haveli	77.64	88.03	66.61	28.21	40.75	15.94
Daman & Diu	79.18	91.85	67.62	52.91	63.58	41.49
Delhi	57.6	68.77	43.82	0	0	0
Lakshadweep	0	0	0	80.58	89.5	71.72
Pondicherry	56.26	66.1	46.28	0	0	0

Appendix–5
Enrolment of Scheduled Tribes at Primary Stage (Class I-V)

(Figure in '000)

Year	*Enrolment of All Categories*			*ST Enrolment*			*% of ST Enrolment*	
	Boys	*Girls*	*Total*	*Boys*	*Girls*	*Total*	*Boys*	*Girls*
1980-81	44576	28112	72688	3133	1527	4660	7.03	5.43
1981-82	44976	28587	73563	3293	1628	4921	7.32	5.69
1982-83	47276	29763	77039	3540	1791	5331	7.49	6.02
1983-84	49322	31775	81097	3765	1964	5729	7.63	6.18
1984-85	50739	33193	83932	3846	2102	5948	7.58	6.33
1985-86	51732	34733	86465	4174	2406	6580	8.07	6.93
1986-87	53850	36143	89993	4150	2407	6557	7.71	6.66
1987-88	55169	37775	92944	4606	2623	7229	8.35	6.94
1988-89	57143	38597	95740	4837	2759	7596	8.46	7.15
1989-90	57732	39587	97319	4948	2850	7798	8.57	7.20
1990-91	58095	41024	99119	4958	2911	7869	8.53	7.0
1991-92	59218	42359	101577	4951	3082	8033	8.36	7.28

Source: Selected Educational Statistics.

Appendix–6
Enrolment of Scheduled Tribes at Middle Stage (Class VI-VIII)

(Figure in '000)

Year	*Enrolment of All Categories*			*ST Enrolment*			*% of ST Enrolment*	
	Boys	*Girls*	*Total*	*Boys*	*Girls*	*Total*	*Boys*	*Girls*
1980-81	13278	6568	19846	537	205	742	4.04	3.12
1981-82	13971	7084	21055	603	232	835	4.31	3.28
1982-83	14689	7524	22213	663	263	926	4.51	3.50
1983-84	16500	8497	24997	758	299	1057	4.59	3.52
1984-85	17084	9069	26153	866	350	1216	5.07	3.86
1985-86	18132	9994	28126	983	390	1373	4.93	3.90
1986-87	18543	10237	28780	988	446	1434	5.33	4.36
1987-88	19208	10706	29914	1008	447	1455	5.25	4.17
1988-89	19752	11188	30940	1037	466	1503	5.25	4.17
1989-90	20368	11820	32188	1075	494	1569	5.28	4.18
1990-91	20844	12439	33283	1131	576	1707	5.43	4.63
1991-92	21449	12997	34446	1214	580	1794	5.66	4.47

Source: Selected Educational Statistics.

Appendix–7
Enrolment of Scheduled Tribes at High/Post Basic Stage (Class IX-X)

(Figure in '000)

Year	Enrolment of All Categories			ST Enrolment			% of ST Enrolment	
	Boys	Girls	Total	Boys	Girls	Total	Boys	Girls
1980-81	4953	2189	7142	193	73	266	3.90	3.36
1981-82	6044	2748	8792	211	81	292	3.50	2.96
1982-83	6650	3063	9713	233	95	328	3.50	3.10
1983-84	6742	3003	9745	237	91	328	3.52	3.03
1984-85	7218	3336	10554	267	110	377	3.70	3.30
1985-86	8029	3588	11617	303	136	439	3.77	3.79
1986-87	8622	3851	12473	292	112	404	3.39	2.90
1987-88	8540	3913	12453	330	128	458	3.86	3.26
1988-89	8906	4243	13149	383	177	560	4.30	4.17
1989-90	9303	4486	13789	423	200	623	4.54	4.45
1990-91	9678	4862	14540	425	188	613	4.39	3.87
1991-92	9979	5050	15029	440	201	641	4.41	3.98

Source: Selected Education Statistics.

Appendix–8
Enrolment of Scheduled Tribes at Senior Secondary Stage

(Figure in '000)

Year	Enrolment of All Categories			ST Enrolment			% of ST Enrolment	
	Boys	Girls	Total	Boys	Girls	Total	Boys	Girls
1980-81	3061	1077	4138	53	10	63	1.73	0.93
1981-82	2965	1120	4085	54	12	66	1.82	1.07
1982-83	3124	1187	4311	69	15	84	2.21	1.26
1983-84	3668	1434	5102	81	18	99	2.21	1.26
1984-85	3916	1601	5517	119	25	144	3.04	1.78
1985-86	3780	1573	5353	117	29	146	3.10	1.84
1986-87	3561	1535	5096	121	32	153	3.40	2.08
1987-88	3738	1669	5407	116	37	153	3.10	2.22
1988-89	3676	1696	5372	118	38	156	3.21	2.24
1989-90	4220	1961	6181	130	44	174	3.08	2.24
1990-91	4326	2032	6358	142	50	192	3.28	2.46
1991-92	4205	1994	6199	150	52	202	3.57	2.61

Source: Selected Education Statistics.

Appendix–9
Drop-Out Rates of Scheduled Tribes 1989-90

State/UT	*Primary I-V*			*Middle I-VIII*			*Secondary I-X*		
	Boys	*Girls*	*Total*	*Boys*	*Girls*	*Total*	*Boys*	*Girls*	*Total*
Andhra Pradesh	63.70	68.97	65.66	84.21	90.14	86.42	88.83	92.77	90.34
Arunachal Pradesh	64.77	59.92	63.01	75.60	79.35	76.95	80.49	89.30	83.37
Assam	71.90	70.71	71.40	66.06	68.17	66.95	86.15	77.21	68.18
Bihar	69.51	77.14	72.19	84.53	88.65	85.94	90.30	93.64	91.42
Goa*	83.79	95.36	89.91	96.63	97.21	96.89	-	-	-
Gujarat	55.61	68.50	61.21	77.70	84.03	80.34	85.68	90.10	87.50
Haryana	-	-	-	-	-	-	-	-	-
Himachal Pradesh	24.39	28.16	25.89	33.97	46.97	38.65	55.88	65.33	59.27
Jammu & Kashmir	-	-	-	-	-	-	-	-	-
Karnataka	35.80	45.77	40.18	59.61	70.07	64.03	69.06	80.52	73.97
Kerala	21.19	16.37	18.94	45.30	37.94	41.82	72.94	67.39	70.43
Madhya Pradesh	47.12	59.69	51.80	70.75	80.85	73.79	83.26	93.18	86.20
Maharashtra	57.89	68.83	62.60	73.00	83.04	77.10	83.34	90.94	86.18
Manipur	77.20	78.09	77.61	84.87	85.82	85.30	85.12	86.79	85.88
Meghalaya	73.21	81.76	77.40	72.85	73.09	72.96	91.63	93.37	92.47
Mizoram	61.88	62.70	62.28	31.17	24.66	28.08	75.91	78.49	77.17
Nagaland	34.94	35.70	35.90	64.41	58.67	61.99	79.64	83.86	81.53
Orissa	75.41	77.74	76.19	83.99	85.72	84.59	87.34	92.69	89.23
Punjab	-	-	-	-	-	-	-	-	-
Rajasthan	66.77	79.07	69.23	72.34	86.07	74.44	83.09	94.33	84.72
Sikkim	66.99	57.19	62.87	70.89	62.25	67.19	86.78	88.83	87.64
Tamil Nadu	42.61	54.31	47.95	51.45	59.72	54.90	75.47	77.13	76.15
Tripura	73.96	78.14	75.86	84.75	88.17	86.17	90.83	93.44	91.81
Uttar Pradesh	41.73	51.60	45.14	55.83	63.69	58.10	79.30	83.88	80.68
West Bengal	63.76	67.55	65.03	83.27	87.03	84.39	92.35	92.74	92.47
A & N Island	8.95	13.33	11.00	35.20	38.13	36.50	42.76	64.31	52.97
Chandigarh	-	-	-	-	-	-	-	-	-
D & N Haveli	41.26	57.58	47.60	69.67	79.74	74.04	87.62	93.01	89.94
Daman & Diu	-	-	-	-	-	-	-	-	-
Delhi	-	-	-	-	-	-	-	-	-
Lakshadweep	-	10.94	10.94	29.72	50.41	39.61	71.11	73.78	72.34
Pondicherry	-	-	-	-	-	-	-	-	-

* Includes Daman & Diu.

Appendix–10
Gross Enrolment Ratios SC/ST

Classes and Age Group	*Scheduled Castes*			*Scheduled Tribes*		
	Boys	*Girls*	*Total*	*Boys*	*Girls*	*Total*
1980-81						
I-V (6-11 years)	105.4	57.8	82.2	94.02	45.9	70.0
VI-VIII (11-14 years)	41.4	16.2	29.1	28.2	10.8	19.5
1985-86						
I-V (6-11 years)	166.6	73.2	95.5	113.22	68.8	91.6
VI-VIII (11-14 years)	57.8	26.2	42.5	41.3	19.2	30.6
1990-91						
I-V (6-11 years)	122.68	80.6	102.21	126.78	78.6	103.35
VI-VIII (11-14 years)	61.4	33.28	47.71	51.33	27.5	39.72
1991-92						
I-V (6-11 years)	121.4	83.6	103.0	125.6	82.6	104.7
VI-VIII (11-14 years)	68.9	36.0	52.9	54.1	27.3	41.1
1992-93						
I-V (6-11 years)	127.99	98.18	110.58	126.71	88.64	108.19
VI-VIII (11-14 years)	75.07	44.04	59.97	58.54	32.04	45.64
1993-94						
I-V (6-11 years)	123.33	91.15	107.81	123.9	88.8	108.97
VI-VIII (11-14 years)	74.21	45.01	60.13	60.17	34.91	47.99

Appendix–11
Estimated Population of Scheduled Tribe-School Going Groups
(as on 1.3.1994)

State/UT	*6-11 Years*			*11-14 Years*		
	Total	*Boys*	*Girls*	*Total*	*Boys*	*Girls*
Andhra Pradesh	4945	2379	2566	4411	1258	3153
Arunachal Pradesh	786	391	395	431	218	213
Assam	3694	1893	1801	2085	1070	1015
Bihar	9717	5069	4648	5307	2760	2547
Goa	12	6	6	8	4	4
Gujarat	7149	3690	3459	4080	2105	1975
Haryana	0	0	0	0	0	0
Himachal Pradesh	275	137	138	162	81	81
Jammu & Kashmir	0	0	0	0	0	0
Karnataka	2506	1290	1216	1463	750	713

Contd...

State/UT	*6-11 Years*			*11-14 Years*		
	Total	*Boys*	*Girls*	*Total*	*Boys*	*Girls*
Kerala	304	154	150	184	93	91
Madhya Pradesh	19864	10317	9547	10996	5704	592
Maharashtra	8428	4350	4078	4783	2470	2313
Manipur	668	346	322	286	186	100
Meghalaya	1892	945	947	1090	538	552
Mizoram	798	411	387	494	252	242
Nagaland	1248	634	614	748	381	367
Orissa	8901	4353	4548	4951	2426	2525
Punjab	0	0	0	0	0	0
Rajasthan	7320	3761	3559	4084	2128	1956
Sikkim	148	75	73	81	42	39
Tamil Nadu	592	304	288	373	191	182
Tripura	872	440	432	484	248	236
Uttar Pradesh	376	199	177	211	112	99
West Bengal	4597	2394	2203	2762	1422	1340
A & N Island	58	28	30	29	15	14
Chandigarh	0	0	0	0	0	0
D & N Haveli	133	70	63	69	41	28
Daman & Diu	0	0	0	0	0	0
Delhi	0	0	0	0	0	0
Lakshadweep	56	28	28	29	15	14
Pondicherry	0	0	0	0	0	0

20

Conclusion

Introduction

Imparting education to tribal children is a challenging task in the present scenario, as they have to grow, acclimatizing themselves, in the changing world of new livelihood patterns and lifestyles. The personal growth of tribal children is beset in developing their abilities and faculties to cope up psychologically as well as culturally in the new social milieu. They have to adopt learning through classroom teaching, contrary to the practice of learning their subsistence patterns and value-systems by participating in their culture and gaining knowledge by experience. The medium of education for tribal children in their pristine environments is lived experience, as a member of a social group.

It is, therefore, imperative for the institutions implementing educational programmes to tribal children to give priority in developing suitable mechanisms of reorienting the tribal children to classroom education, and to the realities of the changes into which they are being drawn into. As a matter of fact, the tribal societies and tribal children are already well entrenched in the transition into the realm of tribal-rural-urban, matrix and modern consumerism.

Classroom education for tribal children is crossing a threshold of learning as a practice of interaction with the natural world to a system of textbook learning. This process has already made much headway in the tribal areas. But this kind of education has not evoked the expected enthusiasm among the tribal societies, apparently because it is not emotionally satisfying. Talking to tribal parents, one could sense an obtuse feeling that medium of modern education is a withdrawal of mediation of culture in shaping their life worlds.

As mention has already been made, children in these traditional societies, as a routine, live in harmony with their environments through culturally encoded norms of hands-on learning and gain practical knowledge. Meeting their survival needs is interwoven with tapping the resource zones in their respective ecosystems with a choice and freedom of managing community resources.

Traditional Patterns *vis-à-vis* Modern Education

If we look at the ground realities in the context of education of tribal children, it becomes obvious that it is linked to economic equity, which cannot be achieved by mere classroom prescriptions. Attempts at even partially fulfilling the goal of economic equity, bring us back to the enterprise of involving tribal children in making best use of their traditional knowledge in harnessing the resources and biodiversity and sustainable management of environments and livelihoods. The grassroot level of education of tribal children needs a combination of three strands: *(a)* their traditional knowledge of livelihoods; *(b)* imparting skills to make them partners in sustainable management of environments; and *(c)* modern education through primary and secondary schooling, to bring awareness of the world around them and to derive benefit from the new opportunities that are being made available.

The linkage between traditional knowledge of livelihoods and learning can be seen by considering some of the tribal societies in Andhra Pradesh. These communities are hunter-gatherers (Chenchu, Yanadi, Yerukula, Boya); marine fishermen (Voda Balije, Pallekaru, Besta, Jalari); shifting cultivators (Konda Reddi, Kondadora, Konda Kapu, Koya, Khond, Savara, Bhagata, etc.); and pastoralists (Golla, Kuruva, Kuruma). The Gonds (and also Kolams) of Adilabad though have now taken to settled and plains, agriculture, they originally practiced shifting cultivation. In these societies, the process of learning for a child has an orientation to the traditional practices of survival of that group to which it belongs. For instance, children in hunting-gathering societies learn about the food resources in their natural world (e.g. a variety of forest plant foods such as fruits, berries, nuts, flowers, tubers and yams, gums, mushrooms; insects; honey and habits and habitats of big and small game, birds and fishes) and they acquire the skills of hunting and fishing (using nets, a variety of traps, bows and arrows), and gathering, as a customary tradition of eking out their living. In the pastoral societies, children learn cattle and sheep/goat herding techniques such as tending of herds, transhumance to pastures and herbal veterinary practices by participating in the pursuit along with the elders. Children in shifting cultivator and peasant societies, likewise, learn about seasonality of crops, sowing and cropping patterns, weeding, control of pests and grain storage from the elders.

Learning in these societies is a behavioural response guided by culture. Culture is institutionalized knowledge, a method of information processing, and also a mechanism in situating individuals within its group and also situating different social groups within a larger social matrix. In these tribal, pastoral and agricultural groups kinship relations and age and sex categories also pattern behaviour. The livelihood norms are cultural traditions with a past-present continuum. Some of the important aspects, which a tribal child learns as a member of a given society, are as follows: Land use pattern, organization of space, territorial divisions and markers. Resource zones, communal sharing and management of resource zones. Social construction of landscapes such as forested, rural and urban, sacral and spatial mobility. Settlement systems, domestic architecture, organization of domestic space and sacral space. Procurement of raw materials and production of artifacts, arts and crafts (material culture). Rituals associated with rights of passage and village rituals. Community participation with reciprocal exchange of foods, goods and services.

Development and Education

Education of children in these tribal societies is a long-term strategy that has been going hand-in-hand with a multitude of tribal development programmes. The guiding principle of state's intervention in development of these communities is poverty alleviation; improving housing, hygiene and sanitation; health care; and education.

A wide spectrum of the tribal groups is becoming increasingly aware of the developmental projects and educational programmes and is expecting proper implementation of these schemes for their benefit. They are adjusting themselves to be partners in a system of hierarchical social order.

Empowerment of women and youth due to the encouragement of progressive bureaucrats has given successful results but such instances are not many. In some districts, women through Sahayaka Sanghams/Self-Help Groups are playing an important role not only in income generation and decision-making but also in literacy programmes.

Elders and youth have come to perceive that literacy and education are important for their future. But they are in a dilemma and ask the question 'in which way the modern education (primary/secondary) can contribute for the betterment of their livelihoods? To answer such predicaments it might be appropriate to include, in the curriculum, the socio-cultural patterns of the 'tribal cultures' as well as those of the 'others' whose mode of 'education' is being imparted in the tribal schools, for an interactive exchange in the sphere of education. Further educational measures should be addressed in a long-term holistic approach against the background of livelihoods, poverty alleviation and the ongoing processes of social transformation and change in the tribal societies.

Strategies for Consideration

Educational programmes should create means for income generation. Promotion of small-scale enterprises, processing or manufacturing units in the tribal areas involving the participation of the concerned social groups, especially youth, would be of great use. Women's Self-Help Groups have demonstrated the potential of such an approach.

These societies have a long history of manufacturing items based on forest resources, and barter and exchange of these goods with other groups. Some of these items consist of raw materials for housing; agricultural implements; baskets made of bamboo, reeds, cane and wicker work for household storage, and bins for grain storage; fuel woods; mats; broomsticks; barks for dying and tanning; nuts and seeds for oil processing; gums; honey; lacquer; herbal medicinal products. These items (which fall under the category of Non-Timber Forest Produce) are procured and marketed by the Girijan Co-operatives and middlemen. Children along with elders take part in the collection and supply of these items, which is a contract labour.

These societies have traditional knowledge systems of the use of endemic flora including herbal medicines. Educational inputs coupled with financial support to these groups, by making them stakeholders in the cultivation of such plants and procurement of forest-based raw materials, can be a strategy for development of small scale industries and local entrepreneurial skills. The meaningfulness of modern education and literacy would be appreciated when it is linked with opportunities for income earning.

Bibliography

Abraham, L., 2004, 'Building Cultural Capital to Combat Poverty: Globalisation, Education and the Urban Poor', See, R. Ruzicka, J.H. Ballantine, Roman Jose (Ed.), *Education Participation Globalisation*, Conference Proceedings, Prague, 2004 Conference.

Achar, *Draft Report on Tribal Development through Education in Karnataka, 2002*, Mysore, Central Institute of Indian Languages (CIIL).

Acharya, P., 1981, 'Politics of Primary Education in West Bengal: The Case of Sahaj Path', *Economic and Political Weekly*, Vol. 16, No. 24.

Acharya, P., 1987, 'Education: Politics and Social Structures', In: R. Ghosh and M. Zachariach (Eds.), *Education and the Process of Change*, New Delhi, Sage Publishers.

Acharya, P., 1988, 'Bengali, Bhadralok and Educational Development in Nineteenth Century Bengal', in S. Shukla and R. Kaul (Eds.), *Education Development and Underdevelopment*, New Delhi: Sage Publishers.

Acharya, P., 1988, 'Is Macaulay Still Our Guru?' *Economic and Political Weekly*, Vol. 23, Issue 22, May 1988.

Acharya, S., 2001, 'Access to Primary Education: Rural Maharashtra and Madhya Pradesh', In A. Vaidyanathan and P.R. Gopinathan Nair (Eds.), *Elementary Education in Rural India: A Grassroots View*, New Delhi: Sage Publishers.

Action Plan for the Education of Tribal Children of Karnataka 1996-2001, Mysore, CIIL.

Agarwal, S., 2003, 'CINI ASHA: Building Bridges for Urban Children', in V. Ramachandran (Ed.), *Getting Children Back to School: Case Studies in Primary Education*, New Delhi, Sage Publication.

Aggarwal, J.C. and Aggarwal, S.P., 1982, *Role of UNESCO in Education*, New Delhi, Vikas Publishing House Pvt. Ltd.

Aggarwal, Y., and Sibou, S., 1994, *Educating Scheduled Castes: A Study of Inter District and Intracast Differentials*. New Delhi: NIEPA.

Ahmad, I., 2003, Educational Development of Minorities in India, In J.B.G. Tilak (Ed.), *Education, Society and Development: National and International Perspective*, New Delhi, NUEPA.

Aikara, J., 1997, *Learner Achievement in Primary School*, Mumbai: Tata Institute of Social Sciences (TISS), Memeograph.

Aiyappan, A., *Report on the Socio-Economic Conditions of the Aboriginal Tribes of the Province of Madras*, New Delhi, Government of India, Management of Publication, 1948.

Aiyappan, A., *Report on the Socio-Economic Conditions of the Aboriginal Tribes of the Province of Madras*, 1948, New Delhi, Government of India.

Alexander, R., 2000, *Culture and Pedagogy: International Comparisons in Primary Education*, Oxford: Blackwell.

Amar Kumar Singh, "Status of the Tribals in India", *Social Change, Vol. 23, No. 2&3*, 1993.

Ambasht, N.K., "Universalisation of Elementary Education, Constitution and Right to Education", *Journal of Indian Education, Vol. 19, No. 6, March 1994*, NCERT.

Ambast, N.K., 1970, *A Critical Study of Tribal Education*, New Delhi, C. Chand and Company.

Ambast, N.K., 1970, *Reducing Educational Wastage in Tribal Areas*, New Delhi, NCERT.

Ambast, N.K., 1986, *An Indepth Analysis of Ashram Schools*, New Delhi, NIEPA.

Anand, G., 1998, *Ashram Schools*, New Delhi, Concept Publishers.

Ananda G., 1994, *Ashram Schools in Andhra Pradesh – A Case Study of Chenchus of Nallamalai Hills*, New Delhi, Commonwealth Publishers.

Annamalai, E., "Tribal Development and Education", http://www.google.com.

Annowitz, Stanley and Henry Giroux, 1987, *Education Under Seize: The Conservative, Liberal and Radical Debate over Schooling*, London, Routledge & Kegan Paul.

Apple, Michael, W., 1979, *Ideology and Curriculum*, London, Routledge & Kegan Paul.

Apte, J.S., 1960, "Talwada Ashram School – An Experiment in Tribal Education, *Vanyajati, Vol. VIII, No. 52*.

Artis, E., C. Doobay and K. Lyons, 2003, Economic, Social and Cultural Rights for Dalits in India: Case Study on Primary Education in Gujarat, Paper presented at the workshop on Human Rights: From Grassroots courage to international influence, Princeton University, January 2003.

Arya Shachi, 1998, *Tribal Activism*, Jaipur, Rawat Publications.

Ashok Kumar, 1991, *Current Trends in Indian Education*, New Delhi, Ashish Publishing House.

Ashram Schools, *Vanyajati, Vol. VI, No. 3, July 1958*, pp. 93-95.

Austin, 1982, *Evaluating Your Agency's Programme*, New Delhi, Sage Publications.

Bairathi, S., 1991, *State of Education, Tribal Culture, Economy and Helath*, Jaipur: Rawat Publications.

Balagopalan, S., 2005, 'An Ideal School and the Schooled Ideal: Education at the Margins', In Chopra, R., and Jeffery, P., (Eds.), *Educational Regimes in Contemporary, India*, New Delhi: Sage Publishers.

Balagopalan, S., 2003, 'Neither Studies for the Home nor for the Fields: Inclusion, Formal Schooling and the Adivasi Child', in R. Subramanian *et al.* (Eds.), *Education Inclusion and Exclusion: Indian and South African Perspectives, IDS Bulletin, Vol. 34, No. 1, January*, Sussex: Institute of Development Studies.

Banerji, R., 1997, 'Why Don't Chlidren Complete Primary School?' A Case Study of a Low-Income Neighbourhood in Delhi, *Economic and Political Weekly*, Vol. 32, No. 32.

Banjerji, R., 2000, Poverty and primary schooling: Field studies from Mumbai and Delhi, *Economic and Political Weekly, Vol. 15, No. 10*, March 2000.

Bapat, N.V., "A Few Thoughts on Tribal Education", *Vanyajati, Vol. XII, No. 4, 1964*, pp. 190-194.

Bapat, N.V., "Tribal Education – A Problem", *Vanyajati, Vol. IX, No. 1, January 1961*, pp. 37-39.

Bara, J., 1997, 'Western Education and Rise of New Identity, Mundas and Orans of Chotanagpur', *Economic and Political Weekly*, Vol. 32, No. 15.

Barnhardt, Ray and Harrison Barbara, "Developing Tribal Education, Strategies in Indigenous Communities", *The Australian Journal of Educational Studies*, October 1993, pp. 1-15.

Basu, M.N., "Suggestions for the Educational Plan of the Aboriginal People of India", *Vanyajati, Vol. IX, No. 3, 1961*, pp. 123-126.

Beeker, H.S., 1961, Schools and Systems of Stratification in Halsey, A.H. *et al.* (Eds.), *Education, Economy and Society*, New York, The Free Press.

Behera, D.K., *et al.*, 1999, *Contemporary Society: Tribal Studies, Vol. 4, Social Concept*, New Delhi: Concept Publications.

Behura, N.K., "Tribes of India: Planned Development", *Social Change, Vol. 23, No. 2 & 3, 1993.*

Behura, N.K., Panigrahi Nilakantha, 2006, *Tribals and the Indian Constitution*, New Delhi, Rawat Publications.

Bernstein, Basil, 1961, Social Class and Linguistic Development: A Theory of Social Learning in Halsey, A.H. *et al.* (Eds), *Education, Economy and Society*, New York: The Free Press.

Bernt Sen, M., 1987, "Obstacles on the path to school: Educational Problems of Backward Class Children", *New Quest, July-August.*

Beteille, A., 1983, 'The Backward Classes and the New Social Order', in A. Beteille, *The Ideal of Natural Inequality and other Essays*, New Delhi, Oxford University Press.

Beteille, A., 1992, *Society and Politics in India, Essays in a Comparative Perspective*, Delhi: OUP.

Beteille, A., 2000, "The Scheduled Castes: An Inter-Regional Perspective", in Andre Beteille (Ed.)., *Journal of Indian School of Political Economy, Vol. 12, Nos. 3 & 4.*

Betelle, A., 1983, *The Idea of Natural Inequality and Other Essays*, New Delhi, Oxford University Press.

Bhanage, N.P., *Tribal Commissions and Committees*, 1993, Bombay, Himalaya Publishing House.

Bhatnagar, G.S., 1972, *Education and Social Change*, Calcutta, The Minerva Associates.

Bhattacharya, S., 2002, 'Introduction: An Approach to Education and Inequality', in S. Bhattacharya (Ed.), *Education and the Dispriviledged: Nineteenth and Twentieth Century India*, Hyderabad, Orient Longman.

Bhatty, K., 1988, 'Educational Deprivation in India: A Survey of Field Investigations, Part I and II, *EPW, Vol. 33, Nos. 27 and 28.*

Bhatty, Kiran, "Educational Deprivation in India – A Survey of Field Investigations", *Economic and Political Weekly, Vol. XXXII, No. 28, July 11, 1998.*

Bhowmick, K.L. (Ed.), *Current Anthropological and Archeological Perspectives (11 Vols.)*, 1988, New Delhi, Inter India Publications.

Bhowmick, K.L. (Ed.), *Some Aspects of Indian Anthropology*, 1980, Calcutta, Subernarekha.

Bhowmick, P.K., 1999, *Tribal Literacy in West Bengal*, Kolkata: R.N. Bhattacharya Publications.

Bibhuti, Mishra, "Reorienting Tribal Education", *The Hindu, 3 August 2004.*

Biligiri, H.S., "Problems of Tribal Languages in India" in *Language and Society in India*, Simla, *IIAS, Vol. 8, 1969*, pp. 245-250.

Biman K. Das Gupta and Ajit K. Danda, 1984, *Tribal Education in India*, Anthropological Survey of India, Ministry of Education and Culture, Government of India, Calcutta.

Binod C. Agarwal, Sudhakar Rao, N. and Gurivi Reddy, P.C., 1985, *Yanadi Response to Change An Attempt in Action Anthropology*, New Delhi, Concept Publishing Company.

Birley, Derek and Dufton Anne, 1971, *An Equal Change: Equalities and Inequalities of Educational Opportunity*, London, Routledge and Kegan Paul.

Bondi, L. and Mathews, M.H. (Eds.), *Education and Society: Studies in Politics, Sociology and Geography of Education*, 1988, London, Routledge.

Boralingaiah, H.C., Prabhakar, A.S. (Ed.), "Budakattu Adhyayana" (*Tribal Studies – Kannada), Vol. 1, No. 1, 2003*, Hampi, Kannada University.

Bose, A.B., "Problems of Educational Development of Scheduled Tribes", *Man in India, Vol. 50, No. 1, March 1970*, pp. 26-50.

Bose, S.K., 1986, *Report on Ashram Schools in Bihar*, New Delhi, NIEPA.

Brunen, J.S., "Poverty and Childhood", *Oxford Review of Education, 1975, Vol. 1*, pp. 47-50.

Buch, M.B. (Ed.), *Fourth Survey of Research in Education, 1983-88*, Baroda, SERD.

Buckman, Peter (Ed.), 1975, *Education Without Schools*, Calcutta, Rupa.

Burman Roy, B.K., "Tribal Identity, Globalisation and Planned Development", *The Eastern Anthropologist, Vol. 56, Nos. 2-4, 2003*, pp. 177-194.

Census 2001 – *Districtwise Details of Schedule Tribe Population and Literacy in Karnataka*, Statistical Institute, Bangalore.

Chakravarthi Moyna and Singhrol, C.S., "Problems of Tribal Education – A Key to Development", *Man and Life, Vol. 14, Nos. 1-2, 1988*, pp. 91-96.

Chalam, K.S., 1988, *Education and Weaker Sections*, New Delhi, Inter India Publications.

Chalam, K.S., 1993, *Educational Policy for Human Resources Development*, Jaipur, Rawat Publications.

Chalam, K.S., 2000, 'Impact of Liberalisation on Tribal Development in India', In P.G. Jogdand (Ed.), *New Economy Policy and Dalits*, Jaipur, Rawat Publications.

Charsley, S.R., and Karanth, G.K., (Eds.), 1998, *Challenging Untouchability: Dablit Initiative and Experience from Karnataka*, Sage Publishers, New Delhi.

Chattapodhyay, K. 1978, *Tribalisation in India*, New Delhi, Vikas Publishing House Pvt. Ltd.

Chatterjee, S.K., 2000, *Educational Development of Scheduled Castes: Looking Ahead*, New Delhi: Gyan Publishing House.

Chattopadhayay, K.P., 1955, *Education: Adivasi*, The Publication Division, Government of India.

Chattopadhyay, K., "Tribal Education", *Man in India, Vol. 33, No. 1*, pp. 1-18.

Chattopadhyay, K., 1978, *Tribalism in India*, New Delhi, Vikas Publishing House.

Chaudhari Maitreyi, "Factors Influencing Tribal Sex Ratio in India", *Political Economy Journal of India, Vol. 5, No. 1*, pp. 47-58.

Chaudhary, N.D., "Dropout and Stagnation in a Tribal Situation", *The Education Quarterly, Vol. 3, 1974*, pp. 26-33.

Chauhan, Brijraj, "Scheduled Caste and Scheduled Tribe", *Economic and Political Weekly, Vol. IV, No. 4, 1969*.

Chaurasia, B.P., 1990, *Scheduled Castes and Scheduled Tribes in India*, Allahabad Chugh Publications.

Chitnis, S., and Velaskar, P., 1988, *Education in Maharashtra; Strengths and Weaknesses*, Mumbai, TISS, Memeograph.

Chitnis, Suma and Naidu, U., 1981, *Identity of Scheduled Caste Students*, Mumbai, TISS, Memeograph.

Chitnis, Suma, 1981, *A Long Way to Go*, Surat, Centre for Social Studies, Mumbai, Allied Publishers.

Chitnis, Suma, 1982, Dropout and low pupil achievement among the urban poor in Bombay, *Paper Prepared for the International Labour Office, Geneva, 30th April, 1982*, Mimeograph.

Chitra Shiva Kumar, 1982, *Education Social Inequality and Social Change in Karnataka*, Delhi, Hindustan Publishing Corporation.

Choudhary, E. (Ed.), 1982, *Tribal Development in India: Problems and Prospects*, Delhi, Inter India Publications.

Clarke, P., 2001, *Teaching and Learning: The Culture of Pedagogy*, New Delhi, Sage Publishers.

Clarke, P., and Fuller, B., 1997, 'Life in Indian Classrooms: The Influence of Culture and Caste', in Krishnakumar, (Ed.), *Studies in Classroom Processes and School Effectiveness at Primary Stage*, NCERT.

Cohen, A.D., 1975, *A Sociolinguistic Approach to Bilingual Education*, Mass, Newbury.

Cohen, S.A., 1969, *Teach Them all to Read Theory, Methods and Materials for Teaching the Disadvantaged*, New York, Random House.

Corner Trevor, 1984, *Education in Multicultural Societies*, London, Groom Helm.

Corson, D., 1993, *Language, Minority Education and Gender, Linking Social Justice and Power*, Toronto, Ontario Institute for Studies in Education.

Cosin, B.R. (Ed.), 1972, *Education, Structure and Society*, Harmondsworth, Penguin Books.

D'Souza, S.J., Lawrence, ND, *Gonds in Karnataka*, Mangalore, UNESCO Co-action Learning Centre.

D'Souza, S.J., Lawrence, ND, *Hakkipikkies*, Mangalore, UNESCO Co-action Learning Centre.

D'Souza, S.J., Lawrence, ND, *Harana Shikaris*, Mangalore, UNESCO Co-action Learning Centre.

D'Souza, S.J., Lawrence, ND, *Jenu Kurubas and Kadu Kurubas*, Mangalore, UNESCO Co-Action Learning Centre.

D'Souza, S.J., Lawrence, ND, *Lambanies in Karnataka*, Mangalore, UNESCO Co-action Learning Centre.

D'Souza, S.J., Lawrence, ND, *Malekudiyas – A Primitive Tribe of South India*, Mangalore, UNESCO Co-action Learning Centre.

D'Souza, S.J., Lawrence, ND, *Maragammas*, Mangalore, UNESCO Co-action Learning Centre.

D'Souza, S.J., Lawrence, ND, *Namma Bhase (Koraga Language)*, Mangalore, UNESCO Co-action Learning Centre.

D'Souza, S.J., Lawrence, ND, *Sudugadu Siddhas*, Mangalore, UNESCO Co-action Learning Centre.

D'Souza, S.J., Lawrence, ND, *Vaddars in Karnataka*, Mangalore, UNESCO Co-action Learning Centre.

Dangle, A. (Ed.), 1992, *Poisoned Bread*, Mumbai, Orient Longman.

Das Gupta, N.K., "Problems of Tribal Education and the Santhals", 1964, *Bharatiya Adimajati Sevak Sangh*, pp. 39-45.

Das, A.R., Naidu, R.V.K. and Sreedhar, N., "Ashram Schools and the Education of Tribal Children", *Man and Life, Vol. 29, Nos. 1-2*, 2003, pp. 83-94.

Das, A.R., Naidu, R.V.K. and Sreedhar, N., "Who Joins Ashram Schools"? *Anthropologist, Vol. 5, No. 3, 2003*, pp. 155-159.

Das, Nityananda, "Reorientation of Ashram School Education", 1963, *Adivasi*, pp. 14-20.

Das, V., *Creating an Alternative Paradigm, Agragamee's Experience in Education in the Tribal Districts of Orissa*, Agragamee, Kashipur, Rayagada, Orissa.

Das, V., Education of Girls: *Perceptions from the Tribal Regions*, Agragamee, Kashipur, Rayagada, Orissa.

Dasgupta, A., 2000, 'In the Citadel of Bhadralok Politicians: The Scheduled Castes in West Bengal', *Journal of Indian School of Political Economy*, Vol. 12, Nos. 3 and 4.

Daswani, C.J., 1993, *Tribal Study Synthesis Report* (Summary of Significant Findings), New Delhi, NCERT.

Datt, Ruddar, "Inequalities in Educational Development with Special Reference to Literacy Status and School Education", *Journal of Educational Planning and Administration, Vol. X, No. 3, 1996*, pp. 255-269.

Dave, P.C., "Ashram Schools in Bombay State", *Vanyajati, Vol. 2, No. 2, 1957*, pp. 94-100.

Dave, P.C., "Report on Ashram Schools, Sevashrams and Training Cadres in Orissa State", *Vanyajati, Vol. 2, No. 3, 1954.*

De Rebello, D.M., "The School Drop Outs", *Journal of Indian Education, Vol. 4, No. 2*, NCERT.

Deb Roy, H.L., 1981, *Tribe in Transition, The Jaintias of Meghalaya*, New Delhi, Cosmo Publications.

Debe, S., 2001, 'Inequality of Access to Elementary Education in Orissa: An Inter and Intra Spatial Analysis', in A. Vaidyanathan and Gopinathan, P.R. (Eds.), *Elementary Education in Rural India: A Grassroots View*, New Delhi, Sage Publications.

Deliege, R., *'The World of the Untouchables': Paraiyas of Tamil Nadu*, New Delhi, Oxford University Press.

Desai, A.R., 1969, *Rural Sociology in India*, Mumbai: Popular Prakashan.

Desai, B. and Patel, A., 1981, *Ashram Schools of Gujarat: An Evaluative Study*, Ahmedabad, Gujarat Vidyapeeth.

Desrochers and Veliyannoor V. Paulson, 2004, *Poverty, Marginalization and Empowerment in Karnataka*, Bangalore, KRCR JPC Publications.

Devendra Thakur and Thakur, D.N., 1994, *Tribal Life in India*, Deep and Deep Publications, New Delhi.

District Primary Education Programme, Karnataka, *Baseline Assessment Study A Report, 1997*, Regional Institute of Education, NCERT, Mysore.

Doshi, S.C., 1997, *Emerging Tribal Image*, New Delhi, Rawat Publishers.

Dreze, J., 2004, 'Mid-Day Meals and Childrens' Rights', *Economic and Political Weekly, Vol. 39, No. 19.*

Dreze, J., and Goyal, A., 2003, 'Future of Mid-Day Meals', *EPW*, Vol. 38, No. 44.

Dreze, J., and Harris, G., 1997, Up: The Burden of Inertia', In J. Dreze and Amartya Sen (Eds.), *Indian Development Selected Regional Perspectives*, New Delhi, Oxford University Press.

Dreze, J., and Sen, Amartya, Eds., 1995, India: *Economic Development and Social Opportunity*, New Delhi: Oxford University Press.

Dreze, Jean and Sen, Amartya, "Basic Education as a Political Issue", *Journal of Educational Planning and Administration, Vol. IX, No. 1, 1995*, pp. 1-26.

Dube, S.C., 1968, *Approaches to Tribal Problems in India* in Vidyarathi, L.P. (Ed.), *Applied Anthropology in India*, Allahabad, Kitab Mahal.

Dube, S.M., 1972, 'Education, Social Change and Political Consciousness among Tribes of North East India', in K.S. Singh (Ed.), *The Tribal Situation in India*, IIAS, Simla.

Duraisamy, M., 2001, 'Demands for and Access to Schooling in Tamil Nadu', in A. Vaidyanathan and P.R. Gopinathan Nair, (Eds.), *Elementary Education in Rural India: A Grassroots View*, Sage, New Delhi.

Education for all by 2000: Indian Perspective, 1990, New Delhi, NIEPA.

Education in a Multilingual World, 2003, UNESCO Position Paper.

Education of Tribal Children in India, http://www.google.com.

Edwards, V., 1984, 'Language Issues in School', in M. Craft, (Ed.), *Education and Cultural Pluralism*, London: Falmer Press.

EFA Advocacy Forum, 1994, Universalization of Primary Education: A Promise to Keep, *Educational Profile in Andhra Pradesh, Hyderabad*, EFA, Advocacy Forum, Osmania University in Collaboration with UNICEF.

Elwin, Vassier, *A New Deal for Tribal India*, 1963, Delhi, Manager of Publications.

Enrolment Details in Ashram Schools Districtwise, 2006-07.

Equality of Educational Opportunity, Washington D.C.: U.S. Office of Education Report, National Centre for Educational Statistics, Coleman, J.S. *et al.*, 1965.

Facts and Figures of Scheduled Tribes of Andhra Pradesh, Tribal Cultural Research and Training Institute, 1969, Hyderabad, Tribal Welfare, Hyderabad (mimeographed).

Fantini, Mario, D. and Weinstein Gerald, 1968, *The Disadvantaged Challenge to Education*, New York, Harper and Row.

Farrell, J., 1982, 'Educational Expansion and the Drive for Social Equality', in P. Altbach *et al.* (Eds.), *Comparative Education*, New York, Macmillan.

Foster, P., 1977, 'Education and Social Differentiation in Less Developed Countries', *Comparative Education Review*, Vol. 21.

Freedman, Samuel, G., 1990, *Small Victories: The Real World of a Teacher, Her Students and their High School*, New York, Harper and Row.

Freire, P., 1970, *Pedagogy of the Oppressed*, Harmondsworth, Penguin.

Freire, Paulo, 1973, *Education for Critical Consciousness*, New York, Continuum Book.

Furer, Haimendorf C. Von, "Aboriginal Education in Hyderabad", *Indian Journal of Social Work, Vol. V, No. 2, 1944.*

Furer-Haimendorf, C.V., 1943, *The Chenchus: The Jungle Folk of the Deccan*, London, Macmillan & Co.

Fuzer-Haimendorf, C.V., 1989, *Tribes of India; The Struggle for Survival*, London, Oxford University Press.

Galanter, M., 184, *Competing Equalities: Law and the Backward Classes in India*, New Delhi, Oxford University Press.

Ganesh Prabhu, "Classes in Dinning Hall of Ashram School in Udupi", *The Hindu, September 7, 2007.*

Gare, G., 2000, *Adivasi Samasyaaani Badalte Sandarbh* (Marathi), Pune, Sugava.

Gautam Vinoba, "Education of Tribal Children in India and the Issue of Medium of Instruction", *http://www.google.com.*

George F. Kneller (Ed.), 1971, *Foundation of Education*, New York, John Wiley and Sons.

Ghatage, B.S., 2006, *Nomadic Tribes and Social Work in India*, Jaipur, Shruti Publications.

Ghatak, N.K., "The Scheduled Tribes of India in the New Millennium", *Anthropological Survey of India, Vol. 52, No. 87, 2003*, pp. 87-115.

Ghurye, G.S., 1943, *The Aborigines – So Called and their Future*, Poona, Gokhale Institute of Politics and Economics.

Ghurye, G.S., 1963, *The Scheduled Tribes*, Bombay, Popular Book Depot.

Gnanasundaram, V., "Use of Tribal Languages in Education *(Seminar Paper), Indian Social Science Congress, November 12-16 November, 1994*, Baroda.

Gogate, B., 1986, *Marathwadyatil Shikshan* (Marathi), Pune, Continental.

Gopalakrishnan and Anita Sharma, "Education Guarantee Scheme", *Economic Times, No. 7, 1998.*

Gopalakrishnan, R., and Sharma, A., (1998), "Education Guarantee Scheme in Madhya Pradesh: Innovative Step to Universalise Education", *Economic and Political Weekly, Vol. 33, No. 39, September 26, 1998.*

Gore, M.S. *et al.*, 1970, *Field Study in Sociology of Education in India*, New Delhi, NCERT.

Gore, M.S., 1967, *Papers in the Sociology of Education in India*, New Delhi, NCERT.

Gore, M.S., 1982, *Education and Modernisation in India*, Jaipur, Rawat Publications.

Gore, M.S., 1993, *The Social Context of an Ideology,; Ambedkar's Political and Social Thought*, New Delhi: Sage.

Govenrment of India, *Census of India, 1991.*

Government of India (GOI) 1990, *The Report of the Commissioner for Scheduled Castes and Scheduled Tribes*, 29th Report, 1987-89, New Delhi, GOI.

Government of India (GOI), 1991, *Education of Scheduled Castes and Scheduled Tribes and Other Backward Castes, 8th Five Year Plan Document*, New Delhi, GOI.

Government of India, 1959, *Report of the Study Team on Social Welfare and Welfare of Backward Classes* (Renuka Roy Committee), Ministry of Home Affairs, New Delhi.

Government of India, 1960, *Report of the Committee on Special Multipurpose Tribal Blocks (Verrier Elwin Committee)*, Ministry of Home Affairs, New Delhi.

Government of India, 1961, *Report of the Scheduled Areas and Scheduled Tribes Commission (Dhebar Commission)*, Ministry of Home Affairs, New Delhi.

Government of India, 1962 and 1963, *Report of the Commissioner for Scheduled Castes and Scheduled Tribes (Part I & II)*, Manager of Publications, New Delhi.

Government of India, 1962, *A New Deal for Tribal India*, Ministry of Home Affairs, New Delhi.

Government of India, 1964-66, *Report of the Education Committee (D.S. Kothari Committee).*

Government of India, 1969, *Report of the Committee on Tribal Development Programme* (P. Shilu Ao Committee), Planning Commission, New Delhi.

Government of India, 1978-79, *Report of the Commissioner for Scheduled Castes and Scheduled Tribes*, Ministry of Home Affairs, New Delhi.

Government of India, 1980, *Report of the Commissioner for Scheduled Castes and Scheduled Tribes*, Ministry of Home Affairs, New Delhi.

Government of India, 1981, *Report on Development of Tribal Areas – National Committee on the Development of Backward Areas* (Sivaraman Committee), Planning Commission, New Delhi.

Government of India, 1984, *Selected Educational Statistics for Scheduled Castes and Scheduled Tribes*, Ministry of Education, New Delhi.

Government of India, 1986, *National Policy on Education*, Ministry of Human Resource Development, Department of Education, New Delhi.

Government of India, 1993, *Education of Scheduled Castes and Scheduled Tribes*, Department of Education, MHRD, Government of India.

Government of India, 1996, *Selected Educational Statistics*, 1995-96, Ministry of Human Resource Development (MHRD), Government of India, New Delhi, 1998.

Government of India, 2000, *Selected Educational Statistics, 1999-2000*, New Delhi, MHRD, GOI.

Government of India, 2001, Census of India, *Socio-Cultural Tables* (C-Series), New Delhi.

Government of India, *Hakkipikki – Trapper and Seller*, A Report, 1980.

Government of India, Ministry of Home Affairs, 1983, *Report of the Commissioner for Scheduled Castes and Scheduled Tribes 1982-83*, New Delhi.

Government of India, Ministry of Human Resource Development, *Programme of Action Report*, 1992, New Delhi.

Government of India, *Report on Development of Tribal Areas – National Committee on the Development of Backward Areas* (Sivaraman Committee), Planning Commission, New Delhi.

Government of Karnataka, 1989, *Perspectives for Education Sector – Policy Paper*, Department of Education, Bangalore.

Government of Karnataka, 1991-92, *Social Welfare Department, Programmes*, Bangalore, ND (Kannada).

Government of Karnataka, 1995, *Neravu Nirdeeshana*, Information and Publicity Department, Bangalore (Kannada).

Government of Karnataka, 1996, *Abyudya – Manual of Welfare Programme for the Development of Scheduled Castes and Scheduled Tribes*, Bangalore (Kannada).

Government of Karnataka, *Annual Report 2000-01*, Social Welfare Directorate, Bangalore.

Government of Karnataka, *Details of Ashram Schools of Scheduled Tribes, 2007*.

Government of Karnataka, *Report of the Directorate of Tribal Welfare*, ND.

Govinda, R. and Verghese, V.V., 1993, *Quality of Primary Schooling in India*, Paris, International Institute of Educational Planning.

Govinda, R., (Ed.), *India Education Report: A Profile of Basic Education*, New Delhi, OUP.

Govinda, R., and Josephine, Y., 2005, 'Para Teachers in India: A Review', in *Contemporary Education Dialogue, Vol. 2, No. 2, Spring*.

Grigson, W.V., 1993, *The Aboriginal Problem in the Central Provinces and Besar*, Bhopal, Vanya Prakashan.

Guha, Ramachandra, 196, *Savaging the Civilized, Verrier Elwin and Tribal Question in Late Colonial India, Economic and Political Weekly, Vols. 31, 35, 36 and 37.*

Gupta P. Lalau, 1998, *Tribal Development Administration*, New Delhi, Classical Publishing Company.

Gupta, S.K., Sharma, V.P. and Sharada, N.K. Ed., 1999, *Tribal Development Appraisal and Alternatives*, New Delhi, Indus Publishing Company.

Haimendorf, C.V., 1995, *Tribes of India: The Struggle for Survival*, Delhi, Oxford University Press.

Halbar, B.G., 1986, *Lamani Economy and Society in Change*, New Delhi, Mittal Publishers.

Hanumantharayappa, P. and Mutharayappa, R., 1986, *Backwardness and Welfare of Scheduled Castes and Scheduled Tribes in India*, New Delhi, Ashish Publishing House.

Haokip Ngamkhohao, "Tribal Education in Manipur", *http://www.google.com*.

Haq, M., and Haq, K., 1998, *Human Development in South Asia – The Educational Challenge*, Karachi, Oxford University Press.

Hasnain, Nadeem, 1992, *Tribal India*, New Delhi, Palaka Prakashan.

Heda, H.C., 1965, *Tribal Education: Integration Aspects, Rashtra Sanatan, A Novel Scheme, Souvenir*, Hyderabad, Andhra Pradesh Adimjati Sevak Sangh.

Hegde, L.R., 1981, *Uttara Kannada Gondaru (Gonds of Uttara Kannada)* (Kannada), Bangalore, IBH Prakashana.

Hellmuth, J., (Ed.), 1970, *Disadvantaged Child – Vol. 3, Contemporary Education: A National Debate*, New York, Burner/Mazel, Inc.

Hemalatha, Talesra, 1990, *Tribal Education*, Udaipur, Himanshu Publications.

Hemlata, Rao, Devendra Babu, M., 1994, *Scheduled Castes and Tribes*, New Delhi, Ashish Publishing House.

Henriques, J., and G.G. Wankhede, 1985, *One Step Forward, Yet Steps Behind: A Study of Wastage and Stagnation in Education of Scheduled Castes and Scheduled Tribes in Maharashtra*, Mumbai, TISS, Mimeograph.

Heredia C. Rodolf, "The Tribal Question: Fundamental Issues", *New Frontiers in Education, Vol. XXV, No. 4, October-December 1995*, pp. 358-376.

Heredia, R.C., (1992), *Tribal Education for Community Development: A Study of Schooling in The Talasari Mission Area*, New Delhi, Concept Publishers.

Heredia, Rudolf, C., 1993, *Tribal Education for Community Development: A Study of Schooling in the Talasari Mission Area*, New Delhi, Concept Publications.

Hilda Raj, "Education of Adivasis", *The Eastern Anthropologist, Vol. 5, No. 4, June-August 1952.*

Hubley, John, British Council Division, British High Commission 1995, *A Report: Our Children: Our Future: A Strategy Paper on School Health in India.*

Husen, Torsten and Postlethwaite, T.N. (Ed.), 1985, *The International Encyclopaedia of Education Research and Studies*, Oxford, Pergamon Press.

Ilaiah, K., 1996, *Why I am not a Hindu: A Sudra Critique of Hindutva Philosophy, Culture and Political Economy*, Kolkata: Samya.

Ilaiah, K., 2001, 'Dalitism Vs. Brahmanism: The Epistemological Conflict in History', In G. Shah (Ed.), *Dalit Identity and Politics: Cultural Subordination and the Dalit Challenge*, Vol. 2, New Delhi, Sage Publishers.

Illaiah, K., 1998, 'Towards the Dalitisation of the Nation, From the Margins to the Centre', In P. Chatterjee (Ed.), *Wages of Freedom: 50 years of the Indian Nation-State*, New Delhi, Oxford University Press.

Illich, Ivan, D., 1971, *Deschooling Society*, London, Calder and Boyars.

India Workshop on Multilingual Education with Special Focus on Tribal Education, Mysore, UNESCO, UNICEF, CIIL, NCERT, 25-27 October, 2005.

India, 2007 – *A Reference Annual*, Publication Division, Ministry of Information and Broadcasting, Government of India, New Delhi.

International Perspectives on the Sociology of Education (Series of Articles), *British Journal of Sociology of Education, Vol. 17, No. 2, 1996*, pp. 125-247.

Iyer, L.K.A., 1988, *The Mysore Tribes and Castes (Five Vols.)*, New Delhi, Mittal Publications.

Jabbi, K.M., and C. Rajyalakshmi, 2001, 'Education of Marginalised Social Groups in Bihar, in A. Vaidyanathan and P.R. Gopinathan Nair, (Eds.), *Elementary Education in Rural India: A Grassroots View*, New Delhi, Sage Publishers.

Jackson, Philip, 1968, *Life in Classrooms*, New York, Holt, Rinehart and Winston.

Jacob John Katta Kayam, 1983, *Social Structure and Change Among the Tribals*, New Delhi, D.K. Publications.

Jagannath Pathy, 1998, *"Tribal Education: Incentives, Realities, Challenges and Tasks – Some Reflections"*, National Conference on Management of School Education in India, April 16-17, New Delhi, NIEPA.

Jain, P.C., 1995, *Christianity, Ideology and Social Change among Tribals*, Jaipur, Rawat Publications.

Jain, S., Sharma, S., and Goyal, V., 2003, 'Muktangan: Breaking Fresh Ground', in V. Ramachandran (Ed.), *Getting Children Back to School, Case Studies in Primary Education*, New Delhi, Sage Publishers.

Jandhyala, B.G. Tilak, 1987, *The Economics of Inequality in Education*, New Delhi, Sage Publications.

Jandhyala, K., 2003, Balajyothi: Bringing Child Labour into Schools, in V. Ramachandran (Ed.), *Getting Children Back to School: Case Studies in Primary Education*, New Delhi, Sage Publishers.

Jay Achandran Usha, Taking Schools to Children, *Economic and Political Weekly, September 1, 2001*, pp. 3347-3352.

Jayaram, N., 1990, *Sociology of Education in India*, Jaipur, Rawat Publishers.

Jayasuriya, J.E., 1981, *Education in the Third World: Some Reflections*, Bombay, Somaiya Publications.

Jayaswal, M., "Minimum Levels of Learning in Tribal School Students of Ranchi District", *Social Change, Vol. 23, No. 2 and 3, 1993.*

Jeevan Chennappa, "Their Lifestyle has been the same for Centuries", *The Hindu, February 14, 2007.*

Jeffery, R., *et al.*, 2005, 'Social Inequalities and the Privatisation of Secondary Schooling in North India', in Chopra, R., and Jeffery, P. (Eds.), *Educational Regimes in Contemporary India*, New Delhi, Sage Publishers.

Jha, H., 2000, 'Promises and Lapses: Understanding the Experience of Scheduled Castes in Bihar in Historical Perspective', in Andre Beteille (Eds.), *Journal of Indian School of Political Economy, Vol. 12, No. 3 and 4,* July-December.

Jha, J. and Jhingran, D., 2002, *Elementary Education for the Poorest and Other Deprived Groups: The Real Challenge of Universalisation*, Centre for Policy Research, New Delhi.

Jha, J., 2003, Primary Schools in West Bengal, *Economic and Political Weekly, Vol. 38, No. 27.*

Jhingran, D., 2005, *Language Disadvantage*, New Delhi, APH Publications.

Jodhka, S.S., 2000, 'Prejudice' without pollution? Scheduled Castes in Contemporary Punjab, *Journal of Indian School of Political Economy, Vol. 11, No. 3 and 4.*

Jodhka, S.S., 2002, 'Caste and Untouchability in Rural Punjab, *Economic and Political Weekly*, Vol. 37, No. 19.

Jogdand, P.G., 2000, *New Economic Policy and Dalits*, Jaipur, Rawat Publications.

Joshi Vidyut, "A Century of Tribal Education in Gujarat", *Seminar Proceedings on Tribal Education in Gujarat*, Surat, 1984, Centre for Social Studies.

Joshi, P.C., "Socio-Economic Factors in Literacy and Education in Rural India", *The Economic Weekly, 1964.*

Joshi, V., 1998, *Tribal Situation in India: Issues in Development*, Jaipur, Rawat Publications.

Kabeer, N., G.B. Nambissan and R. Subramanian (Eds.), 2003, *Child Labour and the Right to Education in South Asia: Needs Versus Rights*, New Delhi, Sage Publishers.

Kabui, G., 1985, *Anal – A Trans – Order Tribe of Manipur*, New Delhi, Mittal Publishers.

Kailash, 1993, *Tribal Education and Occupation – Dynamics of Impact and Change*, Delhi, Manak Publications.

Kailash, 1993, *Tribal Education and Occupation: Dynamics of Impact and Changes*, New Delhi, Manak Publications.

Kailash, n.d., *Schools and Schooling in Jhabua*, TISS, Unpublished Research Paper.

Kakati, Kusum, Kunja, "Education and Social Mobility Among the Scheduled Tribes: A Case Study of Two Villages in Assam, *Indian Journal of Adult Education, April-June 2003*, pp. 14-24.

Kalenahalli, Chandru, *Soligara Samskriti – A Cultural Study* (Kannada), 1993, Bangalore, Kannada Sahitya Academy.

Kalia, N., 1979, *Sexism in Indian Education*, New Delhi, Vikas Publications.

Kamat, A.R., 1985, *Education and Social Change in India*, Mumbai, Somaiya Publications.

Kamble, R., 1999, Images of Servility: Everyday Occupational and Social Experience of Charmakars in Mumbai, Paper presented at *National Seminar of Indian Society at Turn of the Century: Perspective from Below*, New Delhi, JNU, March 25-27.

Kanchan Roy, 1989, *Education and Health Problems in Tribal Development*, New Delhi, Concept Publishing Company.

Kanungo K. Akshaya and Mahapatra Hrushikesh, "Tribal Education in Rayagada: A Review of Language Textbook and Medium of Instruction", *http://www.google.com*.

Karnataka State Gazetteer, Part I, 1982, Government of Karnataka, Bangalore.

Karnataka State Gazetteer, Part II, 1983, Government of Karnataka, Bangalore.

Kasinath, H.M., "National Open School and Universalization of Education", *Yojana, Vol. 41, No. 5, May 1997*.

Kaul, S.K., 1967, Existing Facilties, Coverage, Wastage, Stagnation and Utilization of Financial Assistance in *Report of Tribal Education, Tribal Education in India: Report of the National Seminar*, New Delhi, NCERT.

Kayam Katta John Jacob, 1983, *Social Structure and Change Among the Tribals*, New Delhi, D.K. Publications.

Khora, S., (nd), *Teacher Motivation and Schooling*, Mumbai, TISS, Mimeograph.

Khurana, G., "Approach to Education of Scheduled Tribes", *The Education Quarterly, 1978, Vol. 20, No. 1*.

Kingdon, G.G., 1996, Private Schooling in India: Size, Nature and Equity – Effects, *Economic and Political Weekly, Vol. 31, No. 51*.

Kingdon, Geetha, G., "Private Schooling in India Size, Nature and Equity Effects", *Economic and Political Weekly, December 21, 1996*.

Kingston, Paul, W., 1992, *Sociology of Education, in Encyclopaedia of Sociology*, Vol. 4, New York, Macmillan.

Koppikar, G.K., 1956, *The Education of the Adivasis*, New Delhi, Government of India.

Krishnaji, N., 2001, Poverty, Gender and Schooling: A Study of Two Districts in Andhra Pradesh, in A. Vaidyanathan and P.R. Gopinathan Nair, (Eds.), *Elementary Education in Rural India; A Grassroots View*, New Delhi, Sage Publishers.

Krishnarao, R., 1986, *Case Study of Seven Tribal Area Schools*, Hyderabad, TCRTI, (mimio).

Kulkarni, B., 2001, Marathwada, 2001, *Proceedings of a Seminar, Vols. I and II*, Aurangabad, Organising Committee.

Kumar, B.L., 2004, *Schools and Schooling in Tribal Gujarat, The Quality Dimension, Working Paper No. 150*, Ahmedabad, Gujarat Institute of Development Research.

Kumar, K.M., Priyam, and Sadhna, S., 2001, 'Looking Beyond the Smoke Screen: DPEP and Primary Educatic ` in India, *Economic and Political Weekly, Vol. 36, No. 7*.

Kumar, Krishna, 1983, Educational Experience of Scheduled Castes and Tribes, *Economic and Political Weekly, Vol. XVII, Nos. 36 & 37*.

Kumar, Krishna, 1989, *Social Character of Learning*, New Delhi, Sage Publishers.

Kumar, Krishna, 1991, *The Political Agenda of Education: A Study of Colonialist and Nationalist Ideas*, New Delhi, Sage Publishers.

Kumar, Krishna, 1992, *What is Worth Teaching?* Hyderabad, Orient Longman.

Kumar, R., 2004, Educational Deprivation of the Marginalised – The Case of Mushar Community in Bihar, Paper presented at *Seminar on Towards Quality Education for all: Issues and Challenges Beyond 86th Amendment*, India International Centre, New Delhi, Council for Social Development, New Delhi, 2004.

Kundu, M., 1990, *Cultural Anthropology and Tribal Education*, New Delhi, Amar Prakashan.

Kundu, M., 1994, *Tribal Education, New Perspectives*, New Delhi, Gyan Publishing House.

Kuppuswamy, B., 1966, *Social Change in India*, New Delhi, Vikas.

Kusum Premi, 1998, "Impact of Incentives on Educational Development of Tribes: A Review of Studies and Areas of Future Research", *National Conference on Management of School Education in India*, April 16-17, New Delhi, NIEPA.

Lakshmaiah, "Education and Social Change: A Case Study of Tribal Students", *Man in India, Vol. 71, No. 4, 1991*, pp. 587-599.

Lakshmaiah, T. and Aravind, Y., " A Study of Educational Facilities for Tribal Students – Problems and Impact in Paderu Samithi in Andhra Pradesh", *Man in India, Vol. 68, No. 4, 1988*, pp. 380-400.

Lalitha, A.C., 1993, *Kadu Kuruba Mattu Jenukuruba Samskriti – A Cultural Study* (Kannada), Bangalore, Karnataka Sahitya Academy.

Lalitha, V., 1995, *The Making of Criminal Tribes: Patterns and Transition*, Madras, New Era Publications.

Lawton, D., 1977, *Education and Social Justice*, London, Sage Publishers.

Leclerq, F., 2003, 'EGS and Primary Schooling in Madhya Pradesh: A Reply', *Economic and Political Weekly, Vol. 38, Nos. 51 and 52.*

Leclerq, F., 2003, 'EGS and Primary Schooling in Madhya Pradesh', *Economic and Political Weekly, Vol. 38, No. 19.*

Lidhoo, M., 1987, *Kashmir Tribals, Child Rearing and Psycho-Social Development*, Srinagar, Minakshi Publishers.

Lieten, G.K., 2000, 'Children Work and Education – I: General Parameters', *Economic and Political Weekly, Vol. 35, No. 24.*

Lieten, G.K., Children, Work and Education – II: Field Work in Two Up Villages, *Economic and Political Weekly, Vol. 35, No. 25.*

Lockheed, M.E. and Verspoor, A.M., 1990, *Improving Primary Education in Developing Countries: A Review of Policy Options*, Bangkok.

Lotz Barbara, "Promoting Tribal Languages in Education – A Case Study of Santali in Orissa", *Journal of Social Science, Vol. 8, No. 2, 2004*, pp. 129-142.

Mackenzie Pam, 2005, *Multilingual Education for Tribal Minorities in India.*

Madan, T.N., "Education in Tribal India", *The Eastern Anthropologist, Vol. 5, No. 4.*

Mahendra, M., *Nelupalya, Girijana Kendra Ashrama Shaleya Vidyaritigala Jeevanada Manavashatriya Adayana (Kannada) Field Study Report*, Department of Anthropology, University of Mysore, 2006-07.

Maitra, A., 1993, *Profile of a Little Known Tribe*, New Delhi, Mittal Publishers.

Majumdar, D.N. and Furer Haimendorf C. Von, "Special Tribal Number", *The Eastern Anthropologist, Vol. 3, No. 1, 1949.*

Majumdar, D.N. and Madan, T.N., 1988, *An Introduction to Social Anthropology,* New Delhi, National Publishing House.

Majumdar, D.N., 1950, *The Affairs of a Tribe,* Lucknow, Universal Publication.

Majumdar, M., 2001, 'Educational Opportunities in Rajasthan and Tamil Nadu, Despair and Hope, in A. Vaidyanathan and P.R. Gopinathan Nair (Eds.), *Elementary Education in Rural India: A Grassroots View,* New Delhi, Sage Publishers.

Malhotra, 1998, *Tribal Education – Impact of Education on Tribal Life and Adjustment,* New Delhi, Cosmo Publications.

Malhotra, P.C., "Social disadvantage education and development in India", *Social Change, Vol. 16, Nos. 2 and 3,* 1986.

Malli Gandhi, 2006, *Development of Denotified Tribes: Policy and Practice,* New Delhi, Sarup and Sons.

Mandal, Pushpa, 2000, *Ashram Schools in Action,* New Delhi, Rajat Publication.

Mangal Ghode, 1995, "Status of Ashram Schools in Maharashtra State" in *An Overview of Tribal Studies* (Ed.), Navinchandra Jain and Robin D. Tribhuvan, Tribal Research and Training Institute, Pune.

Manu, R.S., 1980, *Hakkipikki,* Calcutta, Anthropological Survey of India.

Mathur, N.N.G., 1994, *Problems of Tribal Education – Past, Present and Future,* Udaipur, Shiva Publications.

Mathur, P.R.G., 1992, Tribal Education in Kerala, in B. Chaudhari (Ed.), *Education and Literacy Programmes,* Vol. IV, New Delhi, Inter-India Publications.

Mays, John Barren, 1967, *Education Today – The School and its Social Setting,* Harlow, Longman.

Meena Rama Singh, 2006, *Tribal Development Programmes – A Critical Appraisal,* Jaipur, Ritu Publications.

Meenakshi, J.V., *et al.,* 2000, 'Estimates of Poverty for SC, ST and Female Headed Households', *Economic and Political Weekly, Vol. 35, No. 20.*

Mehendale Archana, "Isolated Communities and Ignored Claims: Tribal Children's Right to Education in India", *http://www.google.com.*

Mehta, Arun, C., 1995, *Education For All in India: Myth and Reality,* New Delhi, Kanishka Publishers.

Mendelsohn, O. and M. Vicziany, 1998, *The Untouchables: Subordination, Poverty and the State in Modern India,* Cambridge, Cambridge University Press.

Menon, Madhava, T. (Eds.), 2006, *Encyclopaedia of Dravidian Tribes (3 Vols.),* Thiruvananthapuram, DLA.

Metry, K.M., *"Budakattu Adhyayana" (Tribal Studies – Kannada),* No. 4, 2005, Hampi, Kannada University.

Metry, K.M., *"Budakattu Adhyayana" (Tribal Studies – Kannada),* Vol. 3, Issue 1, January-June 2006, Hampi, Kannada University.

Metry, K.M., 2002, *Budakattu Kulakasubugalu* (Tribal Occupation) (Kannada), Hampi, Kannada University.

Miller, H.L., 1967, *Education for the Disadvantaged,* New York, Free Press.

Mishra K. Mahendra, "Contextualizing Classrooms in Tribal Area Schools in Orissa: An Experimental Learning", *http://www.google.com.*

Mishra, P.K., "Primitive Tribes in Southern Region: A Case Study", *The Eastern Anthropologist, Vol. 56, Nos. 2-4, 2003*, pp. 379-389.

Mishra, R.C., "Education of Tribal Children in India", *http://www.google.com*.

Mittal, A.C. and J.B. Sharma, 1998, *Tribal Movement, Politics and Religion in India: Tribal Movement in India*, Vol. I, New Delhi, Radha Publications.

Mohan Rao, K., 1999, *Tribal Development in Andhra Pradesh: Problems, Performance and Prospects*, Hyderabad, Booklinks Corporation.

Mohanty K. Ajit, "*Education for Multigualism: Role of Mother Tongues in Tribal Education*", Mysore, October 24, 2005.

Mohanty K. Ajit, "*Perpetuating Inequality: Language Disadvantage and Capability Deprivation of Tribal Mother Tongue Speakers in India*", Cornell Conference on Language and Poverty, Cornell University, Ithaca, USA, October 14-16, 2005.

Mohanty, B.B., "Policy for Tribal Development: Protective Discrimination or Discrimination Protected", *The Eastern Anthropologist, Vol. 58, No. 1, 2005*, pp. 27-59.

Mohanty, P.K., "Tribal Education in India", *The Eastern Anthropologist, Vol. XXVIII, No. 38, 2003.*

Moonis, Raza, Ed., 1986, *Educational Planning: A Long Term Perspective*, New Delhi, NIEPA.

Morab, S.G., 1977, *The Soliga of Biligiri Ranganna Hills*, Calcutta, Anthropological Survey of India.

Mubarak, S.M., *Facilities Lacking in Ashram Schools: Special Report*, Mysore Mitra, 18 August, 2006.

Mukherji, S.N., 1957, *Education in India Today and Tomorrow*, Baroda, Acharya Book Depot.

Mukul, 1999, 'The Untouchable Present Everyday Life of Musahars of North Bihar', *Economic and Political Weekly, Vol. 34, No. 49.*

Muralidharan, V., 1997, *Educational Priorities and Dalit Society*, New Delhi, Kanishka Publishers.

Nag, C.R., 1993, *The Mizo Society in Transition*, New Delhi, Vikas Publishers.

Naidu, N.Y. and Pradhan, F.M., 1973, *Elementary Education in a Tribal Development Block*, Hyderabad, NIRD.

Naik, J.P., 1941, *Report on Stagnation and Wastage in Primary Schools*, Bombay, Provincial Board of Primary Education.

Naik, T.B., 1969, *Impact of Education on the Bhils: Cultural Change in the Tribal Life in Madhya Pradesh*, New Delhi, Research Programmes Committee.

Nair, M.K.S., 1987, *Tribal Economy in Transition*, New Delhi, Inter-India Publications.

Nali-Kali, District Primary Education Programme, Mysore.

Nambissan B. Geetha, "Language and Schooling of Tribal Children, *Economic and Political Weekly", 15 October, 1994*, pp. 2747-2754.

Nambissan, G.B. and J.B.G. Sedwal, 1996, 'How Free is Primary Education in India, Part I and II', *Economic and Political Weekly, Vol. 31, No. 5 & 6.*

Nambissan, G.B. and M. Sedwal, 2002, 'Education for All: The Situation of Dalit Children', in R. Govinda (Ed.), *India Education Report: A Profile of Basic Education*, New Delhi, Oxford University Press.

Nambissan, G.B., 1994, 'Language and Schooling of Tribal Children Issues Relating to the Medium of Instruction', *Economic and Political Weekly, Vol. 36, No. 42.*

Nambissan, G.B., 2000, 'Identity, Exclusion and the Education of Tribal Communities', Wazir (Ed.), *Gender Gaps in Literacy and Education*, New Delhi, Sage Publishers.

Nambissan, G.B., 2001, 'Social Diversity and Regional Disparities in Schooling: A Study of Rural Rajasthan', in A. Vaidyanathan and P.R. Gopinathan Nair (Eds.), *Elementary Education in Rural India: A Grassroots View*, New Delhi, Sage Publications.

Nambissan, G.B., 2004, *Terms of Inclusion: Dalits and the Right to Education*, Paper presented at Seminar on Towards Quality Education for All: Issues and Challenges Beyond 86th Amendment at India International Centre, New Delhi.

Nancharaiah, G., 2000, New Economic Policy and its Effects on Dalits, in Jogdand, P.G. (Ed.), *New Economic Policy and Dalits*, Jaipur, Rawat Publications.

Nancharaiah, G., 2002, 'Dalit Education and Economic Inequality', In S. Bhattacharya (Ed.), *Education and the Disprivileged: Nineteenth and Twentieth Century India*, Hyderabad, Orient Longman.

Nanda, B.N., 1994, *Contours of Continuity and Change: The Story of the Bonda Highlanders*, New Delhi, Sage Publications.

Nanjunda Rao, L., 1988, *Tribals in Heggadadevanakote Taluk (Mysore District)*, Bangalore, Government of Karnataka.

Narayan, S., 1986, *Dimensions of Development in Tribal Bihar*, New Delhi, Inter-India Publication.

Narayan, Yaji, 1986, *Gondaru* (Gonds in Kannada), Mysore Uttara Kannada Jilla Samskritika Sangha.

Narendra K. Singhi, 1979, *Education and Social Change*, Jaipur, Rawat Publications.

Narmada Bachao Andolan (n.d.), *Aksharan Olkhan*, Baroda, NB.

Narmada Bachao Andolan (n.d.), *Amra Kanya*, Baroda, NBA.

Narmada Bachao Andolan (n.d.), *Narmada: The Struggle for Life against Destruction*, Baroda, NBA.

Narmada Bachao Andolan (n.d.), *Various Reports on the Andolan, Annual Reports of the Jeevanshalas*, etc., Baroda, NBA.

Narwani, G.S., 2004, *Tribal Law in India*, Jaipur, Rawat Publication.

Natarajan, N., 1977, *The Missionary Among the Khasis*, New Delhi, Sterling Publishers.

National Commission for Women (NCW), 1994, *Report on Development of Female Education Among Tribal Communities*, New Delhi, NCW.

National Council for Educational Research and Training (NCERT), 1999, *Sixth All India Educational Survey, Main Report*, New Delhi, NCERT.

National Council for Teacher Education, 2003, *Discrimination Based on Sex, Caste, Religion and Disability Addressing through Educational Interventions – A Handbook for Sensitising Teachers and Teacher Educators*, New Delhi, NCTE.

National Council of Educational Research and Training (NCERT), (n.d.), *Executive Summary: Learning Achievement of Students at the End of Class V*, New Delhi, NCERT.

National Council of Educational Research and Training (NCERT), 2000, *Fifth Survey of Educational Research, Vol. I and II*, New Delhi, NCERT.

National Council of Educational Research and Training (NCERT), 2002, *Seventh All-India School Educational Survey*, New Delhi, NCERT.

National Curriculum Framework, *National Focus Group Reports, Position Papers, 2005*, NCERT, New Delhi.

National Family Health Survey (NFHS), 2000, *National Family Health Survey*, 2001, International Institute for Population Sciences.

National Seminar on Tribal Transformation and Development (Seminar Papers), Hyderabad, NISRA and NISIEJ, 18-19 December 1998.

Nautiyal, K.C. and Sharma, Y.D., 1979, *Equalisation of Educational Opportunities for Scheduled Castes and Scheduled Tribes*, New Delhi, NCERT.

NCERT, 1966, *Wastage and Stagnation in Primary and Middle Schools in India*, Project Report, New Delhi, Ministry of Education, Government of India.

NCERT, 1967, *Tribal Education in India, Publication No. 20*, Tribal Education Unit, Department of Adult Education.

NCERT, 1980, *Report of Fourth All India Education Survey*, New Delhi.

NCERT, Educational Problems of Tribal Children, *http://www.google.com.*

Nehru, Jawaharlal, 1977, 'An Approach to Tribal Problems', In H.M. Mathur (Ed.), *Anthropology in the Development Process*, New Delhi, Vikas Publishers.

Nikhilesh, K. (Ed.), 1990, *Tribal Demography and Development in North-East India*, New Delhi, B.R. Publishing Corporation.

Nuna, S.C. (Ed.), 1993, *Regional Disparities in Educational Development*, New Delhi, South Asia Publication.

O'Hanlon, R., 1985, Caste, Conflict and Ideology: *Mahatma Jotira Phule and Low Caste Protest in 19th Century Western India*, London, Cambridge University Press.

Ogbu, J.U., 1978, *Minority Education and Caste, The American System in Cross-Cultural Perspective*, New York, Academic Press.

Omvedt, G., 176, *Cultural Revolt in a Colonial Society, Scientific Socialist Education Trust*, Mumbai.

Omvedt, G., 1990, *Jotiba Phule Anistree Mukticha Vichar*, Lokvangmay, Gruh, Mumbai.

Omvedt, Gail, (n.d.), *Adivasis, Culture and Modes of Production in India.*

Page, E., 2005, 'Negotiation and Compromise: Gender and Government Elementary Education', in Chopra, R. and Jeffery, P. (Eds.), *Educational Regimes in Contemporary India*, New Delhi, Sage Publishers.

Pai, S., 2000, 'Changing Socio-Economic and Political Profile of SCs in UP, *Journal of Indian School of Political Economy*, Vol. 12, Nos. 3 & 4.

Panda, B.K., 1996, *Functions and Organisation of Tribal Schools*, New Delhi, Anamika.

Pande, A., 2001, Education of Rural Children in UP Himalayas', in A. Vaidyanathan and P.R. Gopinathan Nair (Eds.), *Elementary Education in Rural India; A Grassroots View*, New Delhi, Sage Publishers.

Pande, N. and Tripathi, R., 1982, 'Scheduled Caste Children in High Caste School: Some Motivational Consequences', in D. Sinha, R.C. Tripathi and G. Misra (Eds.), *Deprivation: Its Social Roots and Psychological Consequences*, New Delhi, Concept Publishing Company.

Pandey, S.N. and Jain, S.K., "Common School System Needs Streamlining", *Yojana, Vol. 42, No. 5, May 1998.*

Pandian, M.S.S., 2000, 'Dalit Assertion in Tamil Nadu; An Exploratory Note', *Journal of Indian School of Political Economy, Vol. 12, Nos. 3 and 4.*

Pandy, K.S. and Satapathy, P.C., *Tribal India*, New Delhi, Ashish.

Panse, R. (n.d.), *Narmada Jeevanshala*, (Marathi), UNICEF.

Pant, V.K. and Visht, B.S. (Ed.), 1999, *Backward Communities: Identity, Development and Transformation*, New Delhi, Gyan Publishing House.

Parameswara, S., *Development and Backwardness: Coexistence or Confrontation*, New Delhi, Reliance.

Parvathamma, C., 1984, *Scheduled Castes and Scheduled Tribes – A Socio-Economic Survey*, New Delhi, Ashish Publishing House.

Pasayat, C., 2000, 'Need of Educating Tribal Children in Orissa', in S.N. Tripathy (Ed.), *Glimpses of Tribal Development*, New Delhi, Discovery Publications.

Patel, H.M., ND, *Jenu Kurubas*, Calcutta, Anthropological Survey of India.

Patel, S.P., 1983, *Equality of Educational Opportunity in India: A Myth or Reality?* New Delhi, National Publishing House.

Patel, Srisha, 1991, *Tribal Education in India*, New Delhi, Mittal Publications.

Patel, Tara, 1984, *Development of Education – Among Tribal Women*, Delhi, Mittal Publications.

Pathak, A., 2002, *Social Implications of Schooling: Knowledge, Pedagogy and Consciousness*, Delhi, Rainbow Publishers.

Pathy, J., 1984, *Tribal Peasantry: Dynamics of Development*, New Delhi, B.R. Publishing Corporation.

Pathy, J., 2000, 'The End of Millennium: Liberalisation and Accentuation of the Tribal Problematique', P.G. Jogdand (Ed.), *New Economic Policy and Dalits*, Jaipur, Rawat Publications.

Patnaik, N., *"An Appraisal of Ashram School Education", Report of the Fourth Conference for Tribes and Tribal (Scheduled) Areas*, New Delhi, Bharatiya Adimavasi Sevak Sangh, 1957.

Pattanaik, B.K., "Better Deal for Children", *Yojana, Vol. 42, No. 7, July 1998.*

Pattanayak, D.P., *"The Teacher and the Language"*, Mysore, 24 October, 2005.

Pattanayak, D.P., 1987, *Multilingualism and Multiculturalism: Britain and India, Occasional Papers, No. 6, Centre for Multicultural Education*, Institute of Education, University of London.

Patwardhan, A., 2000, *Tribal Perceptions of Education: A Case of Adivasis in the SSP Religion of the Narmada Valley*, New Delhi, Department of Education, Delhi University.

Pawar, S.S. and Bhuvanendran, P., "Tribal Education – A Study in Madhya Pradesh", *Kurukshetra, January 1988*, pp. 18-30.

Pfeffer, G., 1997, *Contemporary Studies: Tribal Studies, Vol. II*, New Delhi, Concept Publishing Company.

Phule, J., 1991, *Selections*, Vol. II, Department of Education, Government of Maharashtra.

Phule, J., 1991, *Slavery*, Collected Works of Jotirao Phule, Vol. I, Department of Education, Government of Maharashtra.

Prabakar, A.S., 2004, *Budakattu Abbivruddi Meemamse (Concept of Tribal Development)* (Kannada), Hampi, Kannada University.

Prakash, K., "Some Aspects of Tribal Education", *Vanyajati, Vol. IV, No. 4, October 1956*, pp. 127-133.

Prasad, S., "Tribal Education in Bihar", *Man in India, Vol. 5, No. 4*, December 1971, pp. 364-393.

Pratap, D.R., and others, 1972, *Assessment of Unemployment among the Educated Tribals of Visakhapatnam*, Hyderabad, TCRTI, mimio.

Pratap, D.R., Raju, C.C. and Rao, M.V.K., 1971, *Study of Ashram Schools in Tribal Areas of Andhra Pradesh*, Hyderabad, TCRTI, mimio.

Probe Team, 1999, *Public Report on Basic Education in India*, New Delhi, Oxford University Press.

Programme Manual for Development of Tribals, 2007, Directorate for the Welfare of Scheduled Tribes, Government of Karnataka, Bangalore.

Punalekar, S.P. and Ranadive, J., 1984, *Tribal Education: An Interstate Study*, Surat, CSS.

Punalekar, S.P., 2000, New Economic Policy and Tribal Reality: A Case of Gujarat, in Jogdand, P.G. (Ed.), *New Economy Policy and Dalits*, Jaipur, Rawat Publications.

Punalekar, S.P., 2001, 'Dalit Literature and Dalit Identity', in G. Shah (Ed.), *Dalit Identity and Politics: Cultural Subordination and the Dalit Challenge, Vol. 2*, New Delhi, Sage Publishers.

Rahul, 1999, 'On Education Guarantee Scheme in Madhya Pradesh', *Economic and Political Weekly, Vol. 34, No. 1 & 2.*

Rajagopalan, C., 1974, *Education Progress and Problem of Scheduled Caste and Scheduled Tribe Students in Karnataka*, Bangalore, Department of Sociology, Bangalore University.

Rajappa Dalavai, R., 1993, *Hakkipikkiyara Samskriti – A Cultural Study (Kannada)*, Bangalore, Karnataka Sahitya Academy.

Rajeev, J., Mother Tongue Taught to Haadi Children by ITDP, *Vijaya Karnataka, July 21, 2004.*

Rama, Rao, V., "Tribal Education and the Role of the Teachers", *Man and Life, Vol. 14, No. 1-2, 1988*, pp. 77-83.

Ramachandran, V. and Agarwal, S., 2003, 'Agragamee: Real Life Education for Tribal Children', in V. Ramachandran (Ed.), *Getting Children Back to School: Case Studies in Primary Education*, New Delhi, Sage Publishers.

Ramachandran, V. and Saihjee, A., 2004, An Overview of Microstudies', in Ramachandran, V., (Ed.), *Gender and Social Equity in Primary Education*: Hierarchies of Access, New Delhi, Sage Publishers.

Ramachandran, V., (Ed.), 2003, *Getting Children Back to School: Case Studies in Primary Education*, New Delhi, Sage Publishers.

Ramachandran, V., (Ed.), *Gender and Social Equity in Primary Education: Hierarchies of Access*, New Delhi, Sage Publishers.

Ramana, G.V., 1990, *Problems of Education Among the Tribal Communities of Andhra Pradesh: A Case Study of Ashram Schools*, Ph.D. Thesis (Unpublished), Tirupati, S.V. University.

Ramesh, S.C., 2005, *Alemarigala Sthitigati (Kannada)*, Hampi, Kannada University.

Ramoo, S.K., "Tribals in Karnataka Left in the Lurch", *The Hindu, 21 February 2002.*

Ramphal, A., 2002, Texts in context: Development of Curricula, Text Books and Teaching Learning Materials', in R. Govinda, *Indian Education Report: A Profile of Basic Education*, New Delhi, Oxford University Press.

Rana, K. and Das, S., 2004, 'Primary Education in Jharkhand', *Economic and Political Weekly, Vol. 39, No. 11.*

Rana, K., Rafique, A. and Sengupta, A., 2002, *The Pratichi Education Report*, New Delhi, Pratichi Trust.

Ranasubhe, S., *et al.*, 1997, *Girikandaratoon* (Marathi), Aurangabad, Vasantarao Naik Mahavidyalaya.

Rao Bhaskara, N. and Kulkarni Suresh, "Disparities in School Facilities in India: The Case of Scheduled Castes and Scheduled Tribe Children", *Journal of Educational Planning and Administration, Vol. XIII, No. 2, 1999*, pp. 175-185.

Rao, Mohan, K., 1993, *Socio-Cultural Profile of Tribes of Andhra Pradesh*, Hyderabad, TCRTI.

Rao, Prasada, D.L. and Venkata Rao, P., "Problems of Teachers Working in Tribal Areas", *The Educational Review, Vol. LXXXIX, No. 8.*

Rao, Raghava, K., 1972, *The Law Relating to Scheduled Areas in Andhra Pradesh*, Hyderabad, Venkateswara Printers.

Rao, S.N. (n.d.), *Mobility among the Scheduled Castes of Andhra Pradesh: A Sociological Perspective*, Unpublished Paper.

Rao, Sudha, 1986, *Education and Rural Development*, New Delhi, Sage Publications.

Rashmi Dewan, *"An Analytical Review of Schemes of Incentives at the Primary Stage of Education"*.

Rath, Govinda Chandra, 2006, *Tribal Development in India – The Contemporary Debate*, New Delhi, Sage Publications.

Rath, K.B., "A Study of the Effect of Household, Community and School Factors on the Enrolment, Retention and Achievement of Scheduled Tribe Children at Primary Level", *http://www.google.com.*

Rath, R., Dash, A.S., Dash, U.N., 1979, *Cognitivie Abilities and School Achievements of the Socially Disadvantaged Children in Primary Schools*, New Delhi, Allied Publishers.

Rath, R.N., "Impact of Education in Modernising the Tribals", *New Frontiers in Education, Vol. 33, No. 1, 2003*, pp. 58-62.

Rath, S.N., 1986, *A New Thought on Tribal Education*, Report of U.G.C. Seminar on Tribal Education.

Rathnaiah, E.V., 1977, *Structural Constraints in Tribal Education: Gonds of Adilabad*, AP, New Delhi, Sterling Publishers.

Ratnaiah, E.V., 1977, *Structural Constraints in Tribal Education: A Regional Study*, New Delhi, Sterling Publishers.

Ravi S. Srivastava, "Inequality and Education Security", *The Indian Journal of Labour Economics, Vol. 42, No. 3, 1999.*

Ravi, N., 1997, *The Hindu Speaks on Education*, Chennai, Kasturi and Sons.

Rayappa, P. Hanumantha, "Issues in Tribal Development: A Study of Scheduled Tribes in Dakshina Kannada District of Karnataka", *Journal of Rural Development, Vol. 12, No. 12, 1993.*

Raza, M. Ahmad, and Nuna, S.C., 1985, *Tribal Literacy in India*: The Regional Dimension, Occasional Papers, New Delhi, NUEPA.

Reddy, G.P., "Causes of Wastage in Tribal Education of Andhra Pradesh", *Vanyajati, Vol. XVIII, Vol. 3, 1970*, New Delhi.

Reddy, P. Sudhakar, 1995, *A Report on the Functioning of Ashram Schools in Tribal Areas of Andhra Pradesh and Maharashtra*, New Delhi, Educational Research and Innovations Committee.

Reisman, Frank, 1962, *The Culturally Deprived Child*, New York, Haper and Row.

Renake, B., (n.d.), *Shikshan Paddhati Anivanchit Dalit*, Unpublished Paper.

Roger, Rich (Ed.), 1986, *Education and Social Class*, London, Falmer Press.

Roy Burman, B.K., 1964, *A Preliminary Appraisal of the Scheduled Tribes of India*, New Delhi, Registrar General.

Roy Burman, B.K., 1994, *Tribes in Perspective*, New Delhi, Mittal Publication.

Roy Kanchan, 1989, *Education and Health Problems in Tribal Development*, New Delhi, Concept Publishing Company.

Roy, Burman, B.K., "Issues in Tribal Development", *Mainstream, January 5, 1985.*

Roy, Burman, B.K., 1969, *Educational Problems of the Tribal Communities in India: Social Development of Educability in India*, Ed. by S.P. Ruhela, New Delhi, Jain.

Roy, S., *Koli Culture*, New Delhi, Cosmo Publications, 1983.

Russell, Bertrand, 1977, *Education and the Social Order*, London, Unwin.

Sacchidananda and Ramesh, P. Sinha, 1989, *Education and the Disadvantaged*, New Delhi, Uppal Publishing House.

Sachchidanand, 1902, Tribal India: Past and Present, Kolkata: Institute of Social Research and Applied Anthropology.

Sachchidanand, 1989, Disparities in Elementary Education: A Case Study of Bihar, in Panchmukhi, P.R. (Ed.), Studies in Educational Reform in India, Vol. II, Bombay, Himalaya Publishing House.

Sachchidanand, 1997, "The Harijans in Bihar, in Sachchidananda *et al.* (Eds.), Social Realities in Bihar, Patna, Novelty and Co.

Sachchidanand, 1999, Voluntary Action for Social Development and Empowerment of Marginalised Groups, A.N.S. Institute of Social Studies.

Sachchidananda, *"Community Development and the Tribals"*, Department of Social Welfare, Government of Andhra Pradesh, Vol. II, No. 1, Hyderabad.

Sachchidananda, "Education and Changes in Social Values", *Man in India, Vol. 48, No. 1, Ranchi,* pp. 71-85.

Sachchidananda, "Tribal Education in India", *Vanyajati, Vol. XII, No. 1, 1964,* pp. 3-6.

Sachchidananda, 1967, Socio-Economic Aspects of Tribal Education, *Report of the National Seminar on Tribal Education in India,* New Delhi, NCERT.

Sachidananda and Prasad, R.R. (Ed.), 1996, *Encyclopaedic Profile of Indian Tribes, 4 Volumes,* New Delhi, Discovery Publishing House.

Sahastrabuddhe Milind and Srivasta Sujatha, "School Education of Scheduled Castes and Scheduled Tribes in India, Critical Management Issues", *NFIE, Vol. XXVIII, No. 3, 1998,* pp. 221-231.

Sainath, P., 1996, *Everybody Loves a Good Drought: Stories from India's Poorest Districts,* Penguin Books, New Delhi.

Saksena, H.S., 1999, Putting People Last: Tribal Displacement and Rehabilitation, Inter India Publications, New Delhi.

Saldana, D., 1990, Socialisation of Critical Thought: Responses to Literacy among Adivasis in Thane District, in Krishnakumar (Ed.), *Democracy in India,* New Delhi, Radiant Publishers.

Samavesh, 2003, *Dalit, Adivasi aur School,* Bhopal, Bhopal Rehabilitation.

Sarangapani, P., 2001, Childhood, Growing up and Learning. The Baigas of Northern Kawardha, Report Submitted to the Indira Gandhi National Centre for the Arts, September.

Sarangapani, P., 2003, *'Indigenising Curriculum: Questions Posed by Baiga Vidya', Comparative Education, Vol. 39, No. 2.*

Sarangapani, P., *Constructing School Knowledge: An Ethnography of Learning in an Indian Village,* New Delhi, Sage Publishers.

Sarangapani, Padma, M. and Vijay Simha, Indira, 2005, *Assessment of Utility and Usage of Soliga Siddhi Text Books Developed for Soliga Tribal Ashram Schools of Chamarajanagar District,* Karnataka, Sarvashiksha Abhiyan.

Sarvashiksha Abhiyan – *Perspective Plan 2002 to 2010,* Office of the District Project Coordinator, DPEP, Mysore, ND.

Saxena, S. and Mahendroo, K., 1993, 'Politics of Language', *Economic and Political Weekly, Vol. 28, No. 45.*

Saxena, S., 1995, 'Kis Bhasha Mein Padhen?' *Jan Samplav, 14-16, August-September, 6-22.*

Saxena, S., 1997, 'Language and the Nationality Question', *Economic and Political Weekly, Vol. 32, No. 6.*

Saxena, S., 1998, 'Education of the Poor – A Pedagogy of Resistance', in S. Shukla and R. Kaul (Eds.), *Education, Development and Underdevelopment,* New Delhi, Sage Publishers.

Scarse, T.J., 1993, *Image, Ideology and Inequality: Cultural Domination, Hegemony and Schooling in India,* New Delhi, Sage Publishers.

Shah Beena, "Researches on Tribal Education: An Overview", *Perspectives in Education, Vol. 6, No. 3, July 1990,* pp. 177-92.

Shah, G., 2000, 'Hope and Despair; A Study of Untouchability and Atrocities in Gujarat', In Andre Beteille (Ed.), *Journal of Indian School of Political Economy, Vol. 12, No. 3 and 4.*

Shah, G., Joshi, V., *et al.*, 1985, *Tribal Education in Gujarat*, Centre for Social Studies, Surat.

Shah, V.P. and Patel, T., 1984, *Social Contexts of Tribal Education*, New Delhi, Concept Publishing House.

Shah, V.P. and Patel, T., *Social Contexts of Tribal Education*, Concept Publishing Company.

Shara, G.D. and Sujatha, K., 1983, *Educating Tribals – An Indepth Analysis of Ashram Schools*, New Delhi, NUEPA.

Sharma, B.D., "Resolving the deeping crisis in tribal areas", *Social Change, Vol. 23, Nos. 2 and 3*, 1993.

Sharma, B.D., *Dalits Betrayed*, 1994, New Delhi, Har-Anand Publications.

Sharma, D.K., 1994, *Education and Socialisation among the Tribes*, New Delhi, Common Wealth Publishers.

Sharma, Dasu, 2006, *Primitive Tribals in India*, New Delhi, Serials Publications.

Sharma, G.D. and Sujatha, K., 1983, *Educating Tribals – An Indepth Analysis of Ashram Schools*, New Delhi, NUEPA.

Sharma, G.D., 1991, *An Indepth Analysis of Ashram Schools (A Study)*.

Sharma, K.R., "Absenteeism Among the Tribal Pupils", *Journal of Educational Research and Extension, Vol. 32, No. 2, October 1995*, pp. 64-73.

Sharma, K.R., "A Study of Educational Backwardness of Tribal Students", *Education Quarterly, Vol. XXXV, No. 2.*

Sharma, K.R., "Action Research", *The Primary Teacher, NCERT, Vol. 21, No. 2, April 1996*, pp. 20-22.

Sharma, K.R., "Educational Attitudes of Tribal Students", Bhopal, *Bulletin of the Tribal Research Institute, Vol. XXII, No. 2, December 1994.*

Sharma, K.R., "Improving the Quality of Tribal Education", *The Education Quarterly, Vol. XXXII, No. 3, 1998*, pp. 221-231.

Sharma, K.R., "Language Learning Among Tribals", *Vanyajati, Bhartiya Adimjati Sangh, Vol. XLI, No. 3, July 1993.*

Sharma, K.R., "Tribal Education in India", *The Progress of Education, Vol. XIX, No. 8, March 1995.*

Sharma, K.R., 1991, *Educational Life Style of Tribal Students*, New Delhi, Classical Publishing House.

Sharma, K.R., *Action Research*, New Delhi, The Primary Teacher, NCERT, Vol. 21, No. 2, April 1996.

Sharma, K.R., Educational Attitudes of Tribal Students, Bhopal, *Bulletin of the Tribal Research Institute, Vol. XXII, No. 2, December 1994.*

Sharma, R., 1990, 'What Manner of Teacher: Some Lessons from Madhya Pradesh, *Economic and Political Weekly, Vol. 34, No. 25.*

Sharma, R., 1997, 'Dynamics of Learning Three R's in Madhya Pradesh, *Economic and Political Weekly, Vol. 32, No. 17.*

Sharma, R., 1998, 'Universal Elementary Education, The Question of How', *Economic and Political Weekly, Vol. 33.*

Sharma, Raj Khem, "Educational Life Styles of Tribal Students", *The Indian Journal of Social Work, Vol. LI, No. 3, July 1990*, pp. 457-472.

Shashi, S.S. (Ed.), 1994, *Encyclopaedia of Indian Tribes*, Vol. 2, New Delhi, Anmol Publications.

Shavni, K.R., 1991, *Educational Life Style of Tribal Students*, New Delhi, Classical Publishing Company.

Shaw, B.N., "Success of Ashram School", *Adivasi, Vol. III, No. 2.*

Shaw, B.N., "Vocational Education in the Ashram Schools", *Adivasi, Vol. 3, No. 3*, pp. **31-34**.

Shikshana Darpana, *Public Education Department*, Zilla Panchayat, Mysore District, ND (Kannada).

Shikshana Mukhena Pragathi: *Aadivasigalodane Ondu Prayoga* (a Kannada Booklet), 2000, Hunsur, DEED.

Shiladitya Dev, "Un Double-Talk on the Status of the Indigenous People", *Link, September 6, 1992.*

Shivakumar, Chitra, 1982, *Education, Social Inequality and Social Change in Karnataka*, Delhi, Hindustan Publishing Corporations.

Shukla, S. and Kaul, R. (Eds.), 1998, *Education, Development and Under-development*, New Delhi, Sage Publishers.

Shyamalal, 1987, *Education Among Tribals*, Jaipur, Printwell Publications.

Shyamanand Singh, 1991, *Tribal Education in India*, New Delhi, Uppal Publishing House.

Shyamlal, 1987, *Education Among Tribals*, Lucknow, Printwell Publishers.

Singh, A.K., "Parental Support and Scholastic Achievement", *Social Change, Vol. 13, No. 1, 1983*, pp. 9-14.

Singh, A.K., "Social Disadvantage and Academic Achievement", *Social Change, Vol. 10, Nos. 1 and 2*, 1980, pp. 15-18.

Singh, A.K., 1987 & 1994, *Dropout from Primary Schools in Tribal India: A Case Study of the HO in Parampancho, West Singhbhum*, Unpublished Ph.D. Thesis Submitted to University of London, Department of International and Comparative Education.

Singh, A.K., 1995, *The Cultural Construction of Home and School Knowledge in Tribal India*, Prospects, Vol. 25, No. 4.

Singh, Anil Kumar, 1993, *Tribes and Tribal Life: Approaches to Development in Tribal Context*, Vol. 3, New Delhi, Swarup and Sons.

Singh, B., 1996, 'Education and Development of Tribal in India', *Journal of Education and Social Change*, Vol. 10, No. 2.

Singh, K. Narendra, 1979, *Education and Social Change*, Jaipur, Rawat Publications.

Singh, K.S. (Ed.), 1972, *Tribal Situation in India* – Proceedings of a Seminar, Simla, Indian Institute of Advanced Study.

Singh, K.S., 1985, *Tribal Society in India*, New Delhi, Manohar.

Singh, K.S., 1997, *The Scheduled Tribes, People of India National Series*, New Delhi, Oxford University Press.

Singh, K.S., 2003, *People of India, Karnataka (Part 1, 2 & 3)*, New Delhi, East West Press Private Limited.

Singh, M.T., 1987, 1995, *A Review of Educational Programmes for Tribal Children in Rajasthan, Development Programmes for Children*, in Bedi, M.S. (Ed.), Tribal Development in Rajasthan with special reference to women and children, Jaipur: Himanshu Publications.

Singh, S.N., 1991, *Tribal Education in India*, Delhi, Uppal Publishing House.

Sinha, D., 1982, 'Some Social Disadvantages and Development of Certain Perceptual Skills', In D. Sinha, R.C. Tripathi and Misra G. (Eds.), *Deprivation, Its Social Roots and Psychological Consequences*, New Delhi, Concept Publishing Company.

Sinha, D., Tripathy, R.C. and Mishra, G., 1982, *Deprivation and its Motivational and Personality Correlates*; In: Sinha, D., Tripathi, R.C. and Misra, G. (Eds.), *Deprivation: Its Social Roots and Psychological Consequences*, New Delhi, Concept Publishing House.

Sinha, Surajit, Eds., 1977, *Primitive Tribes – The First Step*, New Delhi, Government of India.

Sinha, Surajit, *Tribes and Indian Civilization: Structure and Transformation*, Varanasi, N.K. Bose Memorial Foundations.

Sita Toppo, "Education in Ashram Schools – A Case of Adilabad District", *Journal of Education and Social Change, Vol. 3, No. 1.*

Sreedhar, M.V., 'Reaching the unreached: Enabling Dalit Girls to get Schooling', *Manushi*, Vol. 111, Nos. 10-20, March-April.

Sridhar, N., *Tribal Education: A Study of Ashram Schools in Karnataka*, Ph.D. Thesis (Unpublished), Ananthpur, Sri Krishnadevaraya University.

Srivastava, 1967, Some Basic Problems of Tribal Education, in *Report of the National Seminar on Tribal Education in India*, New Delhi, NCERT.

Srivastava, L.R.N., 1971, *Developmental Need of the Tribal People*, New Delhi, NCERT.

Srivastava, L.R.N., 1992, 'Development of Curriculum for Tribal Studetns', in B. Chaudhary (Ed.), *Tribal Transformation in India, Vol. 4, Education and Literacy Programmes*, New Delhi, Inter-India Publications.

Statistical Figures of Tribal Population and Tribal Haadis Districtwise, Karnataka.

Status of Scheduled Tribes in Karnataka Paints a Dismal Picture: A Study, *The Hindu, October 14, 2007.*

Subba Reddy, Kethu, *Tribal Education in Andhra Pradesh – A Sociological Exploration*, Ph.D. Thesis, Delhi, Jawaharlal Nehru University.

Subramoniam, V.I. (Ed.), 2006, *Dravidian Encyclopaedia (Three Volumes)*, Thiruvananthapuram, Dravidian Linguistic Association.

Sudarshan, H., "Government Ashram Schools are not Functioning Properly", *Mysore Mitra, January 21, 2008.*

Sudhakara Reddy, P. and Raja Reddy, K., "Tribal Parents Awareness About Educational Incentives in Andhra Pradesh", *Journal of Educational Planning and Administration", Vol. XV, No. 3, 2001.*

Sudhakara Reddy, P. *et al.*, "Functioning of Tribal Ashram Schools in Maharashtra: A Comparative Study", *Tribal Research Bulletin, Vol. XXI, No. 1, March 1999.*

Sudhakara Reddy, P., 2001, *Social Assessment of District Primary Education Programme: Tribal Groups in Andhra Pradesh*, Report submitted to Government of Andhra Pradesh, Hyderabad.

Sujata, K., 1996, *Single-Teacher Schools in Tribal Areas: A Study of Girijan Vidya Vikas Kendras in Andhra Pradesh*, New Delhi, Vikas Publishing House.

Sujata, K., 2002, *Education Among Scheduled Tribes*, in R. Govinda, India Education Report: A Profile of Basic Education, New Delhi, OUP.

Sujatha, K. *et al.*, 1996, *Single Teacher Schools in Tribal Areas: A Study of Girijan Vidya Vikas Kendras in Andhra Pradesh*, New Delhi, Vikas Publishing House Pvt. Ltd.

Sujatha, K. *et al.*, 1998, *Quality Improvement Programmes in Education: A Study in Tribal Areas of Andhra Pradesh*, New Delhi, International Unit, NUEPA.

Sujatha, K., "Ashram Schools for Tribal Children", *New Frontiers in Education, Vol. XVII, No. 40*, pp. 83-85.

Sujatha, K., "Tribal Education in India: A Review of Policies", *Perspectives in Education, Vol. 4, No. 4, 1988.*

Sujatha, K., 1987, *Attitudes and Aspiration Towards Education Among Scheduled Tribes*, Vol. 3, New Delhi, International Congress of Anthropological and Ethnological Science.

Sujatha, K., 1987, *Education of the Forgotten Children of the Forests: A Case Study of Yanadi Tribe*, New Delhi, Konark Publishers.

Sujatha, K., 1990, *Education in Ashram Schools – A Case of Andhra Pradesh*, New Delhi, NIEPA, Occasional Paper.

Sujatha, K., 1994, *Educational Development Among Tribes, A Study of Tribal Sub-plan Areas in Andhra Pradesh*, New Delhi, South Asian Publishers.

Sujatha, K., Education Development among Tribes: A Study of Sub-plan Areas in Andhra Pradesh, New Delhi, South Asian Publishers.

Sunandamma, N., *Mysore Mathu Chamarajanagar Jillegallali Soliga Budakattu Janangada Abivruddige Karnataka Sarkarada Karikramagallu – Vondu Vimarshatmaka Adhyayana* (A Critical Study on the Activities of the Development Programmes initiated by the Government of Karnataka, Tribal Welfare Department, for the development of Soliga Tribes), (Kannada), Ph.D. Thesis (Unpublished), University of Mysore, 2006.

Sundar, N., 'Tribal Politics', In S. Wolpert (Ed.), *Encyclopaedia of India*, New York, Charles Seribners and Sons.

Sundar, N., 2002, 'Indigenise, Nationalise and Spiritualise: An Agenda for Education?', *International Social Science Journal*, Vol. 173.

Sundar, N., 2004, 'Teaching to Hate RSS', Pedagogical Programme, *Economic and Political Weekly, Vol. 36, No. 16*.

Sundar, N., 2005, 'Adivasi Vs. Vanavasi: The Politics of Conversion and re-conversion in Central India', in S. Saberwal, M. Hasan (Eds.), *Assertive Religious Identities*, New Delhi, Permanent Black.

Surabhi, Patel, P., 1983, *Equality of Educational Opportunity A Myth or Reality*, New Delhi, National Publishing House.

Surendra Lawrence, Narayan Kikkeri, Hebbar Ritambhara, 2004, *Adivasis of India and Development Strategies*, Bangalore, Hivos.

Swaminathan, P., Jeyaranjan, J., Sreenivasan, R. and Jayashree, K., 2004, Tamil Nadu's Mid-day Meal Scheme Where Assumed Benefits over Hard Data, *Economic and Political Weekly, Vol. 39, No. 44*.

Talib, M., 1998, 'Educating the Oppressed; Observations from a School in a Working Class Settlement in Delhi', in Shukla, S. and Kaul, R. (Eds.), *Education, Development and Underdevelopment*, New Delhi, Sage Publishers.

Talib, M., 2003, 'Modes of Learning-Labour Relations: Educational Strategies and Child Labour', in N. Kabeer, G.B. Nambissan and R. Subramanian (Eds.), *Child Labour and the Right to Education in South Asia; Needs Versus Rights*? New Delhi, Sage Publishers.

Tara, Patel, 1984, *Development of Education Among Tribal Women*, New Delhi, Mittal Publications.

Taradatt, 2001, *Tribal Development in India*, New Delhi, Gyan Publishing House.

Telegraph, *Tribal Children Alienated in School: Report*, September 12, 1994.

Teltumbde, A., 2000, 'Impact of New Economic Reforms on Dalits', in P.G. Jogdand (Ed.), *New Economic Policy and Dalits*, Jaipur, Rawat Publications.

Teltumbde, A., 2004, Impact of Imperialist Globalisation on Dalits, Paper Presented at Mumbai Resistance, *Seminar, January 2004, Mumbai*.

Teltumbe, A., 1996, *Arthik Sudhar anti Dalit Shoshit*, (Marathi), Aurangabad, Prabhuddha Bharat Publication.

Thapar, Romesh, 1997, *Tribe, Caste and Religion in India*, New Delhi, Macmillan India Limited.

The Probe Team, *Public Report on Basic Education in India*, Oxford University Press, 1999.

Thomas, J.A., 2001, Dynamics of Educational Development: A Case Study of Selected Backward Villages in Kerala', in A. Vaidyanathan and P.R. Gopinathan Nair (Eds.), *Elementary Education in Rural India; A Grassroots View*, New Delhi, Sage Publishers.

Thorat, S. and Deshpande, R.S., 2001, 'Caste System and Economic Inequality: Economic Theory and Evidence', in G. Shah (Ed.), *Dalit Identity and Politics*: Cultural Subordination and the Dalit Challenge, Vol. 2, New Delhi, Sage Publishers.

Thorat, S., 2002, Oppression and Denial: Dalit Discrimination in the 1990's, *Economic and Political Weekly, Vol. 37, No. 6.*

Thurston, E., 1906, *Ethnographic Notes on Southern India*, Madras, Government Press.

Thurston, E., 1975, *Castes and Tribes of South India (Vol. I to VIII)*, New Delhi, Cosmo Publications.

Tilak, J.B.G., 2000, *Education Poverty in India*, Occasional Papers, New Delhi, NUEPA.

Tilak, Jandhyala, B.G., 1987, *Economics of Inequality in Education*, New Delhi, Sage.

Toppo, S., 1979, *Dynamics of Educational Development in Tribal India*, New Delhi, Classical Publications.

Toppo, S., 1979, *Dynamics of Tribal Educational Development in India*, New Delhi, Concept Publications.

Toppo, S., 2000, *Tribes in India*, New Delhi, Indian Publishers and Distributors.

Toppo, Sita, 1979, *Dynamics of Educational Development in Tribal India*, New Delhi, Classical Publications.

Toppo, Sita, 2000, *Tribes in India*, New Delhi, Indian Publishers and Distributors.

Tribal Cultural Research and Training Institute, 1971, *Absenteeism, Stagnation, Wastage in the Primary Schools of Tribal Areas of Andhra Pradesh*, Hyderabad (mimeo).

Tribal Cultural Research and Training Institute, 1971, *Study of Ashram Schools in Tribal Areas of Andhra Pradesh*, Hyderabad (mimeo).

Tribal Education in India, *Report of the National Seminar on Tribal Education in India, 1993.*

Tribal Transformation and Development, (Seminar Papers), 1998, Hyderabad, NIRSA and NISIET.

Tribal Welfare Department – *Facts and Figures, Zilla Panchayat, Mysore*, ND (Kannada).

Tripathi, G.M., 2003, *Musahar Samajaur Shiksha*, in Shiksha Vimarsh, Vol. 5, No. 4.

Tripathy, S.N., 2000, *Glimpses on Tribal Development*, New Delhi, Discovery Publishing House.

Trivedi, H.V., 1985, *Economics of Development of Tribes in India*, Delhi, Himanshu.

Uma, Ramaswamy, "Education and Inequality", *Economic and Political Weekly, Vol. XX, No. 36, September 1985.*

UNESCO Report, 1951, *The Use of Vernacular Languages in Education.*

Upadhyay, H.C., 1991, *Scheduled Castes and Scheduled Tribes in India – A Socio-Economic Profile*, New Delhi, Anmol Publications.

Usha, M.J. Rao, 1981, *Deprived Castes in India: Profile of Karnataka*, Allahabad, Chugh Publications.

Vaidyanathan, A. and Gopinathan, P.R., 2001, 'Introduction', in A. Vaidyanathan and Gopinathan, P.R. Nair (Eds.), Elementary Education in Rural India: A Grassroots View, New Delhi, Sage Publishers.

Vasavi, A.R., 2003, 'Schooling for a New Society? The Social and Political Bases of Education Development in India', in R. Subramanian *et al.*, Education and Exclusion: Indian and South African Perspectives, *IDS Bulletin*, Vol. 34, No. 1.

Velaskar, P. and Abraham, L., Class, Culture and Curriculum; An Evaluation of the Abacus, *Curriculum Enrichment Programme – A Report*, Mumbai, TISS, Mimeograph.

Velaskar, P., 2005, 'Educational Stratification, Dominant Ideology and the Reproduction of Disadvantage in India, in S.M. Dahiwale (Ed.), *Understanding Indian Society*: The Non-Brahmanic Perspective, New Delhi, Rawat.

Velaskar, Padma, 1986, *Inequality in Higher Education: A Study of Scheduled Caste Students in Medical Colleges of Bombay*, Mumbai, TISS, Unpublished Ph.D. Thesis.

Velaskar, Padma, 1992, 'Unequal Schooling as a Factor in the Reproduction of Social Inequality', *Sociological Bulletin, Vol. 39, No. 2.*

Velaskar, Padma, 1998, 'Ideology, Education and the Political Struggle for Liberation: Change and Challenge Among Maharashtra Dalits, in S. Shukla and R. Kaul (Eds.), *Education, Development and Underdevelopment*, New Delhi, Sage Publishers.

Velaskar, Padma, 2000, 'The Politics of Untouchability and Social Change: A Study of the Scheduled Castes of Maharashtra', *Journal of Indian School of Political Economy*, Vol. 12, No. 3 & 4.

Velaskar, Padma, 2003, *Community Participation in Education: A Critique*, Shiksha Vimarsh, Vol. 5, No. 1.

Velaskar, Padma, 2004, *Structural Inequalities and Educational Inequalities: The Case of the Dalits in Maharashtra*, Paper presented at Seminar on Towards Quality Education for all: Issues and Challenges beyond 86th Amendment at India International Centre, New Delhi, Organised by CDC, October 7-8, 2004.

Venkata Rao, P., 1989, New Education Policy: Implications for Scheduled Tribes and Scheduled Castes in Rao and Sharma (Eds.), *Human Resource Development for Rural Development*, Bombay, Himalaya Publishers.

Venkata Rao, P., 2001, *Tribal Development: Policy and Practice*, New Delhi, Sarup and Sons.

Venkateshwarlu, K., "Displaced Development", *The Hindu, January 8, 2006.*

Vidyarathi, L.P. and Rai, B.K., 1977, *The Tribal Culture of India*, New Delhi, Concept Publishing Company.

Vidyarthi, L.P. (Eds.), 1968, *Education for the Tribes: Applied Anthropology in India*, New Delhi, NCERT.

Vidyarthi, L.P., " Education in Tribal Bihar", *Man in India, Vol. 35, No. 1.*

Vidyarthi, L.P., 1976, The Tribal Culture of India, *Concept Publishing Company*, New Delhi.

Vidyarthi, L.P., 1987, *Applied Anthropology in India*, Allahabad, Kitab Mahal.

Vilanilam, J.V., "Whither Development? Whither Education", *Yojana, Vol. 42, No. 8, 1998.*

Vimal, P. Shah, 1984, *Social Contexts of Tribal Education*, New Delhi, Concept Publishing House.

Vimala Ramachandran, "Community Participation in Primary Education", *Economic and Political Weekly, Vol. XXXVI, No. 25, June 2001.*

Visaria, L. and Ramachandran, V., 2004, 'What DPEP and other Data Sources Reveal', in Ramachandran, V. (Ed.), *Gender and Social Equity in Primary Education: Hierarchies of Access*, New Delhi, Sage Publishers.

Vyas, A.N., "Ten Years Progress of Ashram Education in Orissa", *Vanyajathi, Vol. 6, No. 4.*

Wankhede, G.G. and Padma Velaskar, 1999, *The Post-Metric Scholarship Scheme for SC/ST in Maharashtra and Goa – An Evaluation*, Mumbai, TISS, Mimeograph.

Wankhede, G.G., 1987, *The Centrally Sponsored SC-ST Girls' Hostels in Maharashtra and Gujarat: An Evaluation*, Prepared for The Ministry of Human Resource Development, GOI, TISS, Mumbai.

Wankhede, G.G., 1998, *Intercaste Educational Variations Among the Scheduled Castes of Mumbai Metropolis*, Mumbai, TISS, Mimeograph.

Wankhede, G.G., 2001, Educational Inequalities Among Maharashtra's Scheduled Castes, *Economic and Political Weekly, Vol. XXXVI, No. 18.*

Welfare Programmes for Schedule Tribes, 2007, Directorate for the Welfare of Scheduled Tribes, Government of Karnataka, Bangalore.

Welfare Programmes for Scheduled Tribes, 2008, Directorate of Social Welfare, Government of Karnataka, ND (Kannada).

World Bank, 1997, *A Report on Primary Education in India,* World Bank, Washington D.C., 1997

World Bank, *A Report on Primary Education in India,* 1997, World, Washington D.C.

Xaxa, V., 1999, 'Tribes as Indigenous People of Indiä', *Economic and Political Weekly, Vol. 34, No. 51.*

Xaxa, V., 2001, Protective Discrimination: Why Scheduled Tribes Lag Behind Scheduled Castes', *Economic and Political Weekly, Vol. 36, No. 29.*

Yadav, B. and Sharma, A.M. (n.d.), *Economic Uplift of Scheduled Castes, Institute for Development and Communication*, Unpublished Report, Chandigarh.

Index